IDOL dreams

STORY & ART BY

ARINA TANEMURA

5

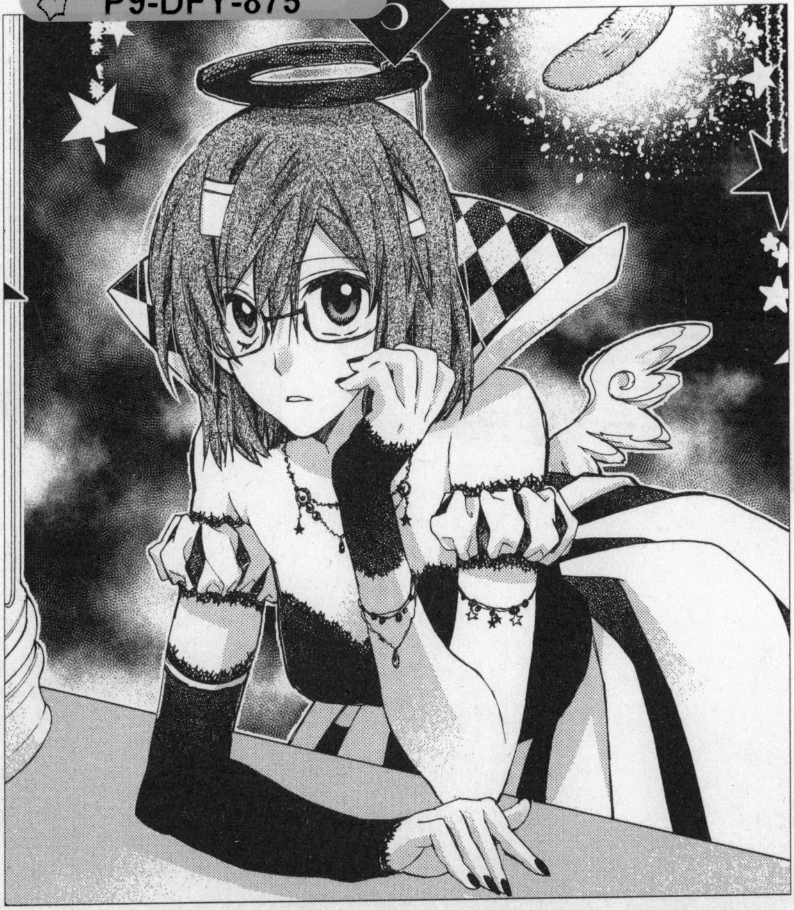

IDOL dreams 5

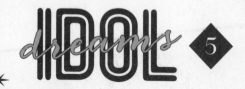

CONTENTS

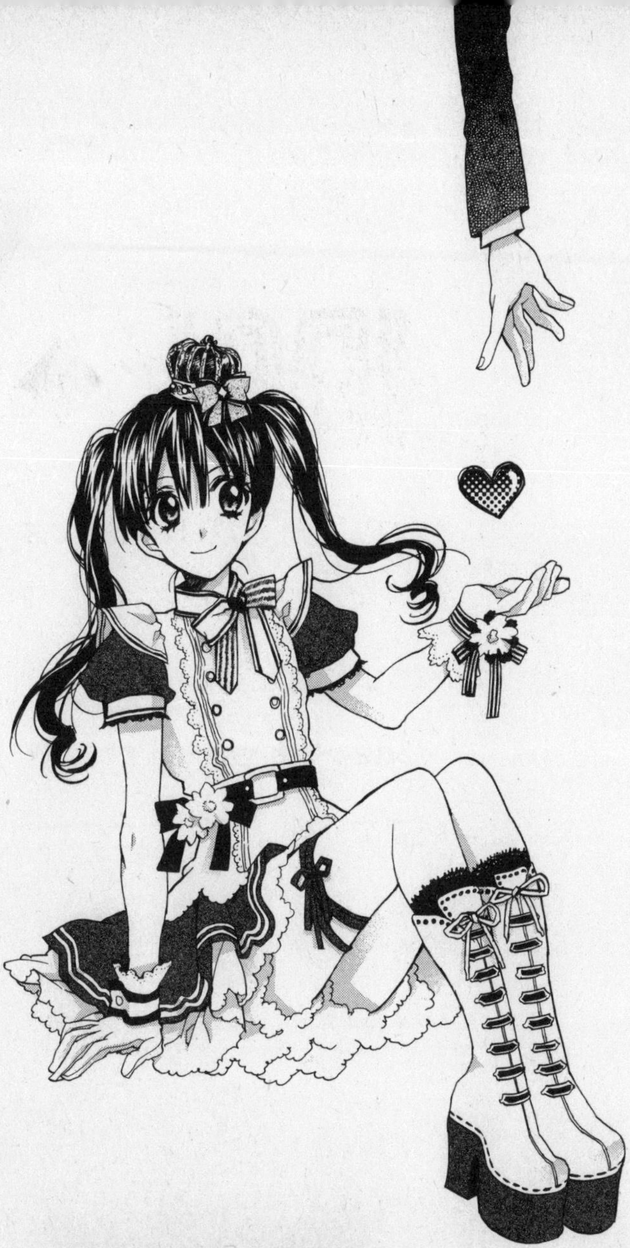

Chapter 21

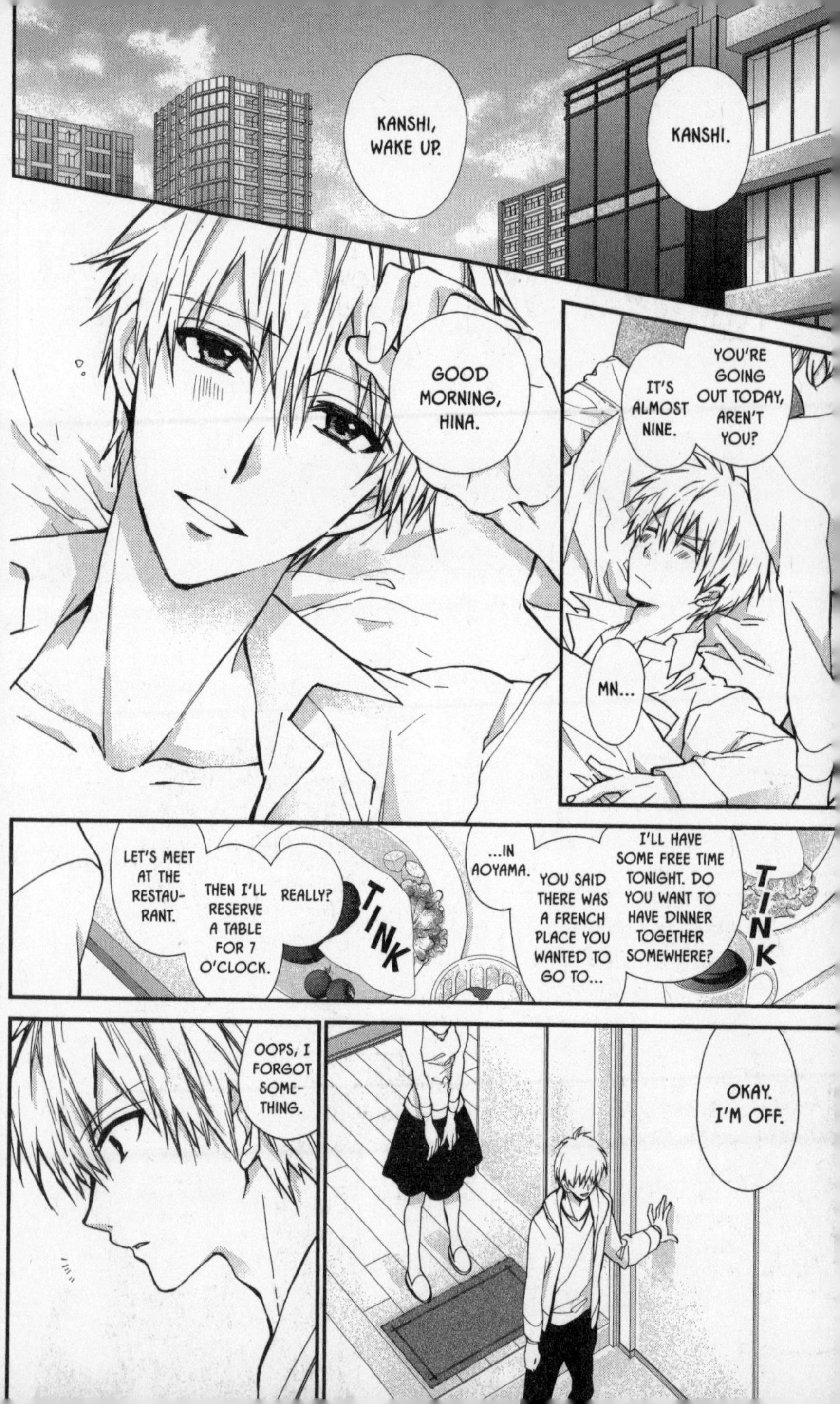
KANSHI.
KANSHI, WAKE UP.
YOU'RE GOING OUT TODAY, AREN'T YOU?
IT'S ALMOST NINE.
MN...
GOOD MORNING, HINA.
TINK
I'LL HAVE SOME FREE TIME TONIGHT. DO YOU WANT TO HAVE DINNER TOGETHER SOMEWHERE?
YOU SAID THERE WAS A FRENCH PLACE YOU WANTED TO GO TO...
...IN AOYAMA.
TINK
REALLY?
THEN I'LL RESERVE A TABLE FOR 7 O'CLOCK.
LET'S MEET AT THE RESTAU-RANT.
OKAY. I'M OFF.
OOPS, I FORGOT SOME-THING.

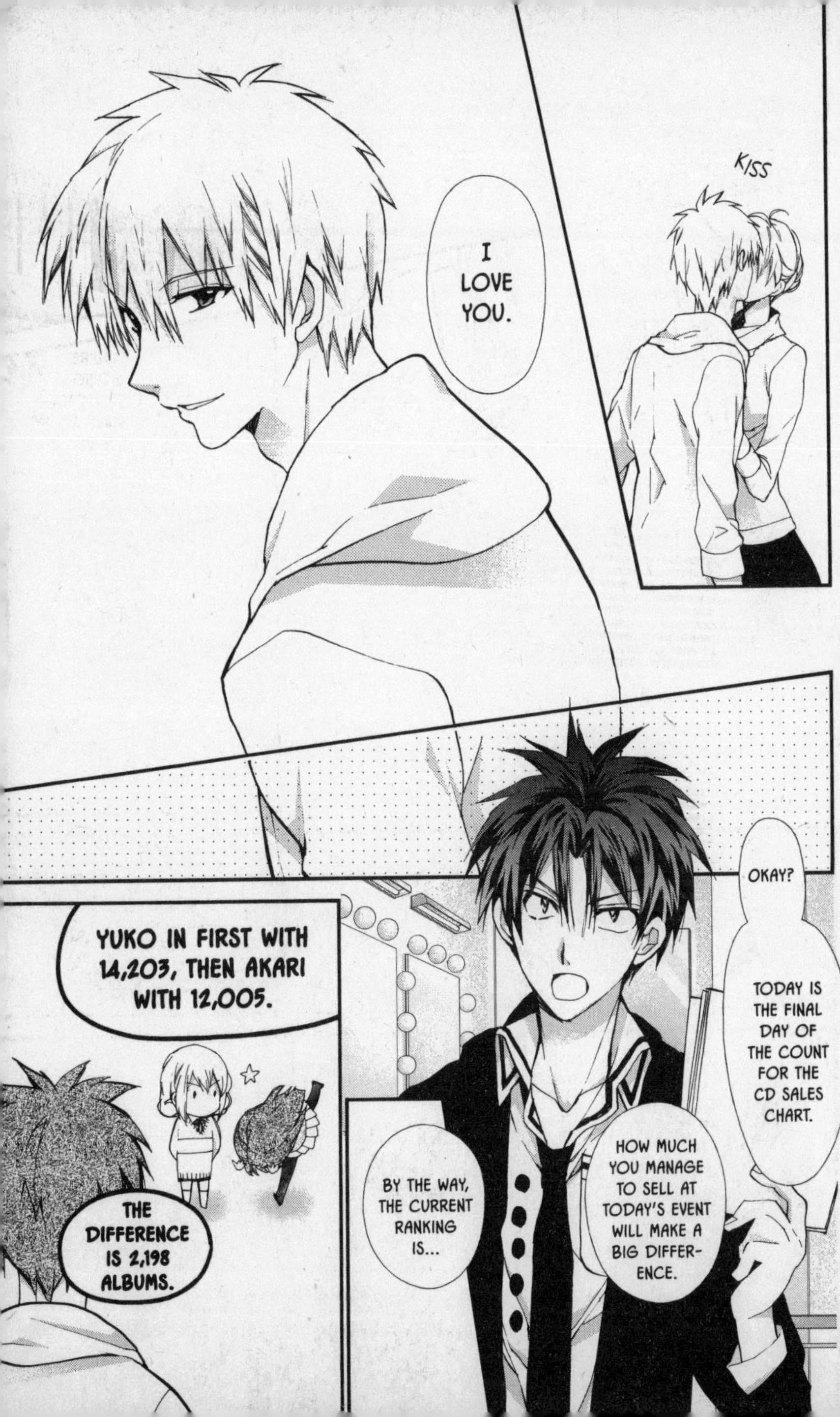
KISS
I LOVE YOU.
OKAY?
TODAY IS THE FINAL DAY OF THE COUNT FOR THE CD SALES CHART.
HOW MUCH YOU MANAGE TO SELL AT TODAY'S EVENT WILL MAKE A BIG DIFFERENCE.
BY THE WAY, THE CURRENT RANKING IS...
YUKO IN FIRST WITH 14,203, THEN AKARI WITH 12,005.
THE DIFFERENCE IS 2,198 ALBUMS.

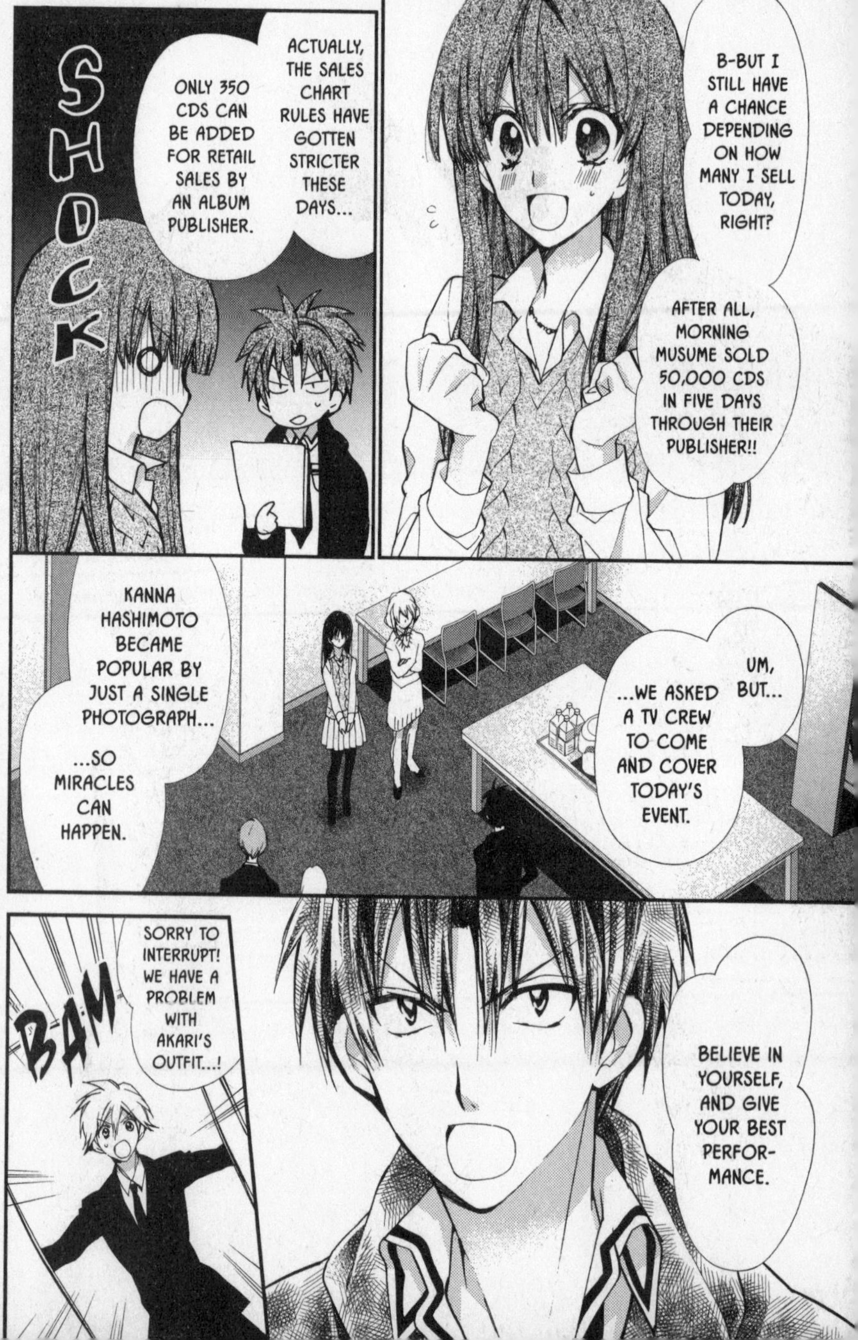
B-BUT I STILL HAVE A CHANCE DEPENDING ON HOW MANY I SELL TODAY, RIGHT?
AFTER ALL, MORNING MUSUME SOLD 50,000 CDS IN FIVE DAYS THROUGH THEIR PUBLISHER!!
ACTUALLY, THE SALES CHART RULES HAVE GOTTEN STRICTER THESE DAYS...
ONLY 350 CDS CAN BE ADDED FOR RETAIL SALES BY AN ALBUM PUBLISHER.
SHOCK
UM, BUT...
...WE ASKED A TV CREW TO COME AND COVER TODAY'S EVENT.
KANNA HASHIMOTO BECAME POPULAR BY JUST A SINGLE PHOTOGRAPH...
...SO MIRACLES CAN HAPPEN.
BELIEVE IN YOURSELF, AND GIVE YOUR BEST PERFOR-MANCE.
SORRY TO INTERRUPT! WE HAVE A PROBLEM WITH AKARI'S OUTFIT...!
BAM

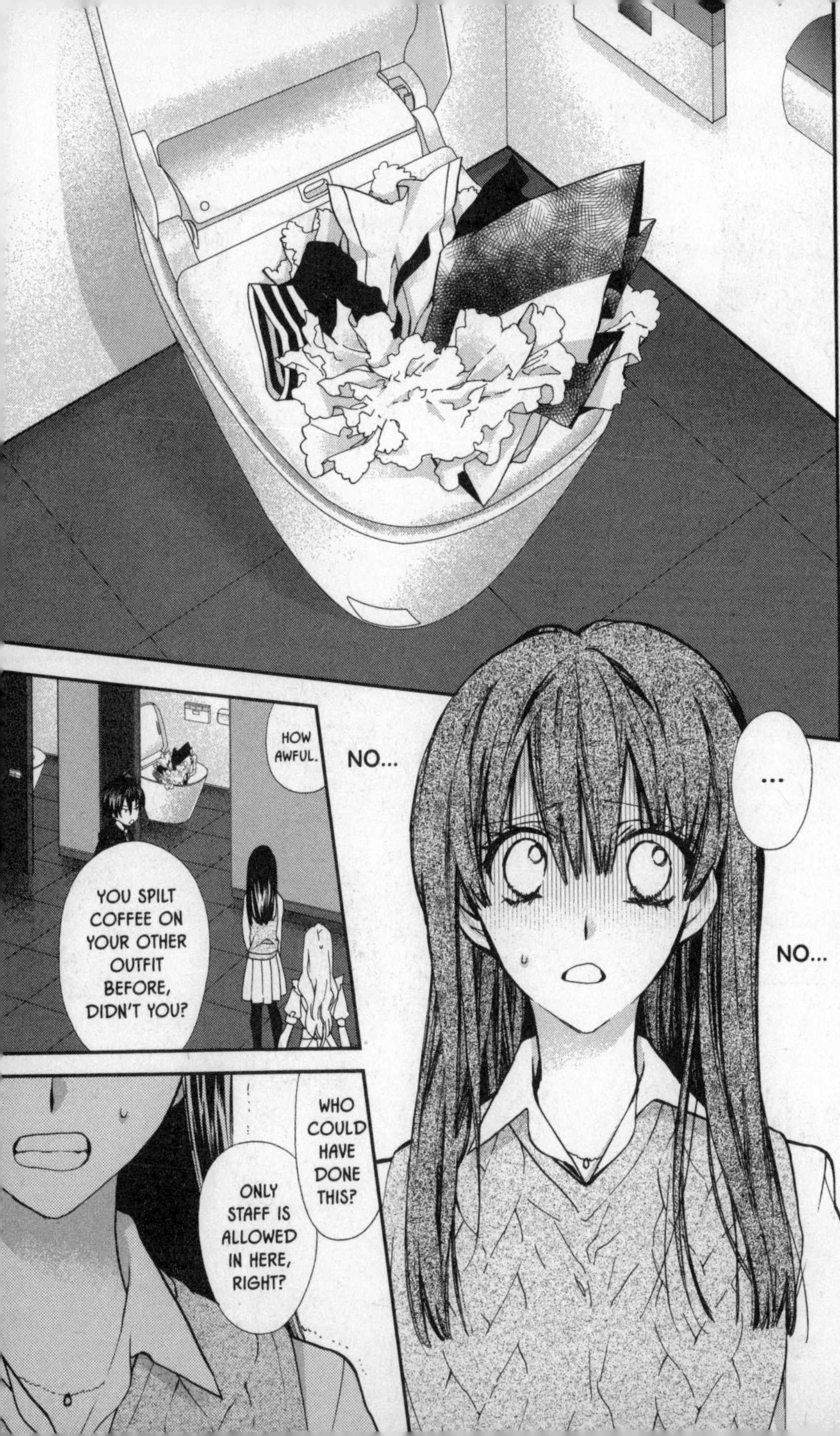
...
NO...
NO...
HOW AWFUL.
YOU SPILT COFFEE ON YOUR OTHER OUTFIT BEFORE, DIDN'T YOU?
WHO COULD HAVE DONE THIS?
ONLY STAFF IS ALLOWED IN HERE, RIGHT?

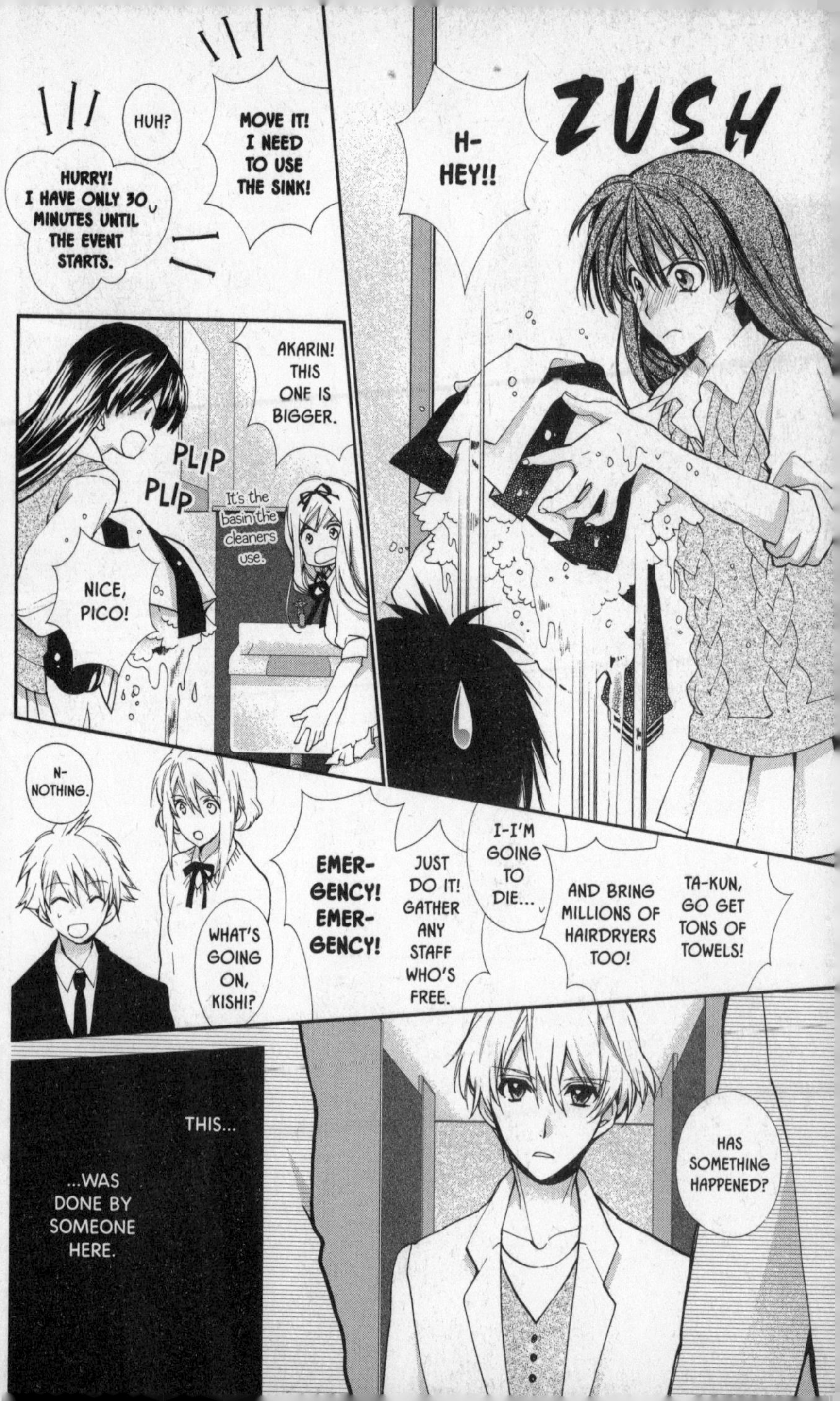
ZUSH
H-HEY!!
MOVE IT! I NEED TO USE THE SINK!
HUH?
HURRY! I HAVE ONLY 30 MINUTES UNTIL THE EVENT STARTS.
AKARIN! THIS ONE IS BIGGER.
PLIP PLIP
It's the basin the cleaners use.
NICE, PICO!
TA-KUN, GO GET TONS OF TOWELS!
AND BRING MILLIONS OF HAIRDRYERS TOO!
I-I'M GOING TO DIE...
JUST DO IT! GATHER ANY STAFF WHO'S FREE.
EMERGENCY! EMERGENCY!
WHAT'S GOING ON, KISHI?
N-NOTHING.
HAS SOMETHING HAPPENED?
THIS...
...WAS DONE BY SOMEONE HERE.

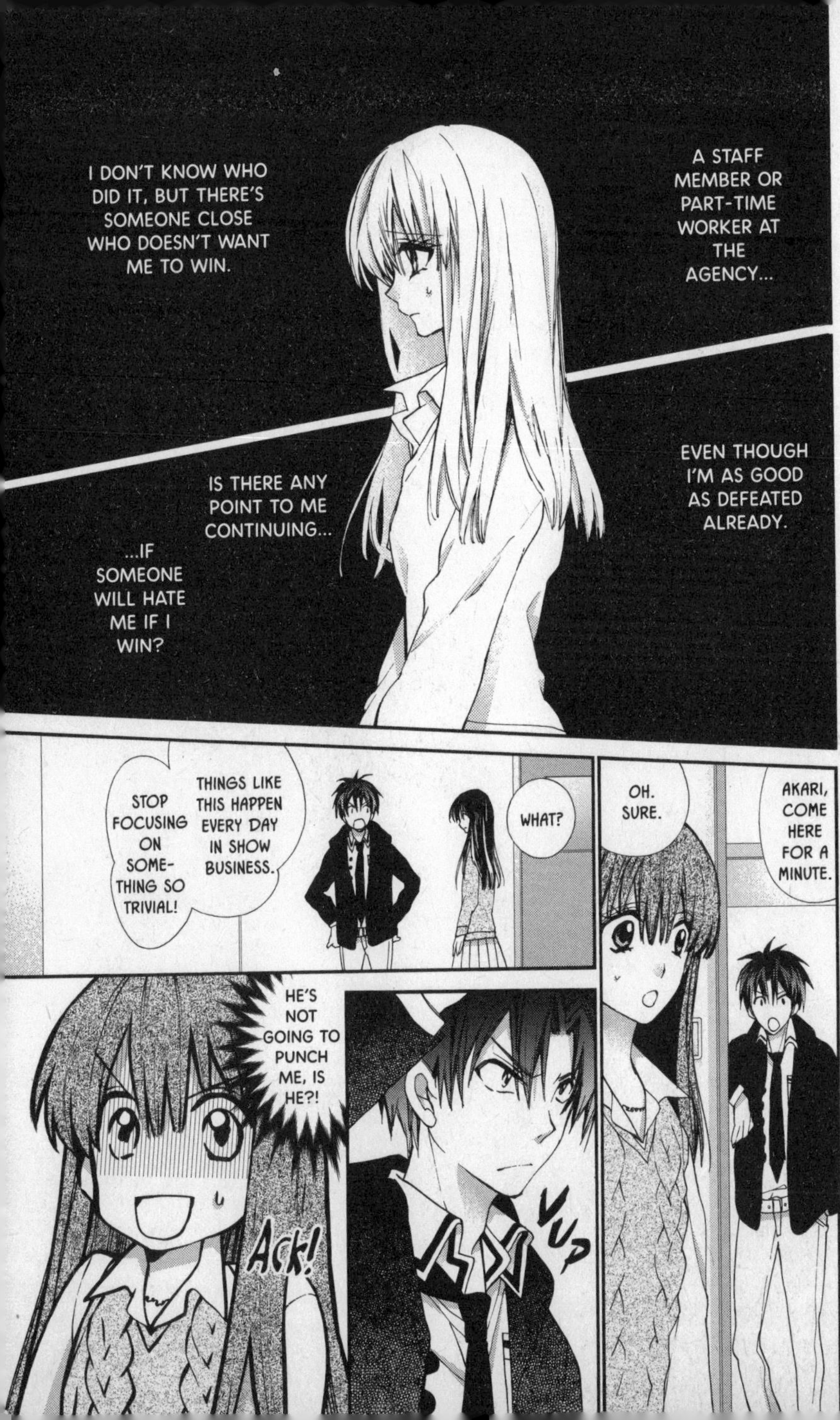
A STAFF MEMBER OR PART-TIME WORKER AT THE AGENCY...
I DON'T KNOW WHO DID IT, BUT THERE'S SOMEONE CLOSE WHO DOESN'T WANT ME TO WIN.
EVEN THOUGH I'M AS GOOD AS DEFEATED ALREADY.
IS THERE ANY POINT TO ME CONTINUING...
...IF SOMEONE WILL HATE ME IF I WIN?
AKARI, COME HERE FOR A MINUTE.
OH. SURE.
WHAT?
THINGS LIKE THIS HAPPEN EVERY DAY IN SHOW BUSINESS.
STOP FOCUSING ON SOME-THING SO TRIVIAL!
YUP
HE'S NOT GOING TO PUNCH ME, IS HE?!
ACK!

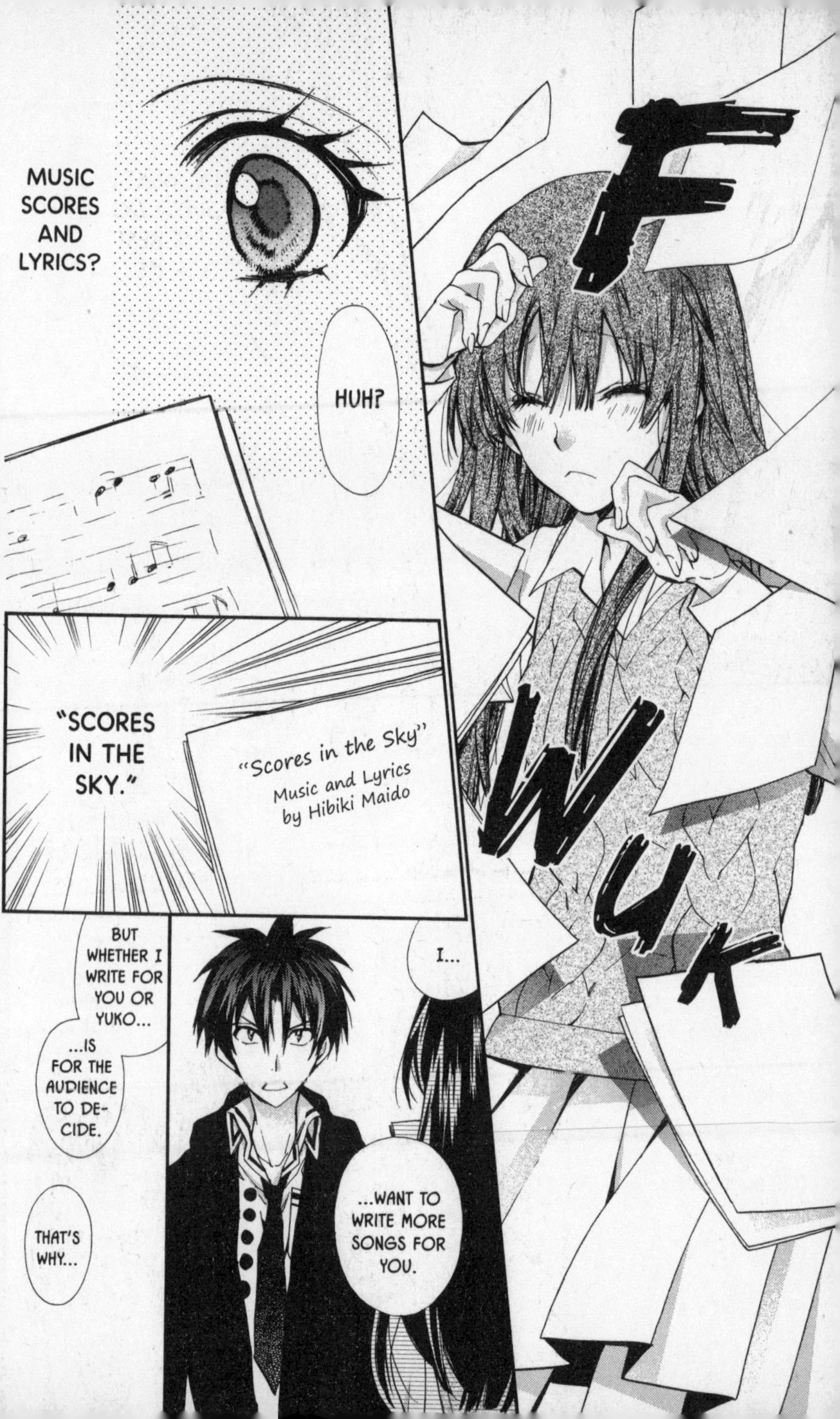
FWUK
HUH?
MUSIC SCORES AND LYRICS?
"SCORES IN THE SKY."
"Scores in the Sky"
Music and Lyrics by Hibiki Maido
BUT WHETHER I WRITE FOR YOU OR YUKO...
...IS FOR THE AUDIENCE TO DECIDE.
THAT'S WHY...
I...
...WANT TO WRITE MORE SONGS FOR YOU.

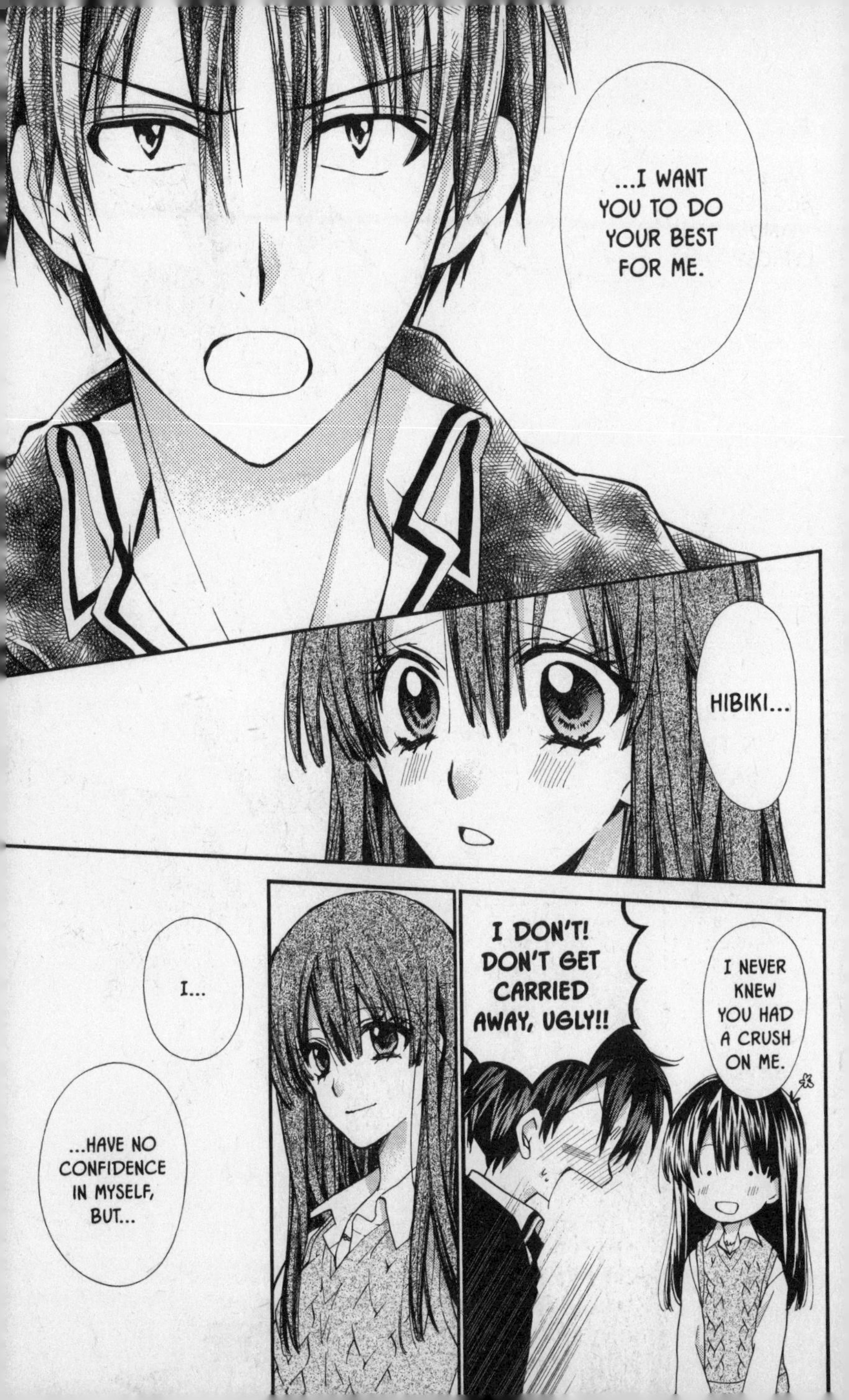
...I WANT YOU TO DO YOUR BEST FOR ME.
HIBIKI...
I NEVER KNEW YOU HAD A CRUSH ON ME.
I DON'T! DON'T GET CARRIED AWAY, UGLY!!
I...
...HAVE NO CONFIDENCE IN MYSELF, BUT...

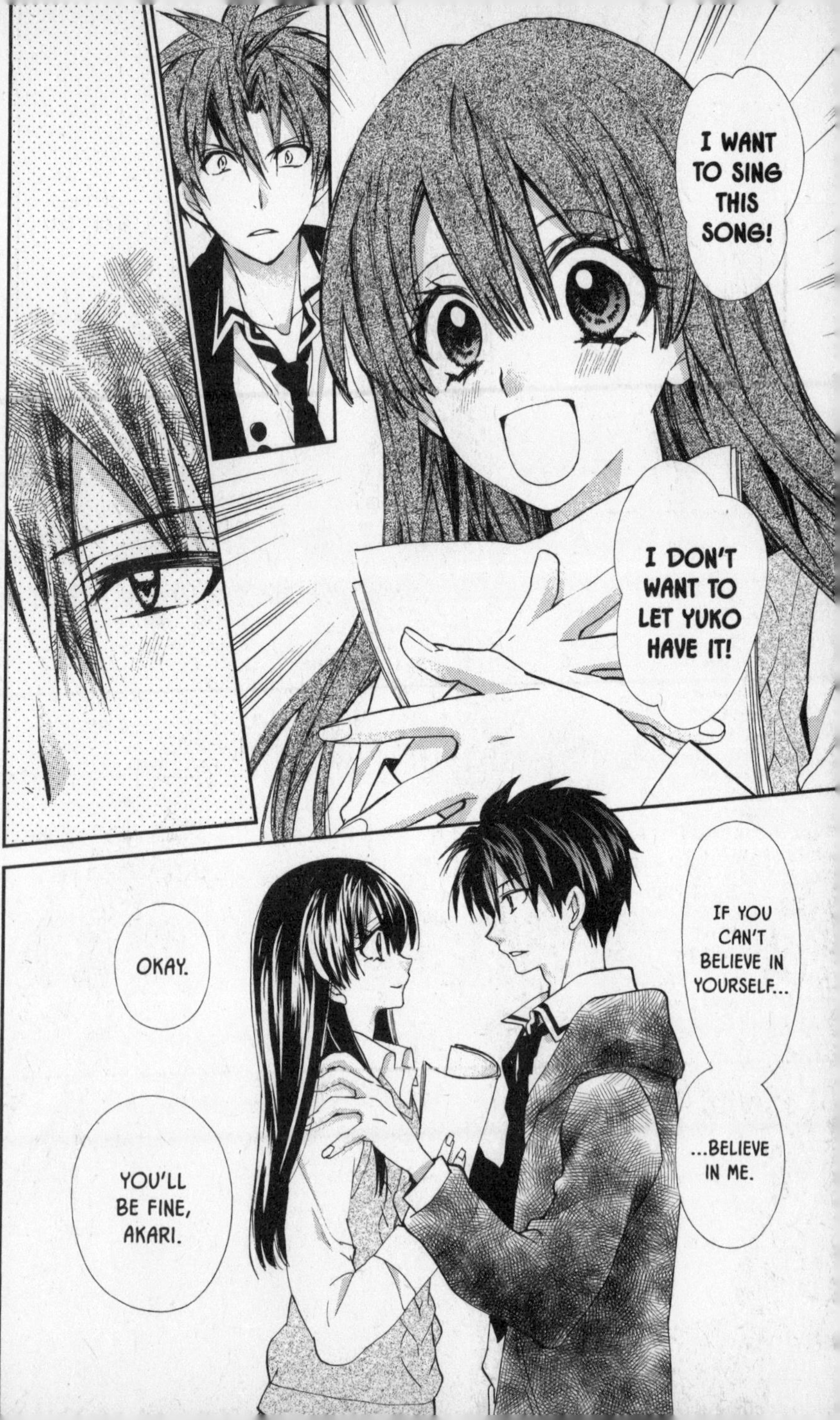
I WANT TO SING THIS SONG!
I DON'T WANT TO LET YUKO HAVE IT!
IF YOU CAN'T BELIEVE IN YOURSELF...
...BELIEVE IN ME.
OKAY.
YOU'LL BE FINE, AKARI.

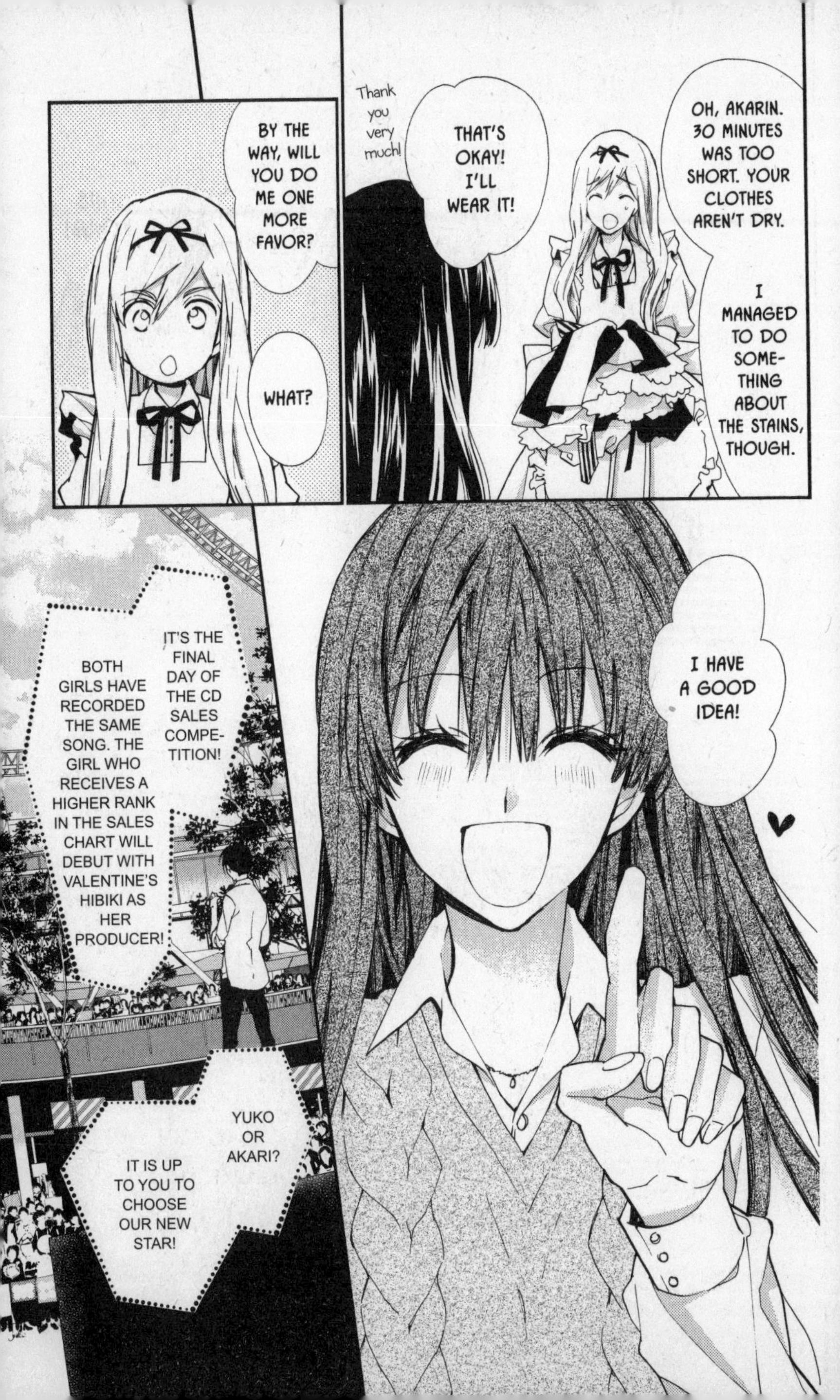
OH, AKARIN. 30 MINUTES WAS TOO SHORT. YOUR CLOTHES AREN'T DRY.
I MANAGED TO DO SOME-THING ABOUT THE STAINS, THOUGH.
THAT'S OKAY! I'LL WEAR IT!
Thank you very much!
BY THE WAY, WILL YOU DO ME ONE MORE FAVOR?
WHAT?
I HAVE A GOOD IDEA!
IT'S THE FINAL DAY OF THE CD SALES COMPE-TITION!
BOTH GIRLS HAVE RECORDED THE SAME SONG. THE GIRL WHO RECEIVES A HIGHER RANK IN THE SALES CHART WILL DEBUT WITH VALENTINE'S HIBIKI AS HER PRODUCER!
YUKO OR AKARI?
IT IS UP TO YOU TO CHOOSE OUR NEW STAR!

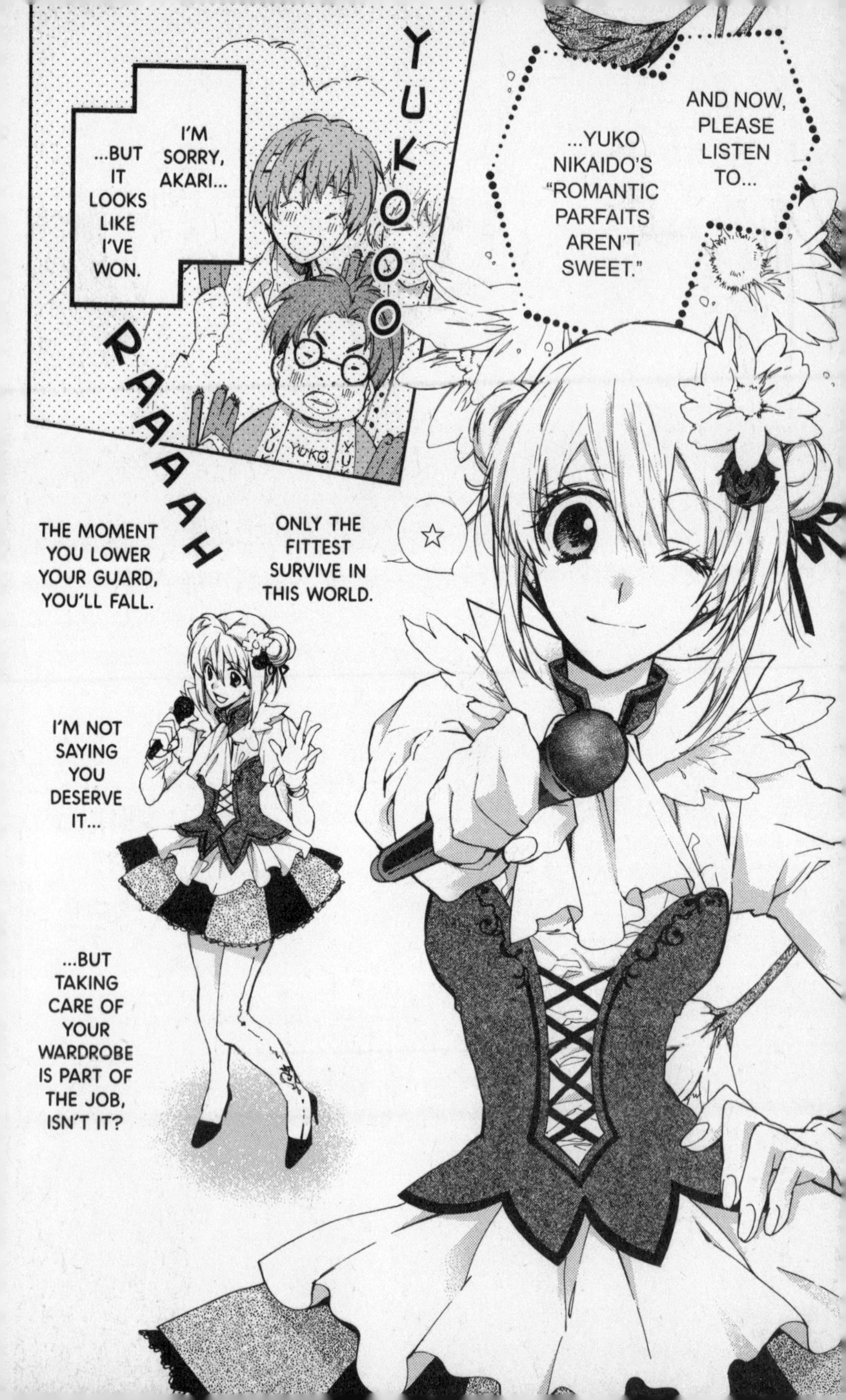
AND NOW, PLEASE LISTEN TO...
...YUKO NIKAIDO'S "ROMANTIC PARFAITS AREN'T SWEET."
I'M SORRY, AKARI...
...BUT IT LOOKS LIKE I'VE WON.
YUKOOOO
RAAAAAH
YUKO
☆
ONLY THE FITTEST SURVIVE IN THIS WORLD.
THE MOMENT YOU LOWER YOUR GUARD, YOU'LL FALL.
I'M NOT SAYING YOU DESERVE IT...
...BUT TAKING CARE OF YOUR WARDROBE IS PART OF THE JOB, ISN'T IT?

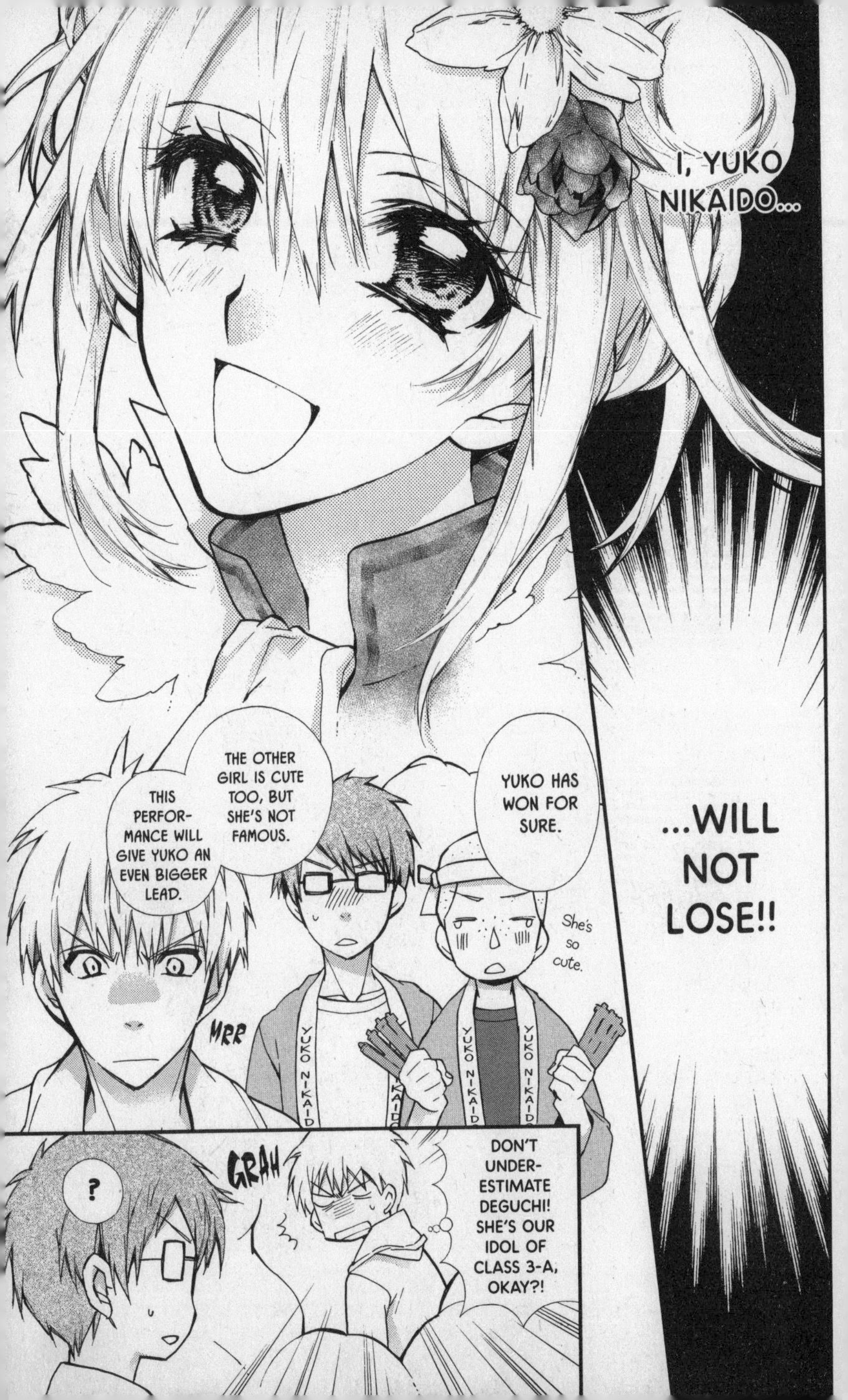
I, YUKO NIKAIDO...
...WILL NOT LOSE!!
YUKO HAS WON FOR SURE.
She's so cute.
THE OTHER GIRL IS CUTE TOO, BUT SHE'S NOT FAMOUS.
THIS PERFOR-MANCE WILL GIVE YUKO AN EVEN BIGGER LEAD.
MRR
DON'T UNDER-ESTIMATE DEGUCHI! SHE'S OUR IDOL OF CLASS 3-A, OKAY?!
GRAH
?

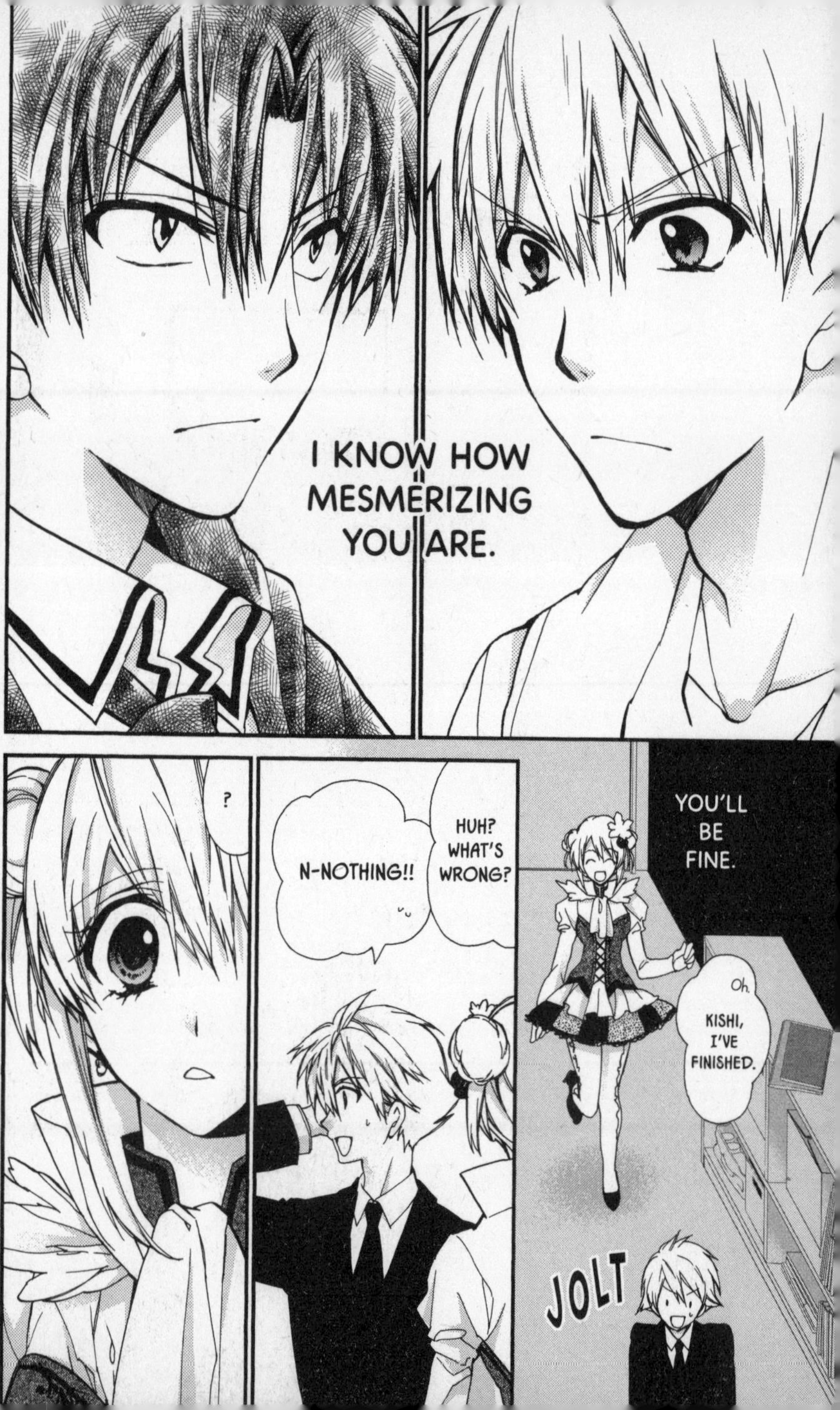
I KNOW HOW MESMERIZING YOU ARE.
YOU'LL BE FINE.
Oh.
KISHI, I'VE FINISHED.
JOLT
HUH? WHAT'S WRONG?
N-NOTHING!!
?

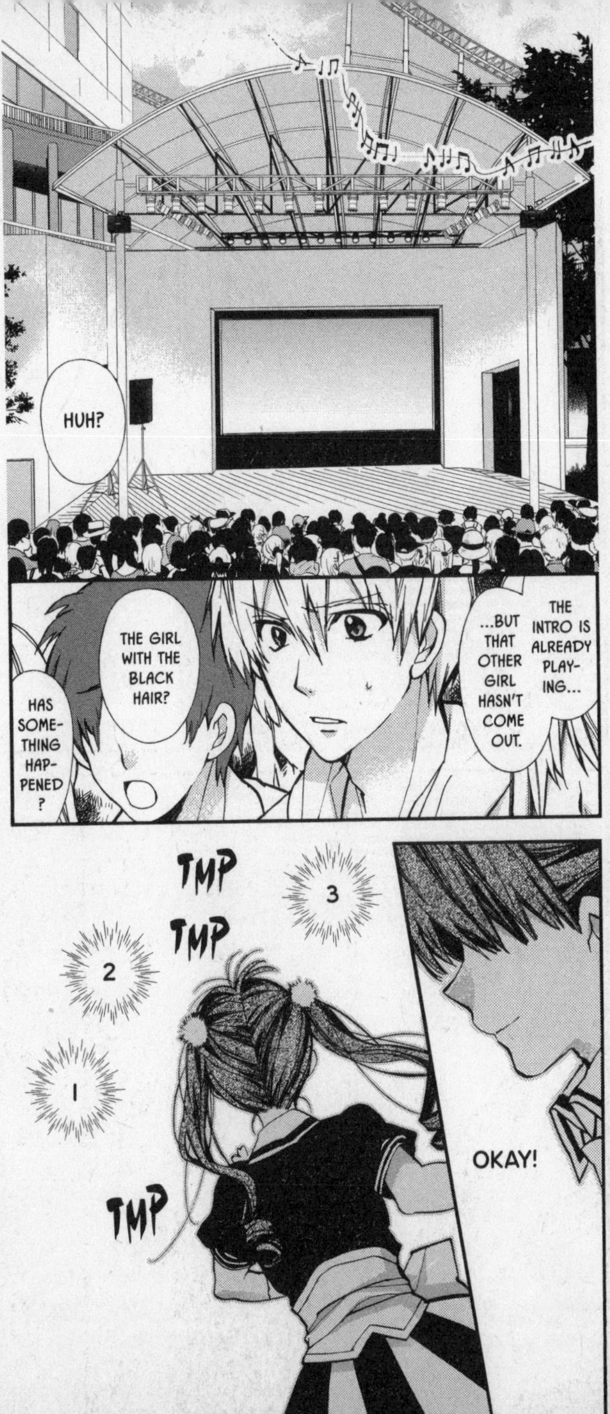
HUH?
THE INTRO IS ALREADY PLAYING...
...BUT THAT OTHER GIRL HASN'T COME OUT.
THE GIRL WITH THE BLACK HAIR?
HAS SOMETHING HAPPENED?
OKAY!
TMP
3
TMP
2
1
TMP

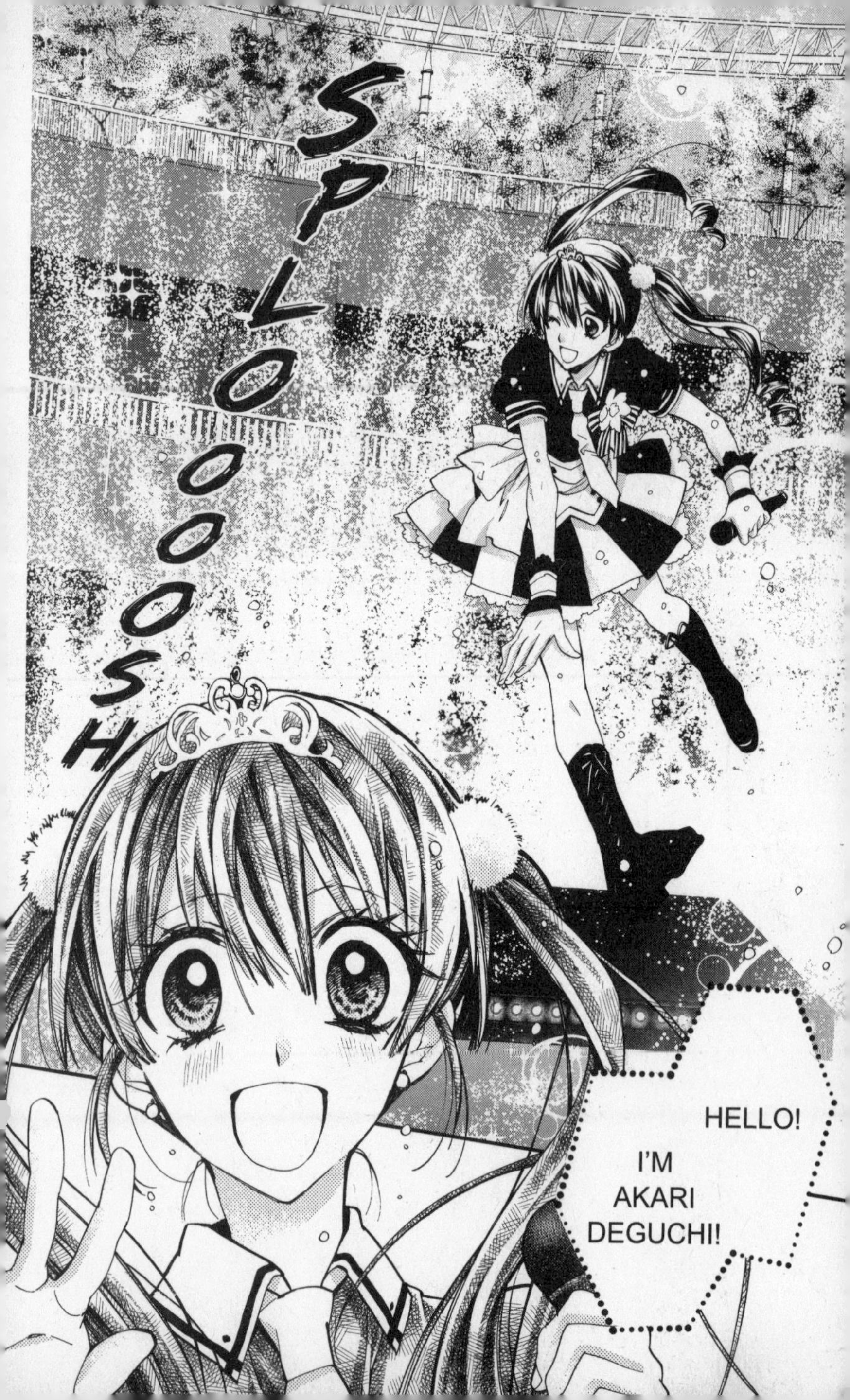
SPLOOOOOOSH
HELLO!
I'M AKARI DEGUCHI!

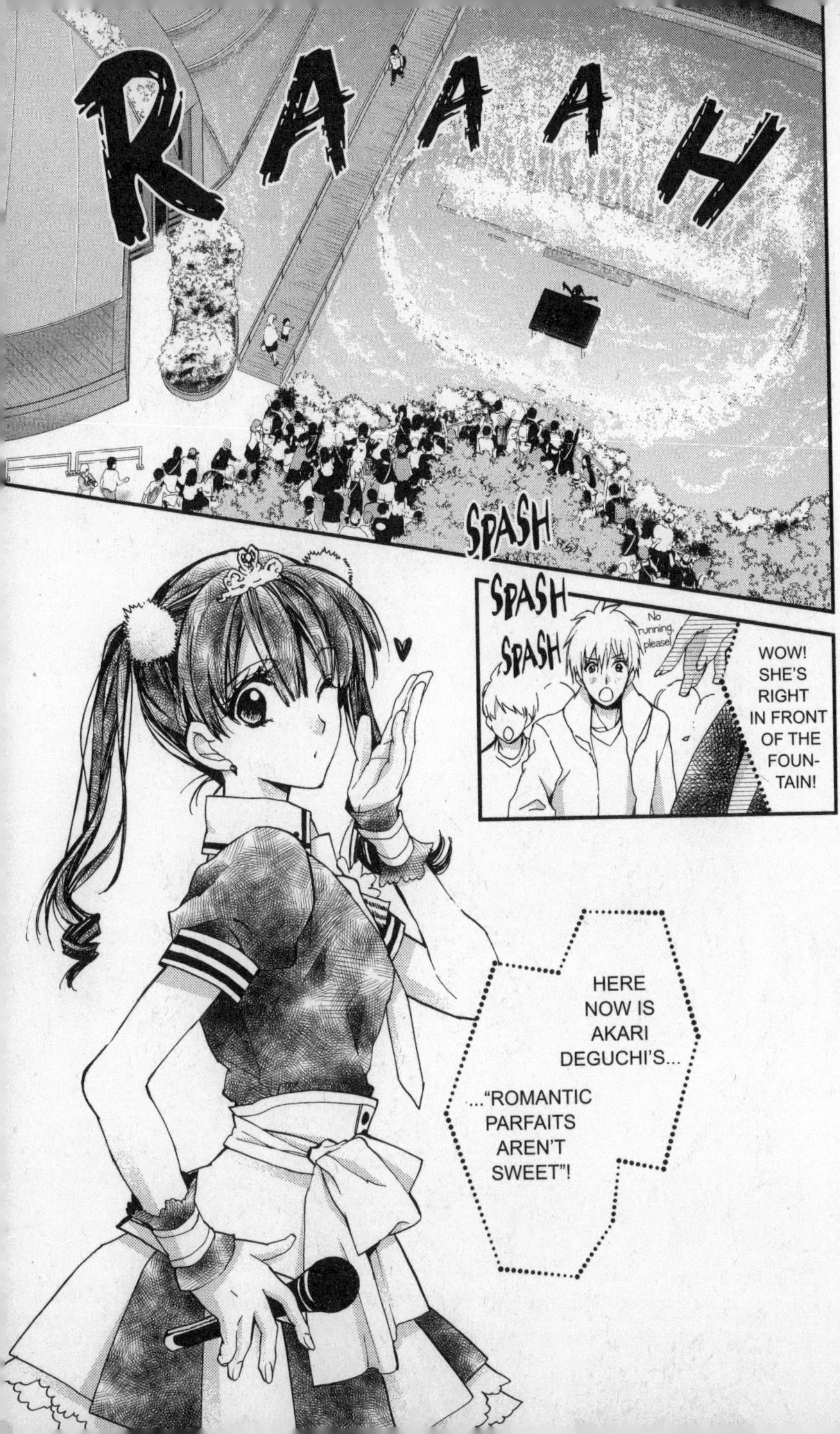
RAAAH
SPASH
SPASH
SPASH
No running, please!
WOW! SHE'S RIGHT IN FRONT OF THE FOUN-TAIN!
HERE NOW IS AKARI DEGUCHI'S...
..."ROMANTIC PARFAITS AREN'T SWEET"!

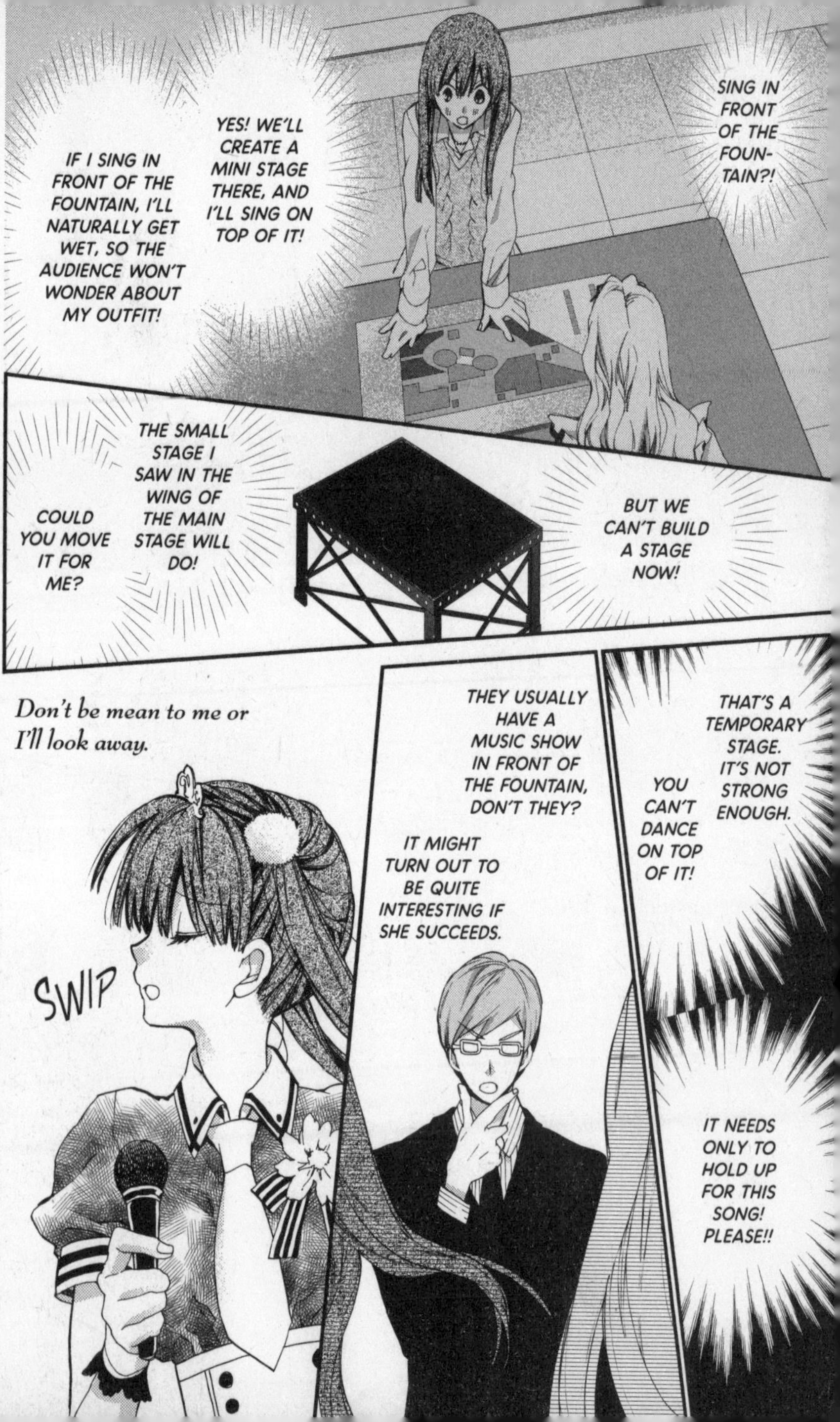
SING IN FRONT OF THE FOUN-TAIN?!
YES! WE'LL CREATE A MINI STAGE THERE, AND I'LL SING ON TOP OF IT!
IF I SING IN FRONT OF THE FOUNTAIN, I'LL NATURALLY GET WET, SO THE AUDIENCE WON'T WONDER ABOUT MY OUTFIT!
BUT WE CAN'T BUILD A STAGE NOW!
THE SMALL STAGE I SAW IN THE WING OF THE MAIN STAGE WILL DO!
COULD YOU MOVE IT FOR ME?
THAT'S A TEMPORARY STAGE. IT'S NOT STRONG ENOUGH.
YOU CAN'T DANCE ON TOP OF IT!
IT NEEDS ONLY TO HOLD UP FOR THIS SONG! PLEASE!!
THEY USUALLY HAVE A MUSIC SHOW IN FRONT OF THE FOUNTAIN, DON'T THEY?
IT MIGHT TURN OUT TO BE QUITE INTERESTING IF SHE SUCCEEDS.
Don't be mean to me or I'll look away.
SWIP

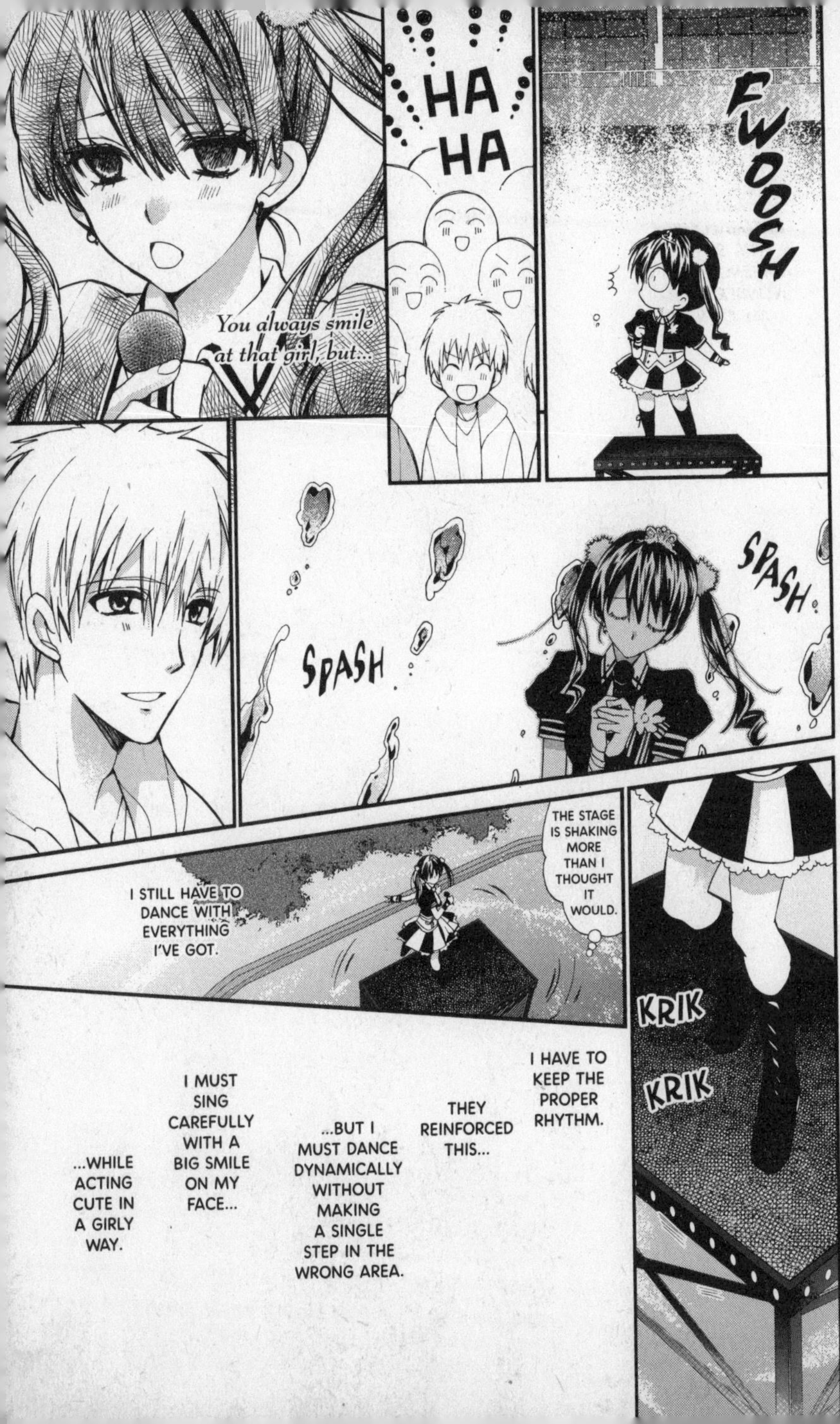
FWOOSH
HA HA
You always smile at that girl, but...
SPASH
SPASH
THE STAGE IS SHAKING MORE THAN I THOUGHT IT WOULD.
KRIK
KRIK
I STILL HAVE TO DANCE WITH EVERYTHING I'VE GOT.
I HAVE TO KEEP THE PROPER RHYTHM.
THEY REINFORCED THIS...
...BUT I MUST DANCE DYNAMICALLY WITHOUT MAKING A SINGLE STEP IN THE WRONG AREA.
I MUST SING CAREFULLY WITH A BIG SMILE ON MY FACE...
...WHILE ACTING CUTE IN A GIRLY WAY.

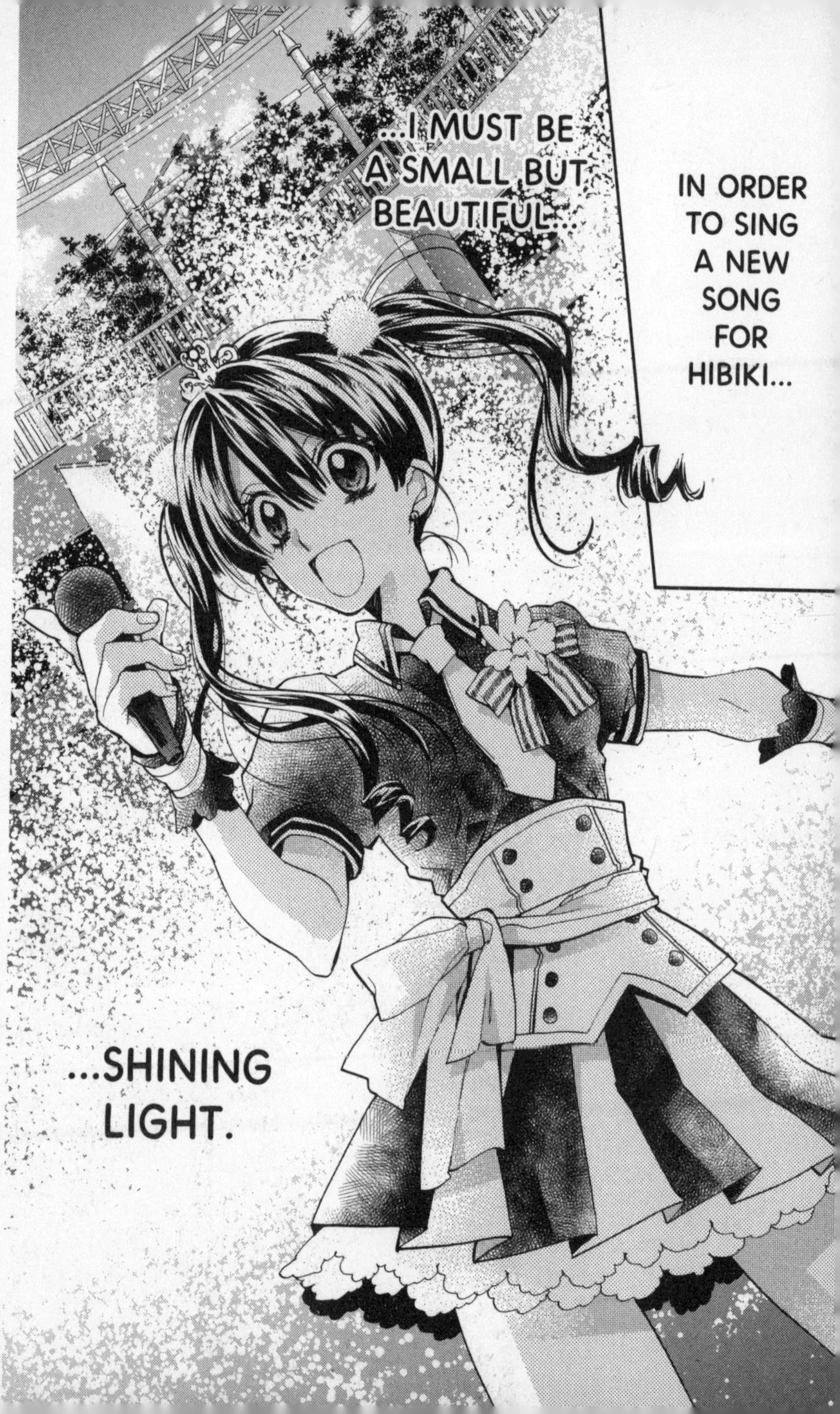
IN ORDER TO SING A NEW SONG FOR HIBIKI...
...I MUST BE A SMALL BUT BEAUTIFUL...
...SHINING LIGHT.

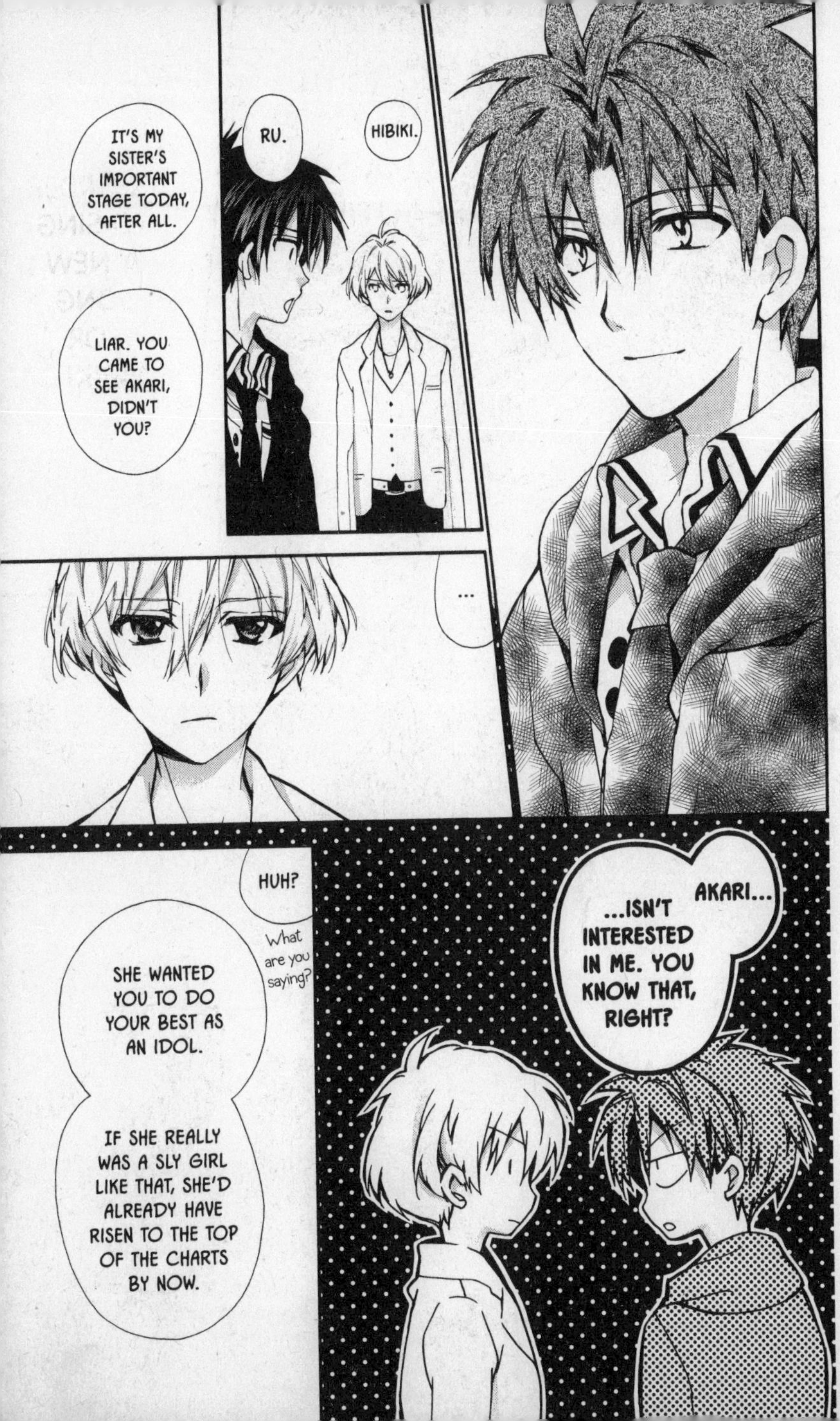
HIBIKI.
RU.
IT'S MY SISTER'S IMPORTANT STAGE TODAY, AFTER ALL.
LIAR. YOU CAME TO SEE AKARI, DIDN'T YOU?
...
AKARI...
...ISN'T INTERESTED IN ME. YOU KNOW THAT, RIGHT?
HUH?
What are you saying?
SHE WANTED YOU TO DO YOUR BEST AS AN IDOL.
IF SHE REALLY WAS A SLY GIRL LIKE THAT, SHE'D ALREADY HAVE RISEN TO THE TOP OF THE CHARTS BY NOW.

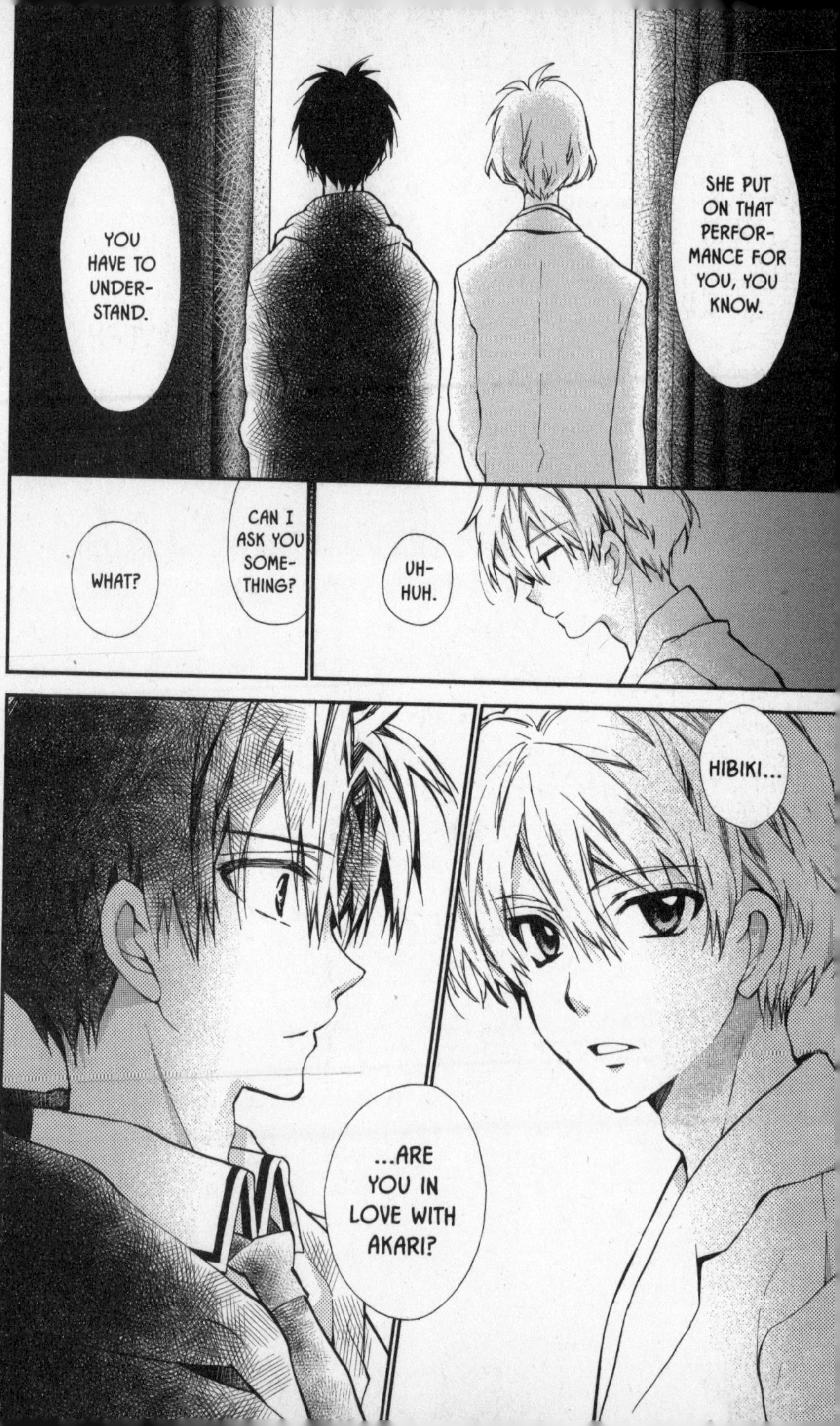
SHE PUT ON THAT PERFORMANCE FOR YOU, YOU KNOW.
YOU HAVE TO UNDERSTAND.
UH-HUH.
CAN I ASK YOU SOMETHING?
WHAT?
HIBIKI...
...ARE YOU IN LOVE WITH AKARI?

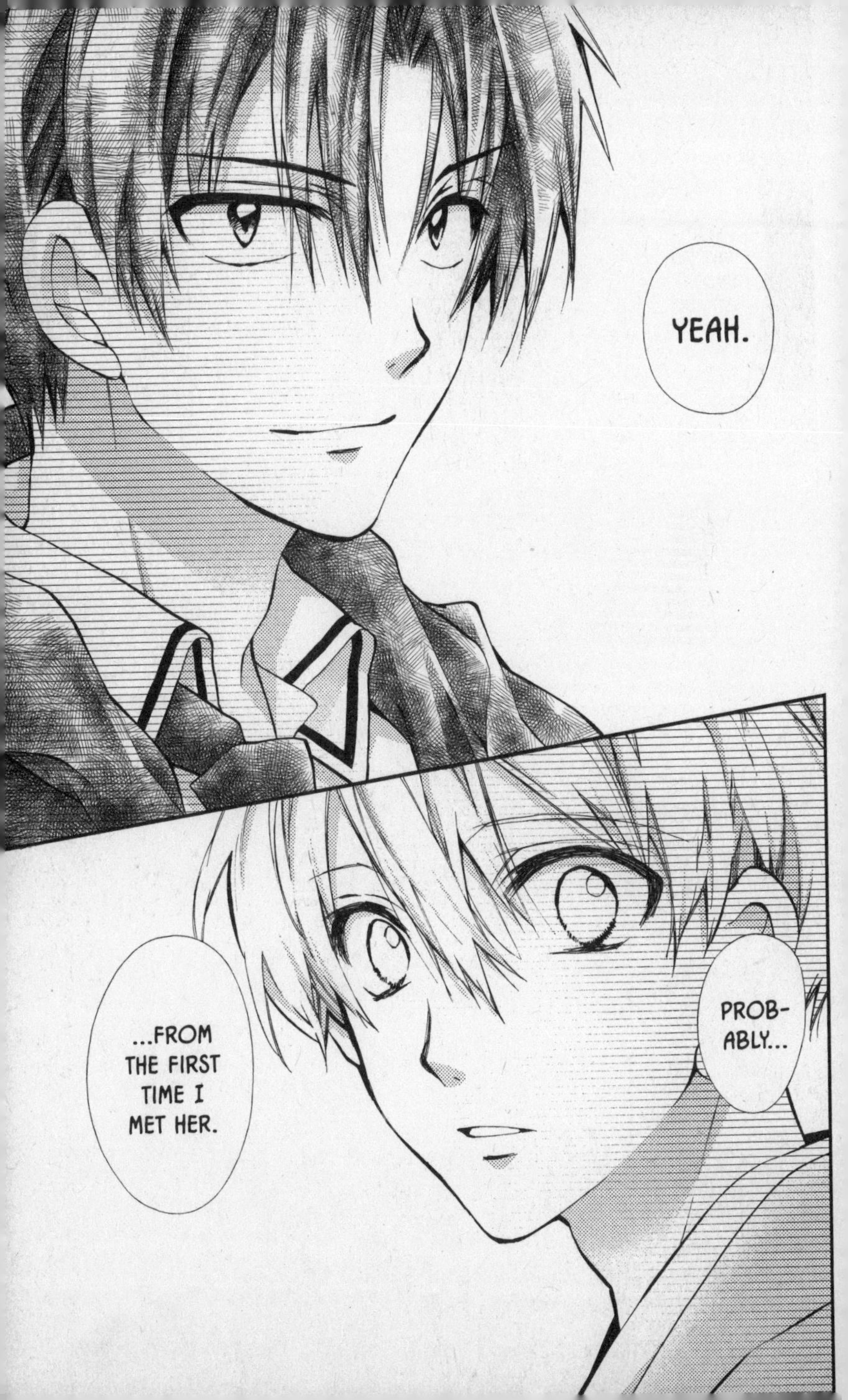
YEAH.
PROB-ABLY...
...FROM THE FIRST TIME I MET HER.

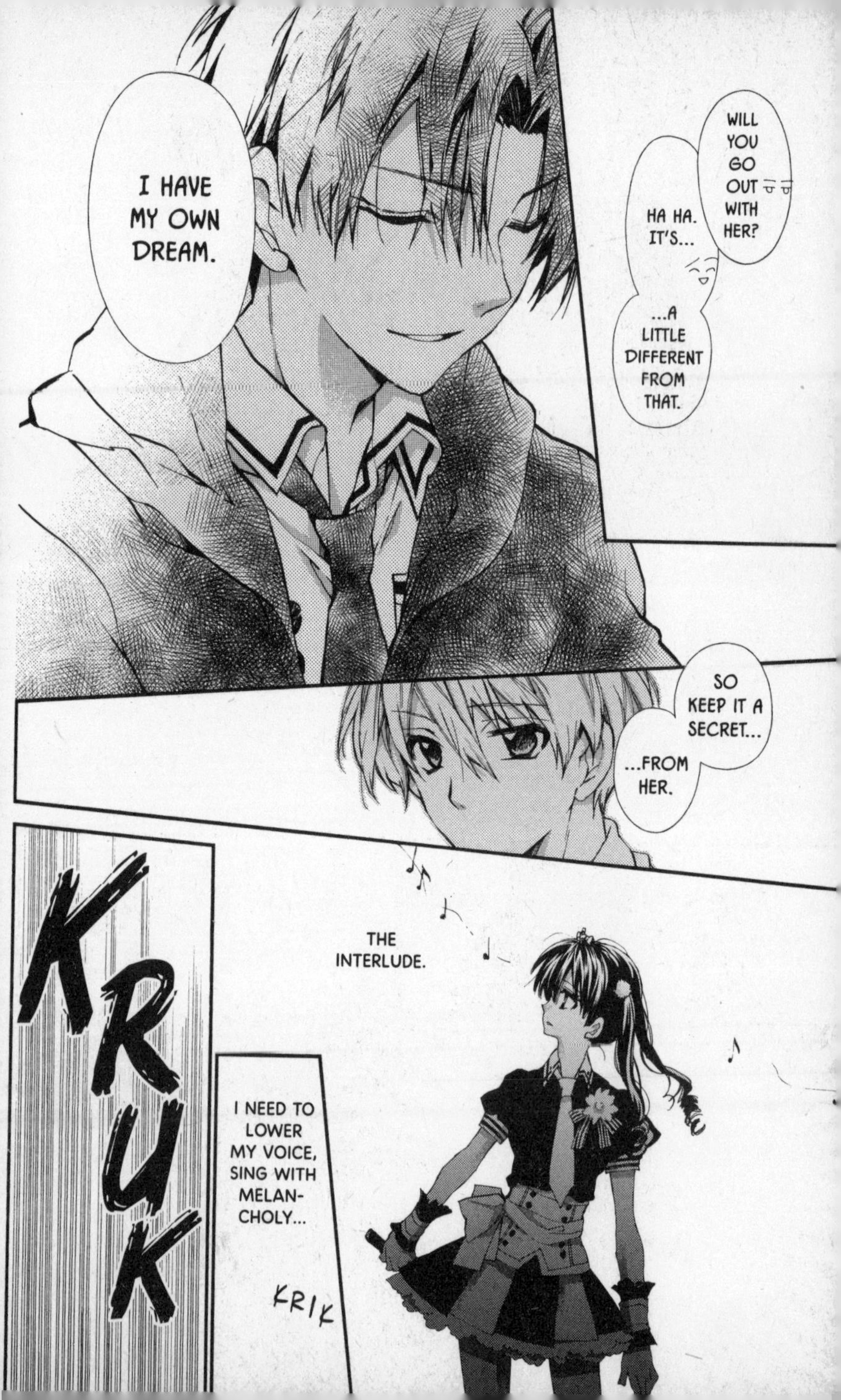
WILL YOU GO OUT WITH HER?
HA HA. IT'S...
...A LITTLE DIFFERENT FROM THAT.
I HAVE MY OWN DREAM.
SO KEEP IT A SECRET...
...FROM HER.
THE INTERLUDE.
I NEED TO LOWER MY VOICE, SING WITH MELAN-CHOLY...
KRIK
KRUK

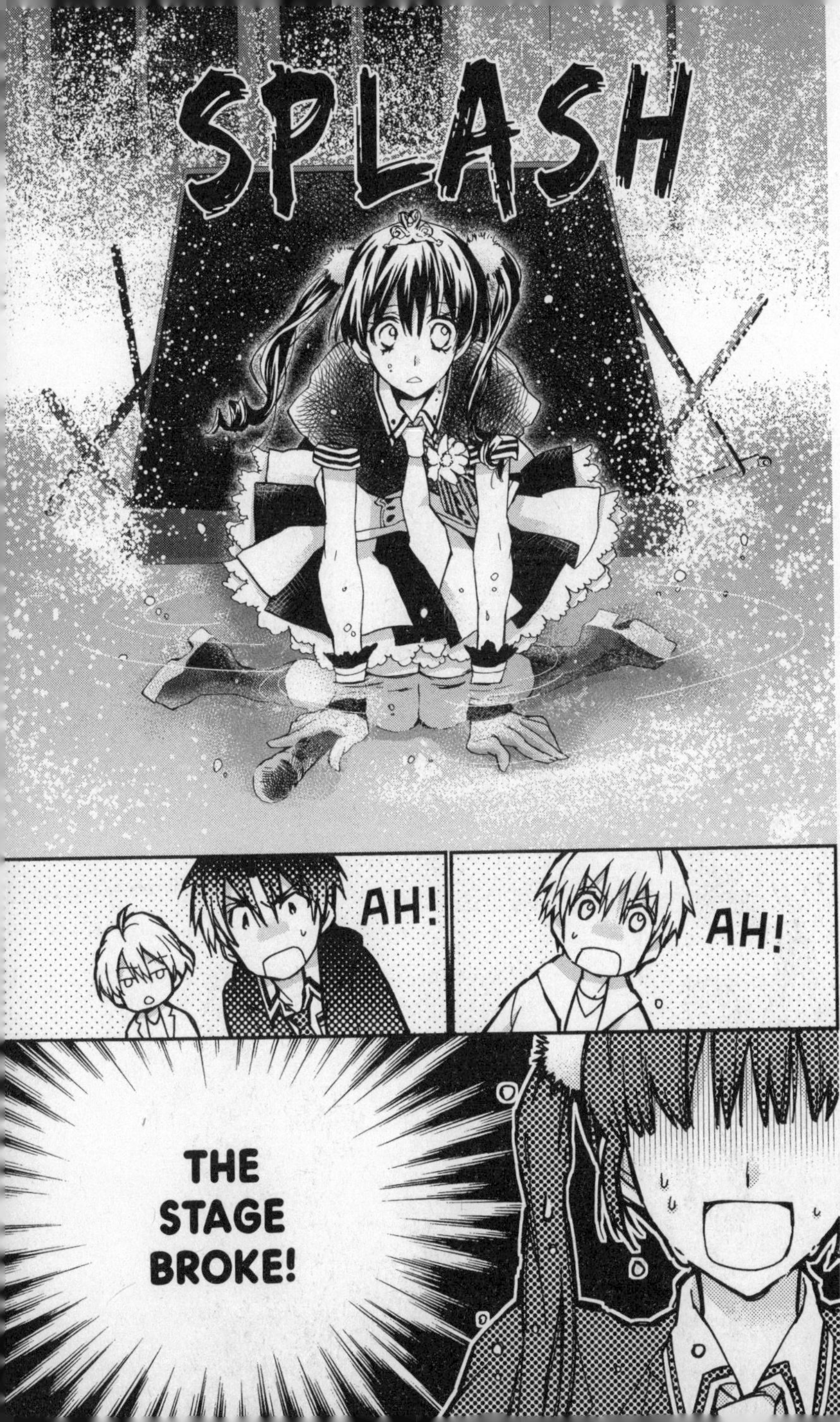
SPLASH
AH!
AH!
THE STAGE BROKE!

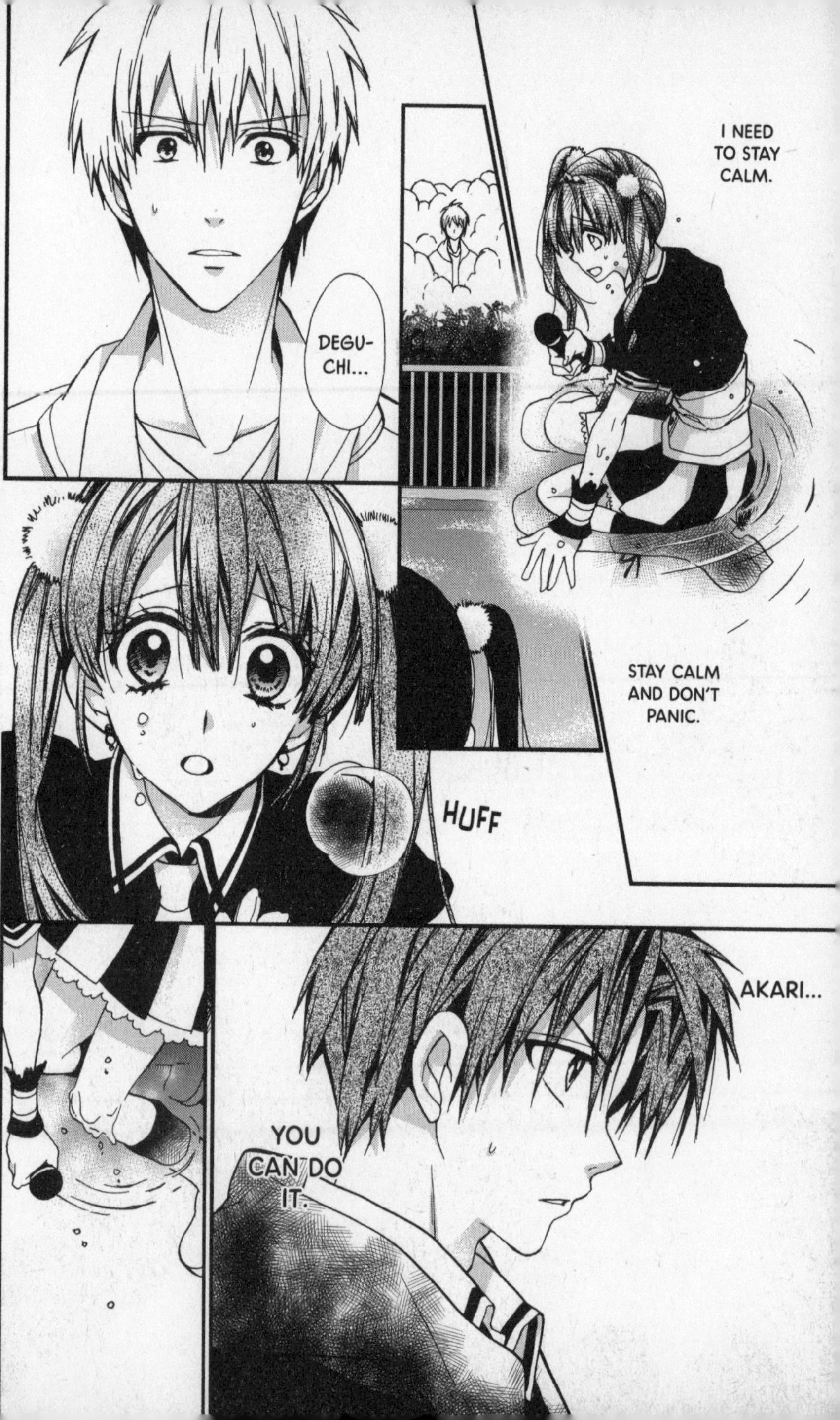
I NEED TO STAY CALM.
STAY CALM AND DON'T PANIC.
DEGU-CHI...
HUFF
AKARI...
YOU CAN DO IT.

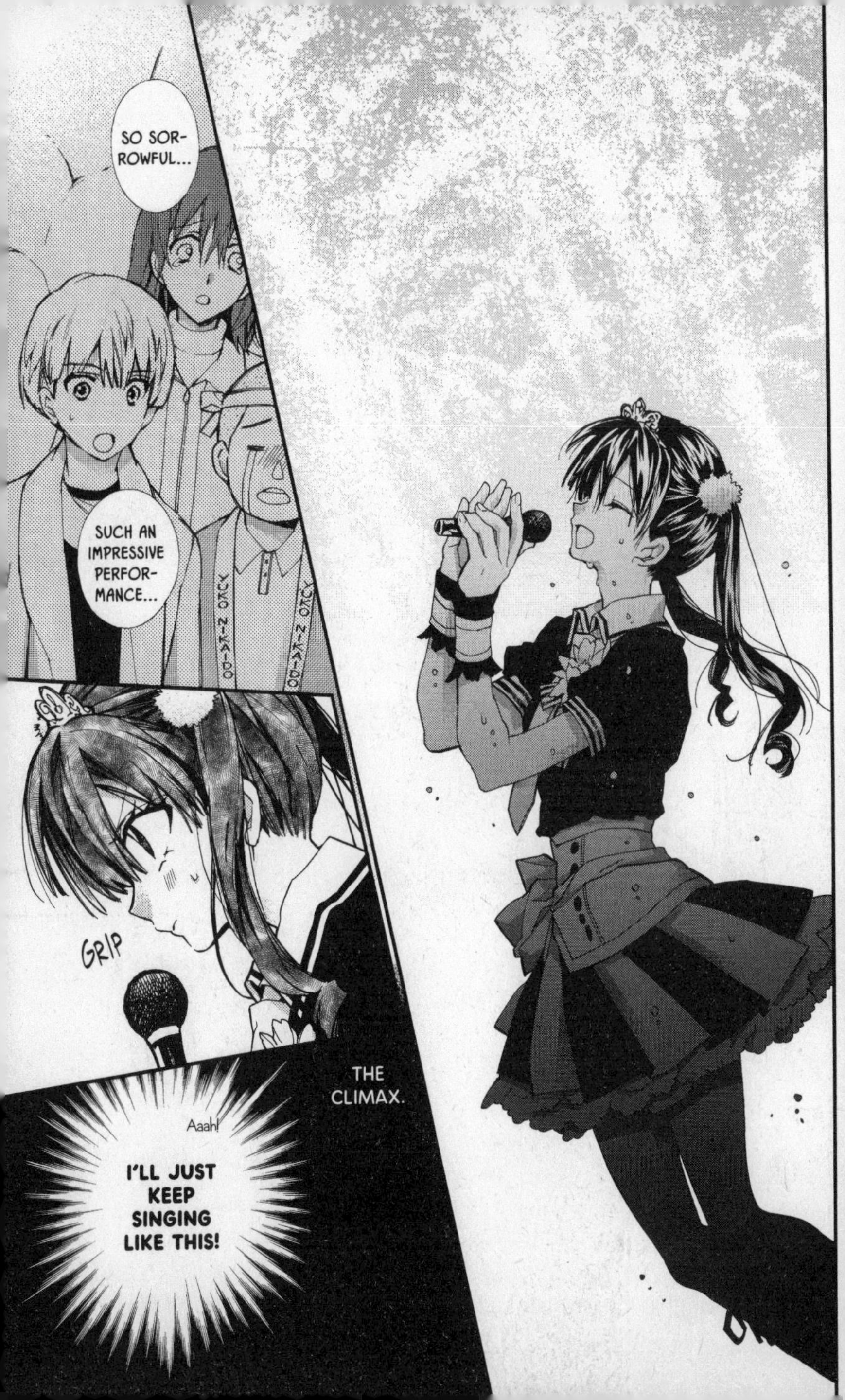
THE CLIMAX.
SO SOR-ROWFUL...
SUCH AN IMPRESSIVE PERFORMANCE...
YUKO NIKAIDO
YUKO NIKAIDO
GRIP
Aaah!
I'LL JUST KEEP SINGING LIKE THIS!

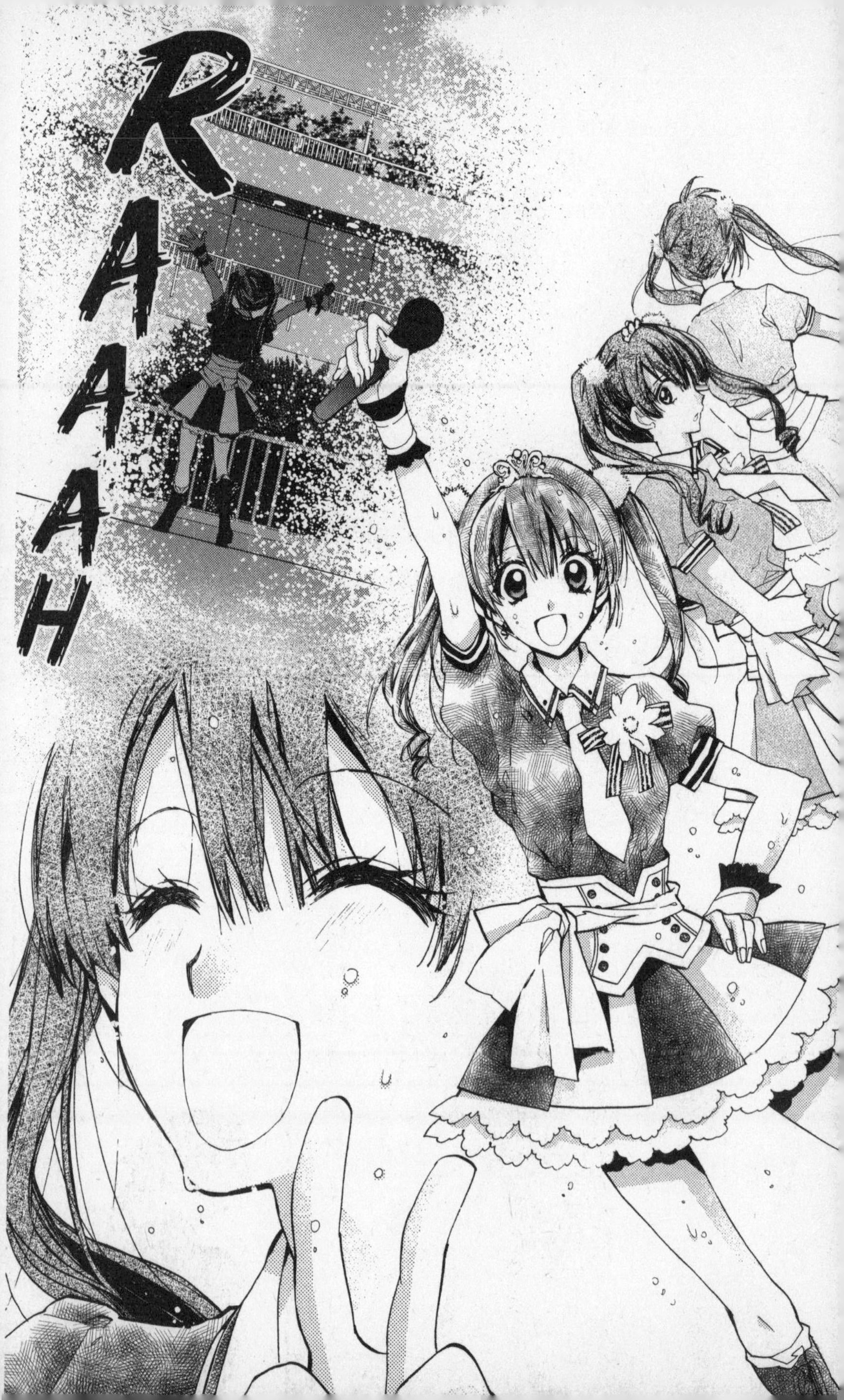
RAAAAH

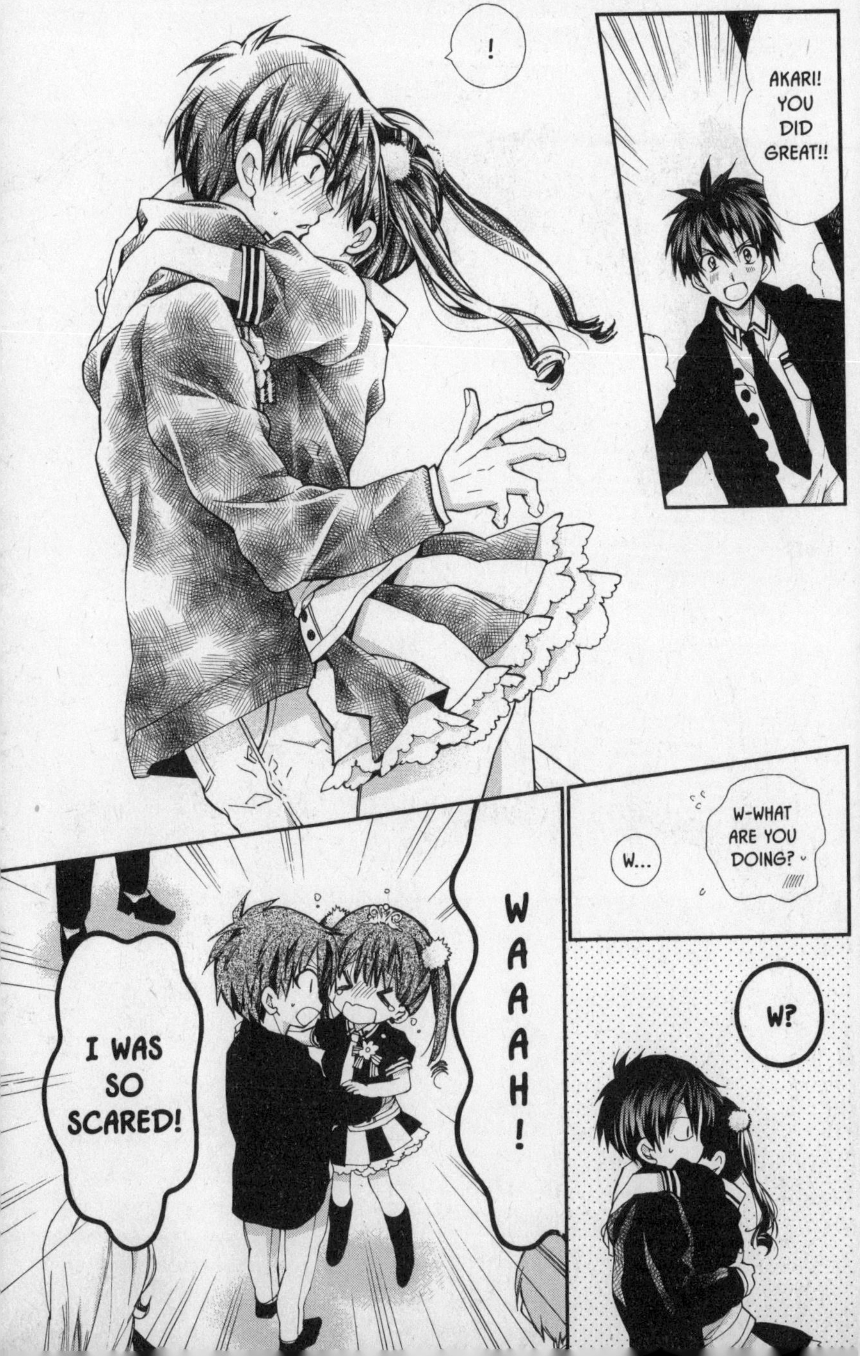
AKARI! YOU DID GREAT!!
!
W-WHAT ARE YOU DOING?
W...
W?
WAAAAH!
I WAS SO SCARED!

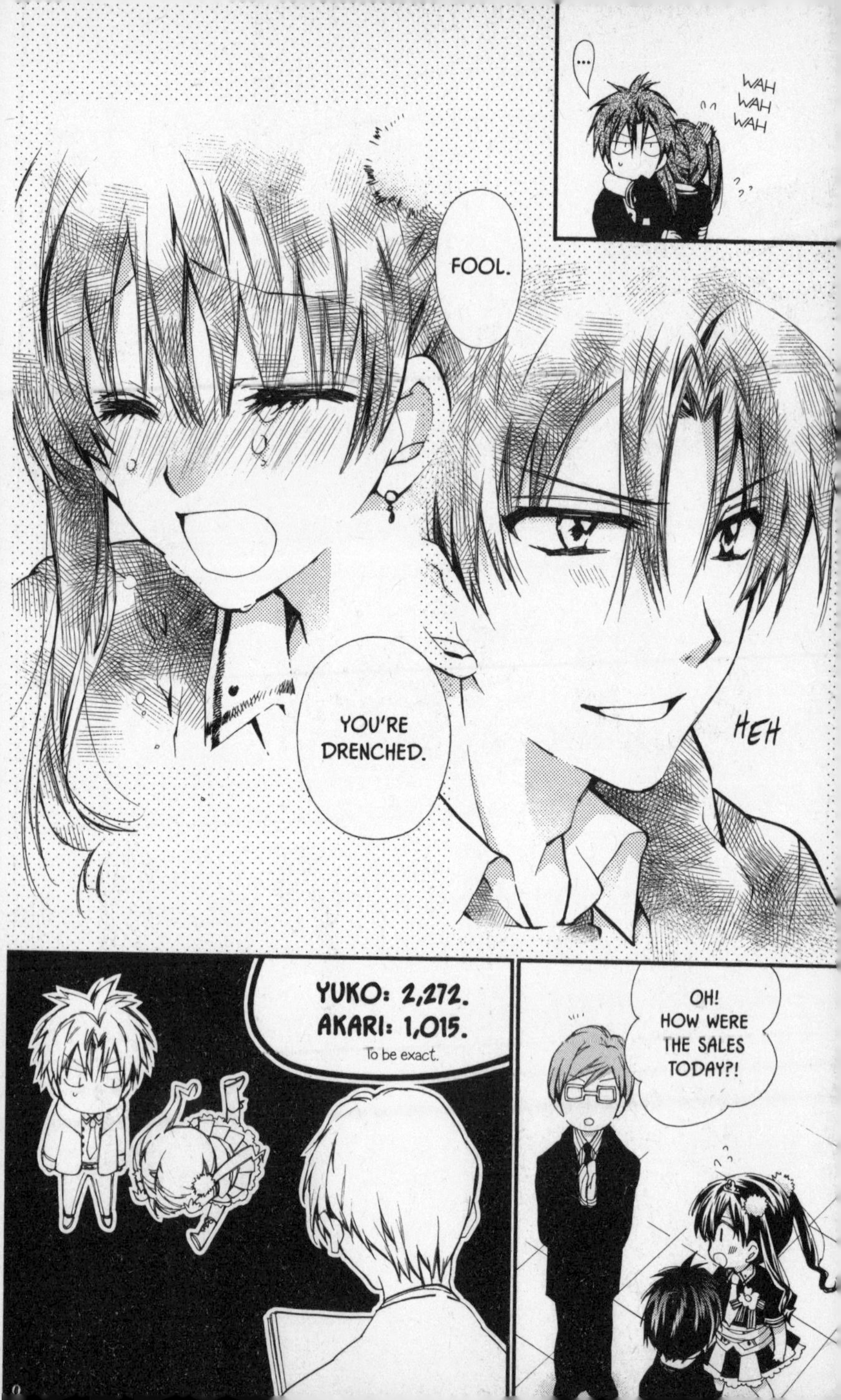
...
WAH WAH WAH
FOOL.
YOU'RE DRENCHED.
HEH
OH! HOW WERE THE SALES TODAY?!
YUKO: 2,272. AKARI: 1,015.
To be exact.

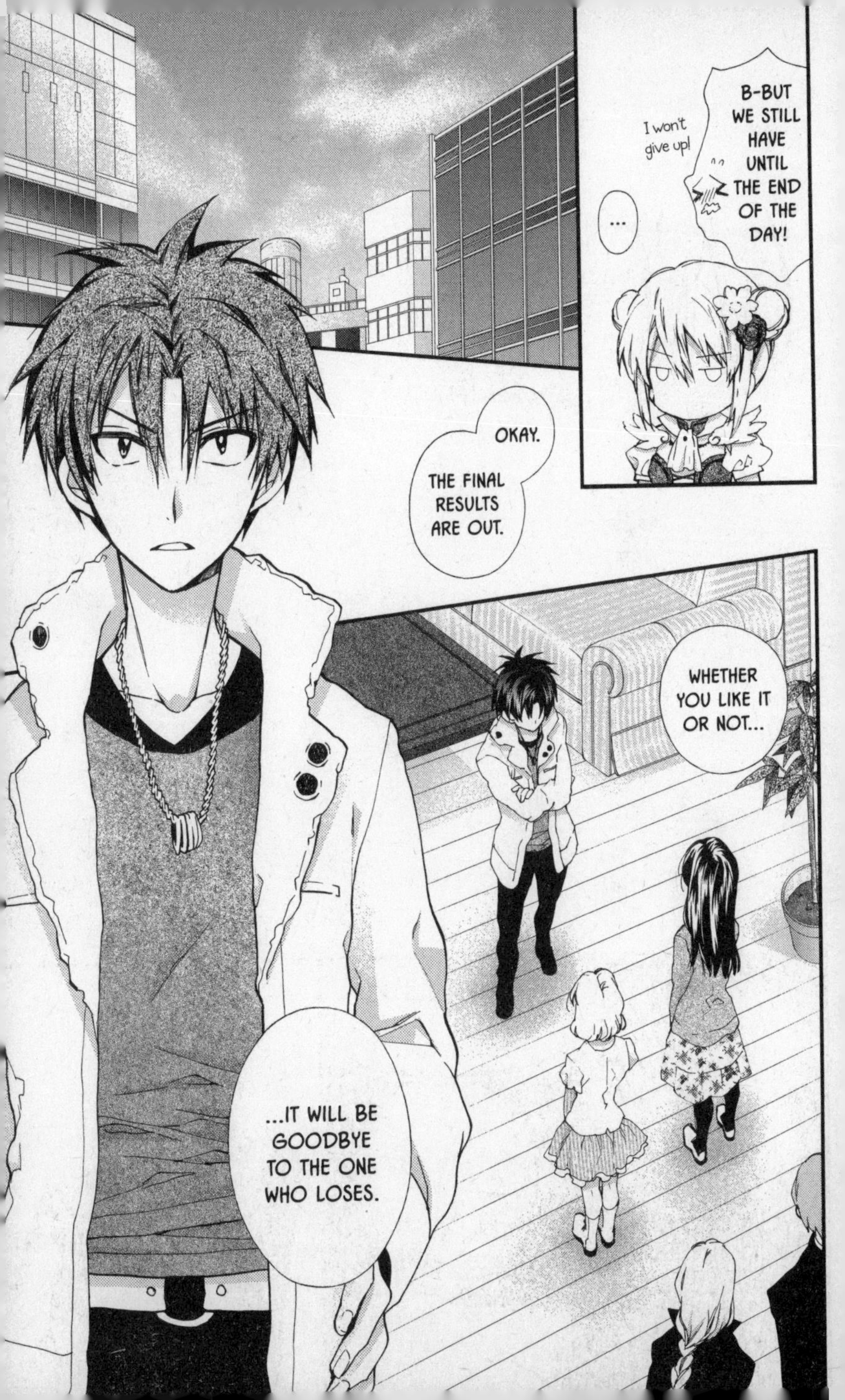

I won't give up!
B-BUT WE STILL HAVE UNTIL THE END OF THE DAY!
...
OKAY.
THE FINAL RESULTS ARE OUT.
WHETHER YOU LIKE IT OR NOT...
...IT WILL BE GOODBYE TO THE ONE WHO LOSES.

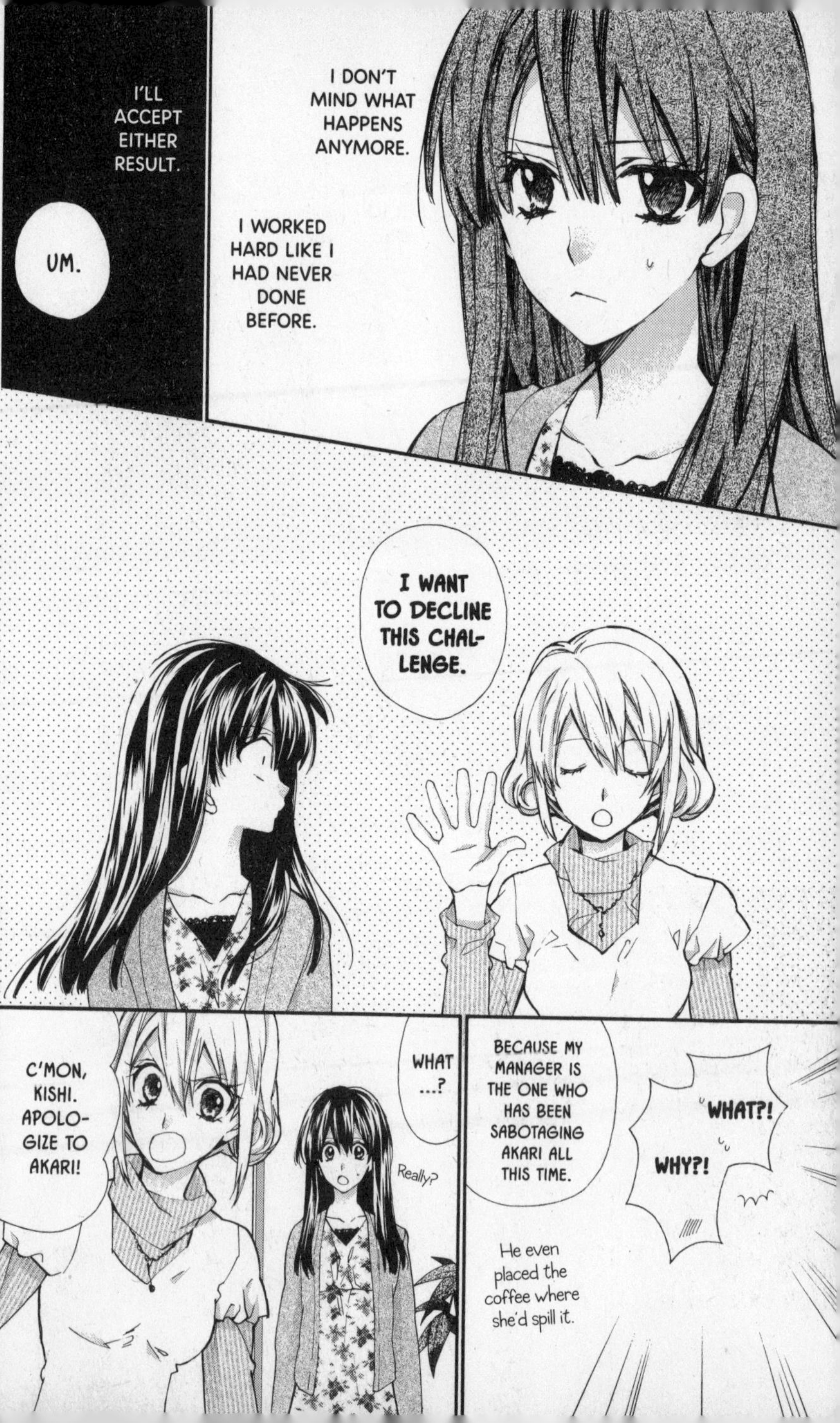
I DON'T MIND WHAT HAPPENS ANYMORE.
I WORKED HARD LIKE I HAD NEVER DONE BEFORE.
I'LL ACCEPT EITHER RESULT.
UM.
I WANT TO DECLINE THIS CHAL-LENGE.
BECAUSE MY MANAGER IS THE ONE WHO HAS BEEN SABOTAGING AKARI ALL THIS TIME.
WHAT?!
WHY?!
He even placed the coffee where she'd spill it.
WHAT ...?
C'MON, KISHI. APOLO-GIZE TO AKARI!
Really?

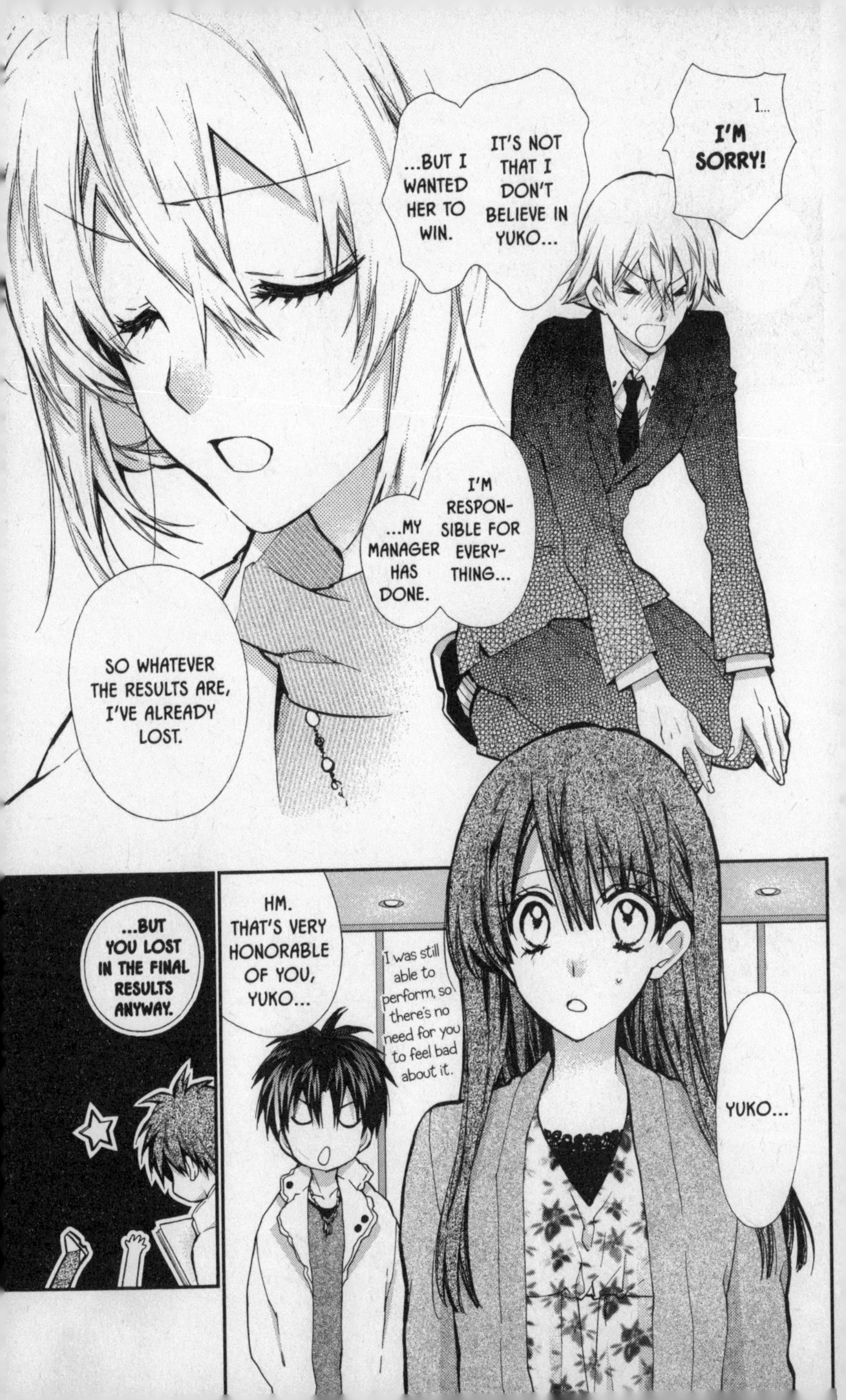
I... I'M SORRY!
IT'S NOT THAT I DON'T BELIEVE IN YUKO...
...BUT I WANTED HER TO WIN.
I'M RESPONSIBLE FOR EVERYTHING...
...MY MANAGER HAS DONE.
SO WHATEVER THE RESULTS ARE, I'VE ALREADY LOST.
YUKO...
I was still able to perform, so there's no need for you to feel bad about it.
HM. THAT'S VERY HONORABLE OF YOU, YUKO...
...BUT YOU LOST IN THE FINAL RESULTS ANYWAY.

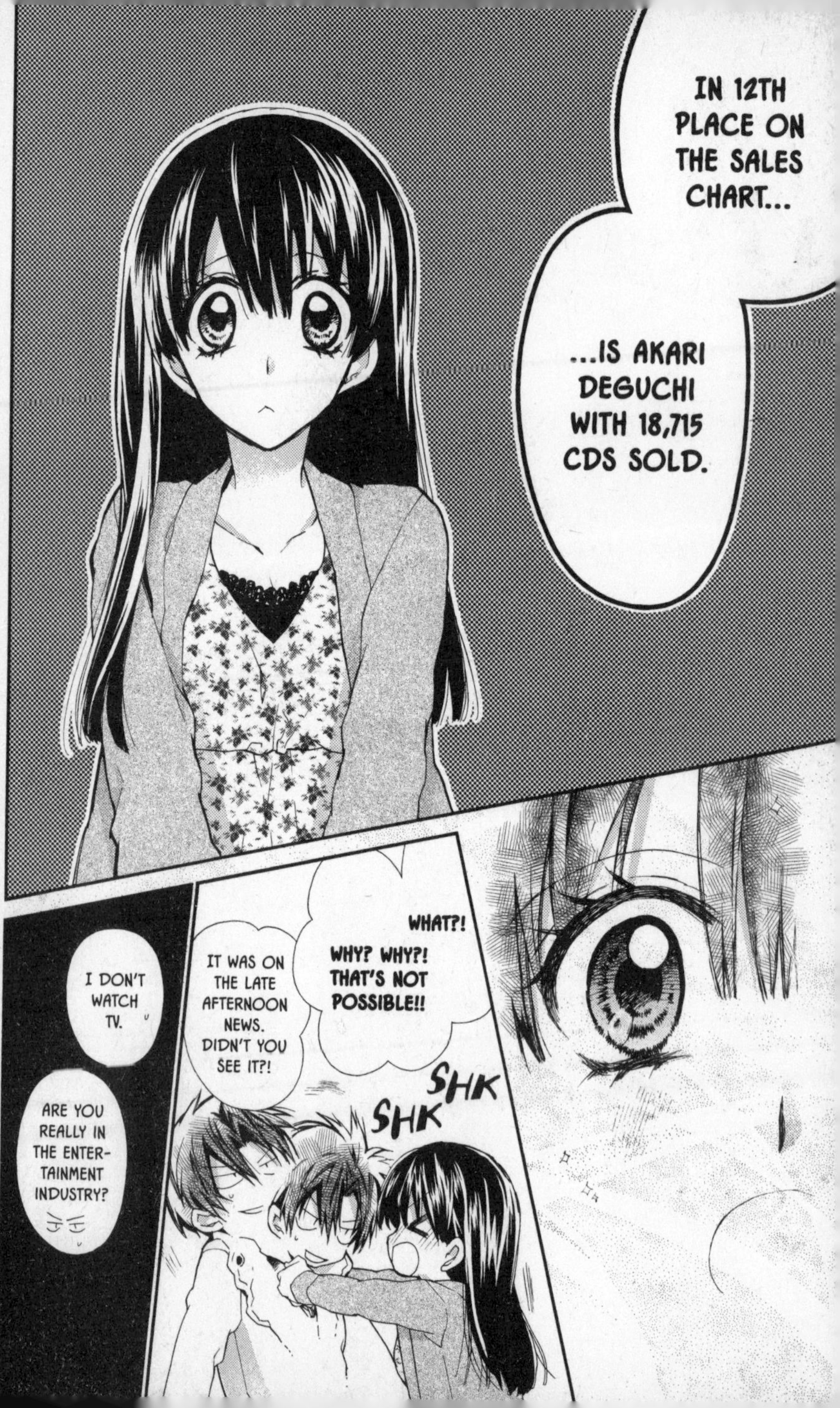
IN 12TH PLACE ON THE SALES CHART...
...IS AKARI DEGUCHI WITH 18,715 CDS SOLD.
WHAT?!
WHY? WHY?! THAT'S NOT POSSIBLE!!
IT WAS ON THE LATE AFTERNOON NEWS. DIDN'T YOU SEE IT?!
SHK
SHK
I DON'T WATCH TV.
ARE YOU REALLY IN THE ENTER-TAINMENT INDUSTRY?

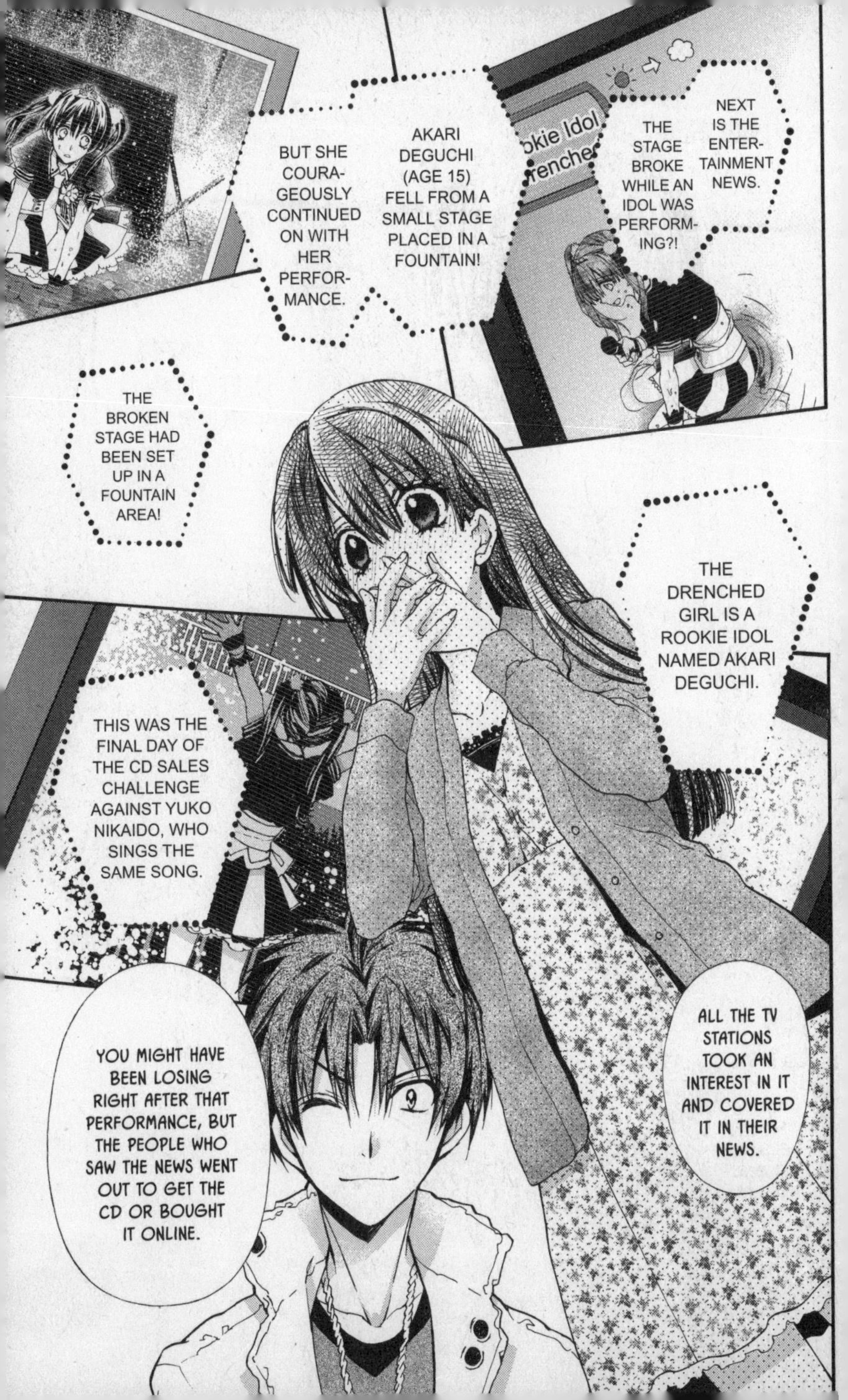
NEXT IS THE ENTER-TAINMENT NEWS.
THE STAGE BROKE WHILE AN IDOL WAS PERFORM-ING?!
AKARI DEGUCHI (AGE 15) FELL FROM A SMALL STAGE PLACED IN A FOUNTAIN!
BUT SHE COURA-GEOUSLY CONTINUED ON WITH HER PERFOR-MANCE.
THE BROKEN STAGE HAD BEEN SET UP IN A FOUNTAIN AREA!
THE DRENCHED GIRL IS A ROOKIE IDOL NAMED AKARI DEGUCHI.
THIS WAS THE FINAL DAY OF THE CD SALES CHALLENGE AGAINST YUKO NIKAIDO, WHO SINGS THE SAME SONG.
ALL THE TV STATIONS TOOK AN INTEREST IN IT AND COVERED IT IN THEIR NEWS.
YOU MIGHT HAVE BEEN LOSING RIGHT AFTER THAT PERFORMANCE, BUT THE PEOPLE WHO SAW THE NEWS WENT OUT TO GET THE CD OR BOUGHT IT ONLINE.

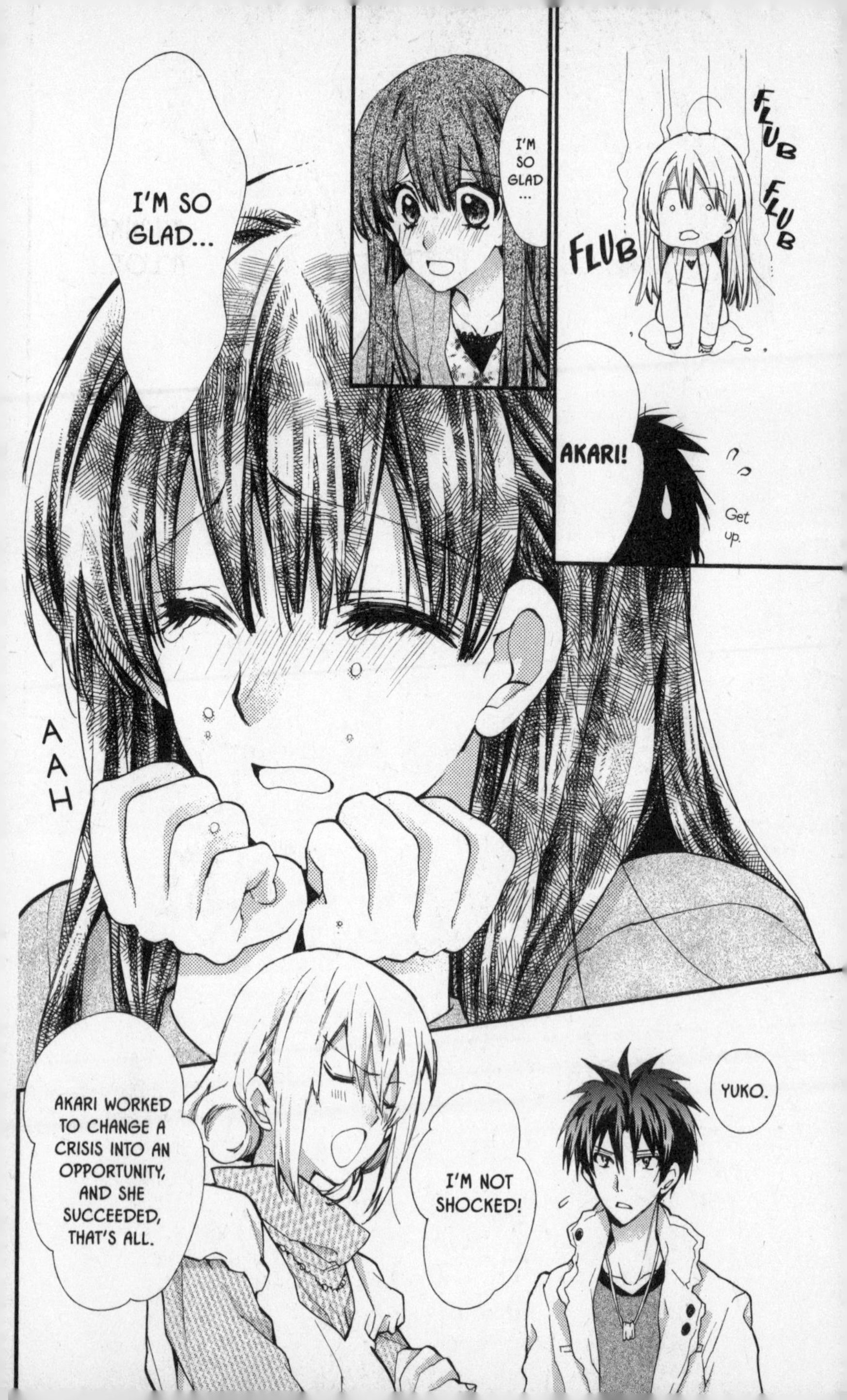

FLUB
FLUB
FLUB
AKARI!
Get up.
I'M SO GLAD ...
I'M SO GLAD...
AAH
YUKO.
I'M NOT SHOCKED!
AKARI WORKED TO CHANGE A CRISIS INTO AN OPPORTUNITY, AND SHE SUCCEEDED, THAT'S ALL.

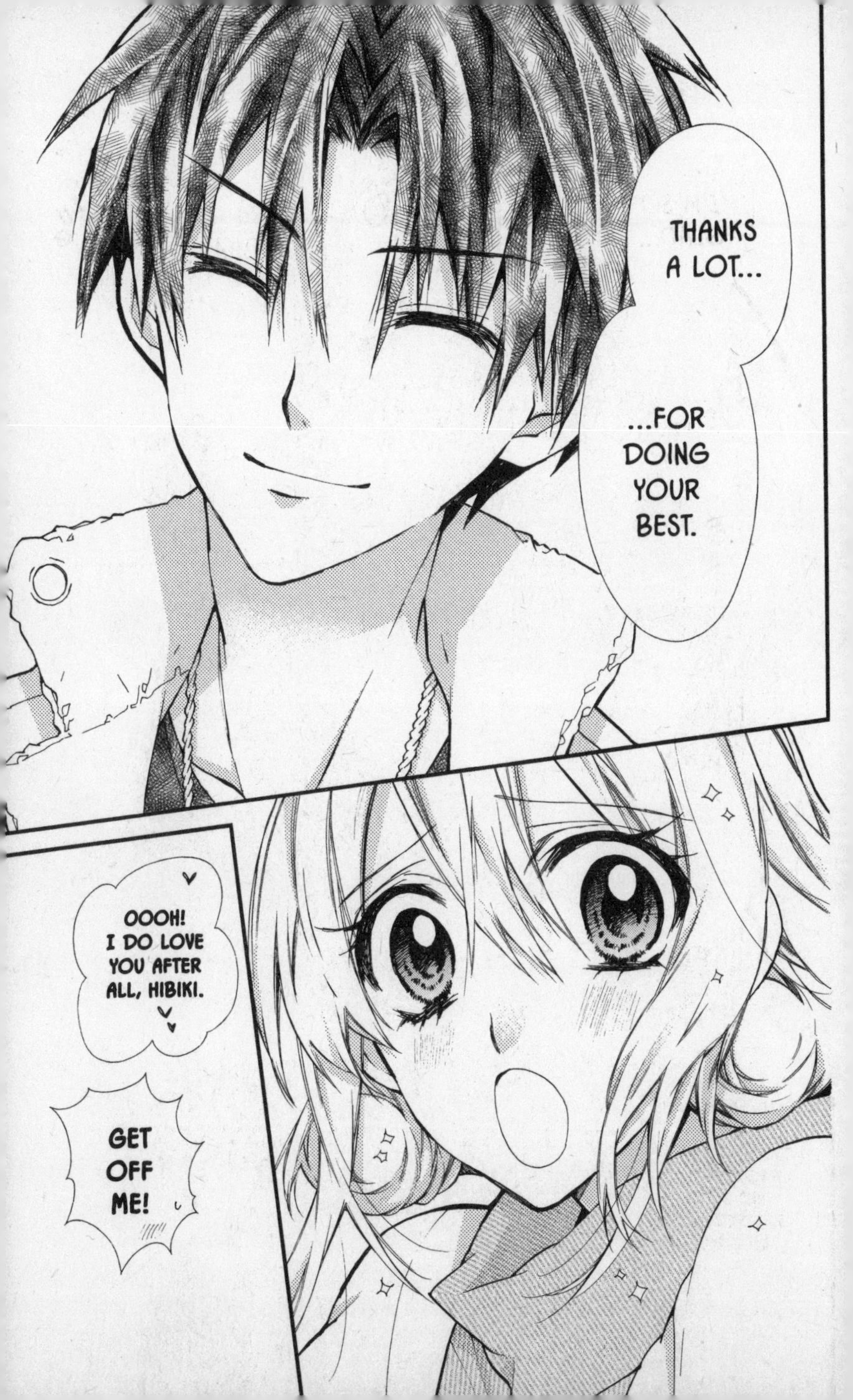
THANKS A LOT...
...FOR DOING YOUR BEST.
OOOH! I DO LOVE YOU AFTER ALL, HIBIKI.
GET OFF ME!

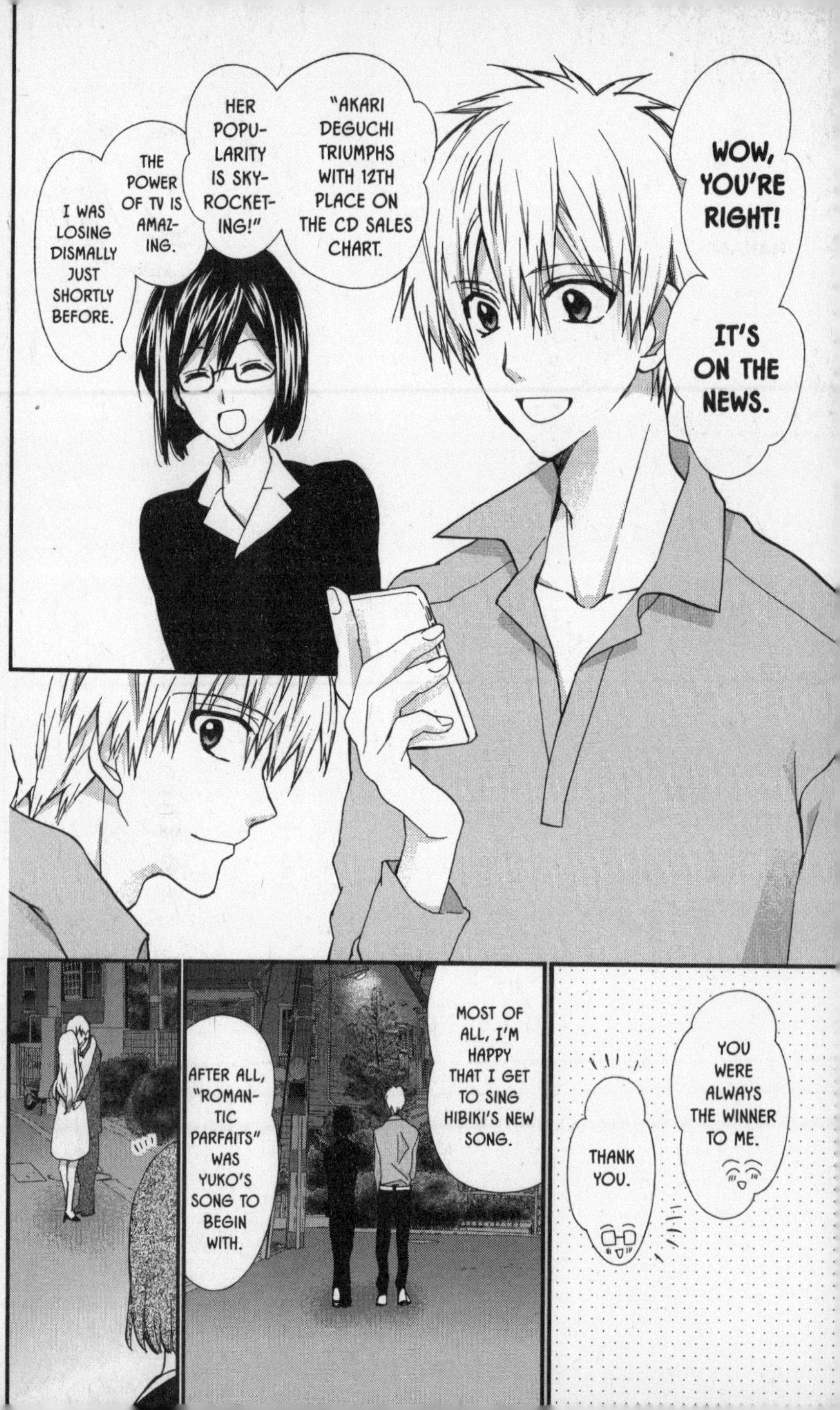
WOW, YOU'RE RIGHT!
IT'S ON THE NEWS.
"AKARI DEGUCHI TRIUMPHS WITH 12TH PLACE ON THE CD SALES CHART.
HER POPU-LARITY IS SKY-ROCKET-ING!"
THE POWER OF TV IS AMAZ-ING.
I WAS LOSING DISMALLY JUST SHORTLY BEFORE.
YOU WERE ALWAYS THE WINNER TO ME.
THANK YOU.
MOST OF ALL, I'M HAPPY THAT I GET TO SING HIBIKI'S NEW SONG.
AFTER ALL, "ROMAN-TIC PARFAITS" WAS YUKO'S SONG TO BEGIN WITH.

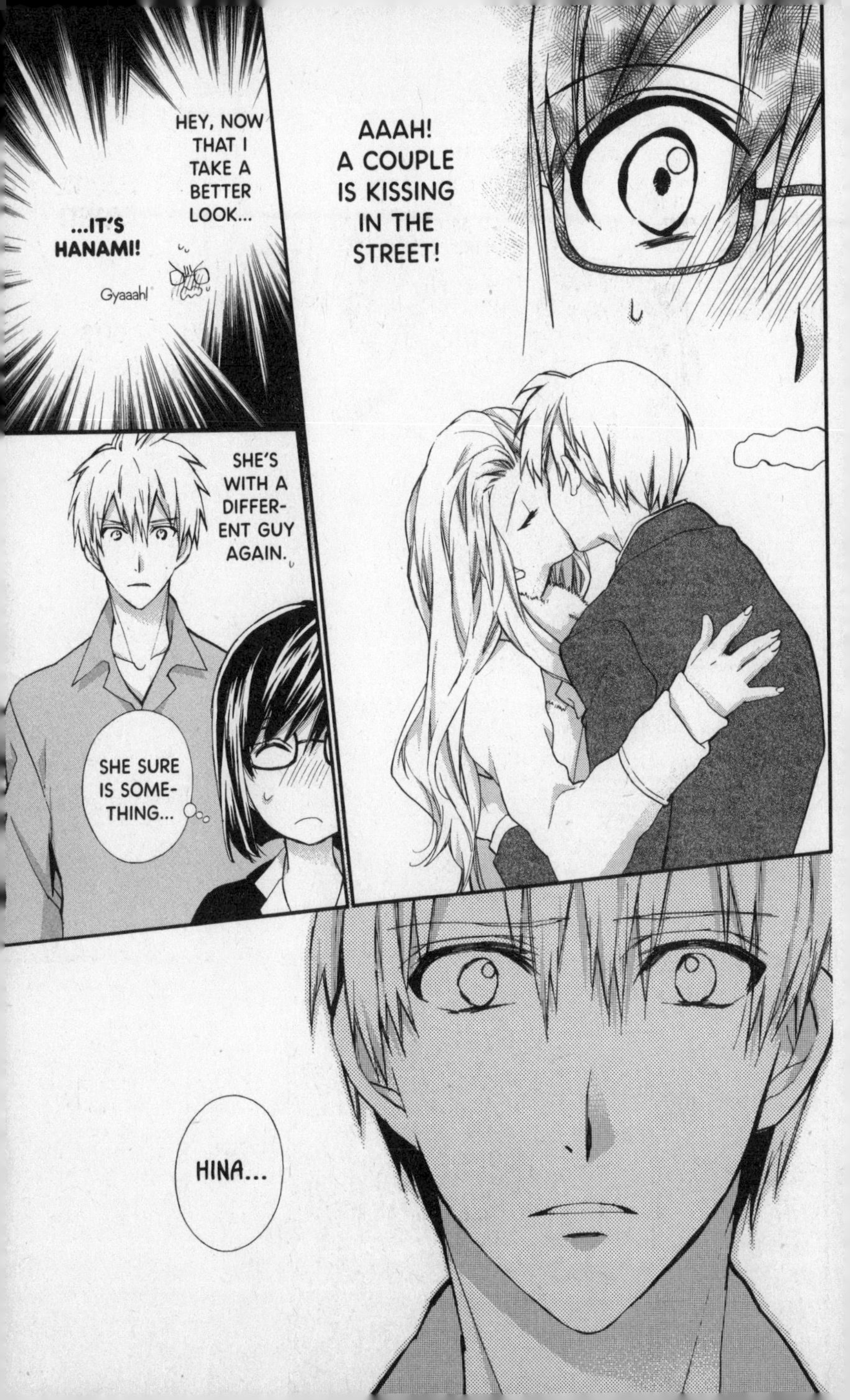
AAAH! A COUPLE IS KISSING IN THE STREET!
HEY, NOW THAT I TAKE A BETTER LOOK...
...IT'S HANAMI!
Gyaaah!
SHE'S WITH A DIFFERENT GUY AGAIN.
SHE SURE IS SOMETHING...
HINA...

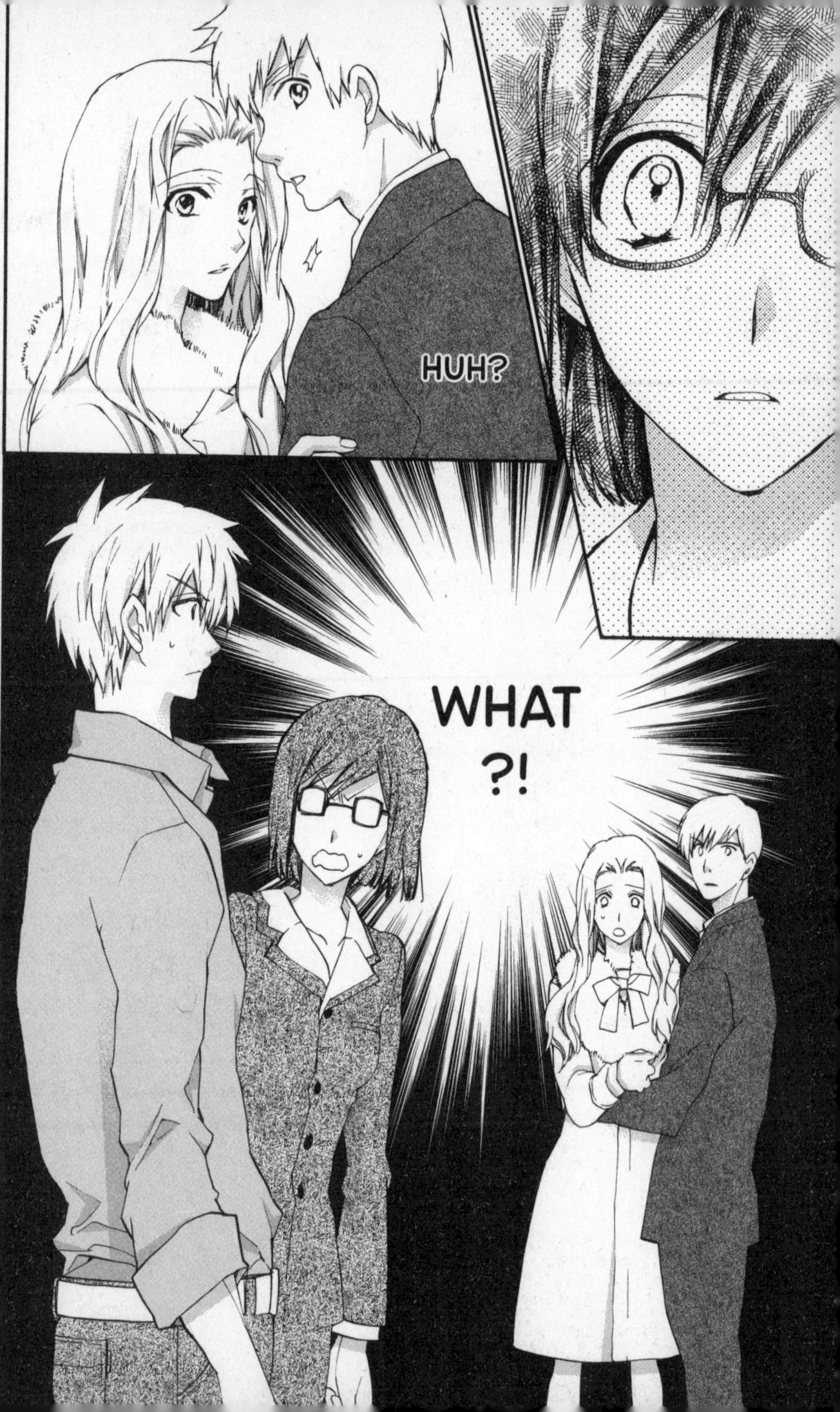
HUH?
WHAT
?!

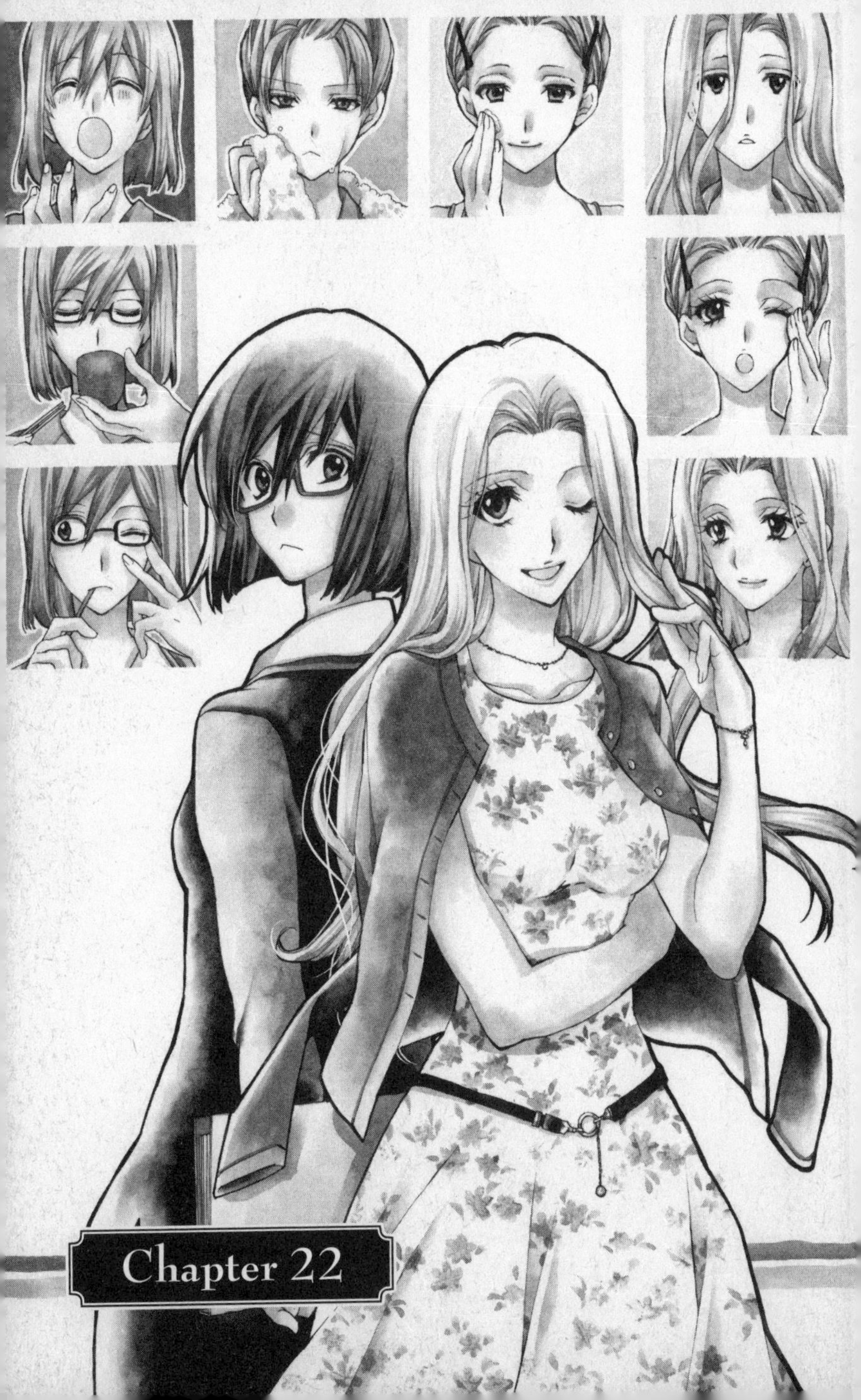
Chapter 22

IDOL dreams

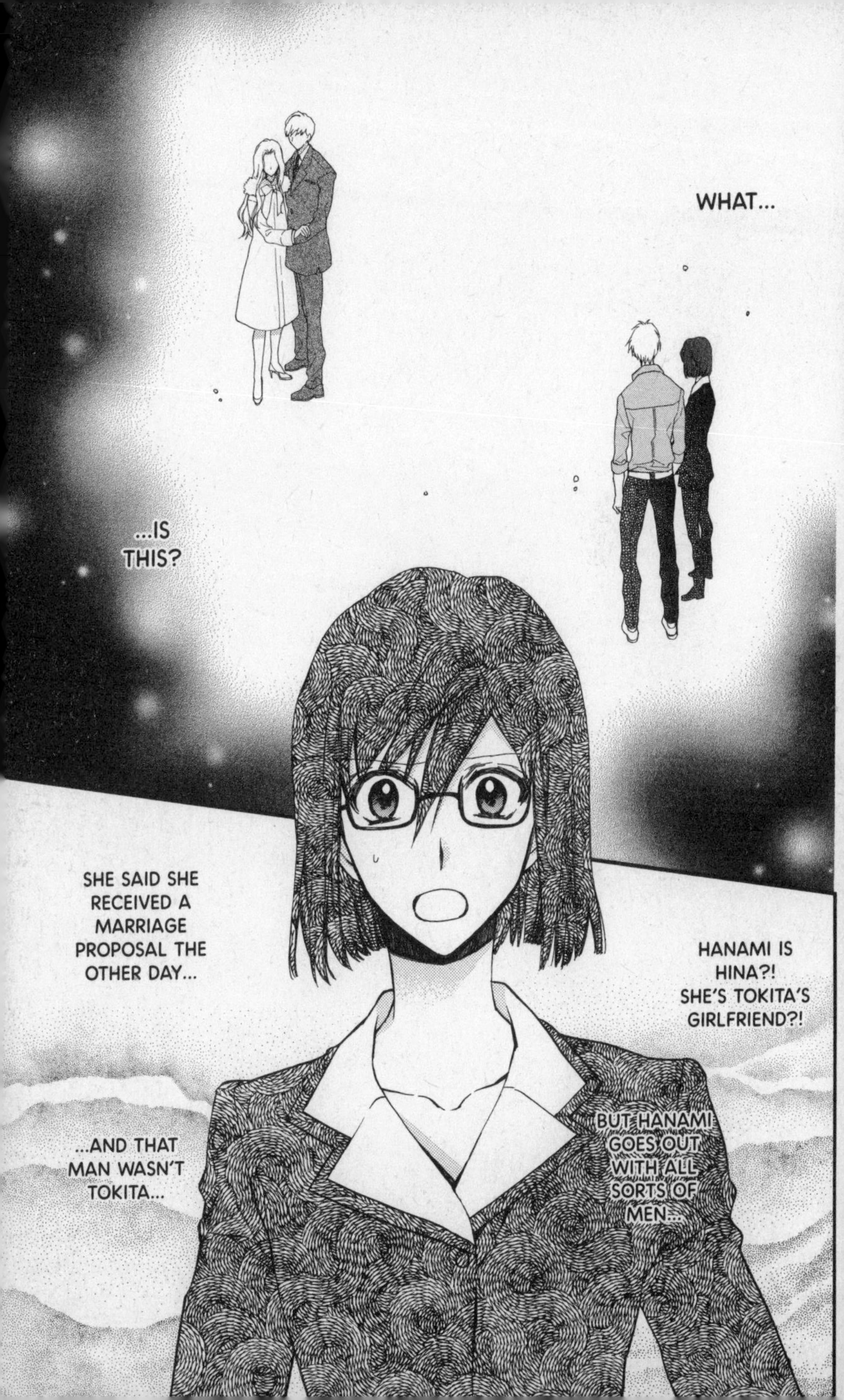
WHAT...
...IS THIS?
HANAMI IS HINA?! SHE'S TOKITA'S GIRLFRIEND?!
BUT HANAMI GOES OUT WITH ALL SORTS OF MEN...
SHE SAID SHE RECEIVED A MARRIAGE PROPOSAL THE OTHER DAY...
...AND THAT MAN WASN'T TOKITA...

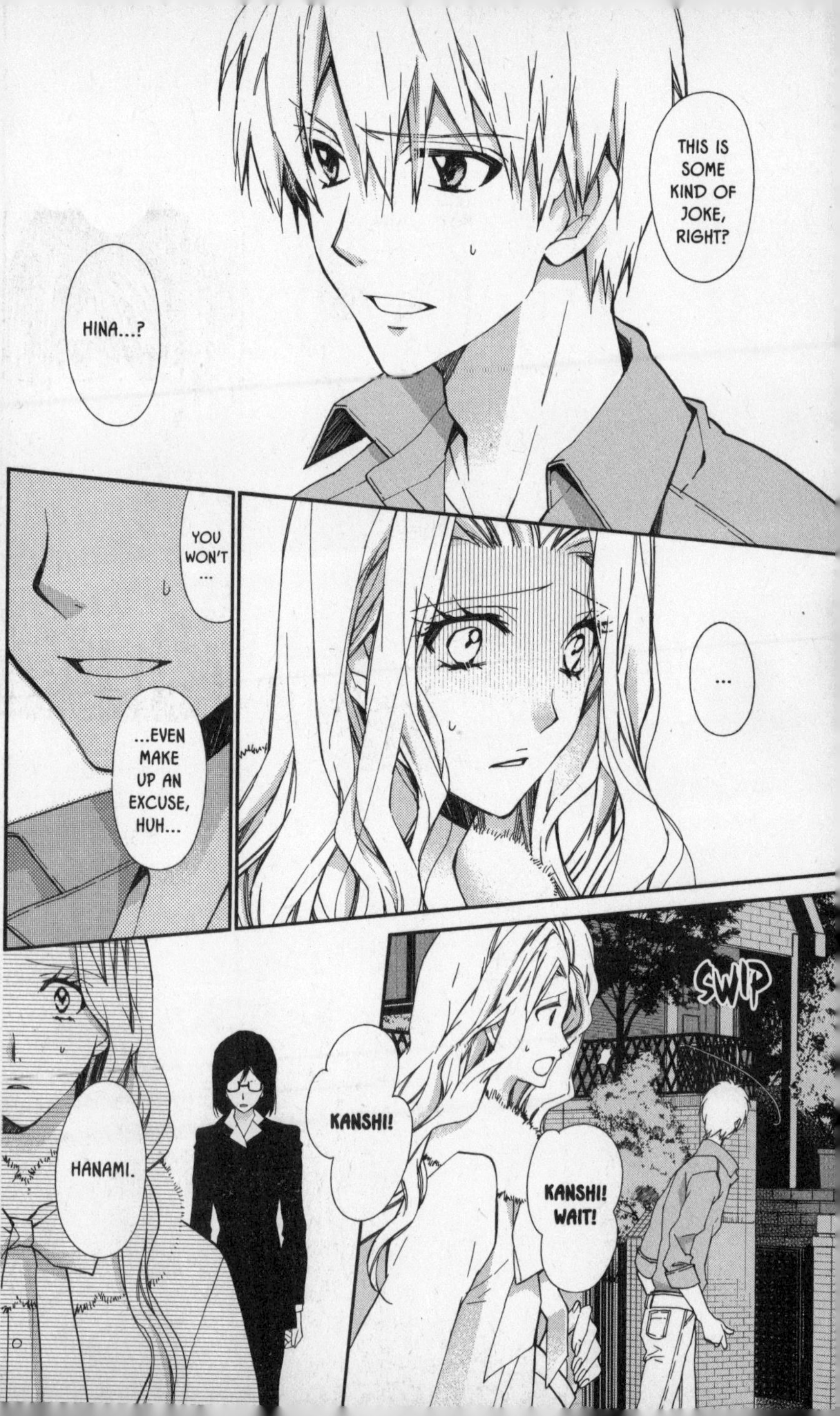
THIS IS SOME KIND OF JOKE, RIGHT?
HINA...?
...
YOU WON'T ...
...EVEN MAKE UP AN EXCUSE, HUH...
SWIP
KANSHI! WAIT!
KANSHI!
HANAMI.

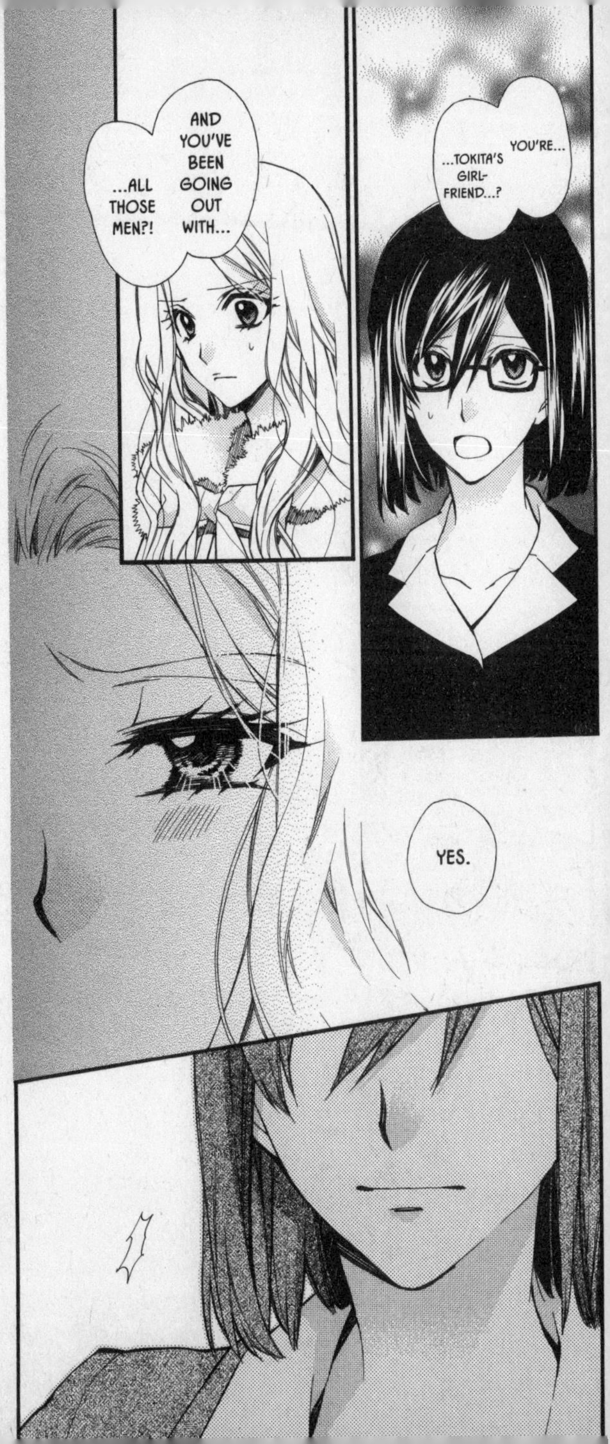
YOU'RE... ...TOKITA'S GIRL-FRIEND...?
AND YOU'VE BEEN GOING OUT WITH... ...ALL THOSE MEN?!
YES.

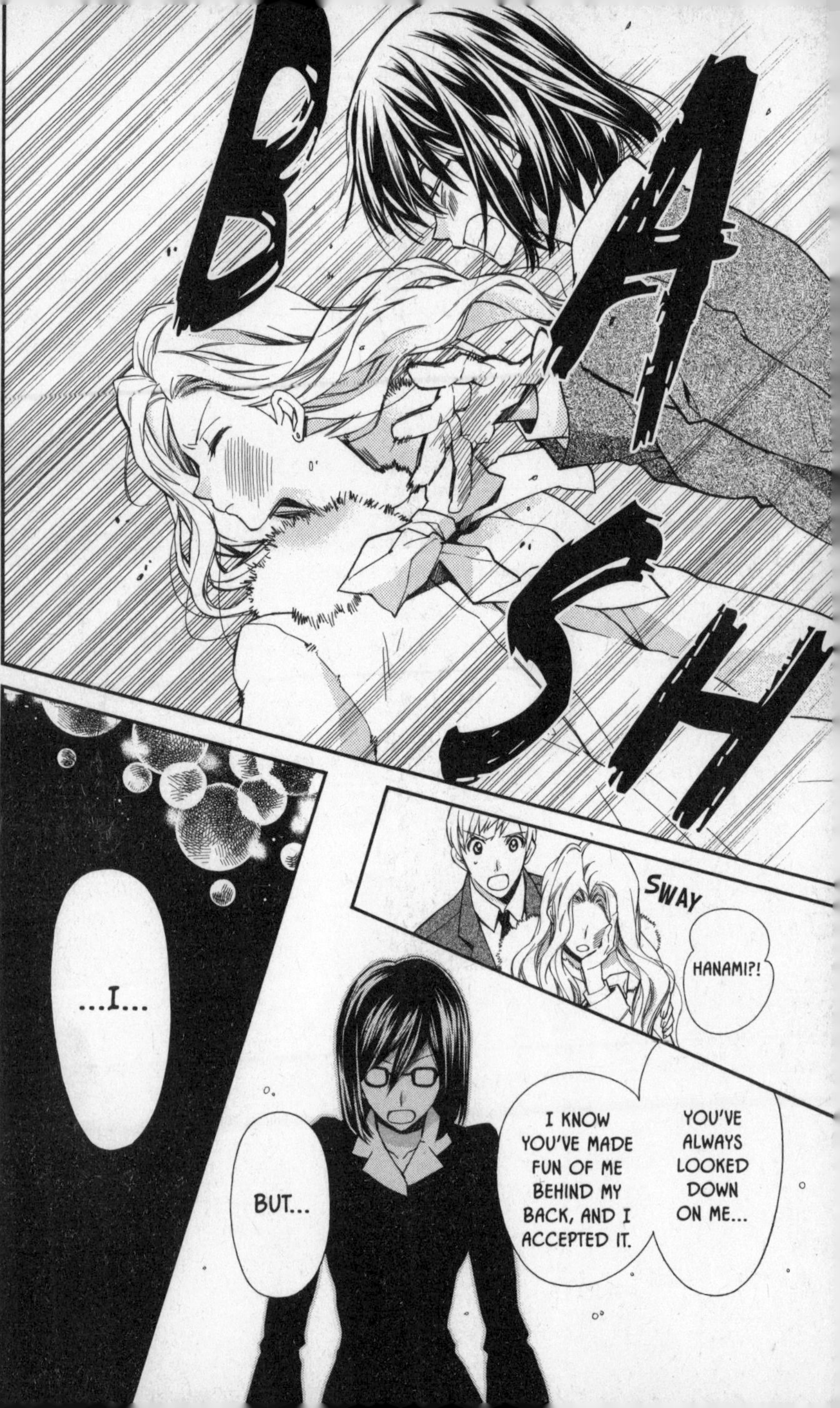
BASH
SWAY
HANAMI?!
YOU'VE ALWAYS LOOKED DOWN ON ME...
I KNOW YOU'VE MADE FUN OF ME BEHIND MY BACK, AND I ACCEPTED IT.
BUT...
...I...

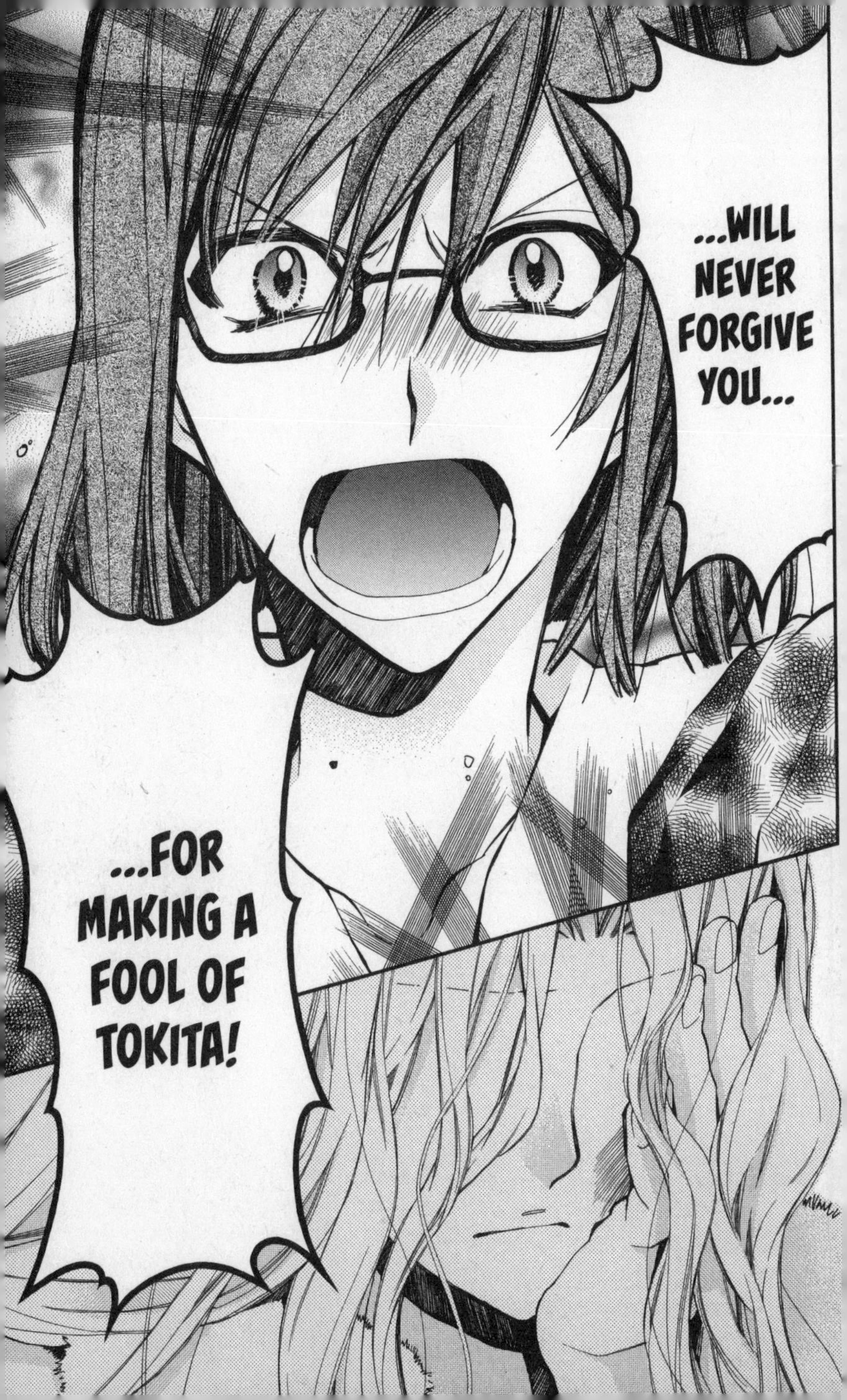
...WILL NEVER FORGIVE YOU...
...FOR MAKING A FOOL OF TOKITA!

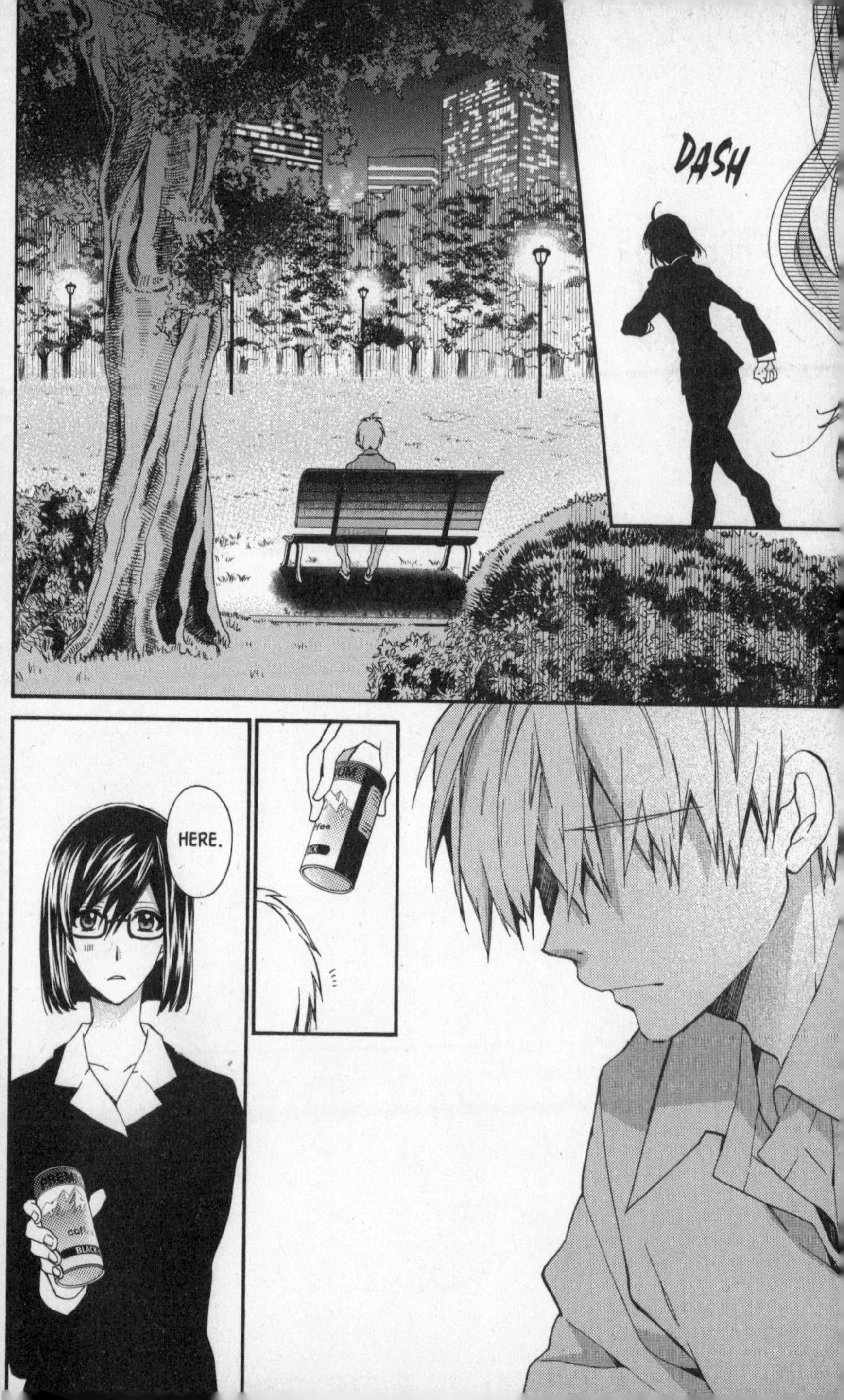
DASH
HERE.

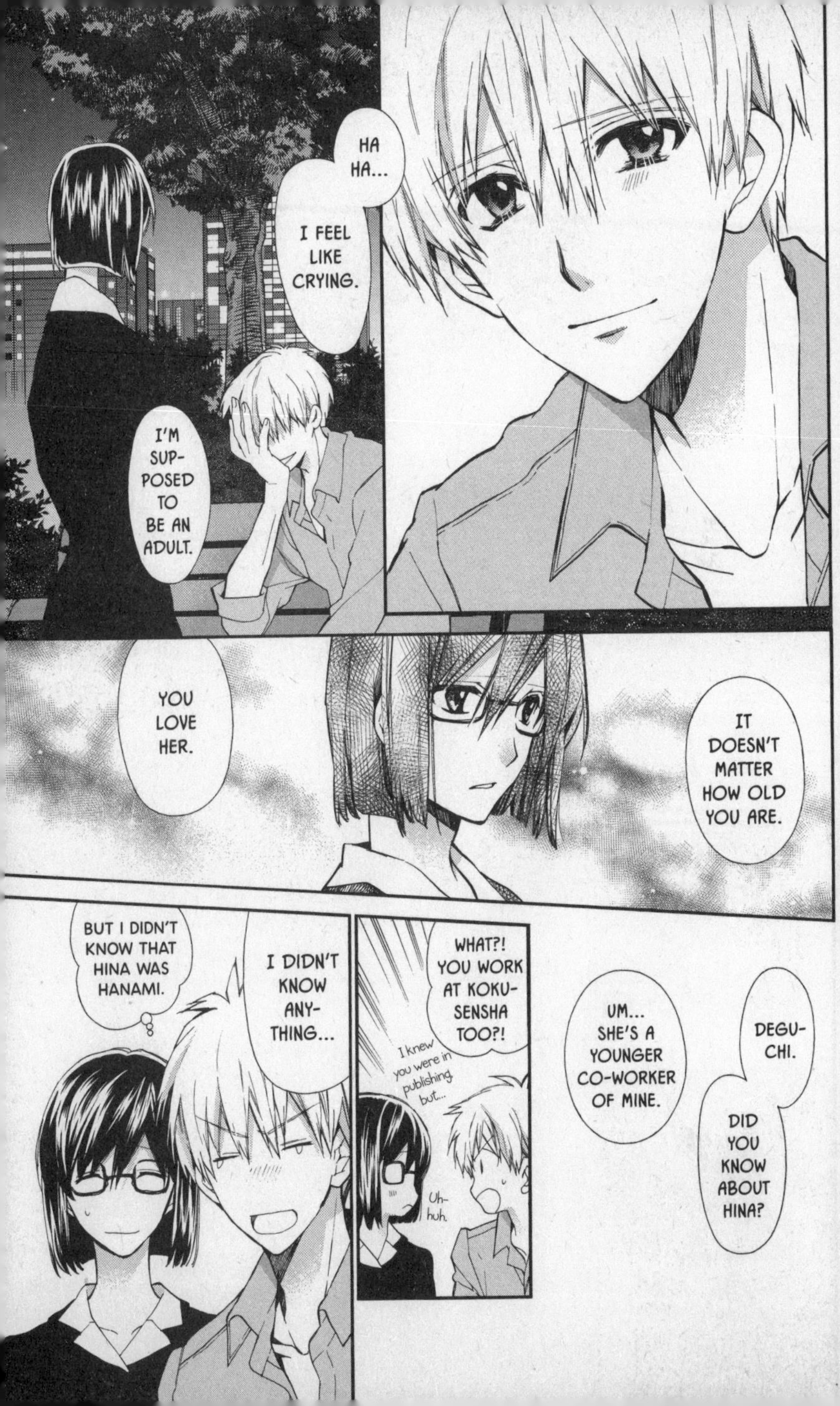
HA HA...
I FEEL LIKE CRYING.
I'M SUP-POSED TO BE AN ADULT.
IT DOESN'T MATTER HOW OLD YOU ARE.
YOU LOVE HER.
DEGU-CHI.
DID YOU KNOW ABOUT HINA?
UM... SHE'S A YOUNGER CO-WORKER OF MINE.
WHAT?! YOU WORK AT KOKU-SENSHA TOO?!
I knew you were in publishing, but...
Uh-huh.
I DIDN'T KNOW ANY-THING...
BUT I DIDN'T KNOW THAT HINA WAS HANAMI.

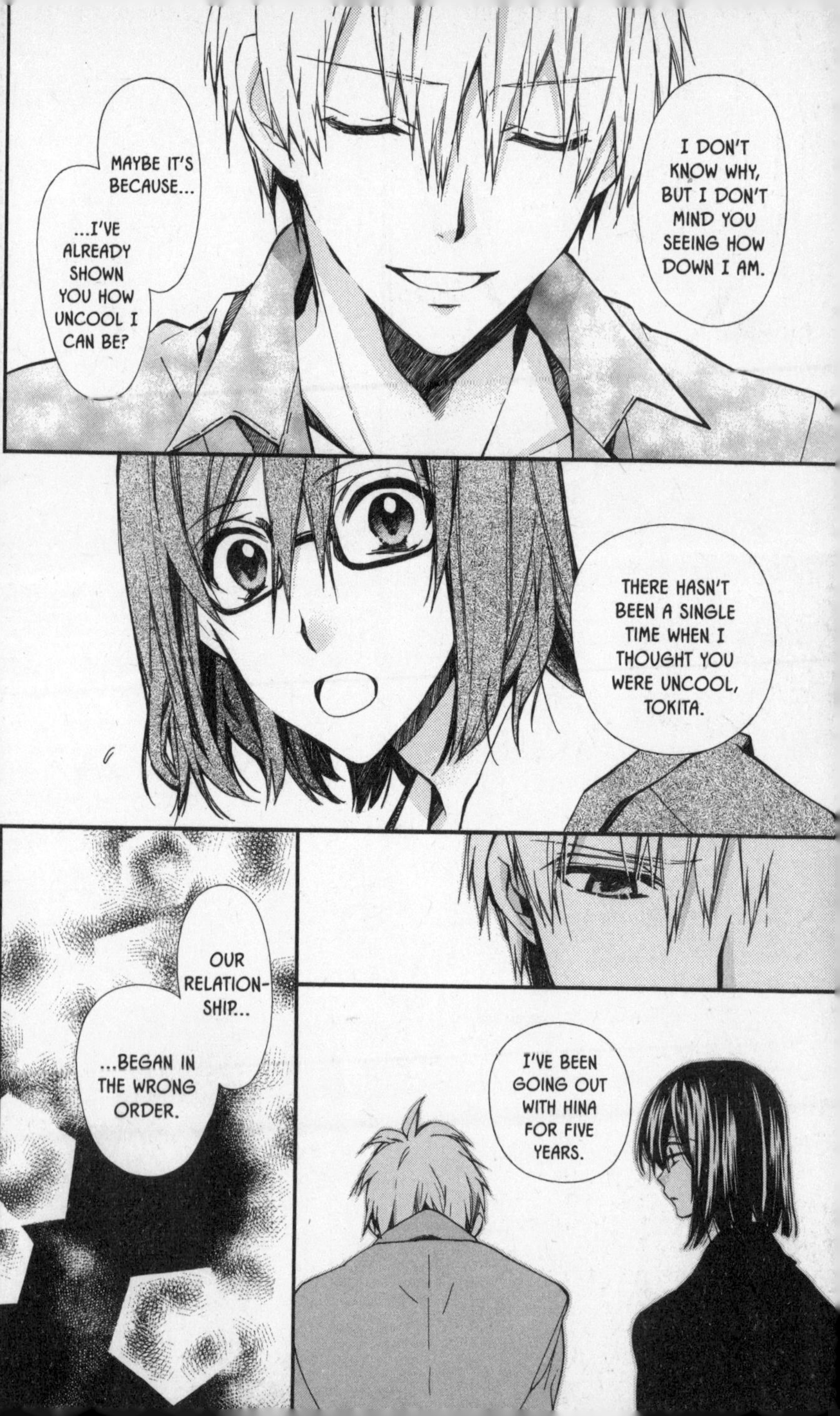
I DON'T KNOW WHY, BUT I DON'T MIND YOU SEEING HOW DOWN I AM.
MAYBE IT'S BECAUSE...
...I'VE ALREADY SHOWN YOU HOW UNCOOL I CAN BE?
THERE HASN'T BEEN A SINGLE TIME WHEN I THOUGHT YOU WERE UNCOOL, TOKITA.
I'VE BEEN GOING OUT WITH HINA FOR FIVE YEARS.
OUR RELATION-SHIP...
...BEGAN IN THE WRONG ORDER.

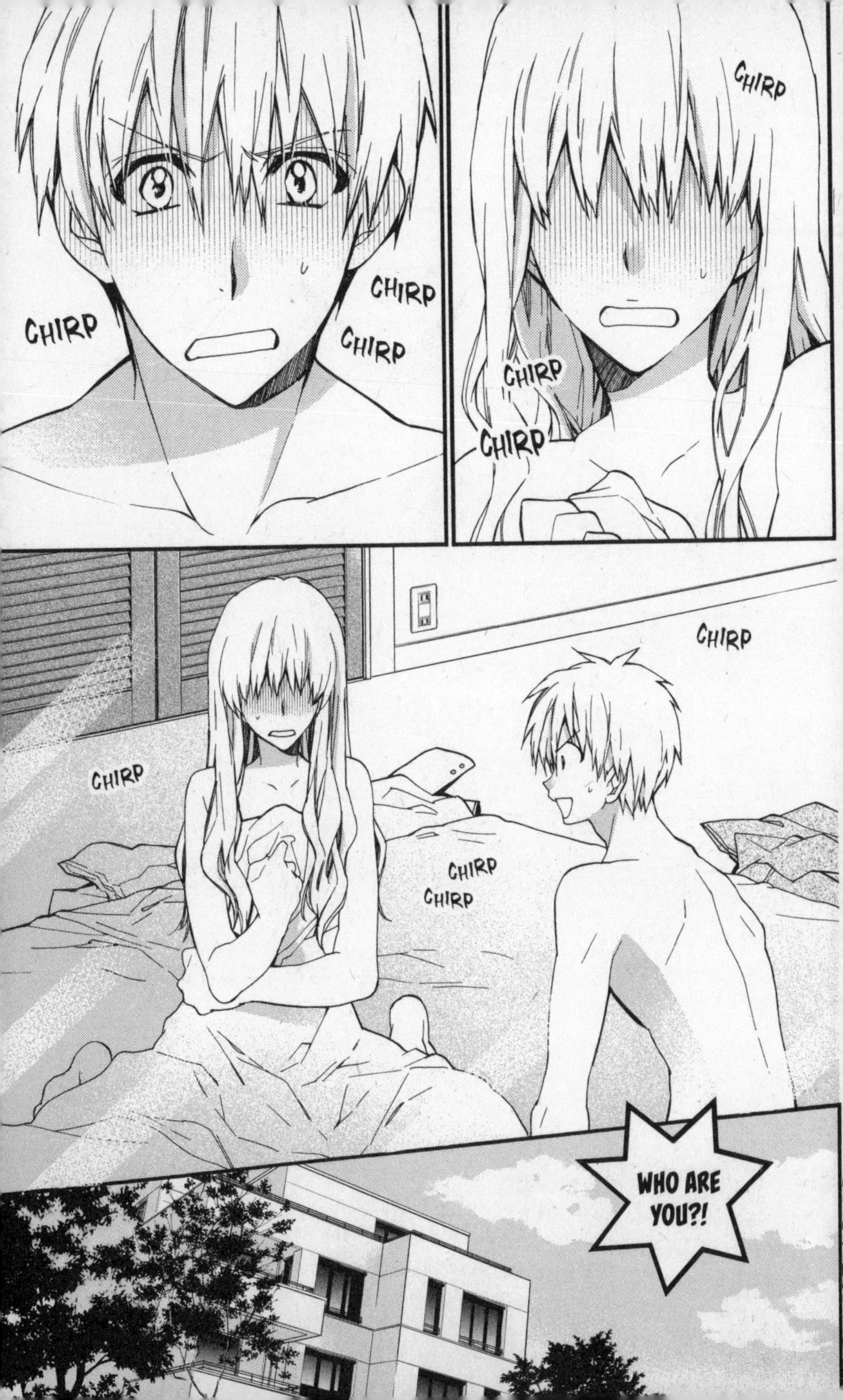
CHIRP
CHIRP
CHIRP
CHIRP
CHIRP
CHIRP
CHIRP
CHIRP
CHIRP
CHIRP
WHO ARE YOU?!

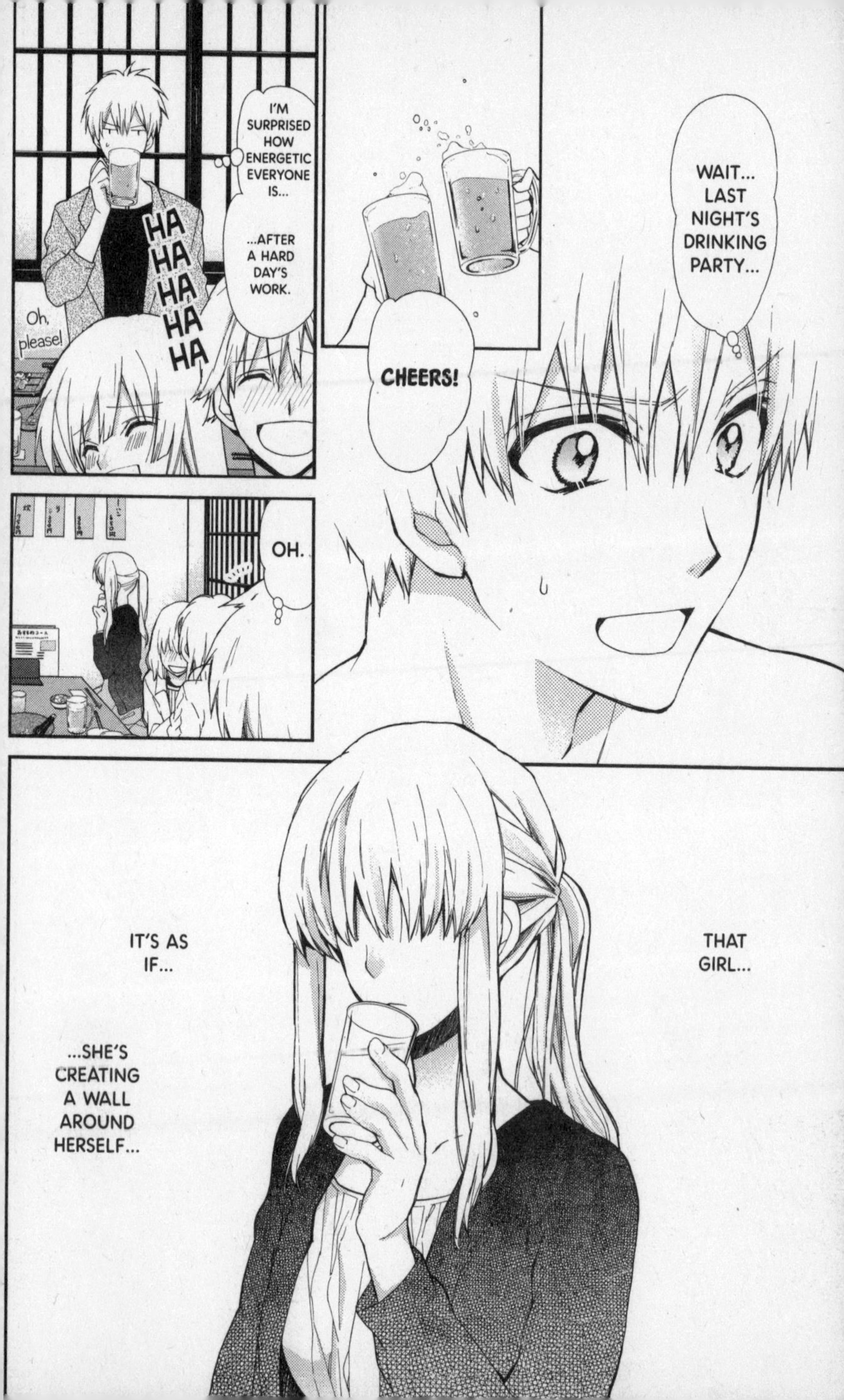
WAIT... LAST NIGHT'S DRINKING PARTY...
CHEERS!
I'M SURPRISED HOW ENERGETIC EVERYONE IS...
...AFTER A HARD DAY'S WORK.
HA HA HA HA HA
Oh, please!
OH.
THAT GIRL...
IT'S AS IF...
...SHE'S CREATING A WALL AROUND HERSELF...

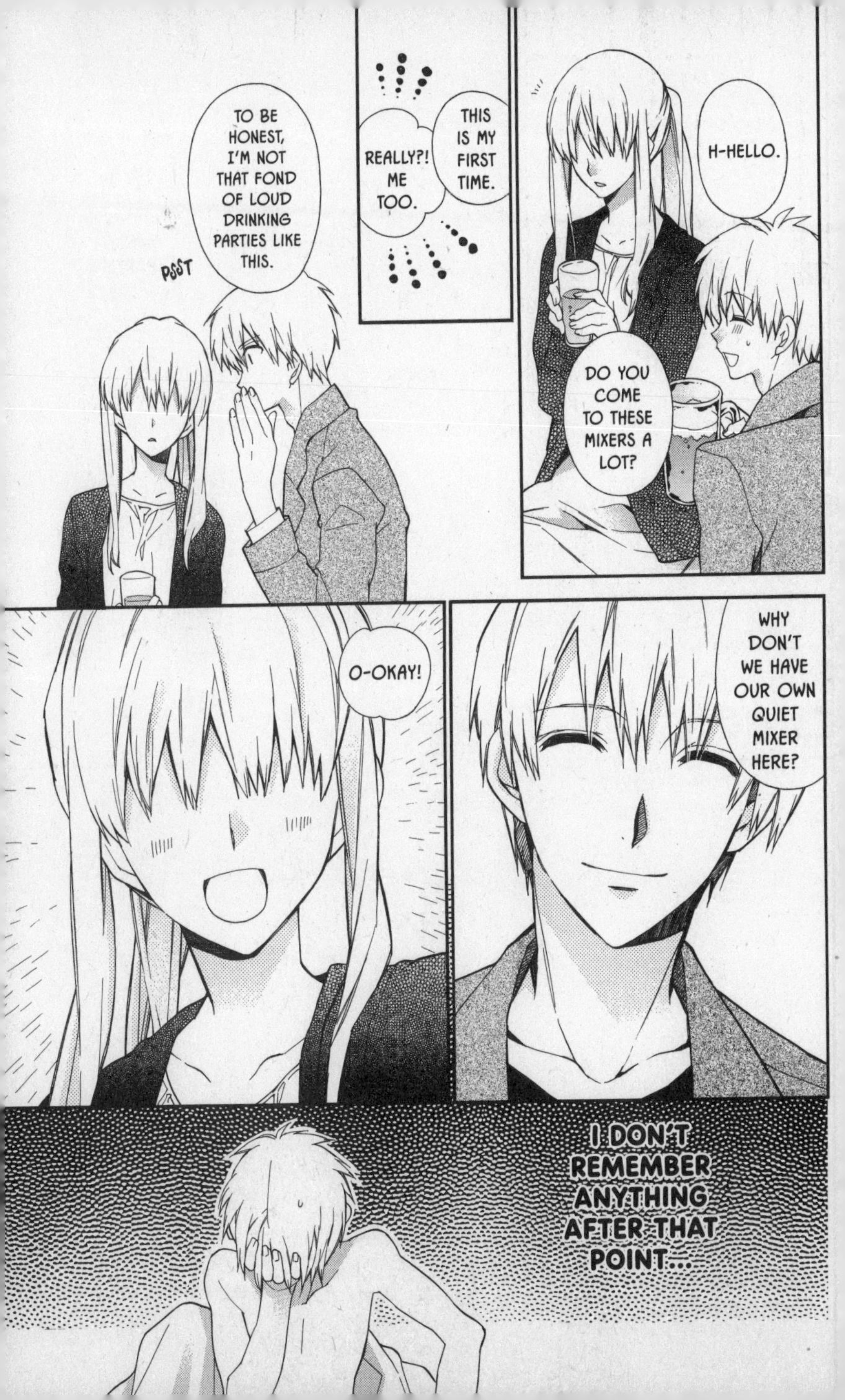
H-HELLO.
DO YOU COME TO THESE MIXERS A LOT?
THIS IS MY FIRST TIME.
REALLY?! ME TOO.
TO BE HONEST, I'M NOT THAT FOND OF LOUD DRINKING PARTIES LIKE THIS.
PSST
WHY DON'T WE HAVE OUR OWN QUIET MIXER HERE?
O-OKAY!
I DON'T REMEMBER ANYTHING AFTER THAT POINT...

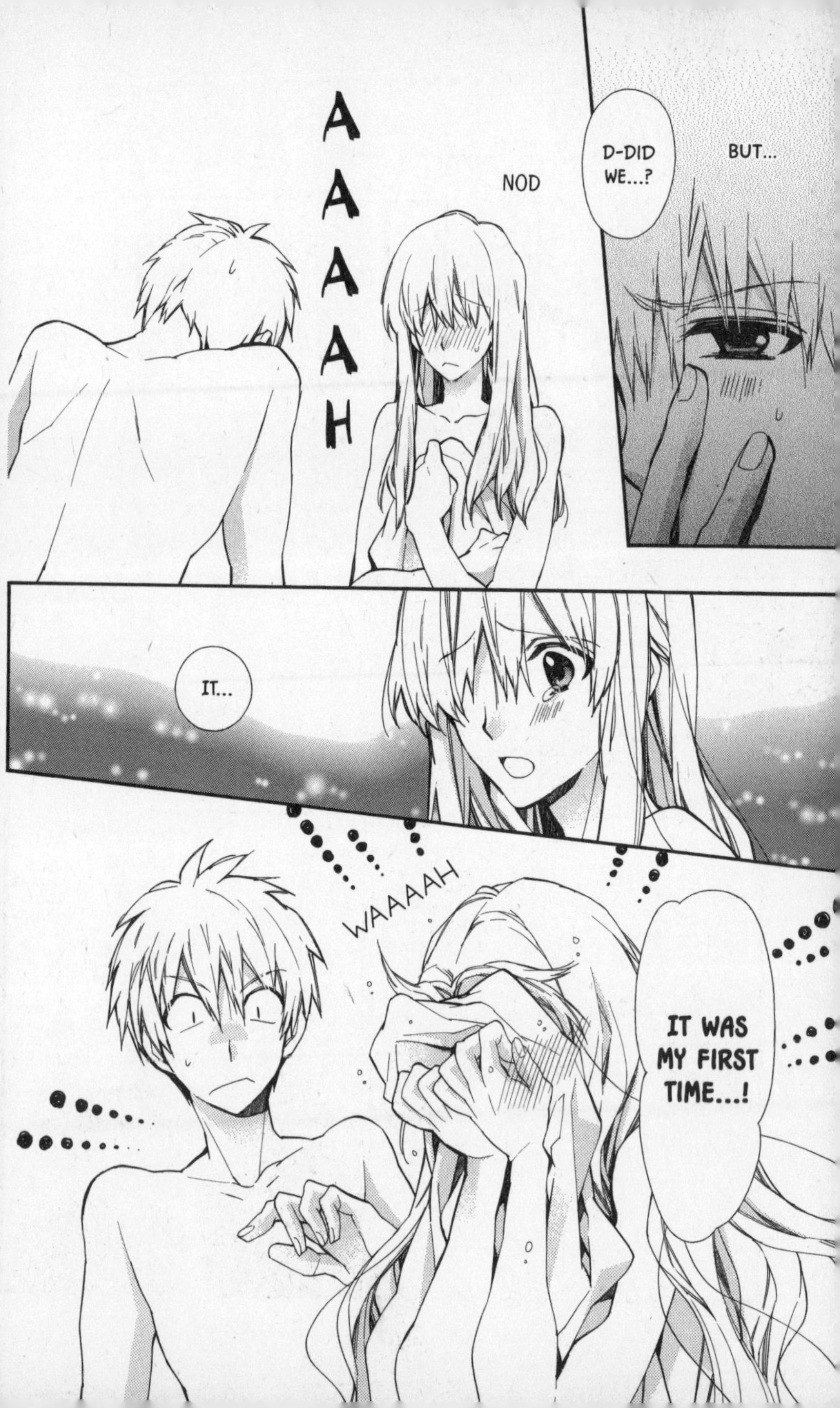
D-DID WE...?
BUT...
NOD
AAAAH
IT...
WAAAAH
IT WAS MY FIRST TIME...!

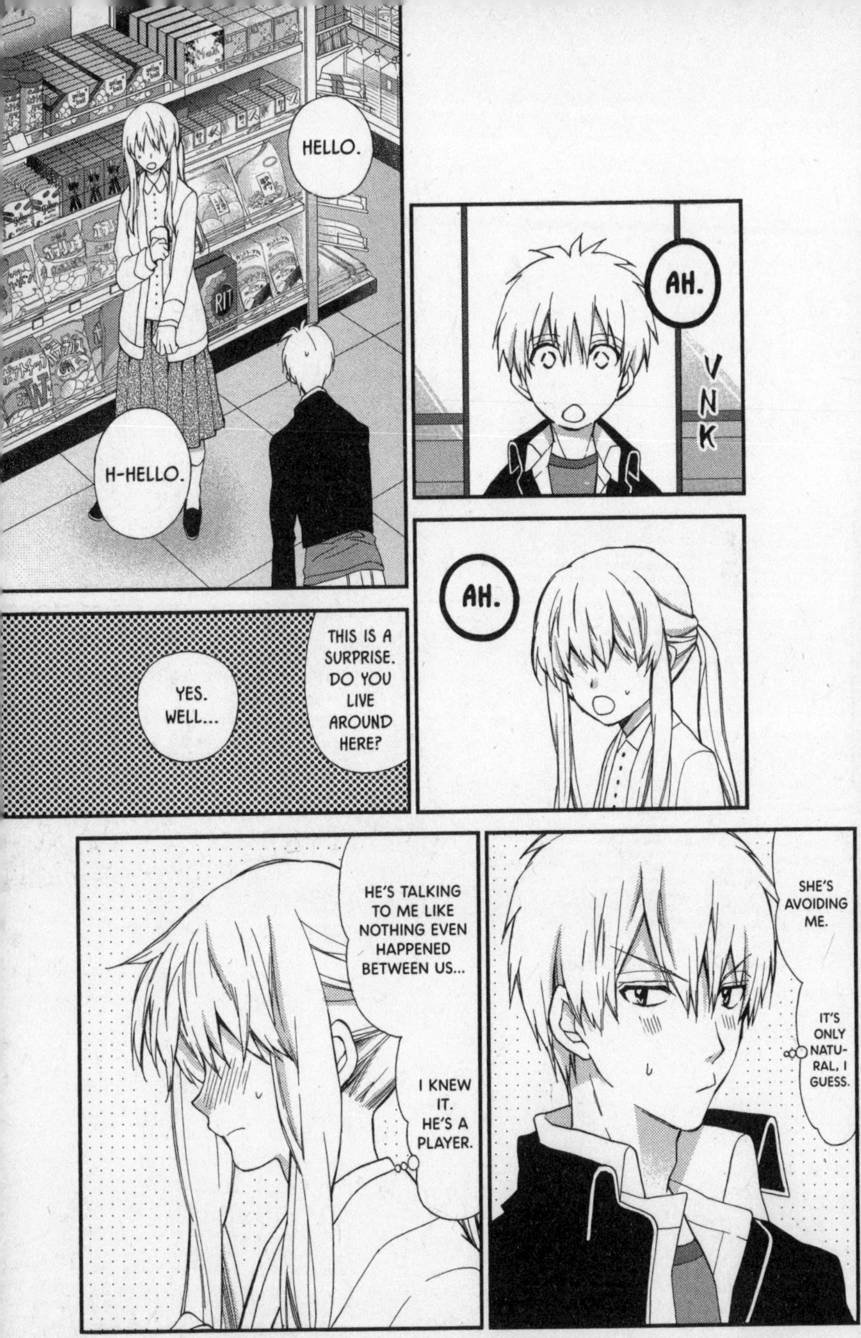
AH.
VNK
AH.
HELLO.
H-HELLO.
THIS IS A SURPRISE. DO YOU LIVE AROUND HERE?
YES. WELL...
SHE'S AVOIDING ME.
IT'S ONLY NATU-RAL, I GUESS.
HE'S TALKING TO ME LIKE NOTHING EVEN HAPPENED BETWEEN US...
I KNEW IT. HE'S A PLAYER.

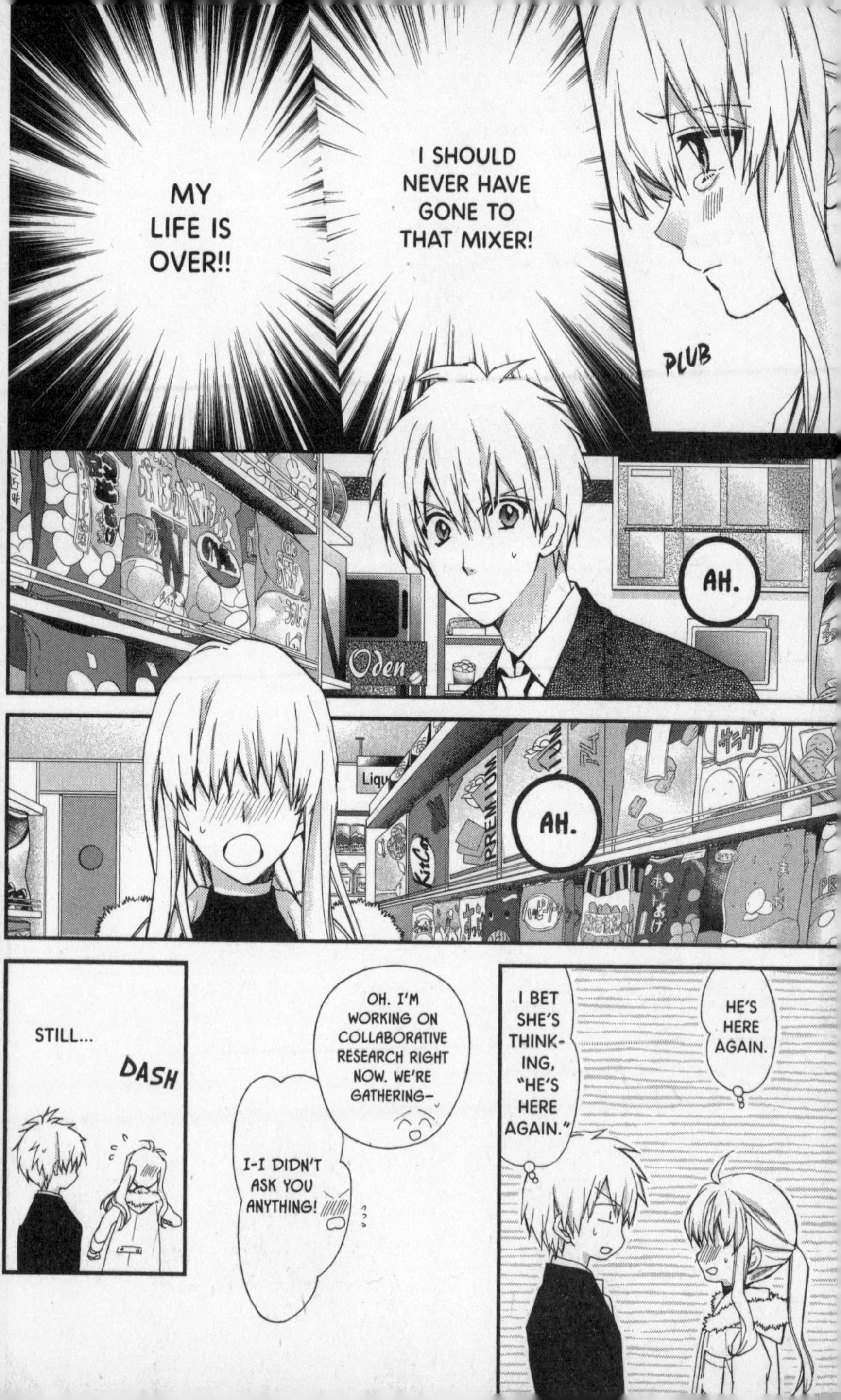
PLUB
I SHOULD NEVER HAVE GONE TO THAT MIXER!
MY LIFE IS OVER!!
AH.
AH.
HE'S HERE AGAIN.
I BET SHE'S THINKING, "HE'S HERE AGAIN."
OH. I'M WORKING ON COLLABORATIVE RESEARCH RIGHT NOW. WE'RE GATHERING—
I-I DIDN'T ASK YOU ANYTHING!
STILL...
DASH

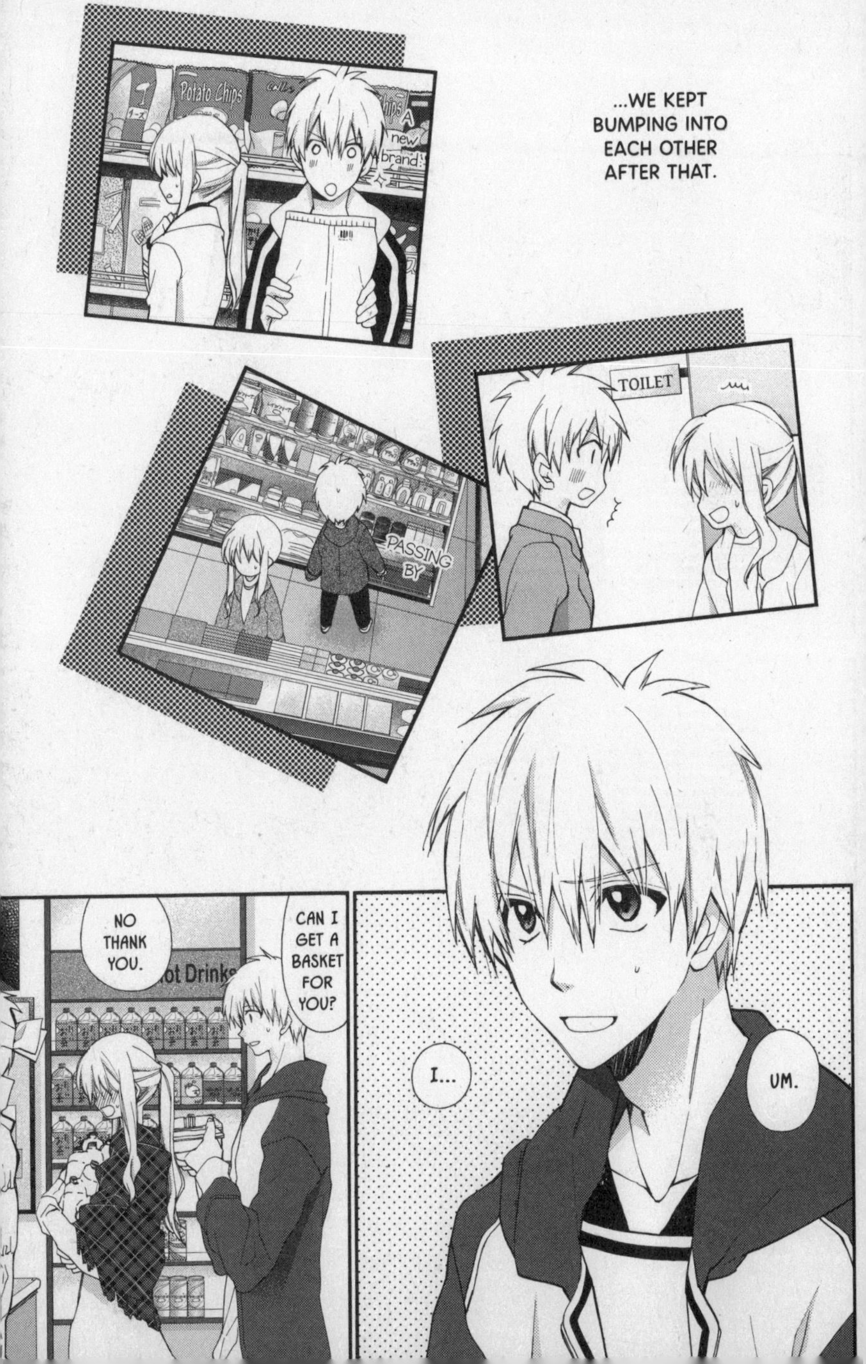
...WE KEPT BUMPING INTO EACH OTHER AFTER THAT.
Potato Chips
A new brand!
TOILET
PASSING BY
UM.
I...
CAN I GET A BASKET FOR YOU?
NO THANK YOU.

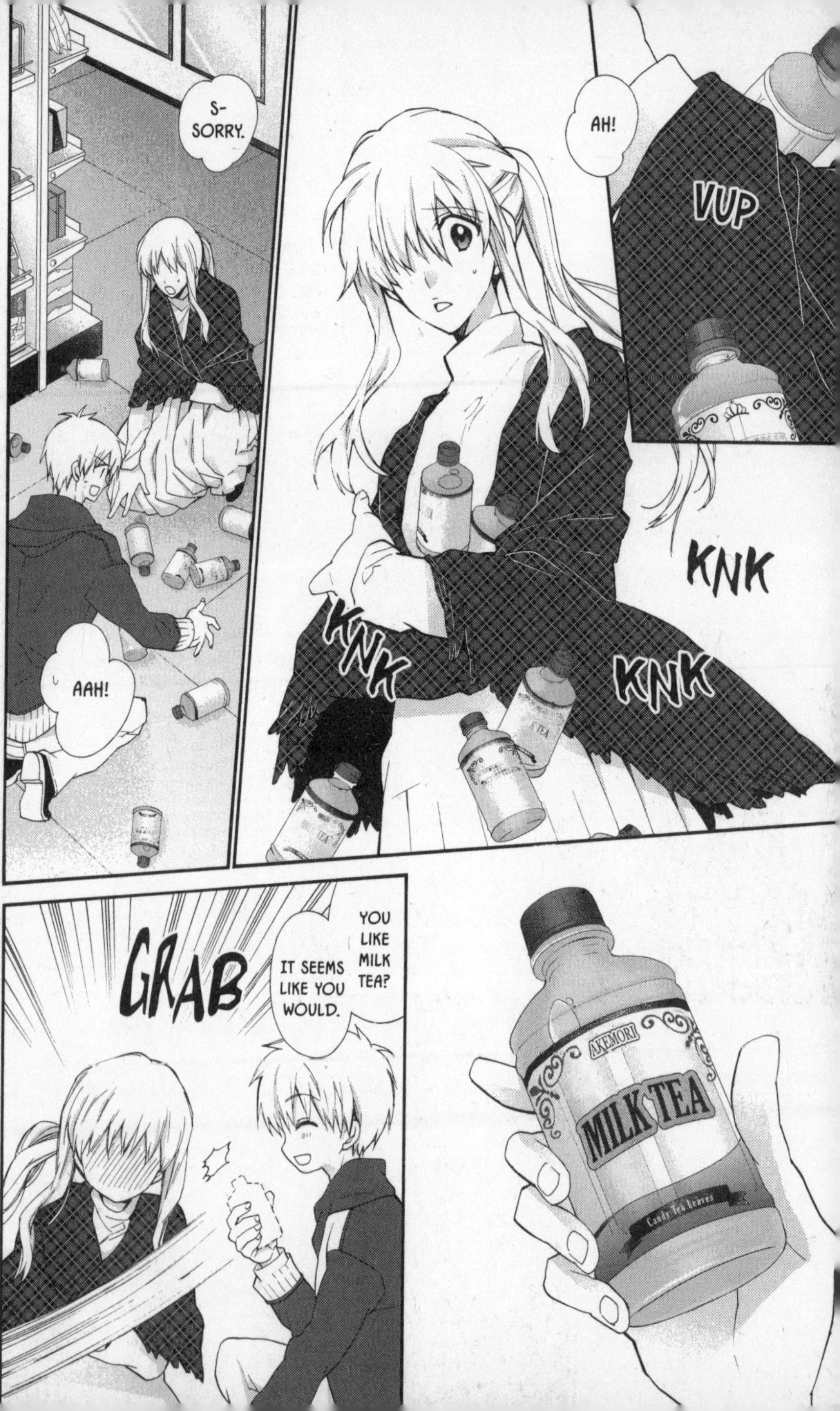
AH!
VUP
KNK
KNK
KNK
S-SORRY.
AAH!
AKEMORI
MILK TEA
Candy Tea Leaves
GRAB
YOU LIKE MILK TEA?
IT SEEMS LIKE YOU WOULD.

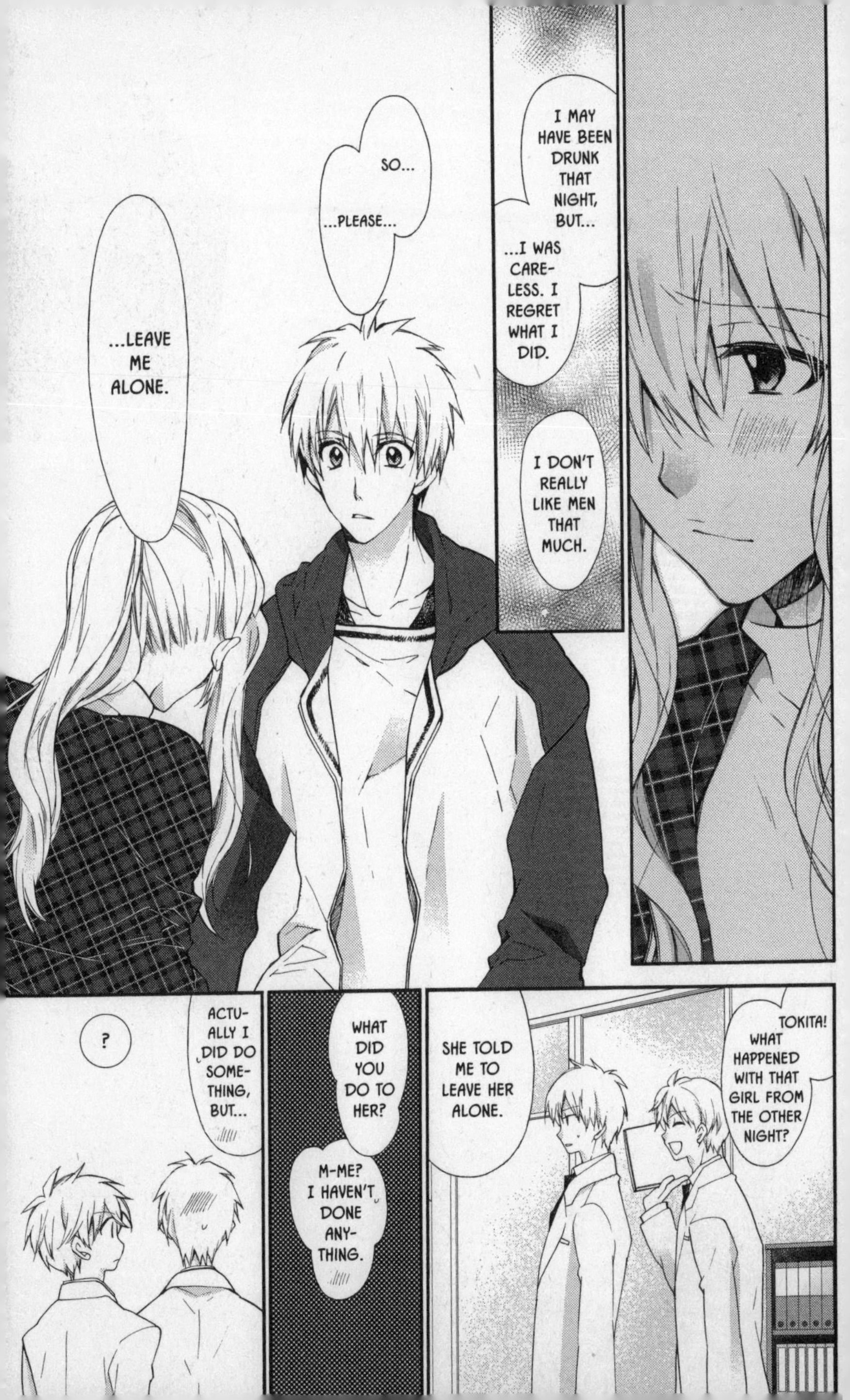
I MAY HAVE BEEN DRUNK THAT NIGHT, BUT...
...I WAS CARE-LESS. I REGRET WHAT I DID.
I DON'T REALLY LIKE MEN THAT MUCH.
SO...
...PLEASE...
...LEAVE ME ALONE.
TOKITA! WHAT HAPPENED WITH THAT GIRL FROM THE OTHER NIGHT?
SHE TOLD ME TO LEAVE HER ALONE.
WHAT DID YOU DO TO HER?
M-ME? I HAVEN'T DONE ANY-THING.
ACTU-ALLY I DID DO SOME-THING, BUT...
?

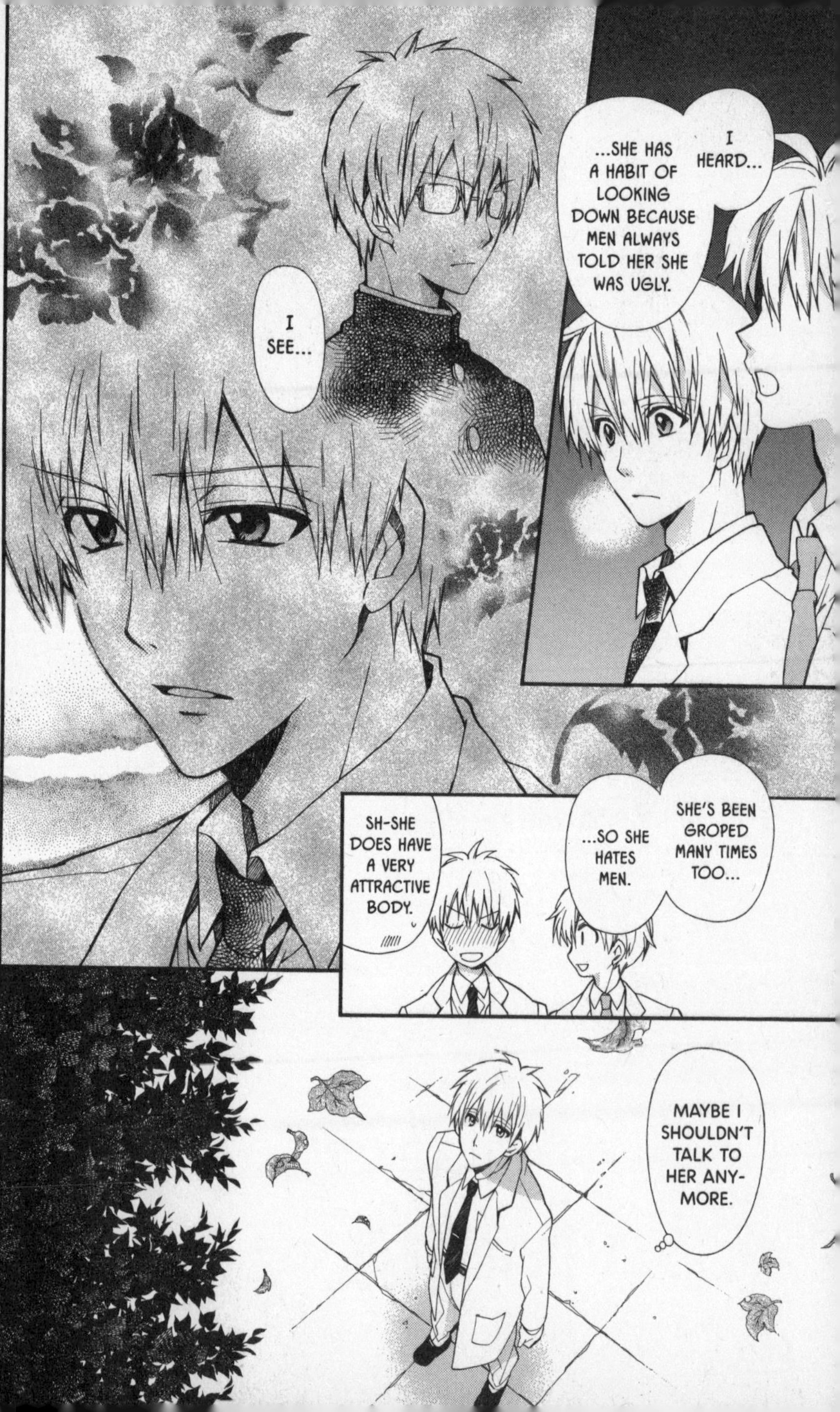
I HEARD...
...SHE HAS A HABIT OF LOOKING DOWN BECAUSE MEN ALWAYS TOLD HER SHE WAS UGLY.
I SEE...
SHE'S BEEN GROPED MANY TIMES TOO...
...SO SHE HATES MEN.
SH-SHE DOES HAVE A VERY ATTRACTIVE BODY.
MAYBE I SHOULDN'T TALK TO HER ANY-MORE.

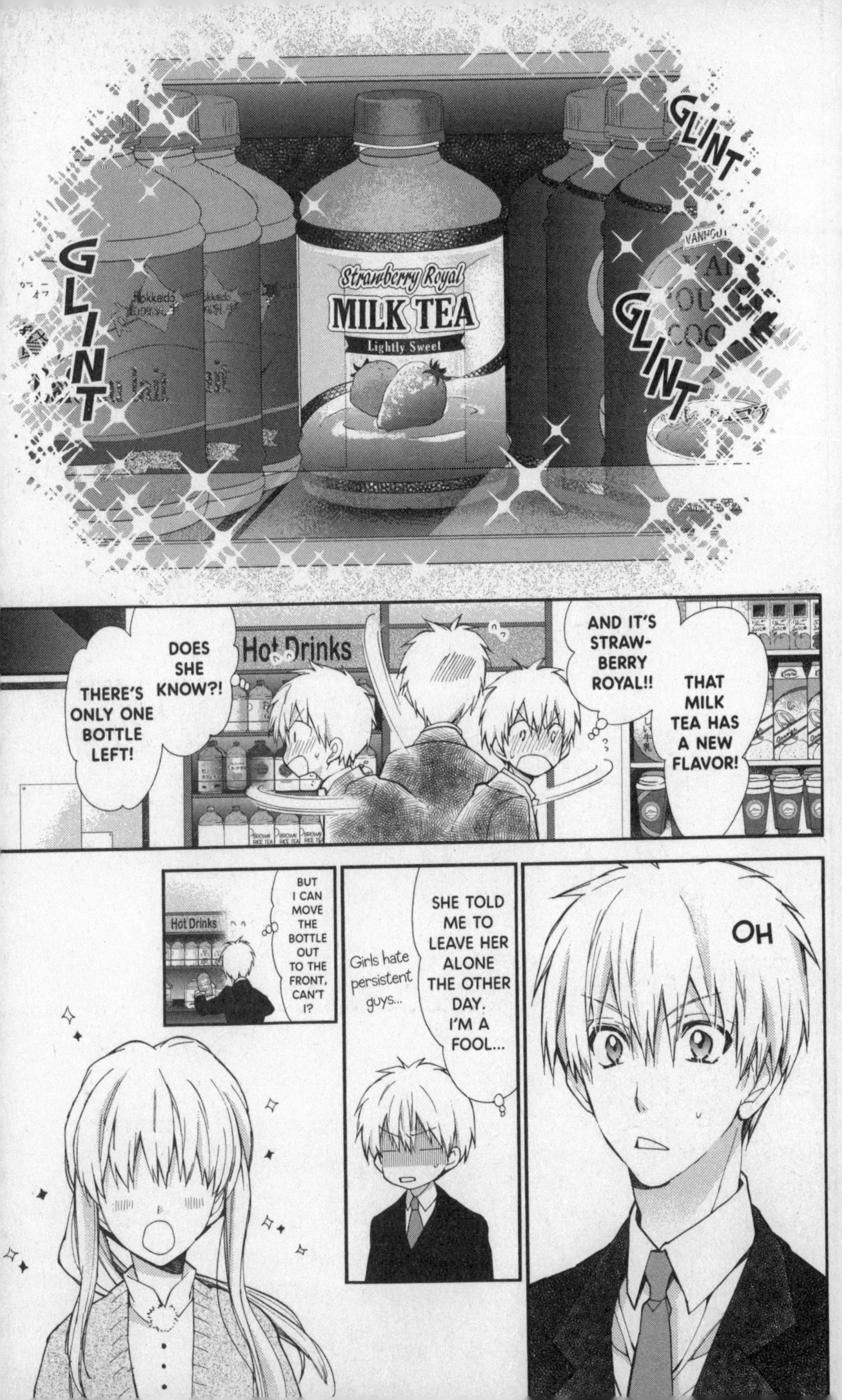
GLINT
GLINT
Strawberry Royal
MILK TEA
Lightly Sweet
GLINT
THAT MILK TEA HAS A NEW FLAVOR!
AND IT'S STRAW-BERRY ROYAL!!
Hot Drinks
DOES SHE KNOW?!
THERE'S ONLY ONE BOTTLE LEFT!
OH
SHE TOLD ME TO LEAVE HER ALONE THE OTHER DAY. I'M A FOOL...
Girls hate persistent guys...
BUT I CAN MOVE THE BOTTLE OUT TO THE FRONT, CAN'T I?
Hot Drinks

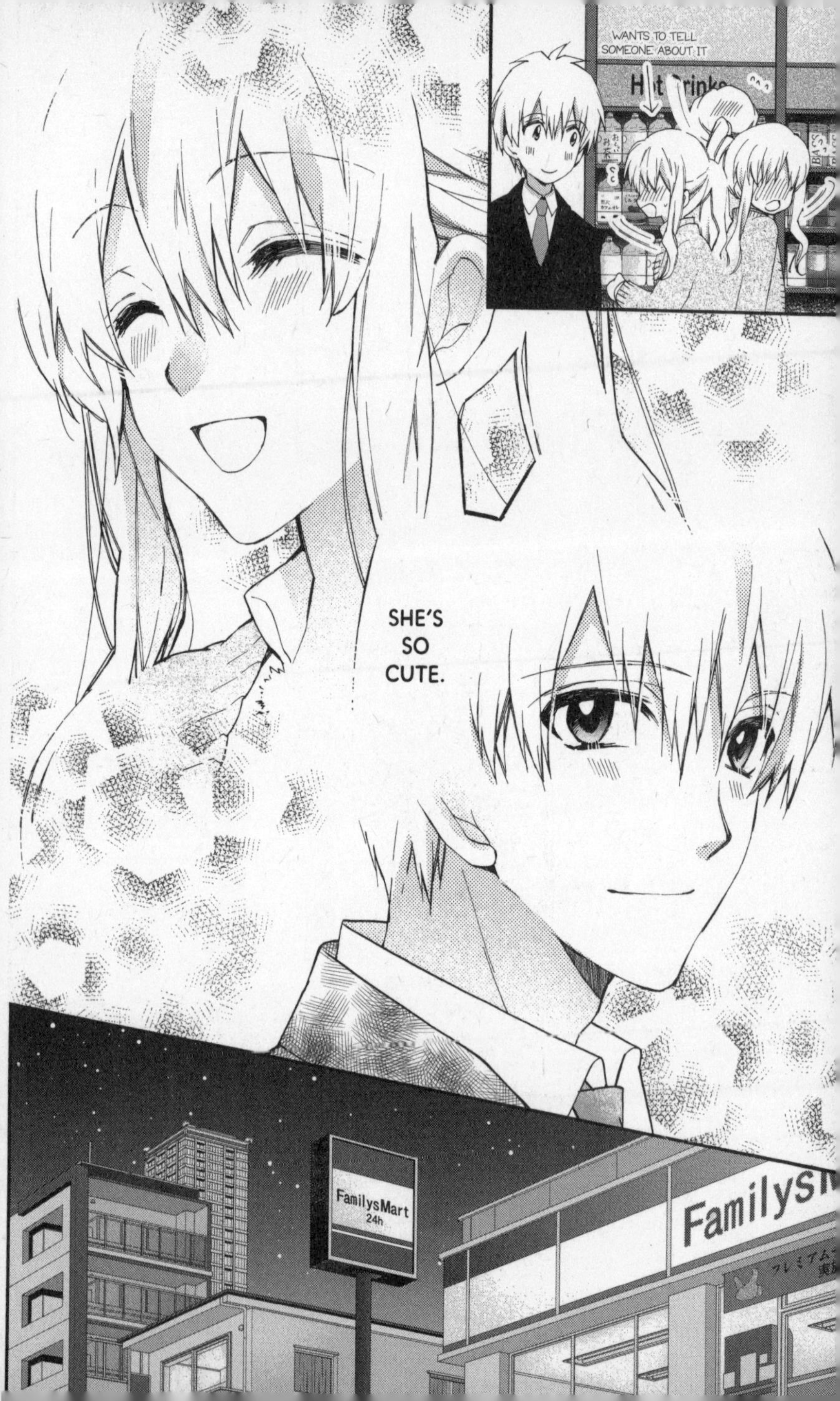
WANTS TO TELL SOMEONE ABOUT IT
SHE'S SO CUTE.
FamilysMart 24h

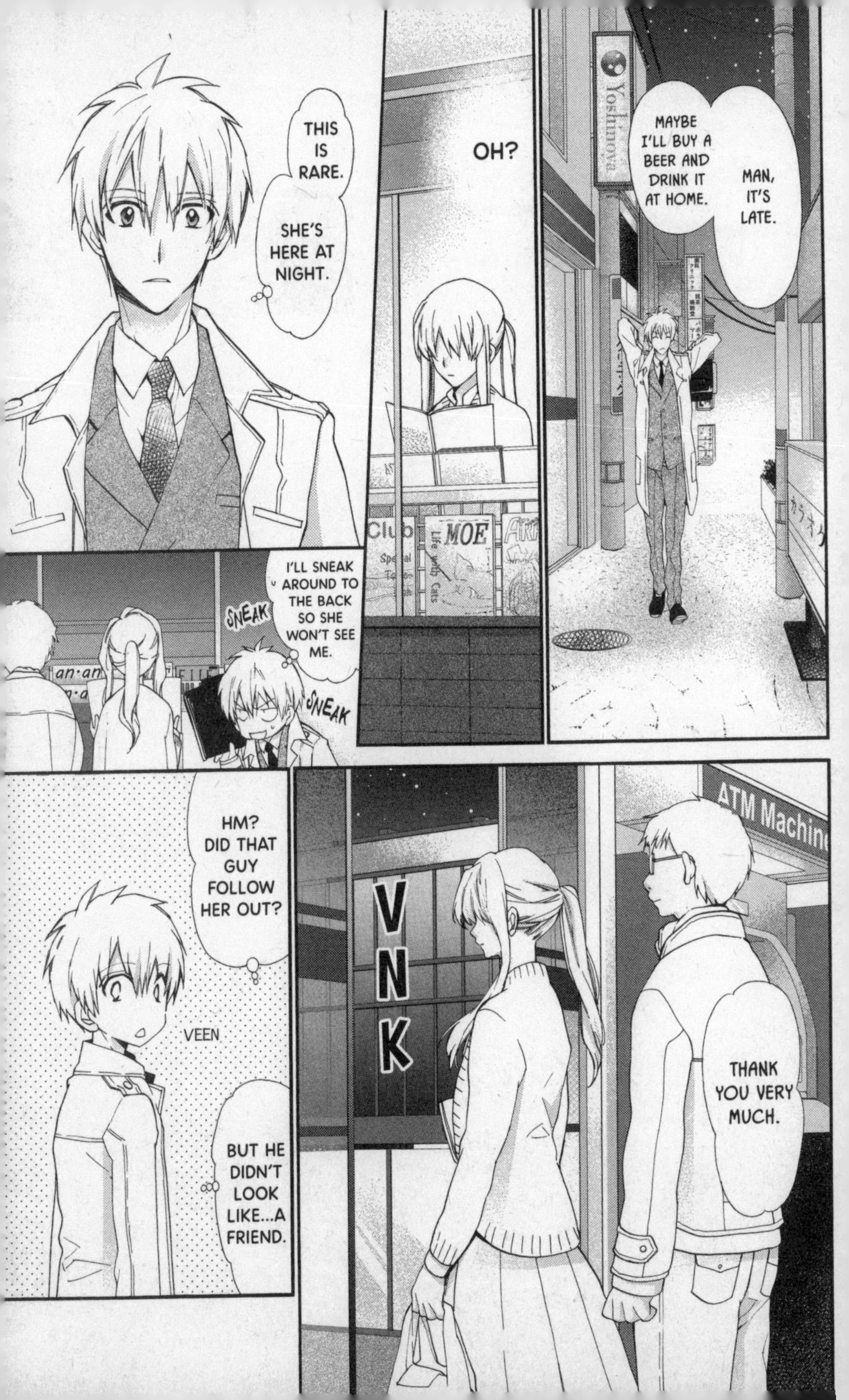
Yoshinoya
MAN, IT'S LATE.
MAYBE I'LL BUY A BEER AND DRINK IT AT HOME.
OH?
MOE
THIS IS RARE.
SHE'S HERE AT NIGHT.
I'LL SNEAK AROUND TO THE BACK SO SHE WON'T SEE ME.
SNEAK
SNEAK
THANK YOU VERY MUCH.
VNK
HM? DID THAT GUY FOLLOW HER OUT?
VEEN
BUT HE DIDN'T LOOK LIKE...A FRIEND.

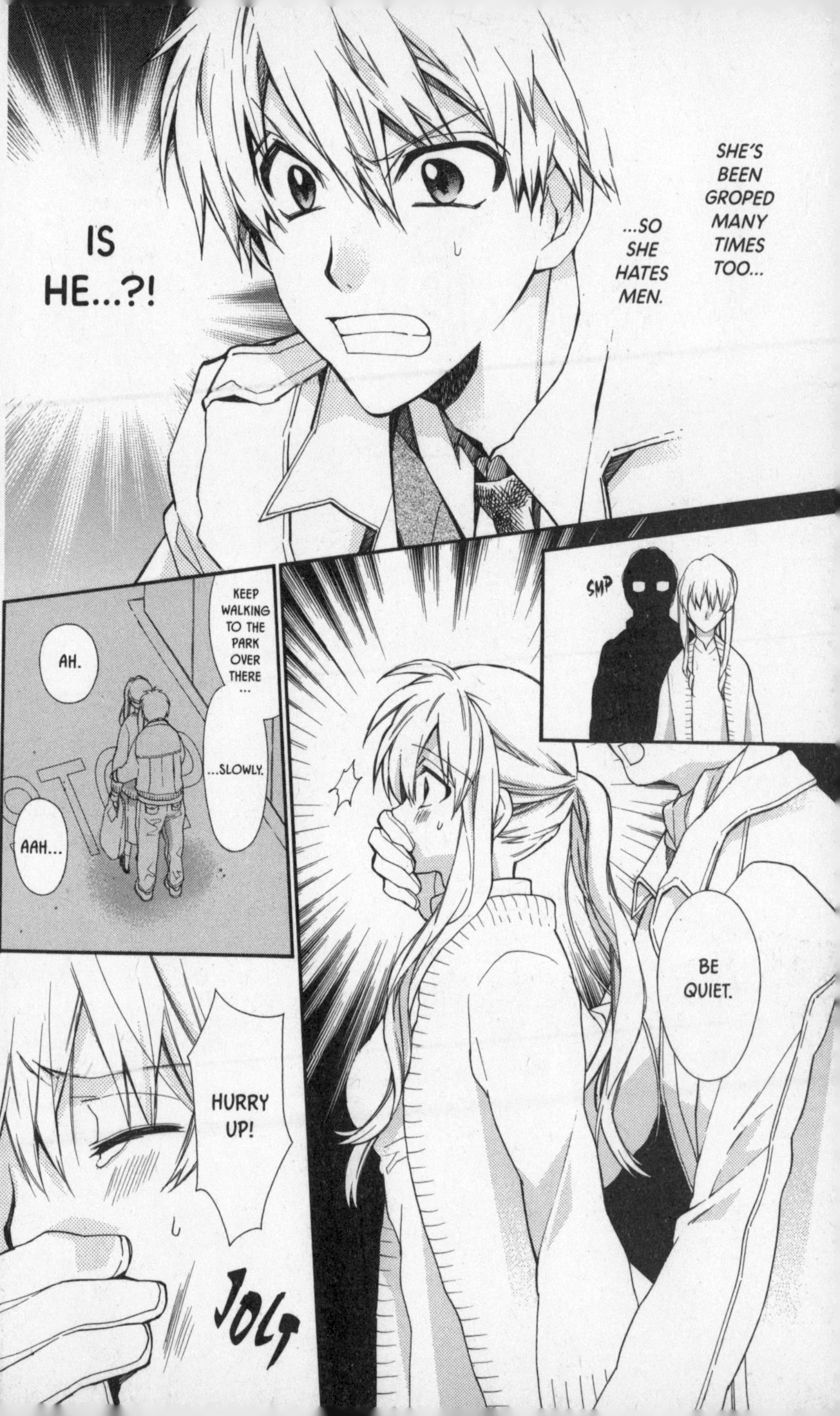
SHE'S BEEN GROPED MANY TIMES TOO...
...SO SHE HATES MEN.
IS HE...?!
SMP
BE QUIET.
KEEP WALKING TO THE PARK OVER THERE ...
...SLOWLY.
AH.
AAH...
HURRY UP!
JOLT

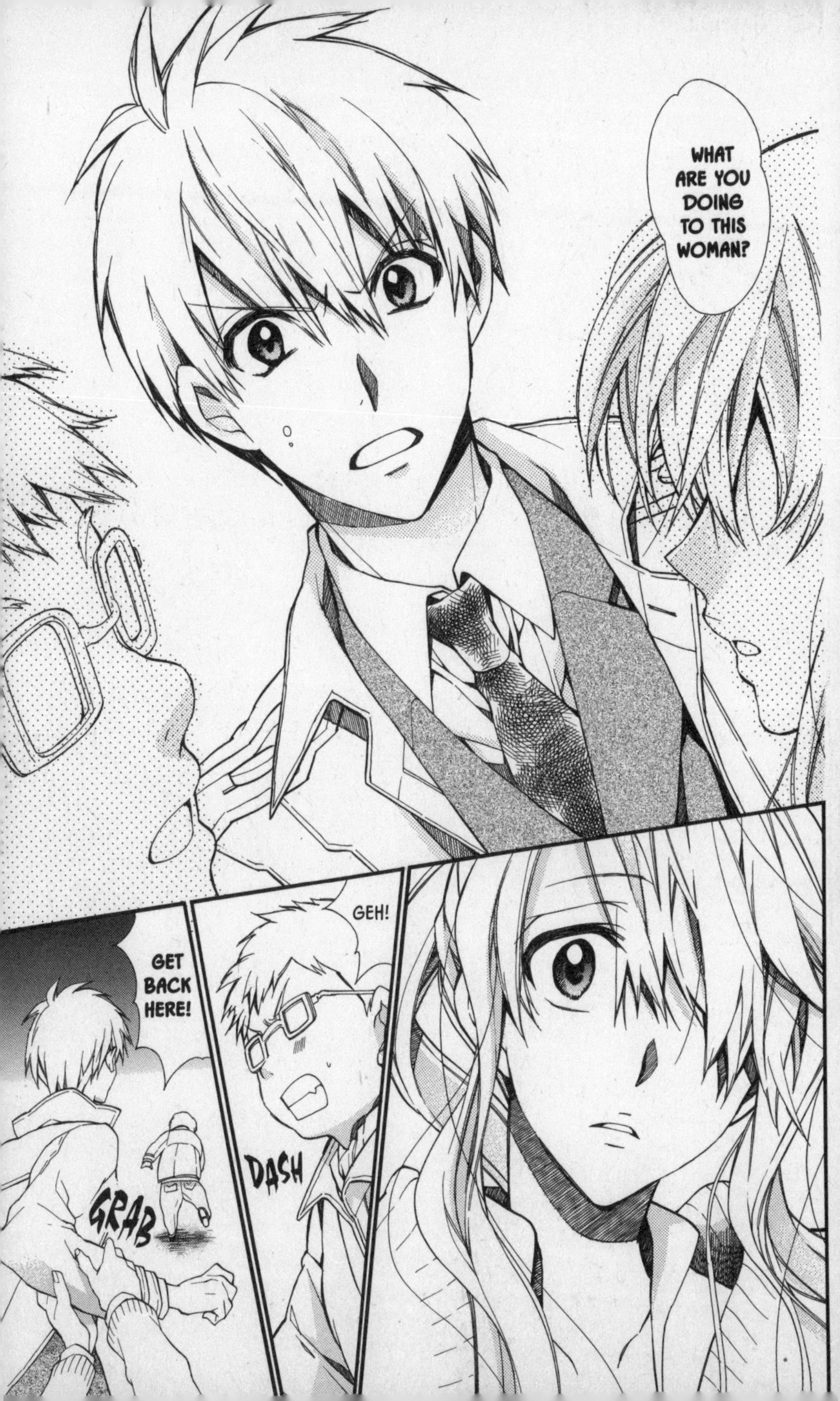
WHAT ARE YOU DOING TO THIS WOMAN?
GEH!
DASH
GET BACK HERE!
GRAB

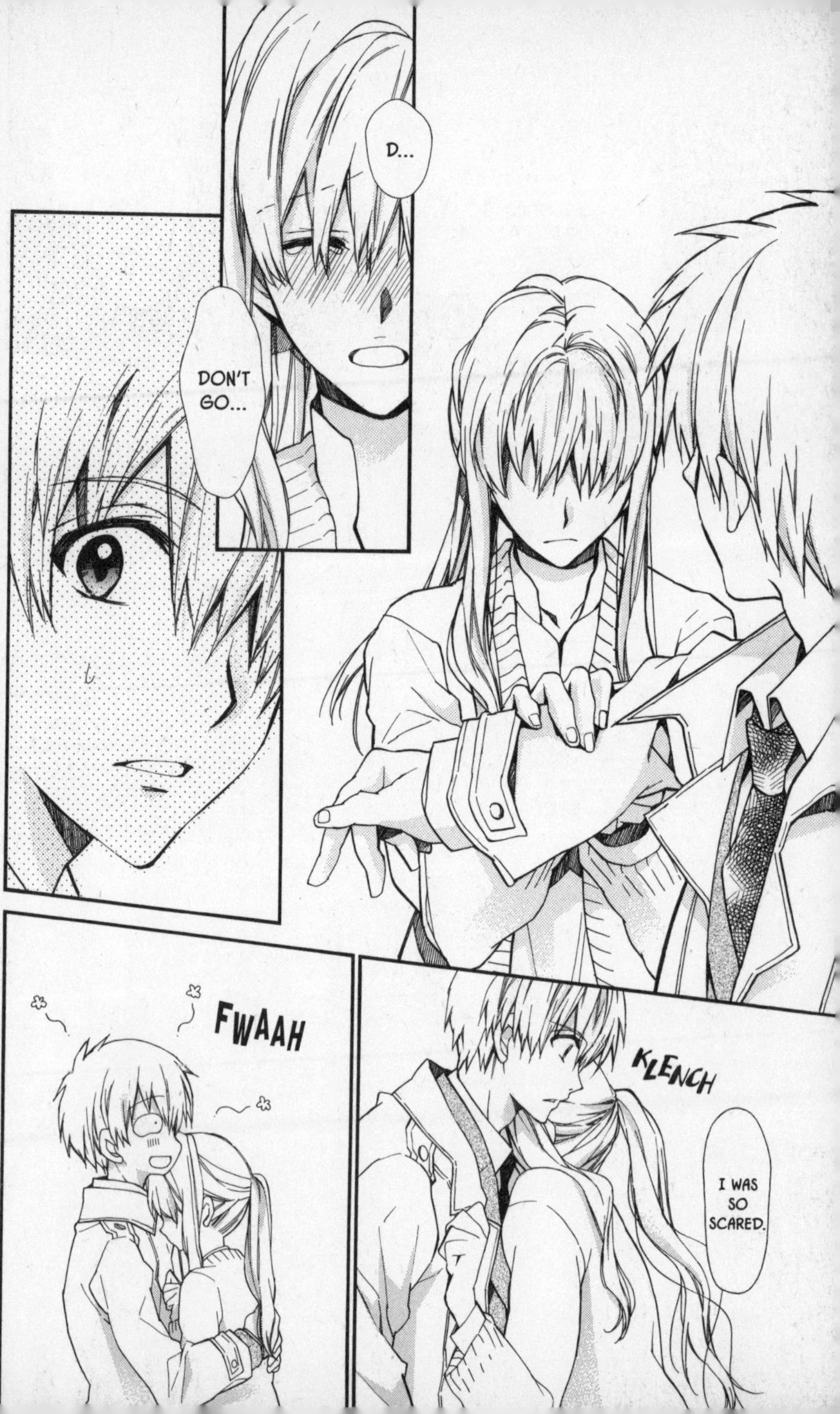
D...
DON'T GO...
KLENCH
I WAS SO SCARED.
FWAAH

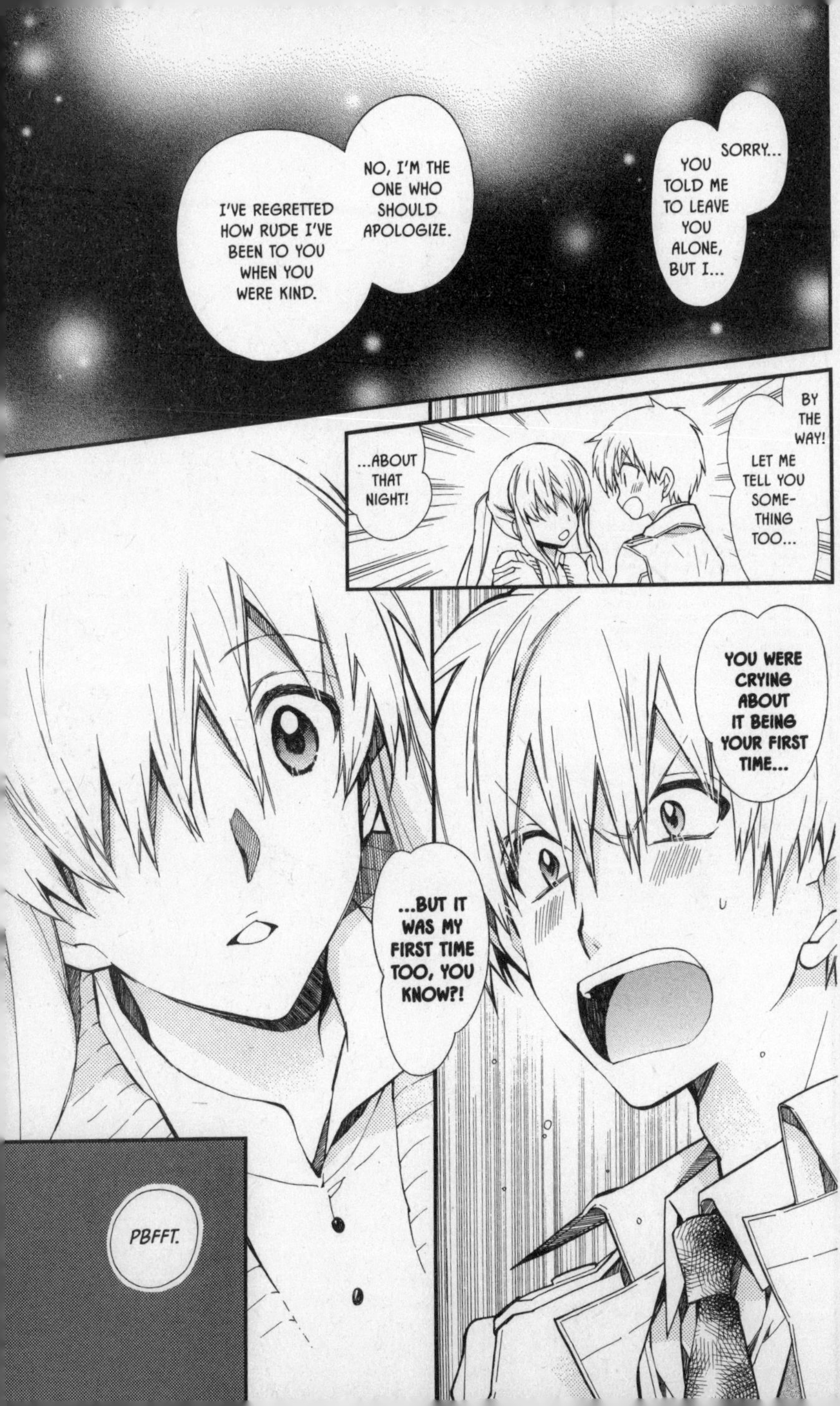
SORRY... YOU TOLD ME TO LEAVE YOU ALONE, BUT I...
NO, I'M THE ONE WHO SHOULD APOLOGIZE.
I'VE REGRETTED HOW RUDE I'VE BEEN TO YOU WHEN YOU WERE KIND.
BY THE WAY! LET ME TELL YOU SOME-THING TOO...
...ABOUT THAT NIGHT!
YOU WERE CRYING ABOUT IT BEING YOUR FIRST TIME...
...BUT IT WAS MY FIRST TIME TOO, YOU KNOW?!
PBFFT.

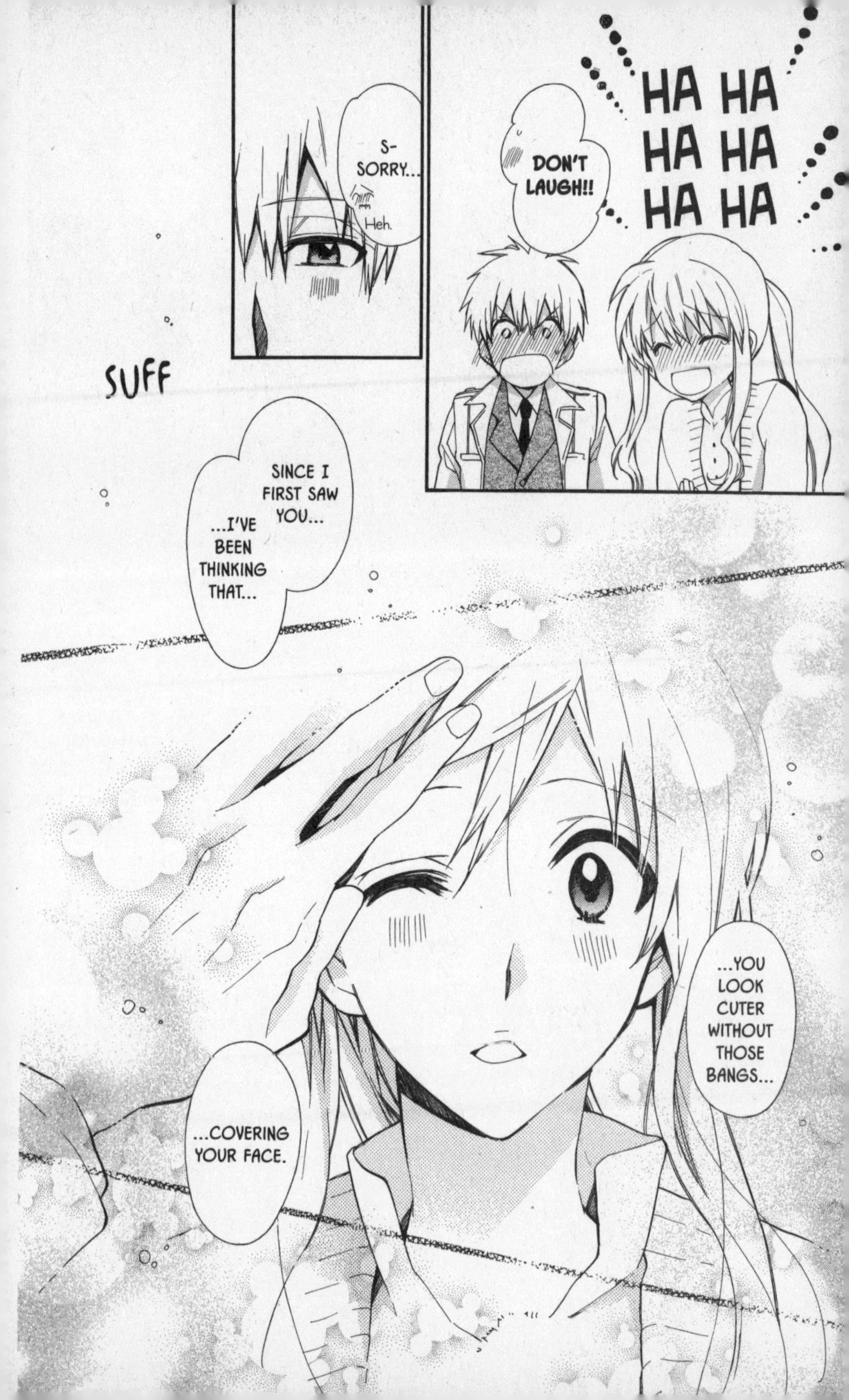
HA HA HA HA HA HA
DON'T LAUGH!!
S-SORRY...
Heh.
SUFF
SINCE I FIRST SAW YOU...
...I'VE BEEN THINKING THAT...
...YOU LOOK CUTER WITHOUT THOSE BANGS...
...COVERING YOUR FACE.

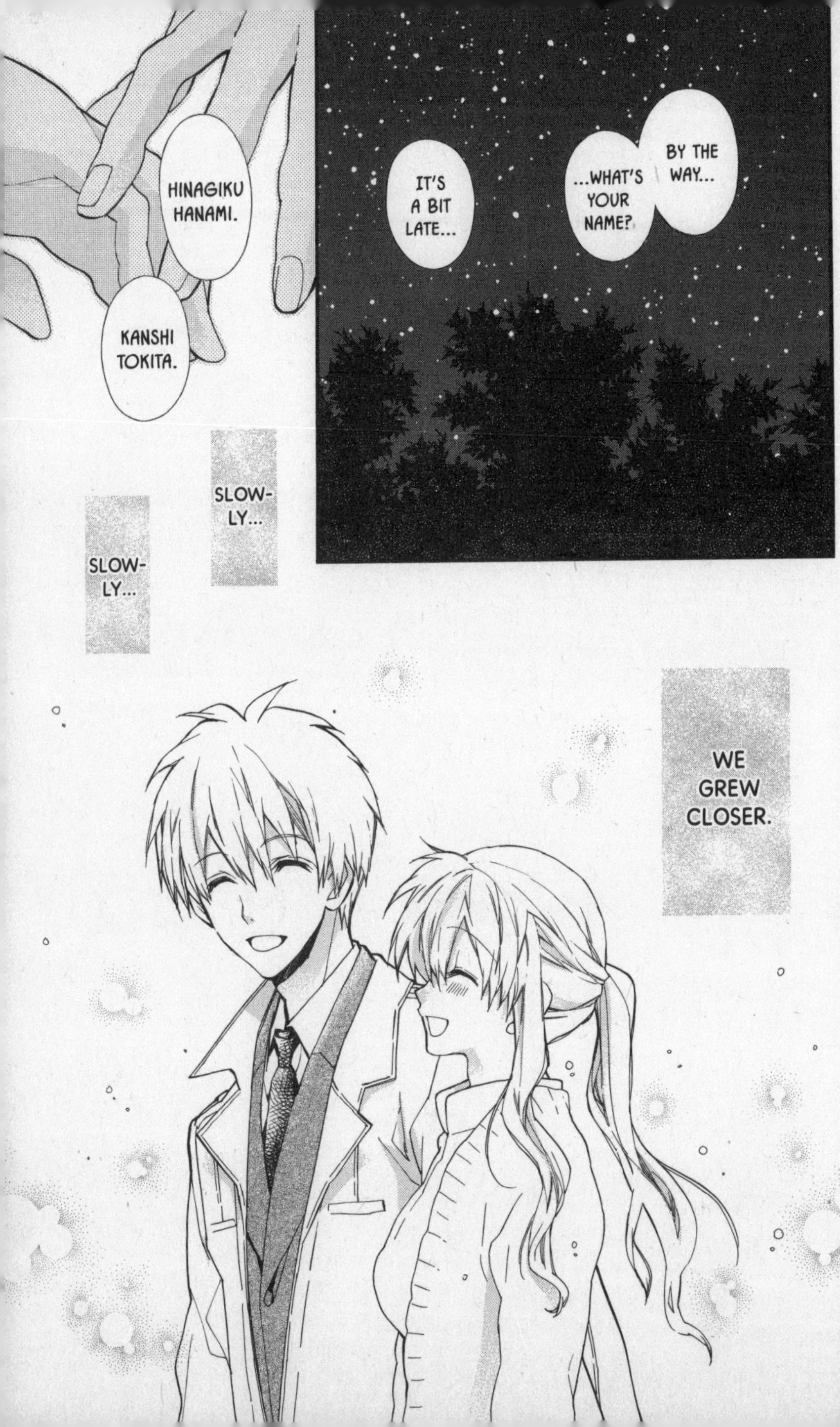

BY THE WAY...
...WHAT'S YOUR NAME?
IT'S A BIT LATE...
HINAGIKU HANAMI.
KANSHI TOKITA.
SLOW-LY...
SLOW-LY...
WE GREW CLOSER.

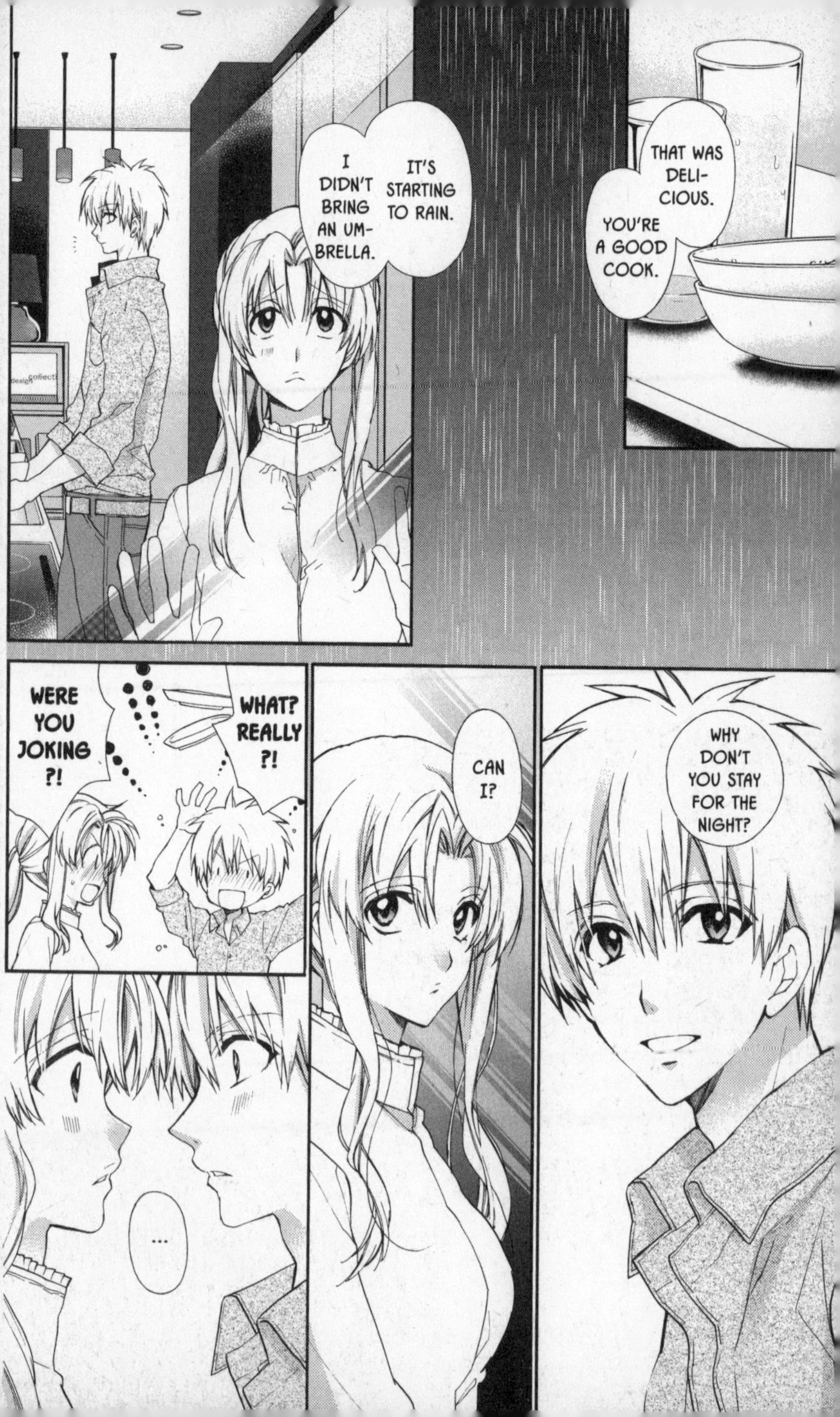
THAT WAS DELICIOUS.
YOU'RE A GOOD COOK.
IT'S STARTING TO RAIN.
I DIDN'T BRING AN UMBRELLA.
WHY DON'T YOU STAY FOR THE NIGHT?
CAN I?
WHAT? REALLY?!
WERE YOU JOKING?!
...

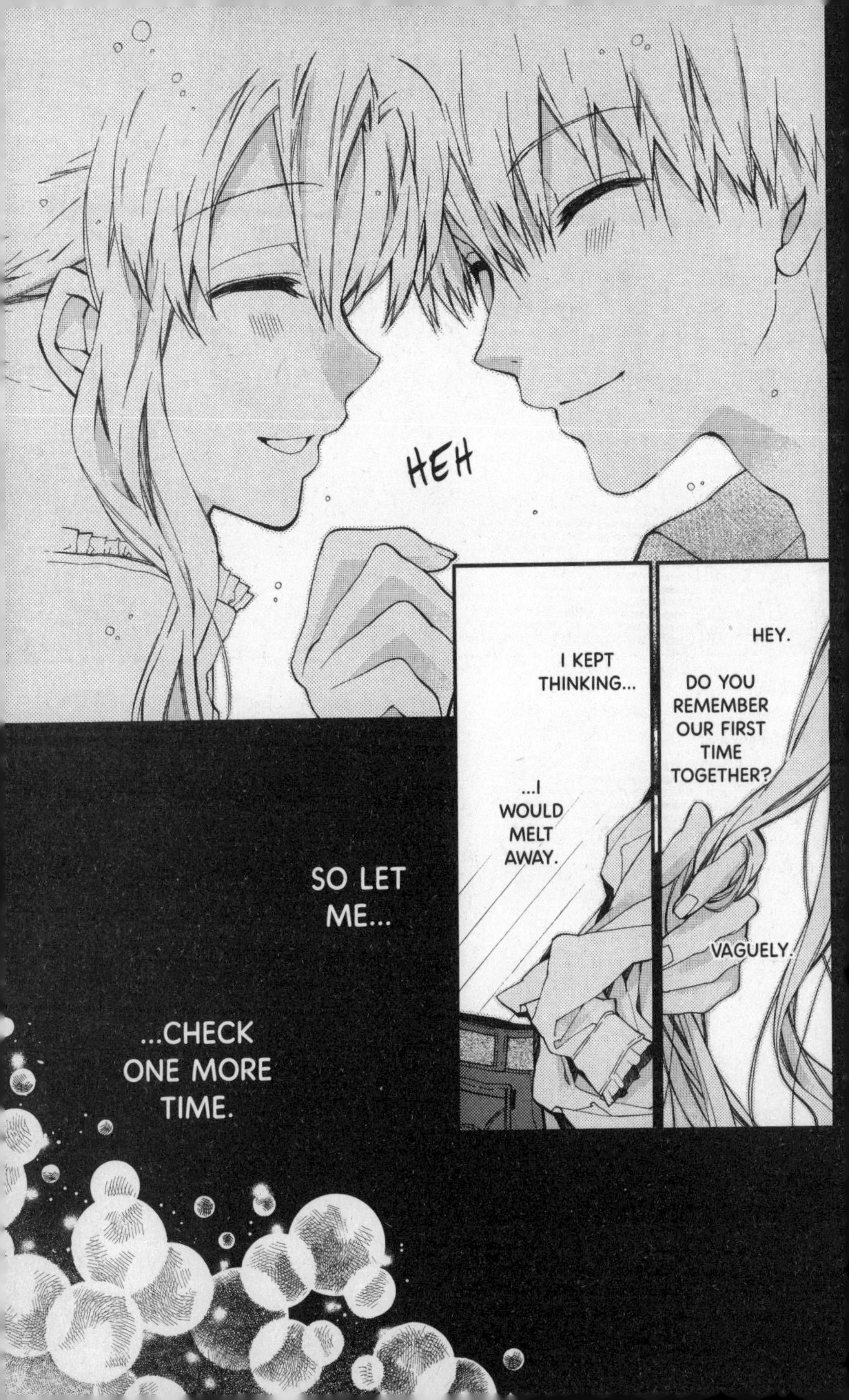
HEH
HEY.
DO YOU REMEMBER OUR FIRST TIME TOGETHER?
VAGUELY.
I KEPT THINKING...
...I WOULD MELT AWAY.
SO LET ME...
...CHECK ONE MORE TIME.

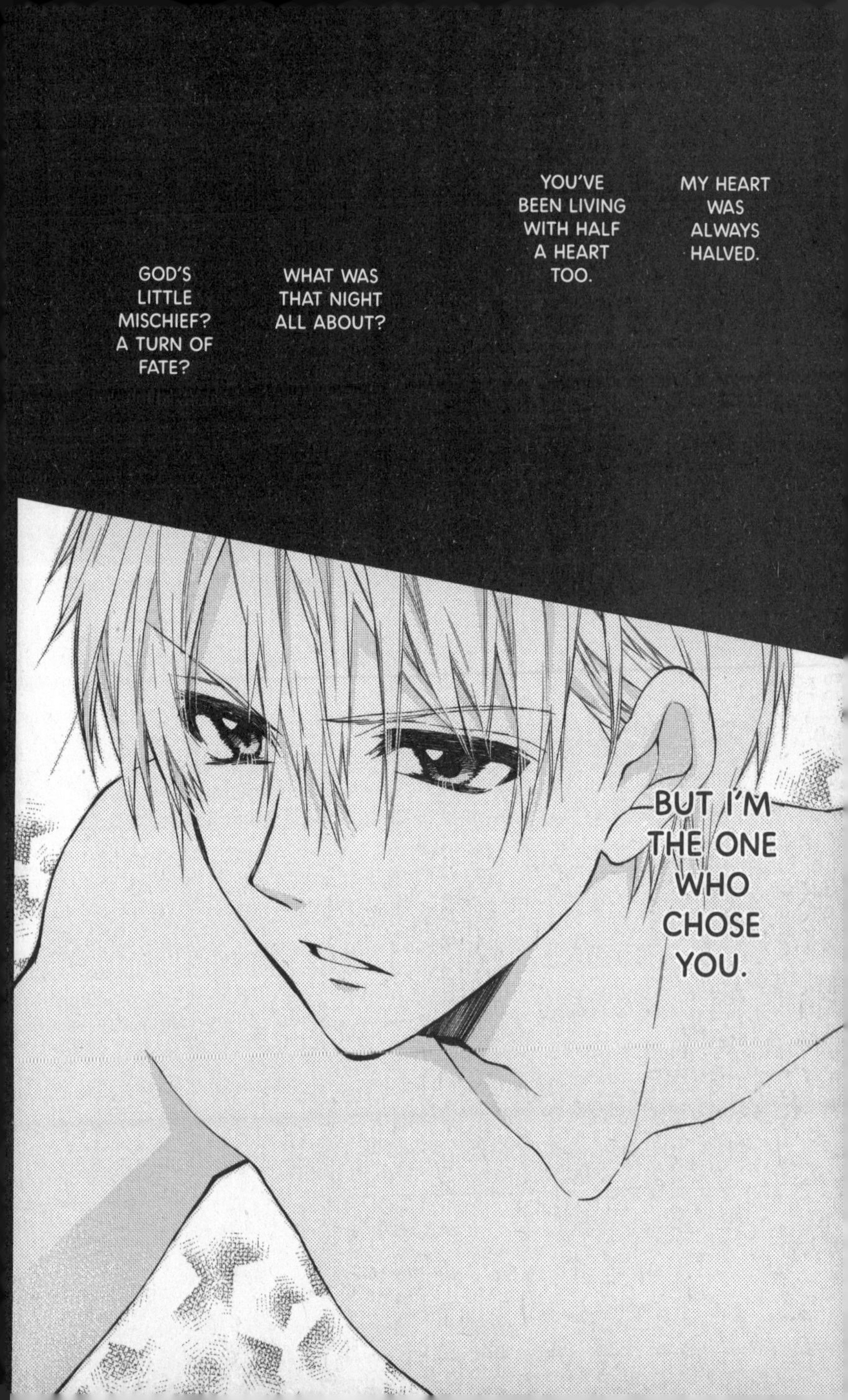
MY HEART WAS ALWAYS HALVED.
YOU'VE BEEN LIVING WITH HALF A HEART TOO.
WHAT WAS THAT NIGHT ALL ABOUT?
GOD'S LITTLE MISCHIEF? A TURN OF FATE?
BUT I'M THE ONE WHO CHOSE YOU.

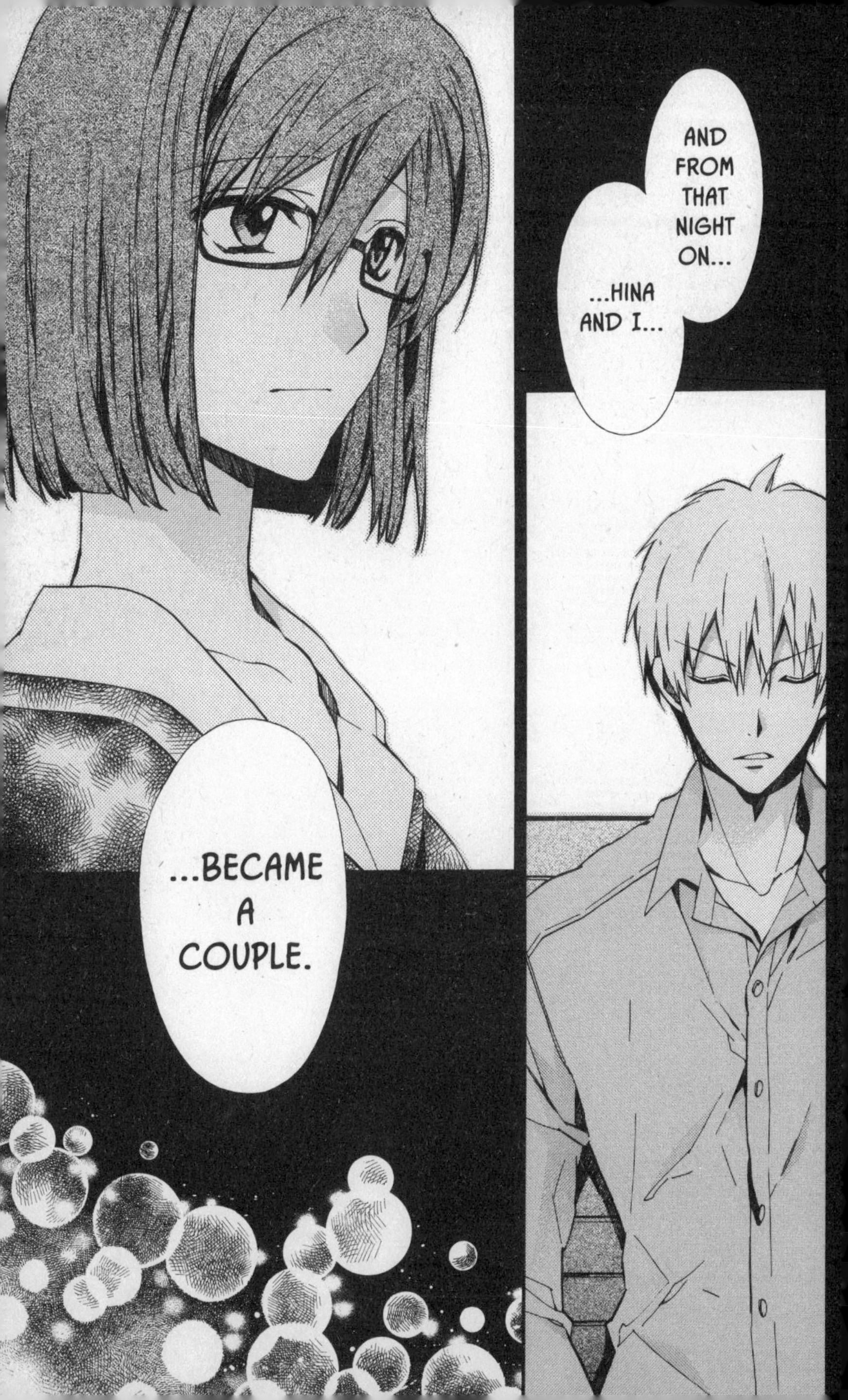
AND FROM THAT NIGHT ON...
...HINA AND I...
...BECAME A COUPLE.

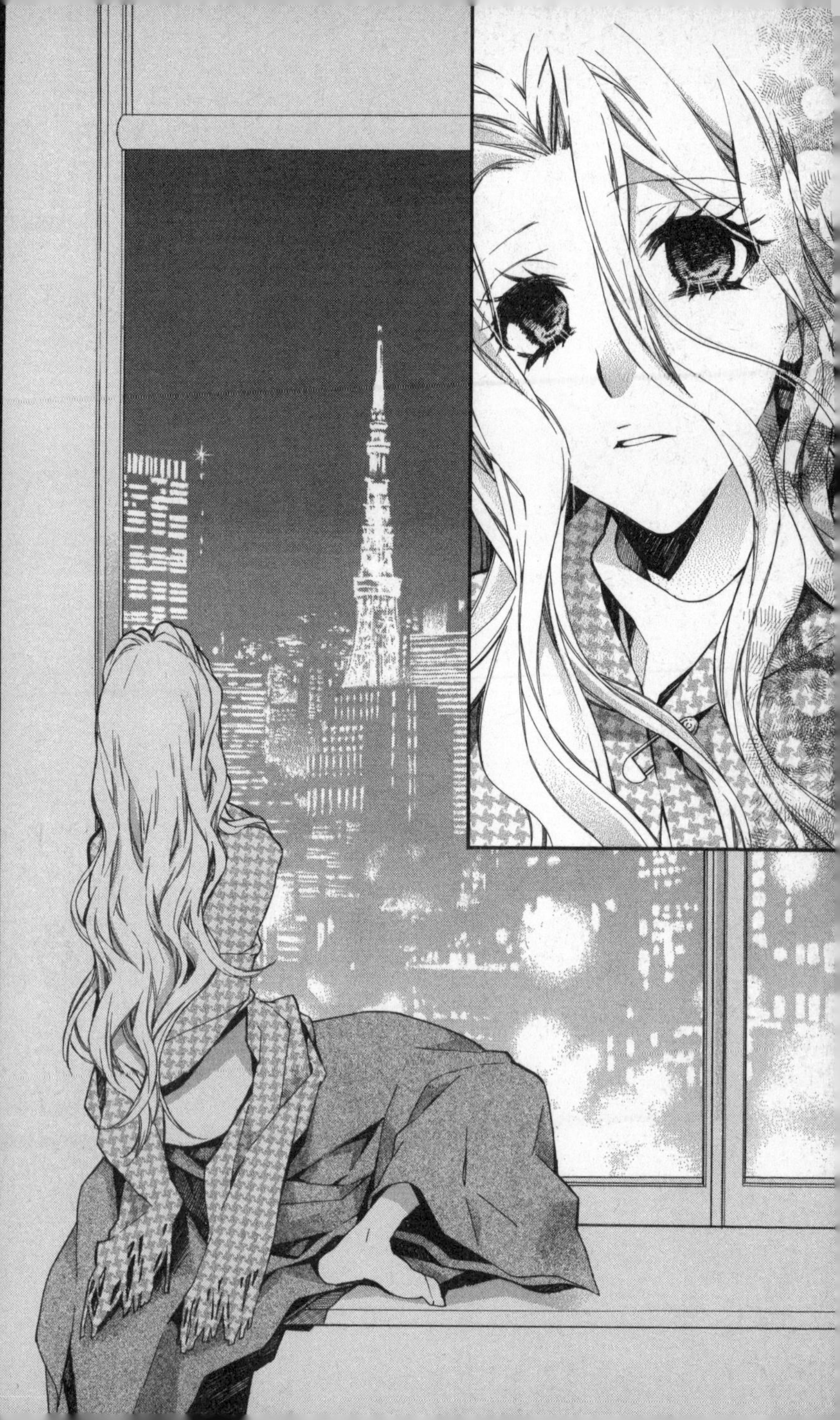

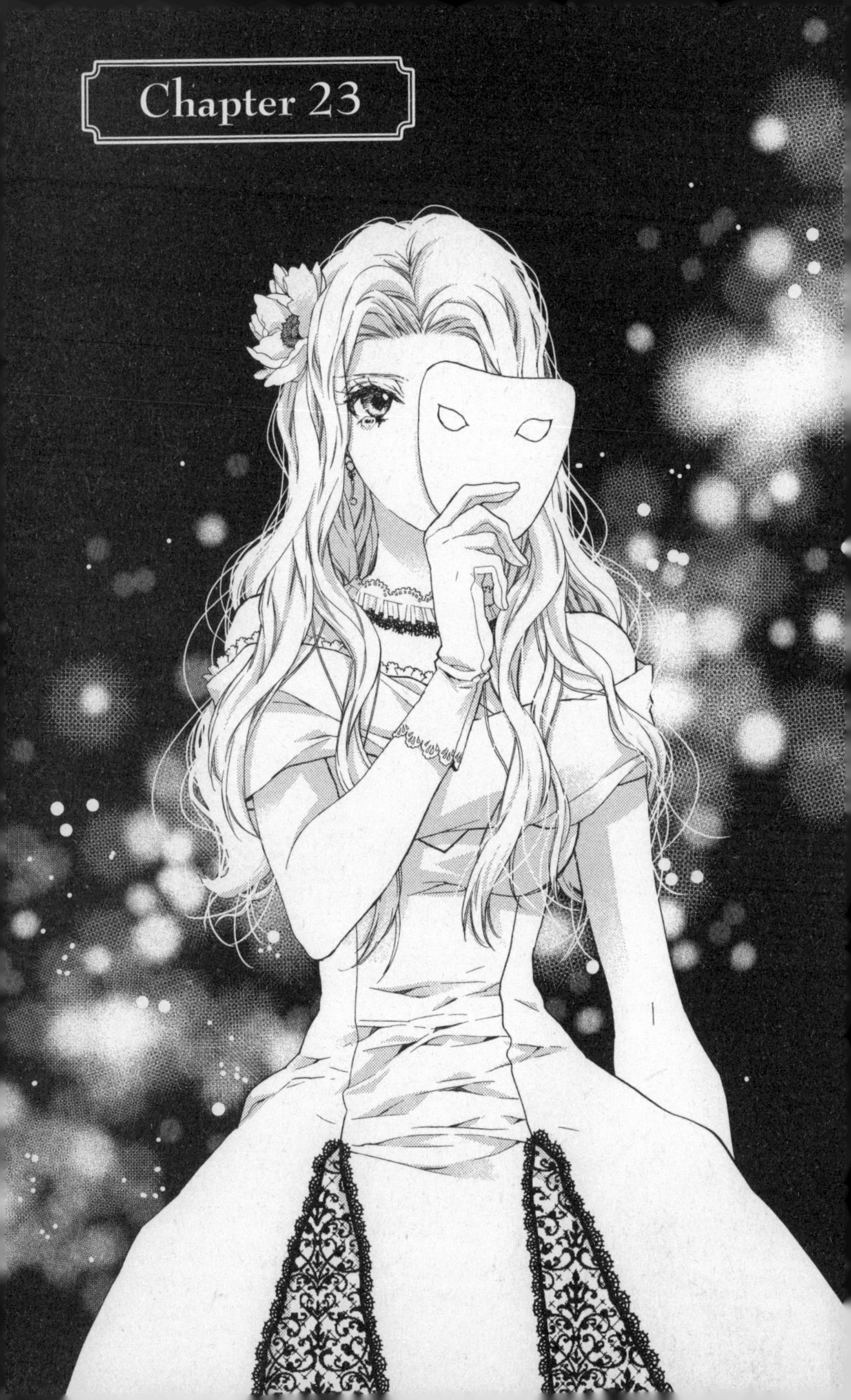
Chapter 23

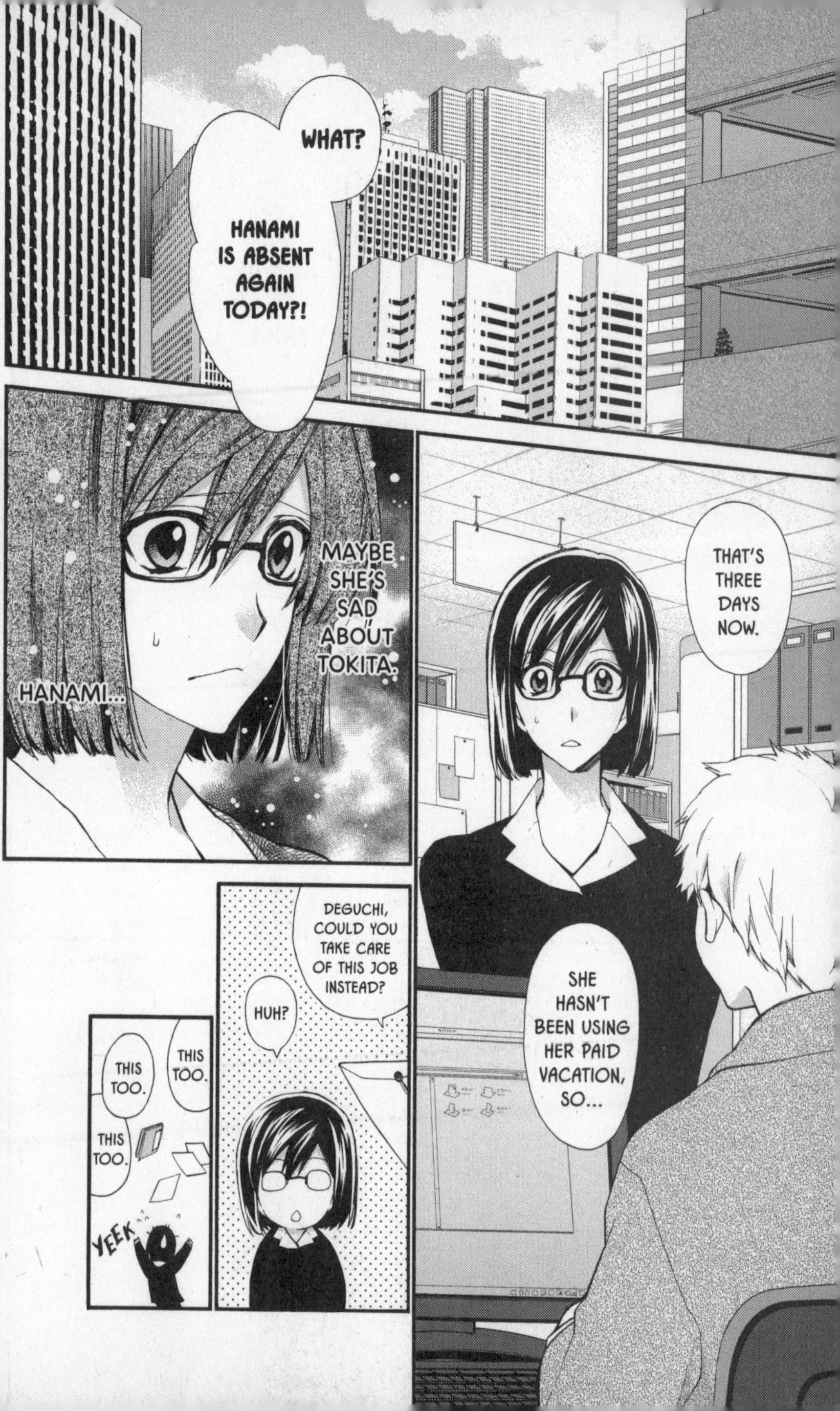
WHAT?
HANAMI IS ABSENT AGAIN TODAY?!
THAT'S THREE DAYS NOW.
SHE HASN'T BEEN USING HER PAID VACATION, SO...
MAYBE SHE'S SAD ABOUT TOKITA.
HANAMI...
DEGUCHI, COULD YOU TAKE CARE OF THIS JOB INSTEAD?
HUH?
THIS TOO.
THIS TOO.
THIS TOO.
YEEK

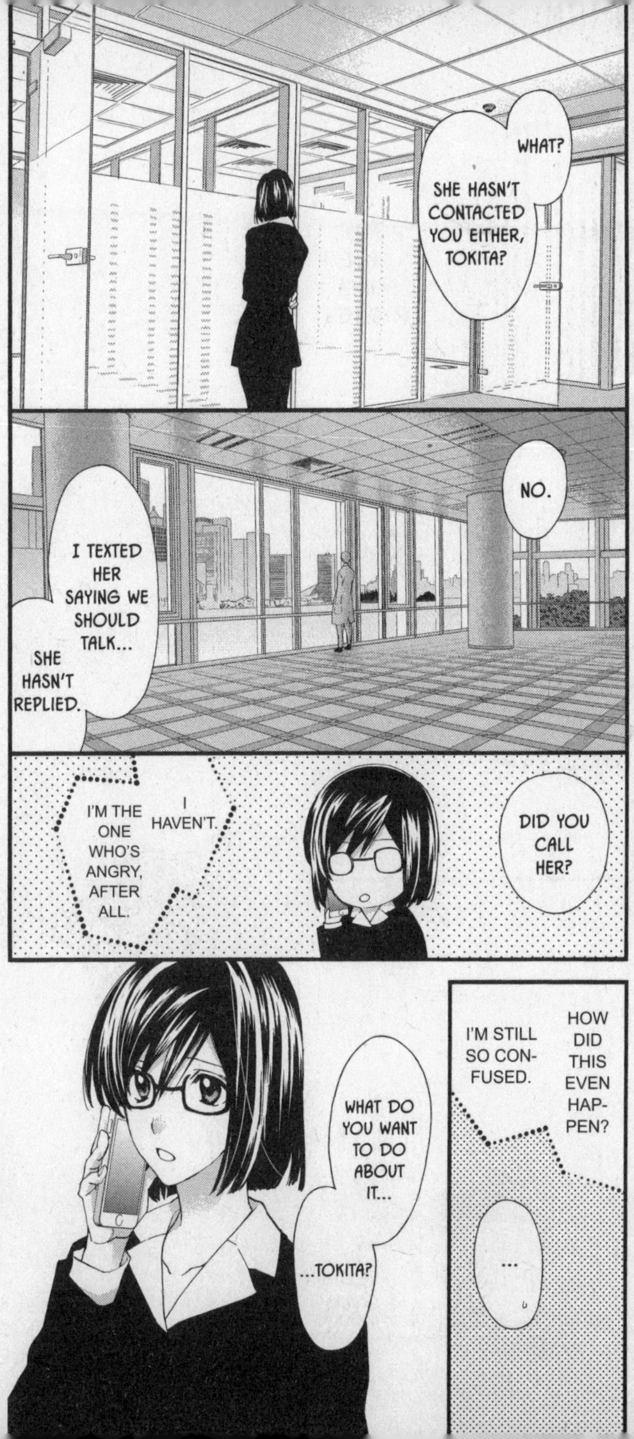
WHAT?
SHE HASN'T CONTACTED YOU EITHER, TOKITA?
NO.
I TEXTED HER SAYING WE SHOULD TALK...
SHE HASN'T REPLIED.
DID YOU CALL HER?
I HAVEN'T.
I'M THE ONE WHO'S ANGRY, AFTER ALL.
HOW DID THIS EVEN HAP-PEN?
I'M STILL SO CON-FUSED.
...
WHAT DO YOU WANT TO DO ABOUT IT...
...TOKITA?

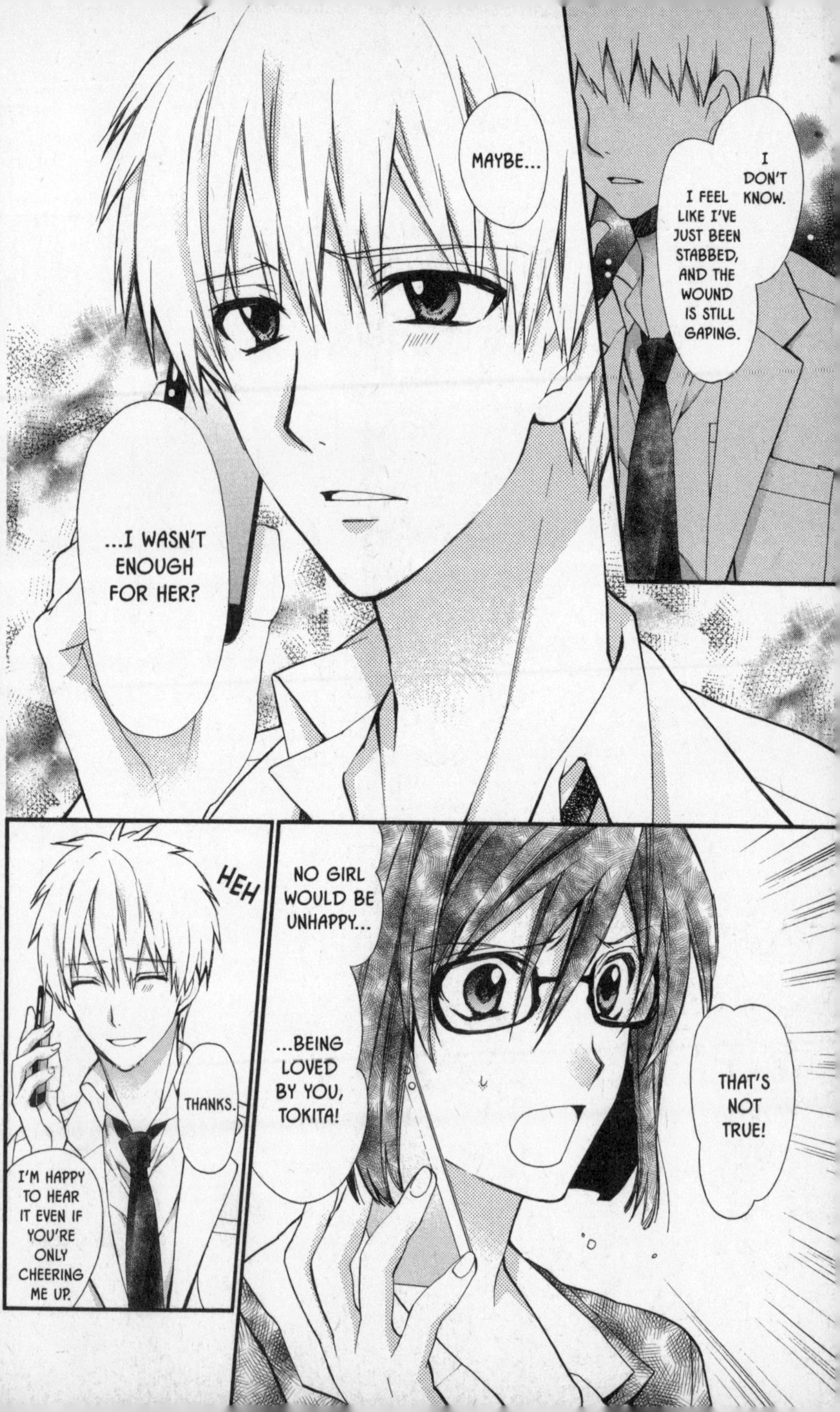
I DON'T KNOW.
I FEEL LIKE I'VE JUST BEEN STABBED, AND THE WOUND IS STILL GAPING.
MAYBE...
...I WASN'T ENOUGH FOR HER?
THAT'S NOT TRUE!
NO GIRL WOULD BE UNHAPPY...
...BEING LOVED BY YOU, TOKITA!
HEH
THANKS.
I'M HAPPY TO HEAR IT EVEN IF YOU'RE ONLY CHEERING ME UP.

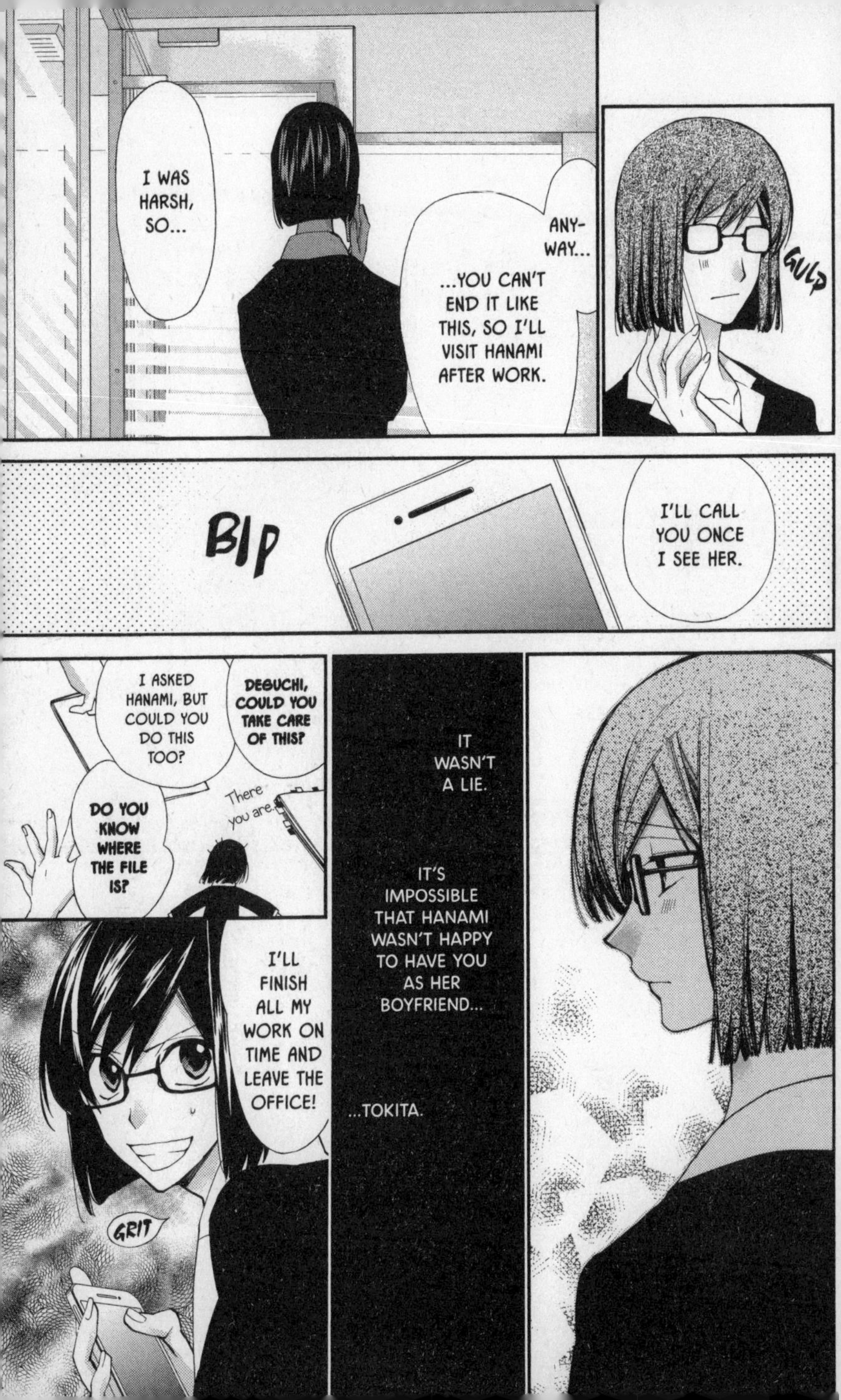
GULP
I WAS HARSH, SO...
ANYWAY...
...YOU CAN'T END IT LIKE THIS, SO I'LL VISIT HANAMI AFTER WORK.
I'LL CALL YOU ONCE I SEE HER.
BIP
IT WASN'T A LIE.
IT'S IMPOSSIBLE THAT HANAMI WASN'T HAPPY TO HAVE YOU AS HER BOYFRIEND...
...TOKITA.
DEGUCHI, COULD YOU TAKE CARE OF THIS?
I ASKED HANAMI, BUT COULD YOU DO THIS TOO?
There you are.
DO YOU KNOW WHERE THE FILE IS?
I'LL FINISH ALL MY WORK ON TIME AND LEAVE THE OFFICE!
GRIT

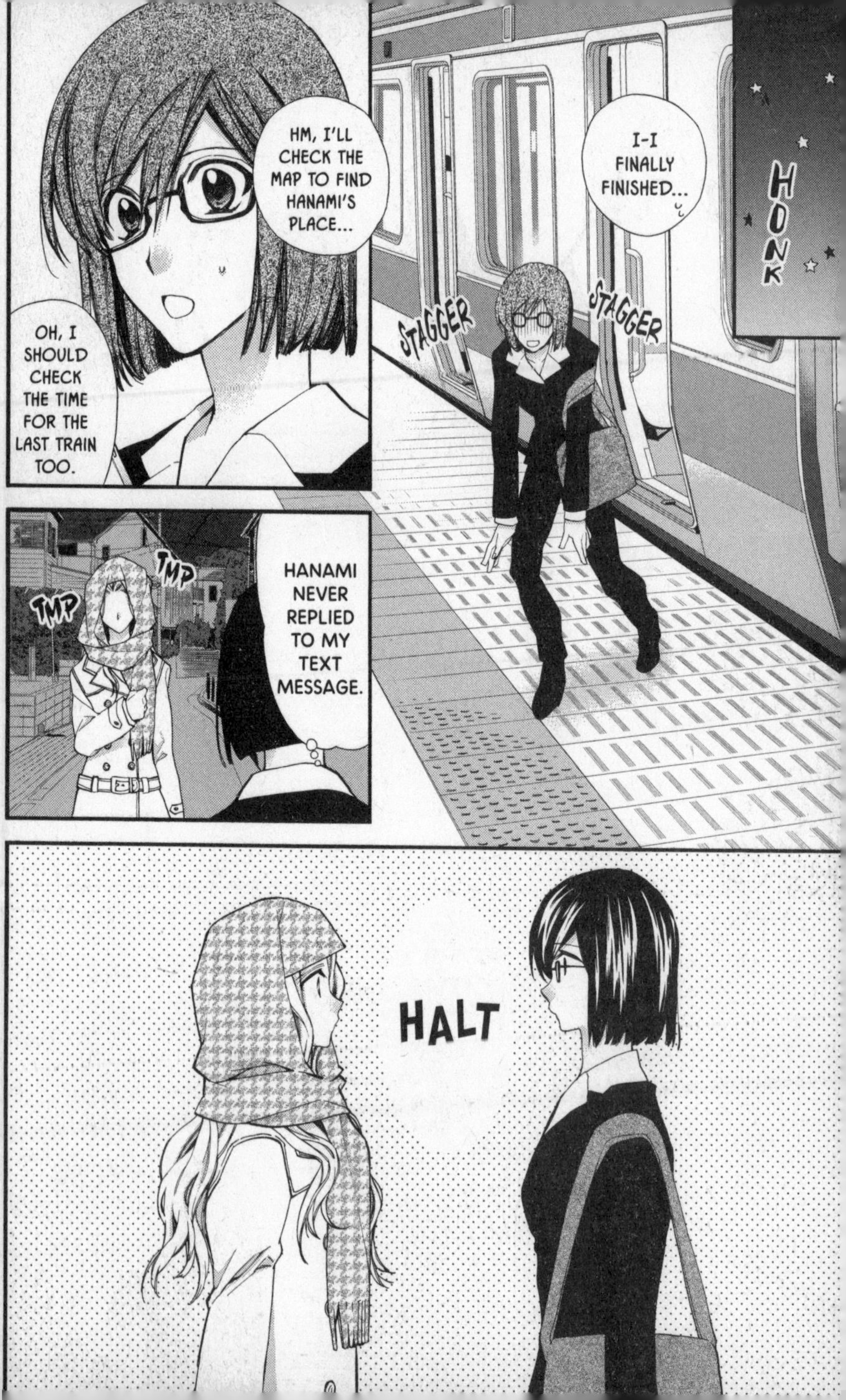
HONK
I-I FINALLY FINISHED...
STAGGER
STAGGER
HM, I'LL CHECK THE MAP TO FIND HANAMI'S PLACE...
OH, I SHOULD CHECK THE TIME FOR THE LAST TRAIN TOO.
TMP
TMP
HANAMI NEVER REPLIED TO MY TEXT MESSAGE.
HALT

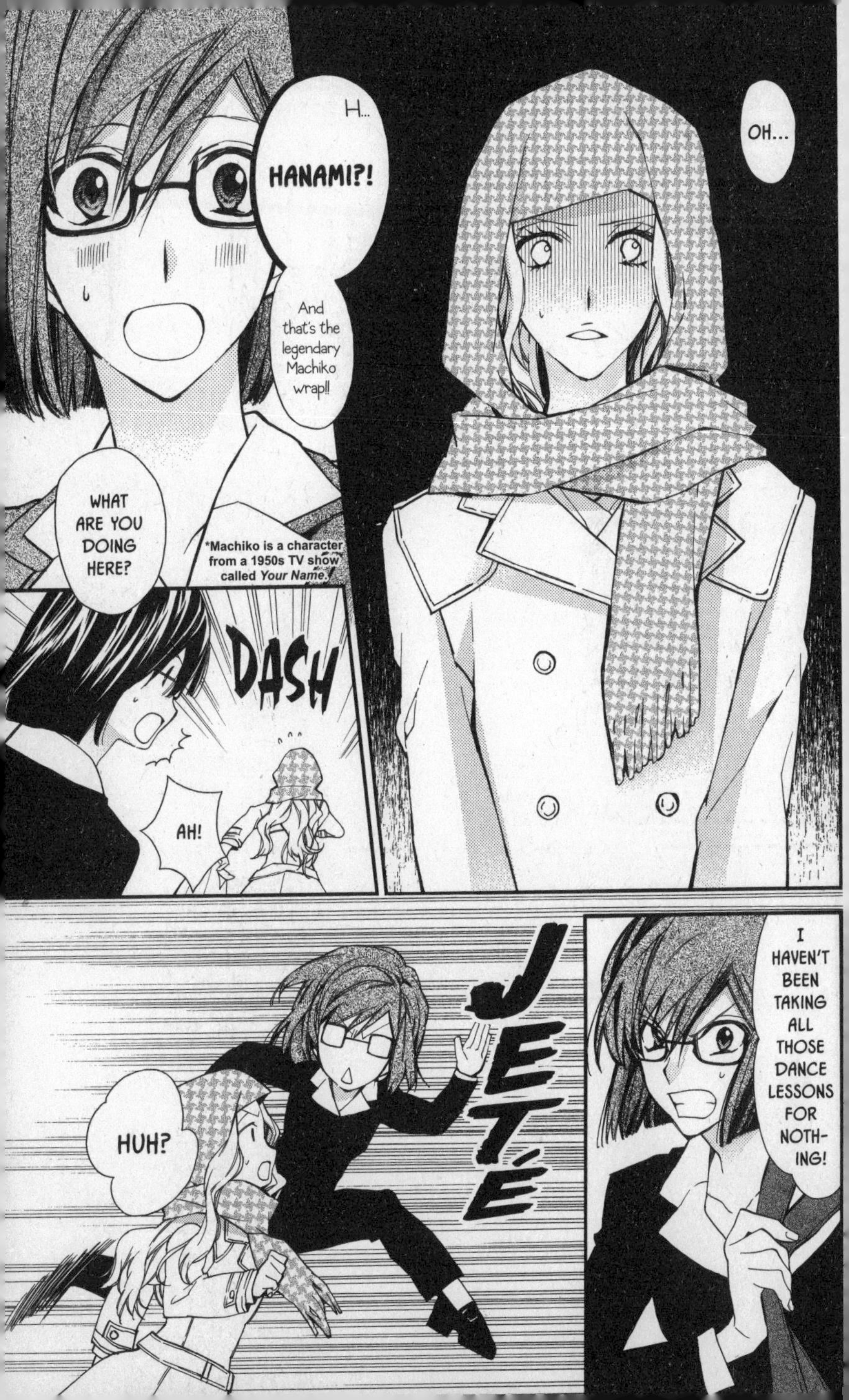
OH...
H...
HANAMI?!
And that's the legendary Machiko wrap!!
WHAT ARE YOU DOING HERE?
*Machiko is a character from a 1950s TV show called Your Name.
DASH
AH!
I HAVEN'T BEEN TAKING ALL THOSE DANCE LESSONS FOR NOTH-ING!
JETÉ
HUH?

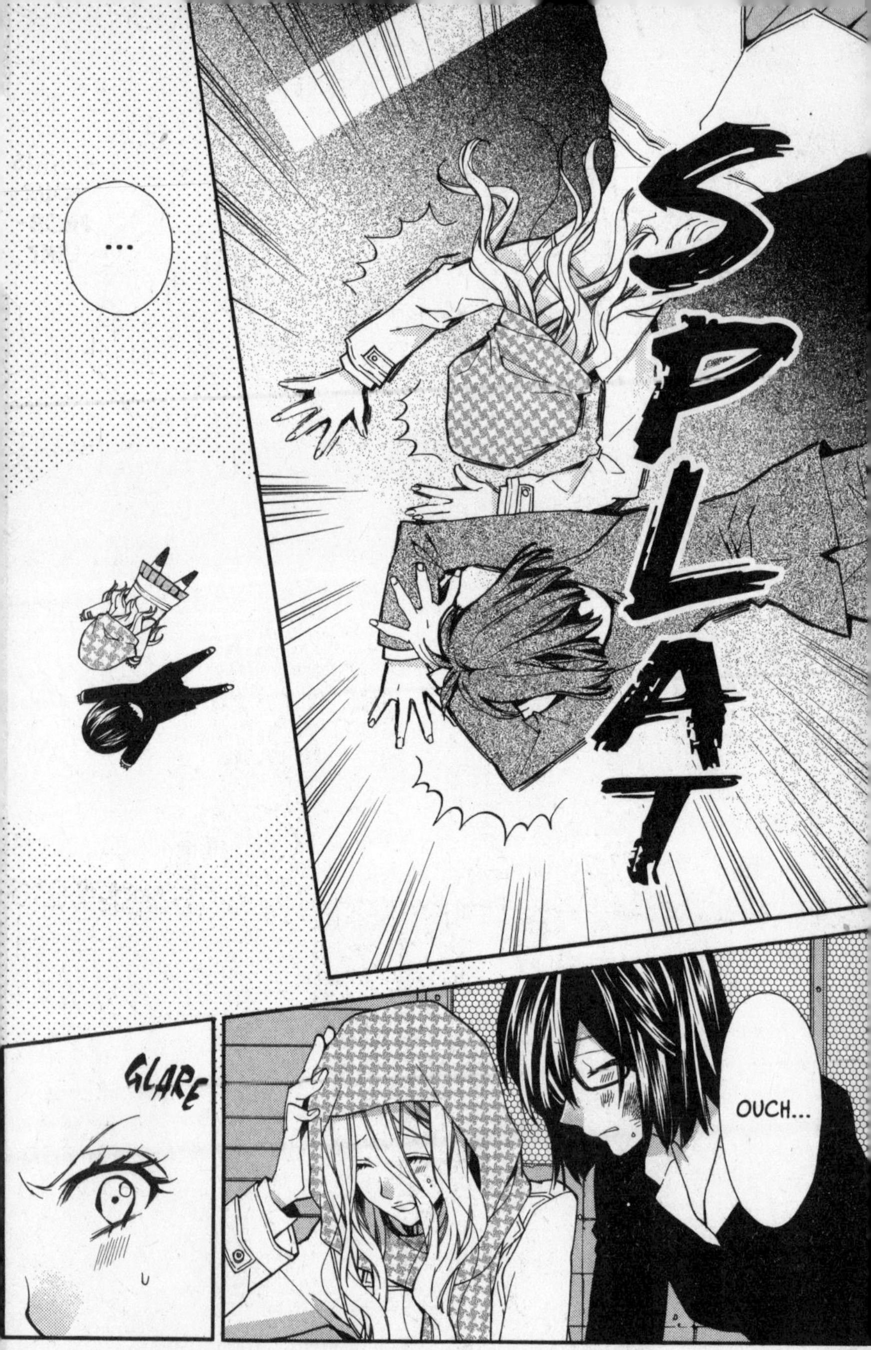
SPLAT
...
OUCH...
GLARE

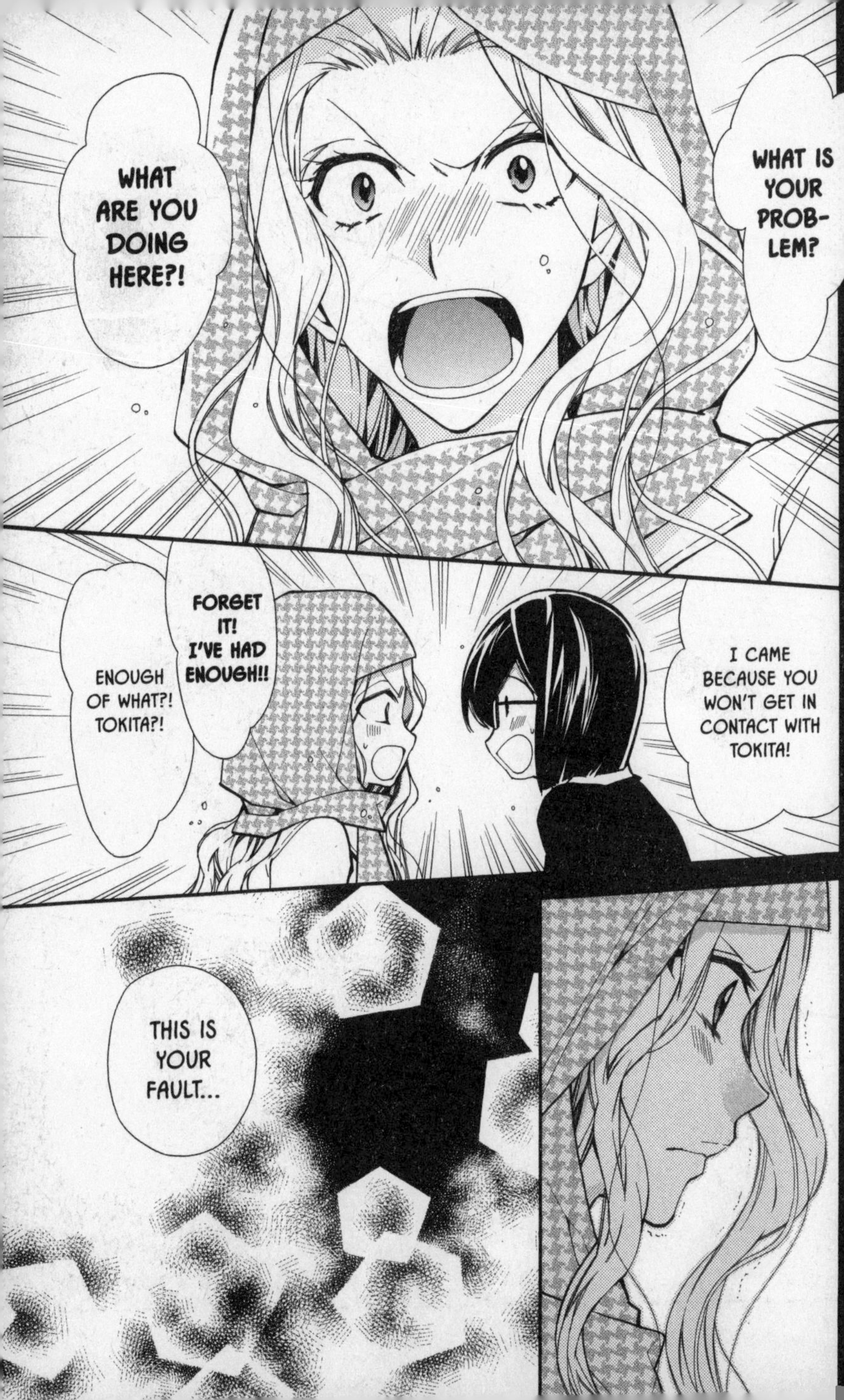
WHAT IS YOUR PROB-LEM?
WHAT ARE YOU DOING HERE?!
I CAME BECAUSE YOU WON'T GET IN CONTACT WITH TOKITA!
FORGET IT! I'VE HAD ENOUGH!!
ENOUGH OF WHAT?! TOKITA?!
THIS IS YOUR FAULT...

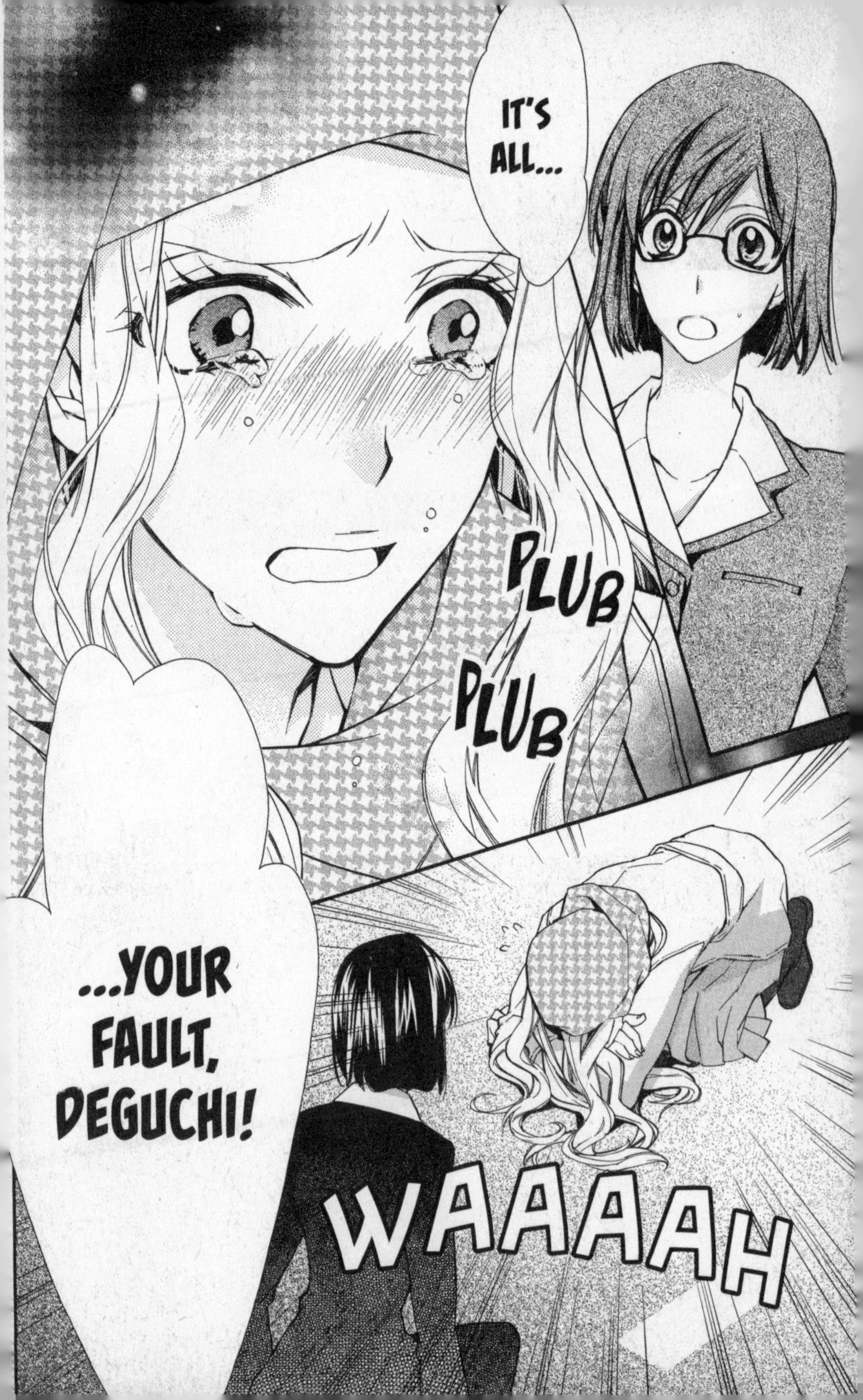
IT'S ALL...
PLUB
PLUB
...YOUR FAULT, DEGUCHI!
WAAAAH

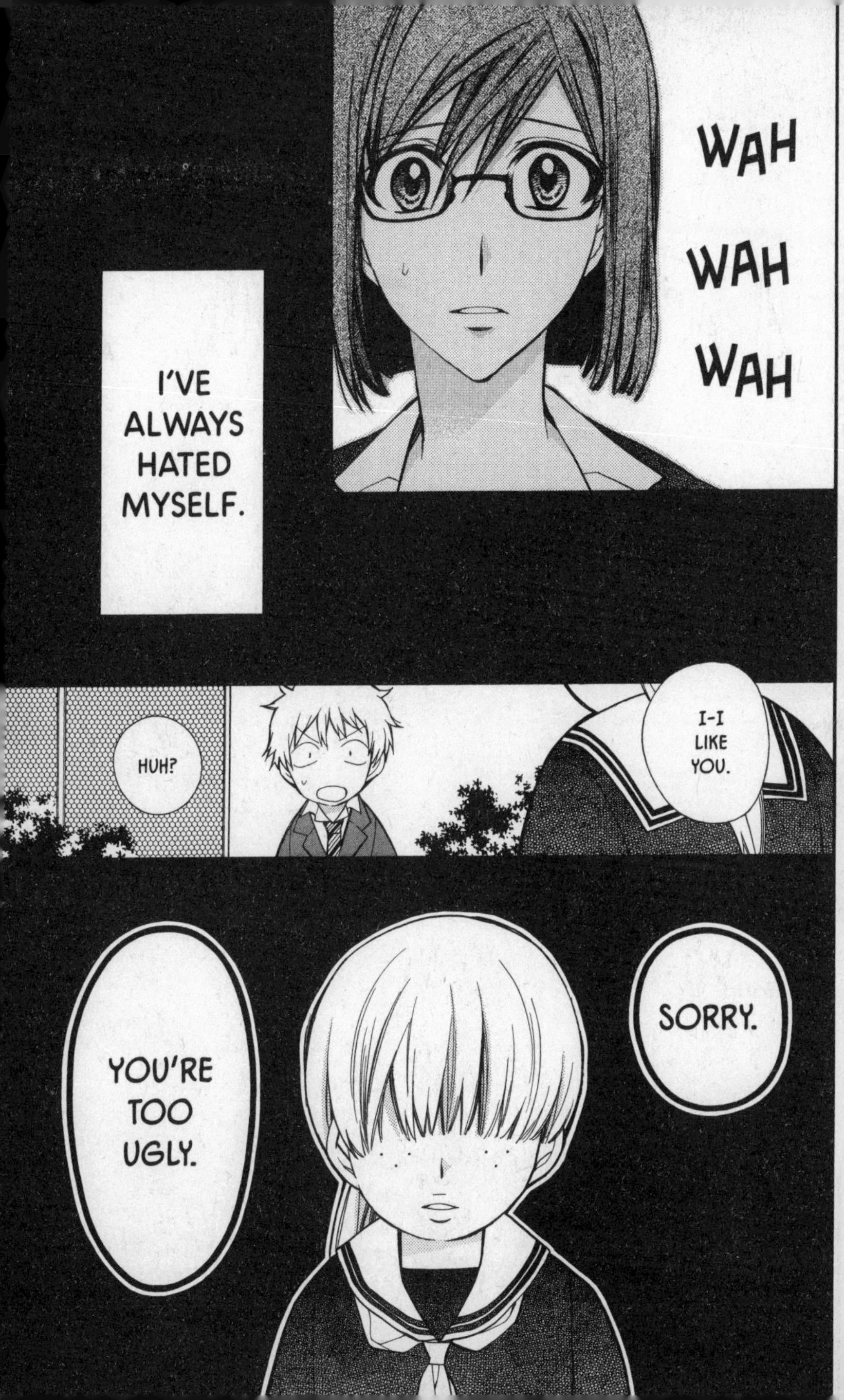
WAH WAH WAH
I'VE ALWAYS HATED MYSELF.
I-I LIKE YOU.
HUH?
SORRY.
YOU'RE TOO UGLY.

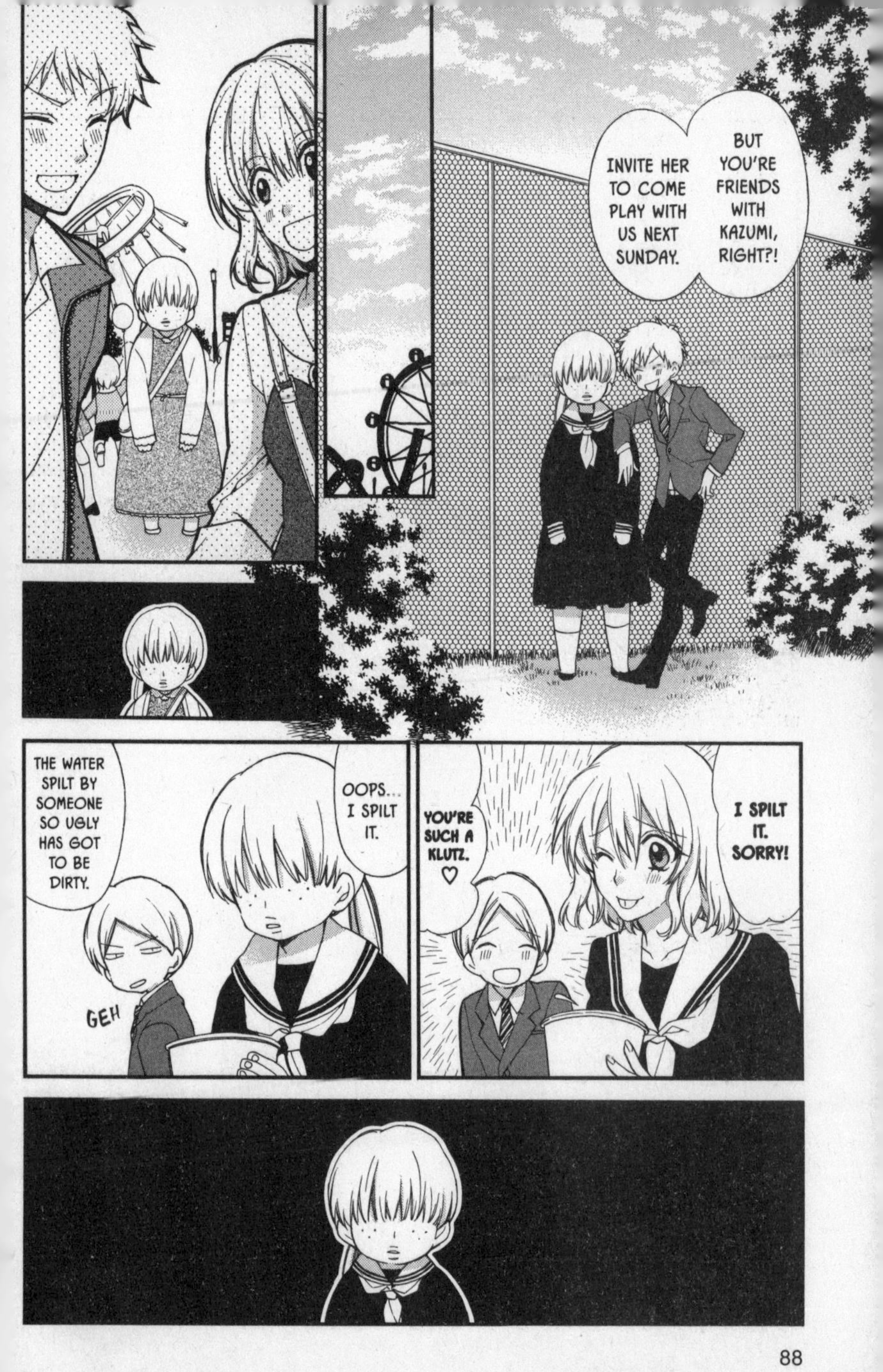
BUT YOU'RE FRIENDS WITH KAZUMI, RIGHT?!
INVITE HER TO COME PLAY WITH US NEXT SUNDAY.
I SPILT IT. SORRY!
YOU'RE SUCH A KLUTZ. ♡
OOPS... I SPILT IT.
THE WATER SPILT BY SOMEONE SO UGLY HAS GOT TO BE DIRTY.
GEH

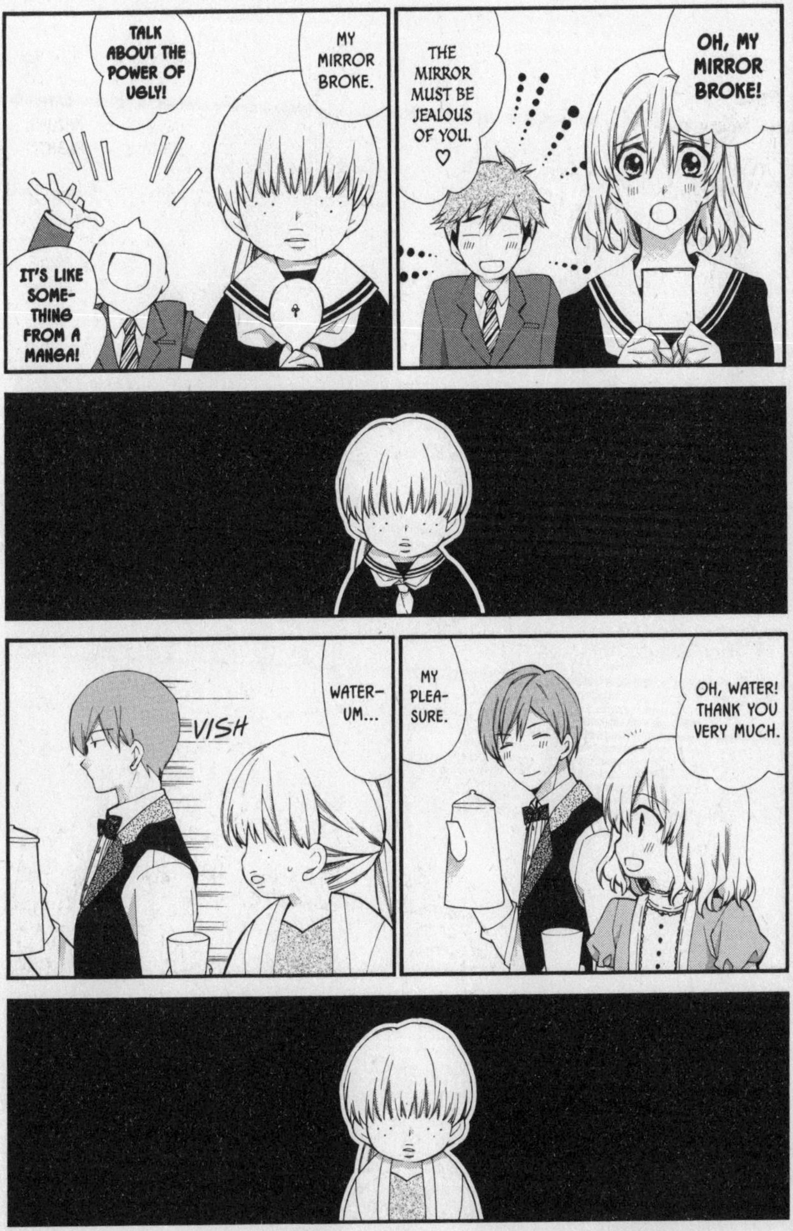
OH, MY MIRROR BROKE!
THE MIRROR MUST BE JEALOUS OF YOU. ♡
MY MIRROR BROKE.
TALK ABOUT THE POWER OF UGLY!
IT'S LIKE SOMETHING FROM A MANGA!
OH, WATER! THANK YOU VERY MUCH.
MY PLEASURE.
WATER-UM...
VISH

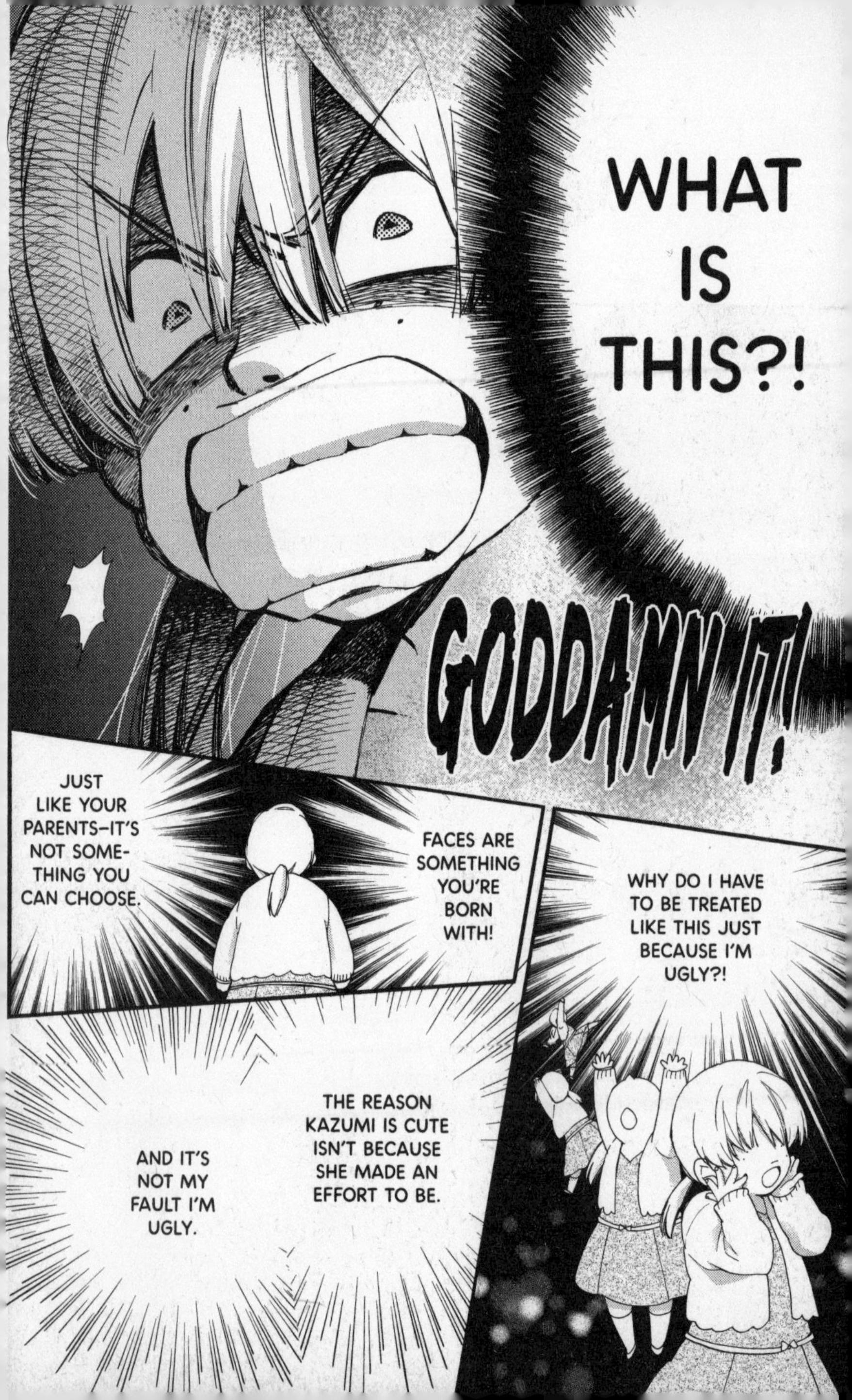

WHAT IS THIS?!
GODDAMN IT!
WHY DO I HAVE TO BE TREATED LIKE THIS JUST BECAUSE I'M UGLY?!
FACES ARE SOMETHING YOU'RE BORN WITH!
JUST LIKE YOUR PARENTS—IT'S NOT SOMETHING YOU CAN CHOOSE.
THE REASON KAZUMI IS CUTE ISN'T BECAUSE SHE MADE AN EFFORT TO BE.
AND IT'S NOT MY FAULT I'M UGLY.

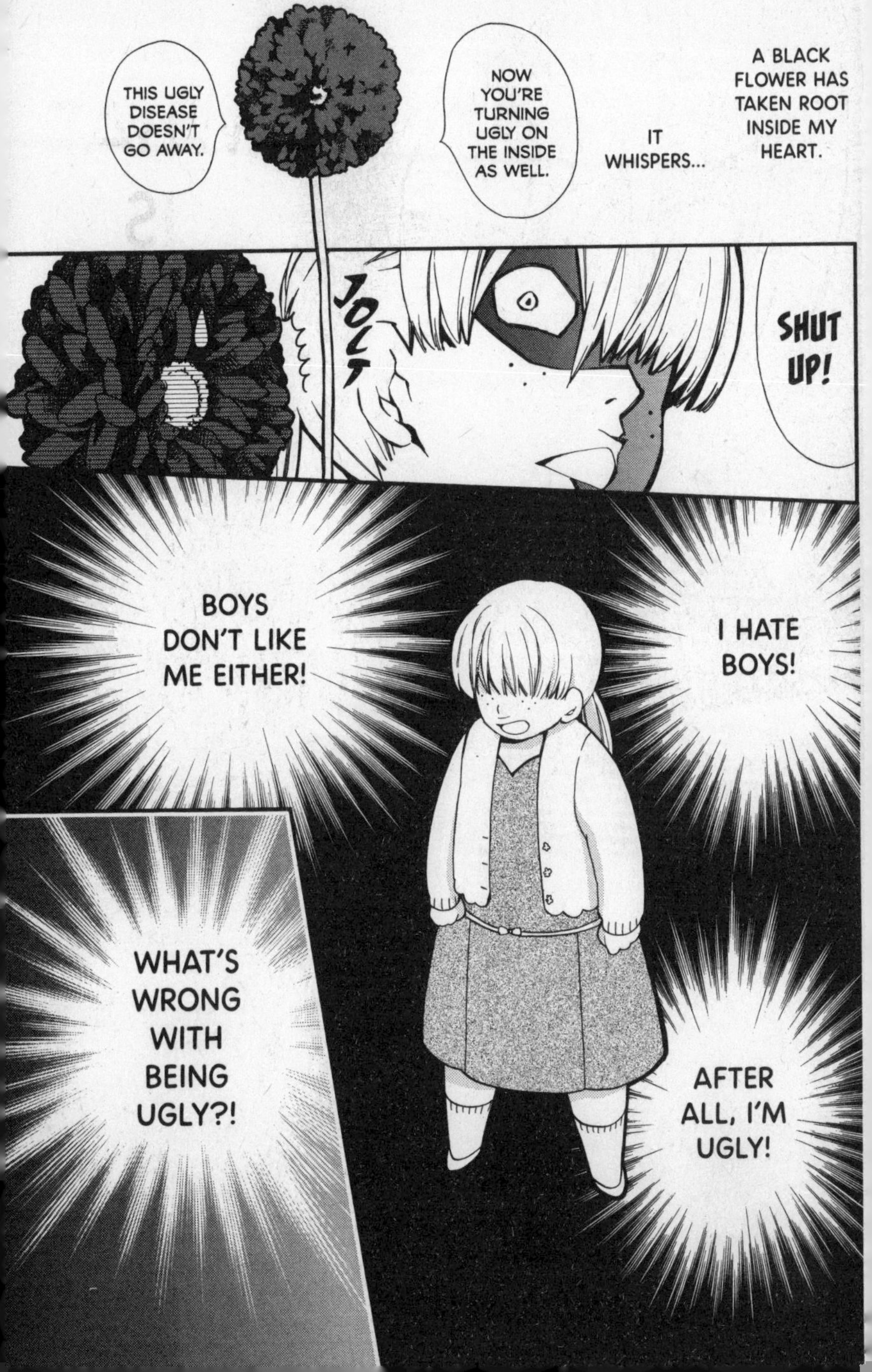
A BLACK FLOWER HAS TAKEN ROOT INSIDE MY HEART.
IT WHISPERS...
NOW YOU'RE TURNING UGLY ON THE INSIDE AS WELL.
THIS UGLY DISEASE DOESN'T GO AWAY.
SHUT UP!
JOLT
I HATE BOYS!
BOYS DON'T LIKE ME EITHER!
AFTER ALL, I'M UGLY!
WHAT'S WRONG WITH BEING UGLY?!

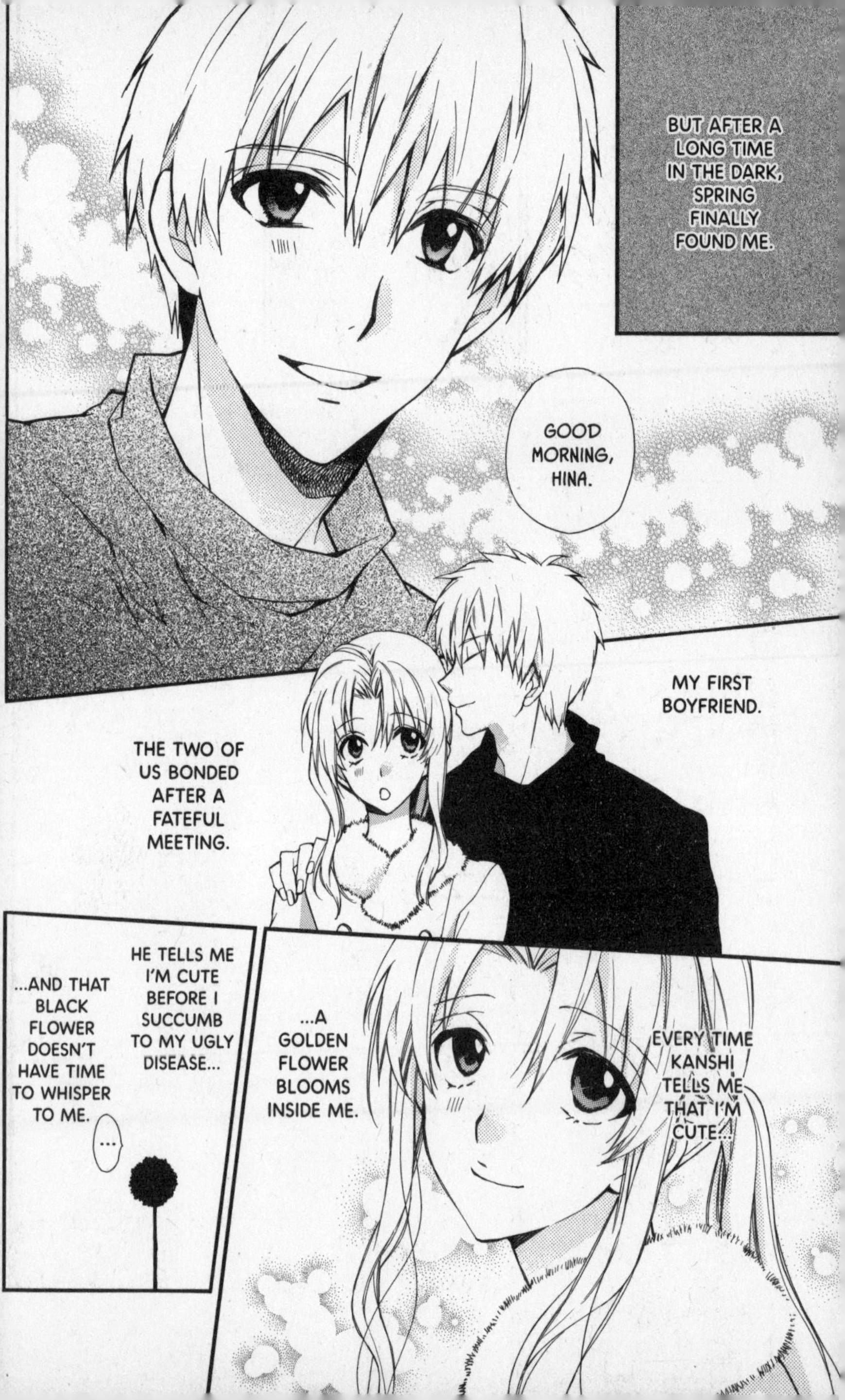
BUT AFTER A LONG TIME IN THE DARK, SPRING FINALLY FOUND ME.
GOOD MORNING, HINA.
MY FIRST BOYFRIEND.
THE TWO OF US BONDED AFTER A FATEFUL MEETING.
EVERY TIME KANSHI TELLS ME THAT I'M CUTE...
...A GOLDEN FLOWER BLOOMS INSIDE ME.
HE TELLS ME I'M CUTE BEFORE I SUCCUMB TO MY UGLY DISEASE...
...AND THAT BLACK FLOWER DOESN'T HAVE TIME TO WHISPER TO ME.
...

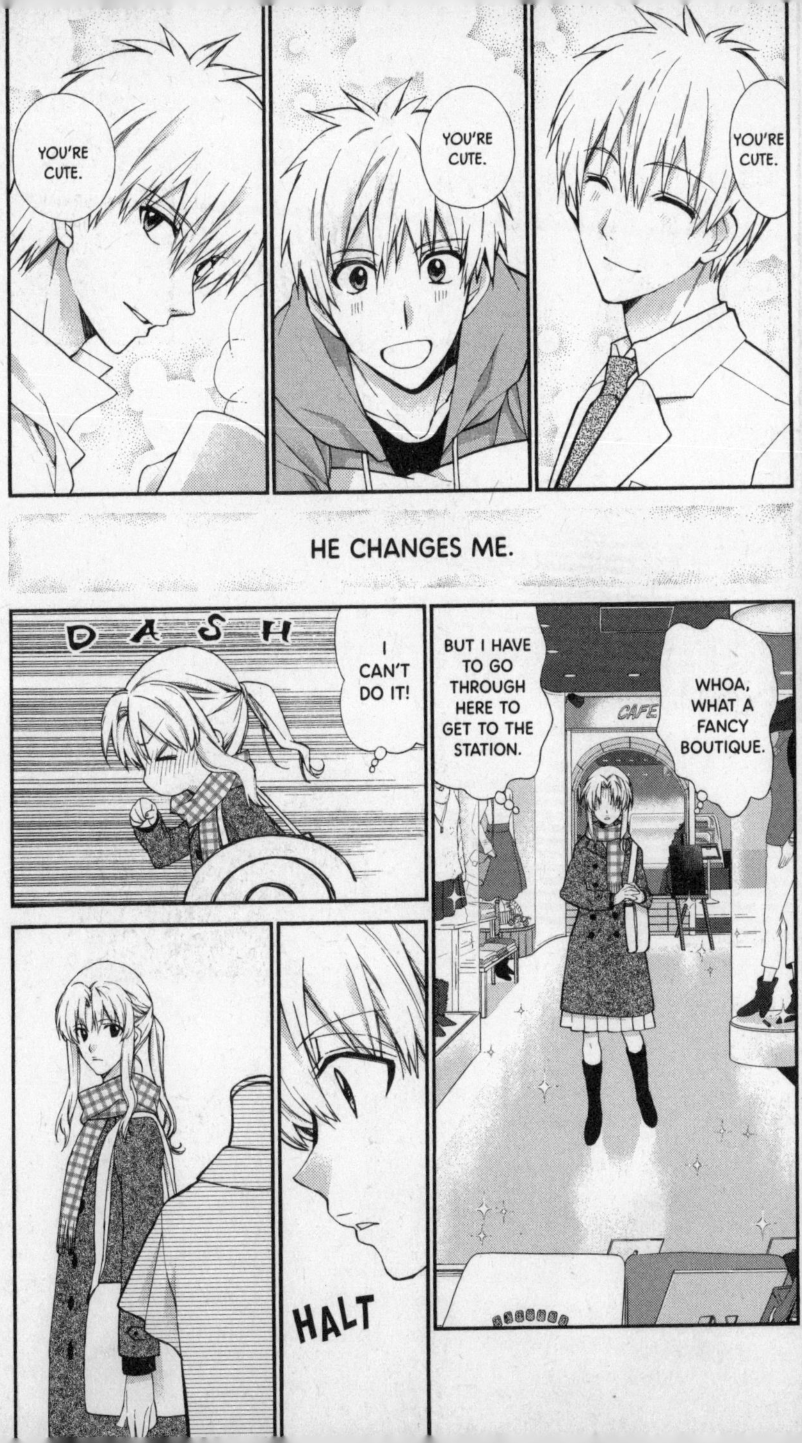
YOU'RE CUTE.
YOU'RE CUTE.
YOU'RE CUTE.
HE CHANGES ME.
WHOA, WHAT A FANCY BOUTIQUE.
BUT I HAVE TO GO THROUGH HERE TO GET TO THE STATION.
CAFE
I CAN'T DO IT!
DASH
HALT

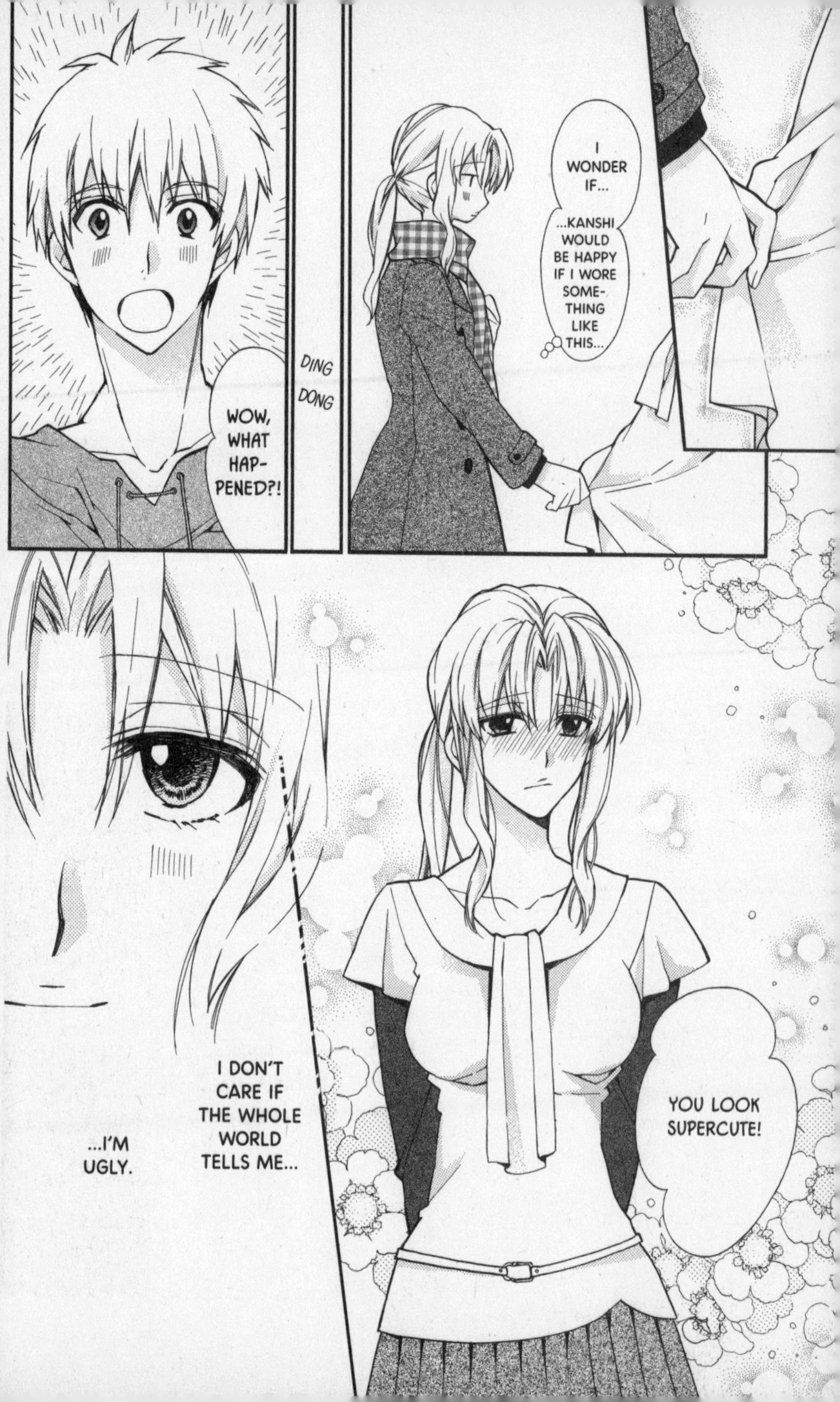
I WONDER IF...
...KANSHI WOULD BE HAPPY IF I WORE SOME-THING LIKE THIS...
DING DONG
WOW, WHAT HAP-PENED?!
YOU LOOK SUPERCUTE!
I DON'T CARE IF THE WHOLE WORLD TELLS ME...
...I'M UGLY.

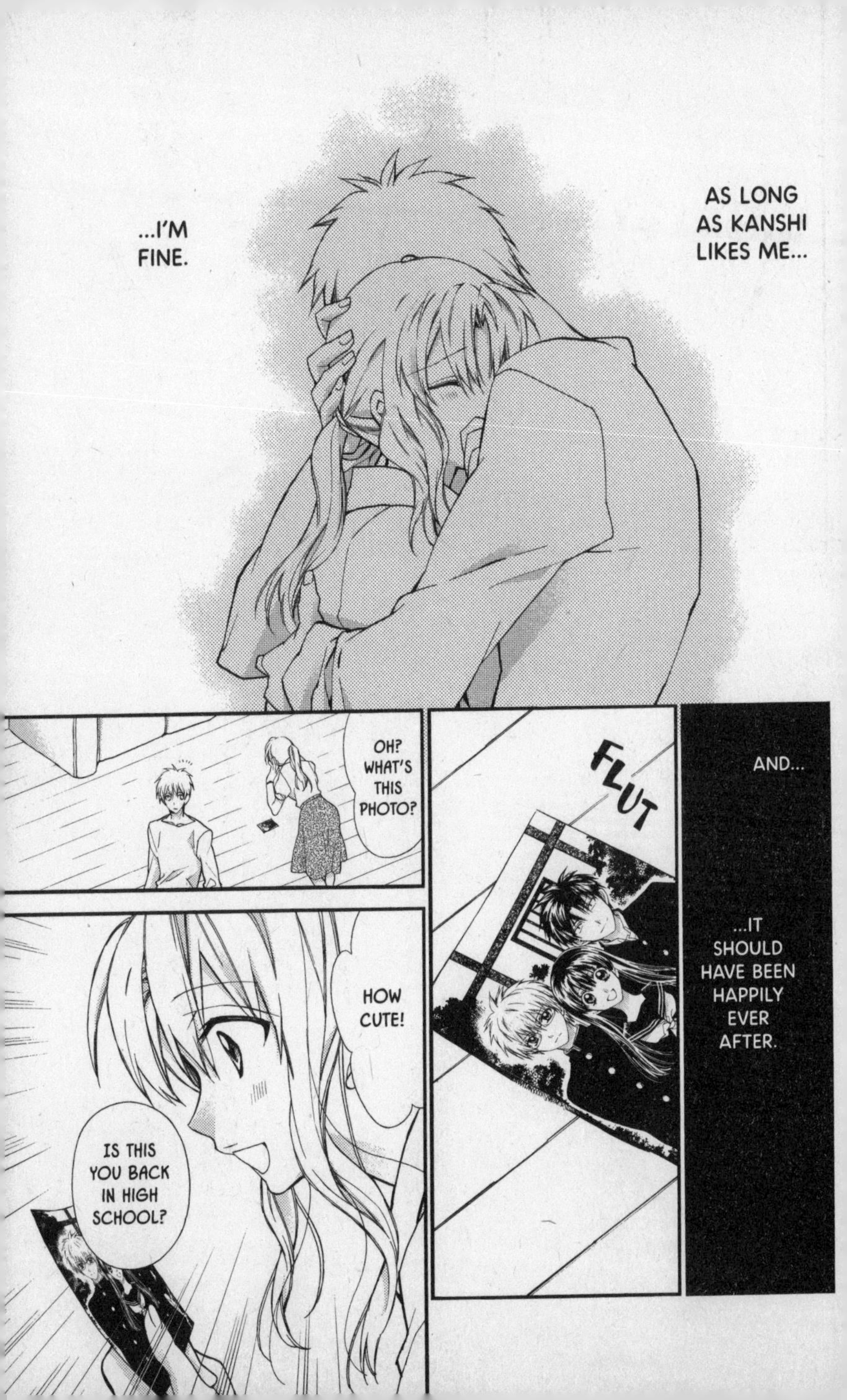
AS LONG AS KANSHI LIKES ME...
...I'M FINE.
AND...
...IT SHOULD HAVE BEEN HAPPILY EVER AFTER.
FLUT
OH? WHAT'S THIS PHOTO?
HOW CUTE!
IS THIS YOU BACK IN HIGH SCHOOL?

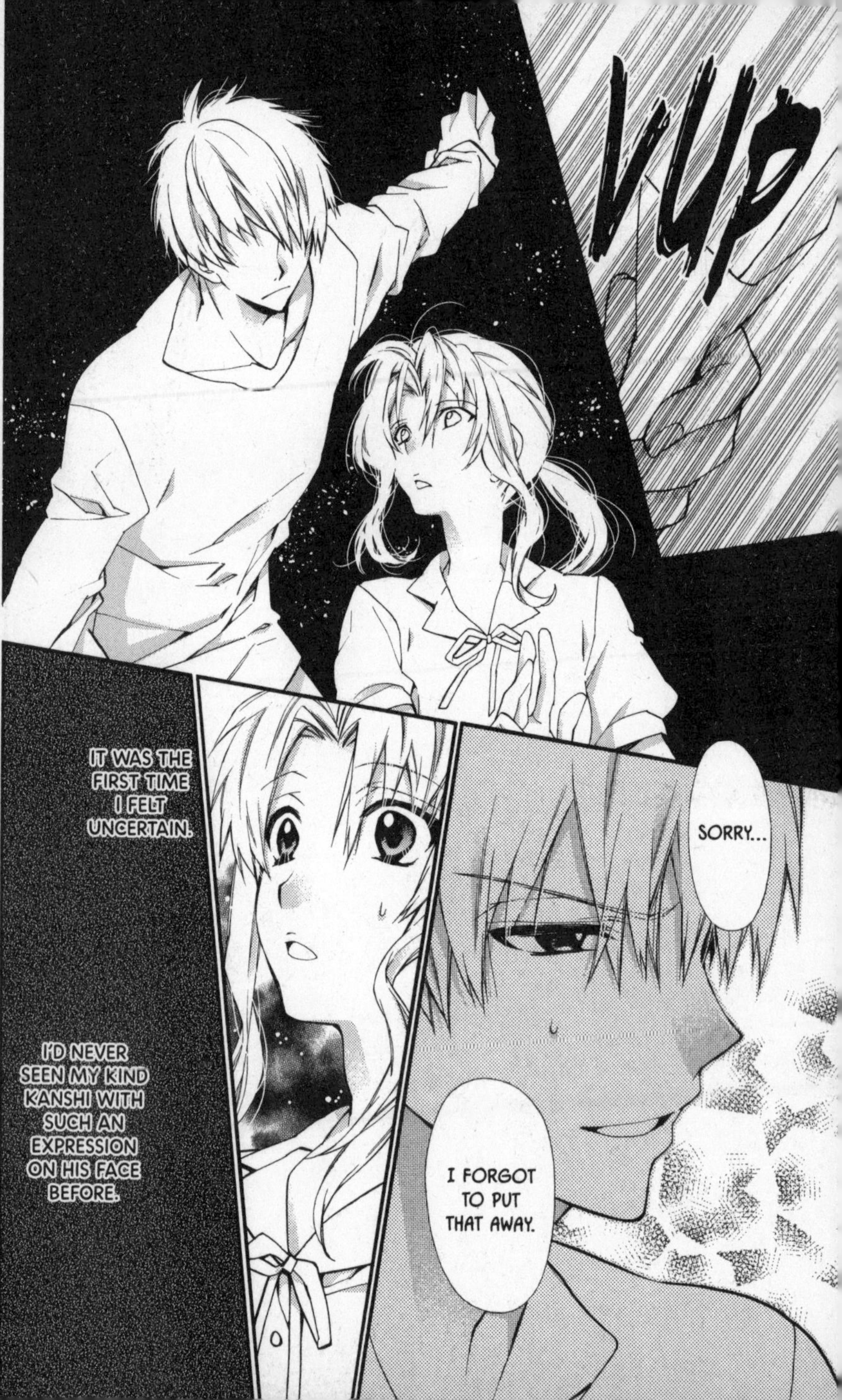
VUP
SORRY...
I FORGOT TO PUT THAT AWAY.
IT WAS THE FIRST TIME I FELT UNCERTAIN.
I'D NEVER SEEN MY KIND KANSHI WITH SUCH AN EXPRESSION ON HIS FACE BEFORE.

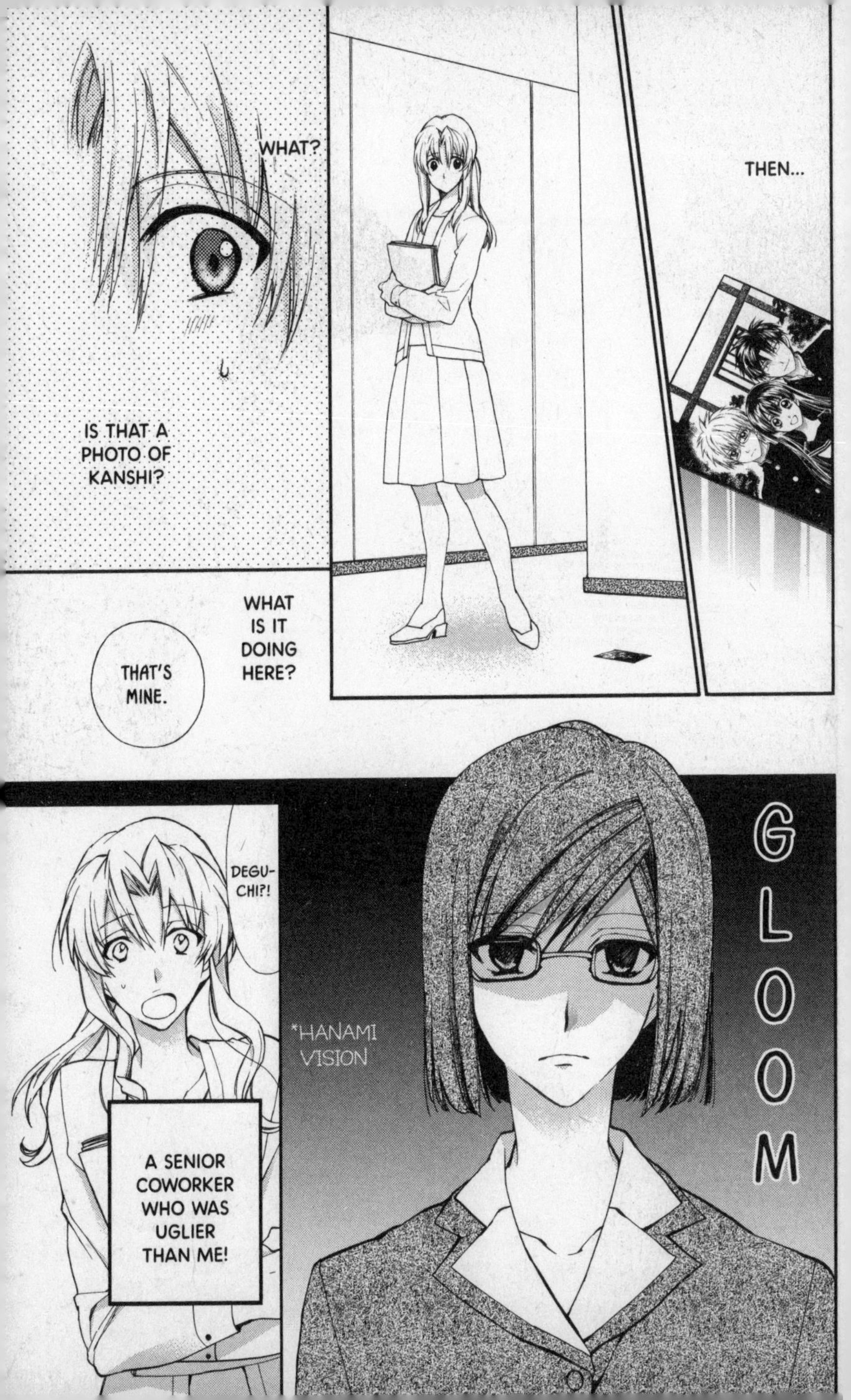
THEN...
WHAT?
IS THAT A PHOTO OF KANSHI?
WHAT IS IT DOING HERE?
THAT'S MINE.
GLOOM
*HANAMI VISION
DEGU-CHI?!
A SENIOR COWORKER WHO WAS UGLIER THAN ME!

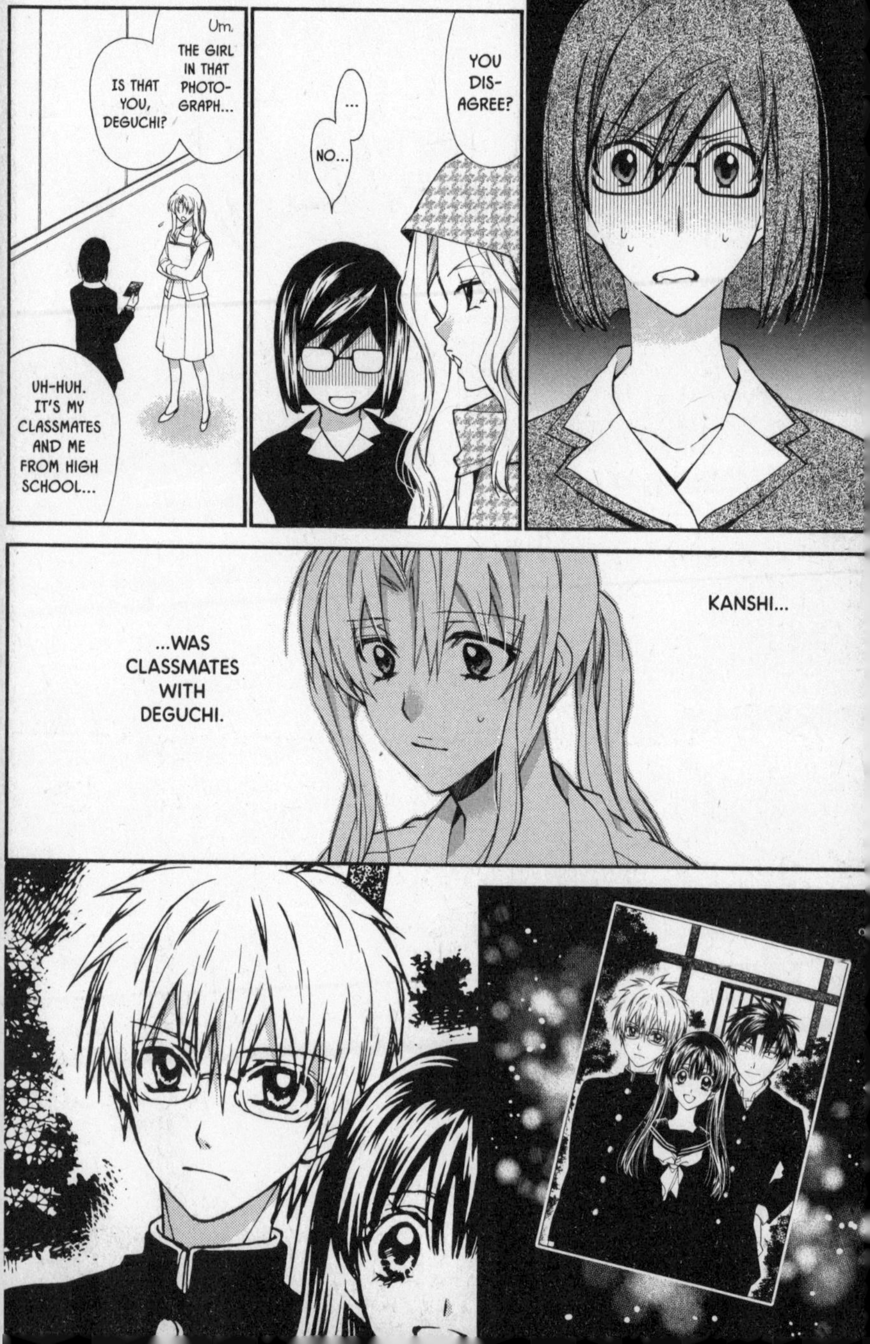
YOU DIS-AGREE?
...
NO...
Um. THE GIRL IN THAT PHOTOGRAPH...
IS THAT YOU, DEGUCHI?
UH-HUH. IT'S MY CLASSMATES AND ME FROM HIGH SCHOOL...
KANSHI...
...WAS CLASSMATES WITH DEGUCHI.

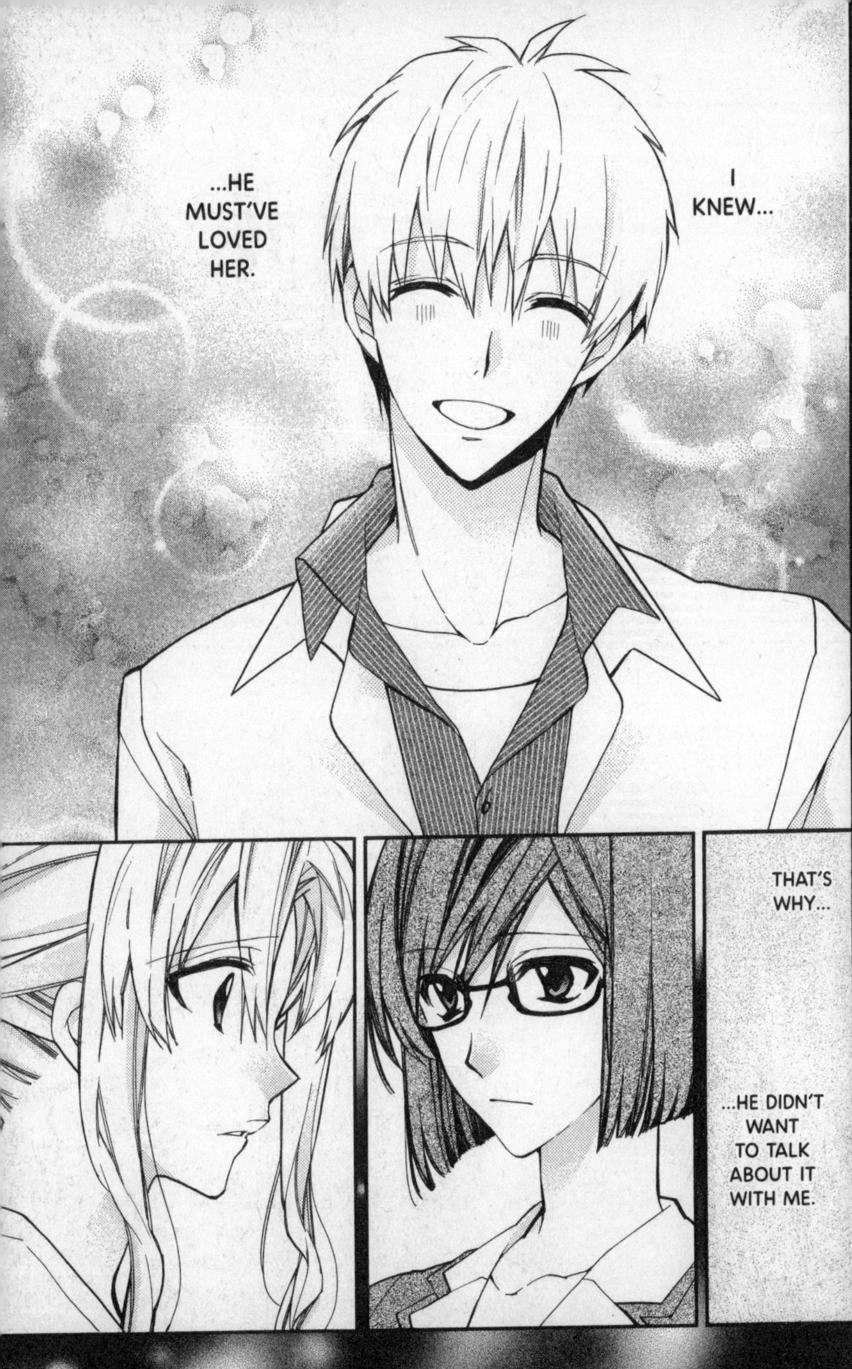
I KNEW...
...HE MUST'VE LOVED HER.
THAT'S WHY...
...HE DIDN'T WANT TO TALK ABOUT IT WITH ME.

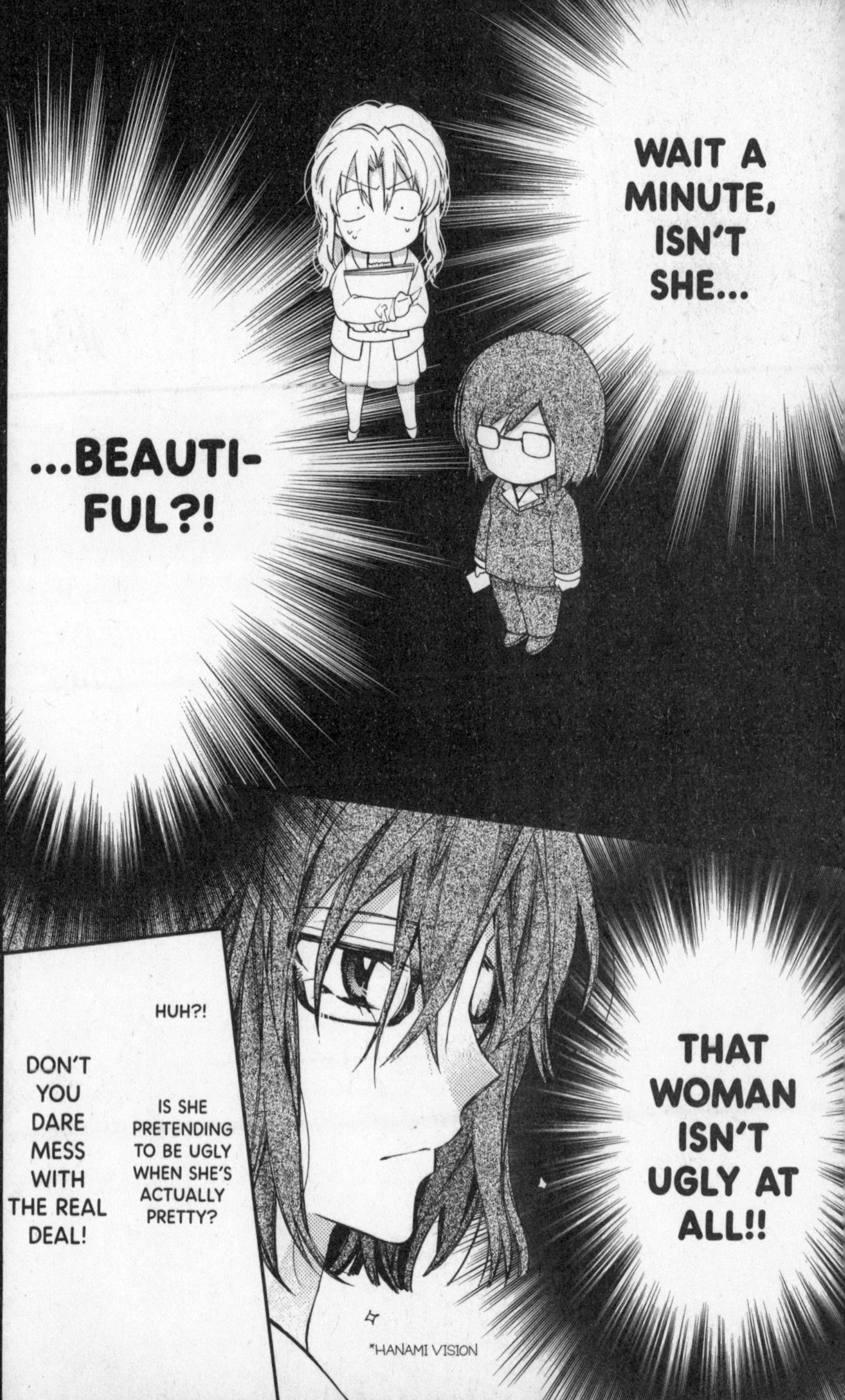
WAIT A MINUTE, ISN'T SHE...
...BEAUTI-FUL?!
THAT WOMAN ISN'T UGLY AT ALL!!
HUH?!
IS SHE PRETENDING TO BE UGLY WHEN SHE'S ACTUALLY PRETTY?
DON'T YOU DARE MESS WITH THE REAL DEAL!
*HANAMI VISION

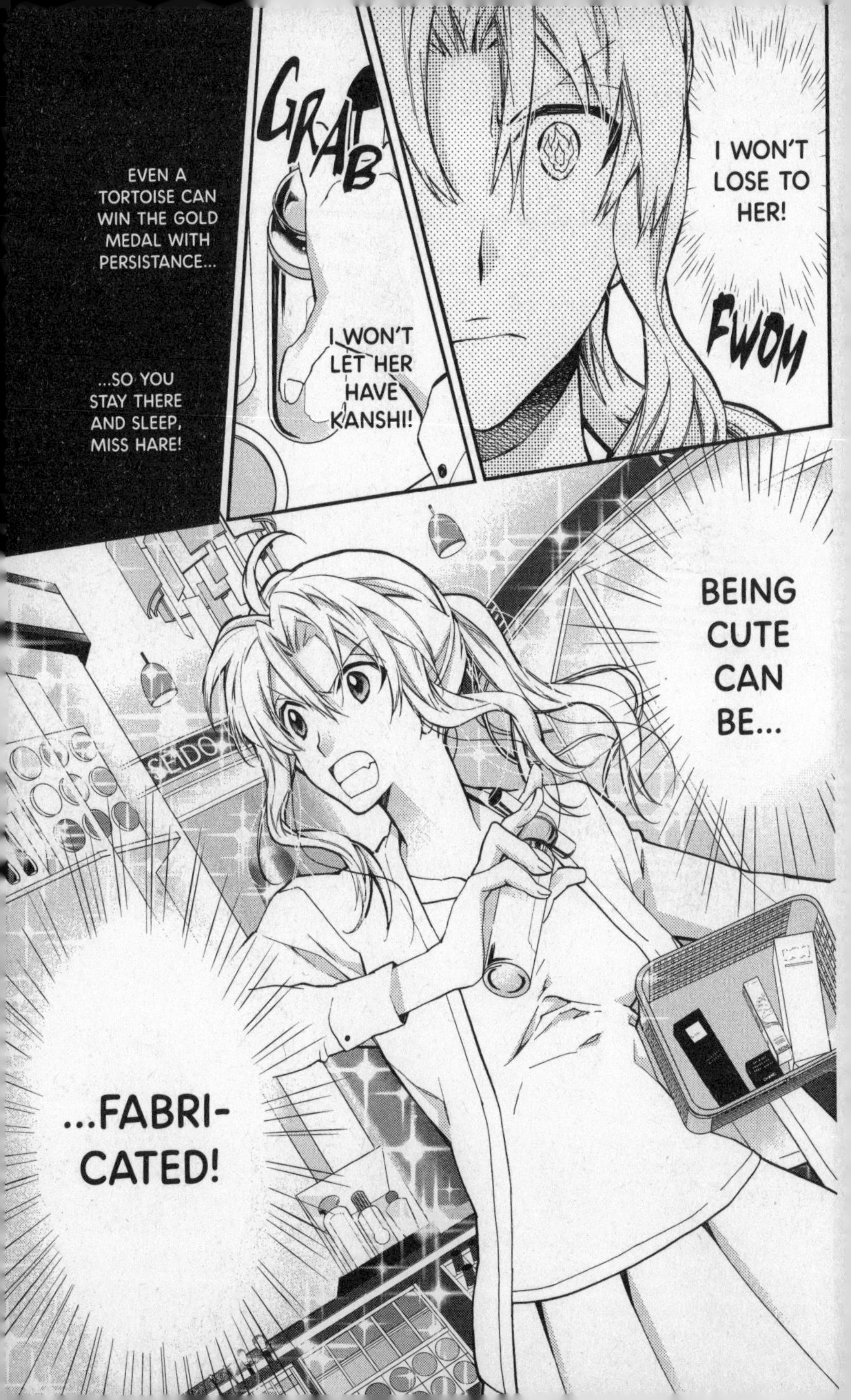
I WON'T LOSE TO HER!
FWOM
GRAB
I WON'T LET HER HAVE KANSHI!
EVEN A TORTOISE CAN WIN THE GOLD MEDAL WITH PERSISTANCE...
...SO YOU STAY THERE AND SLEEP, MISS HARE!
BEING CUTE CAN BE...
SEIDO
...FABRI-CATED!

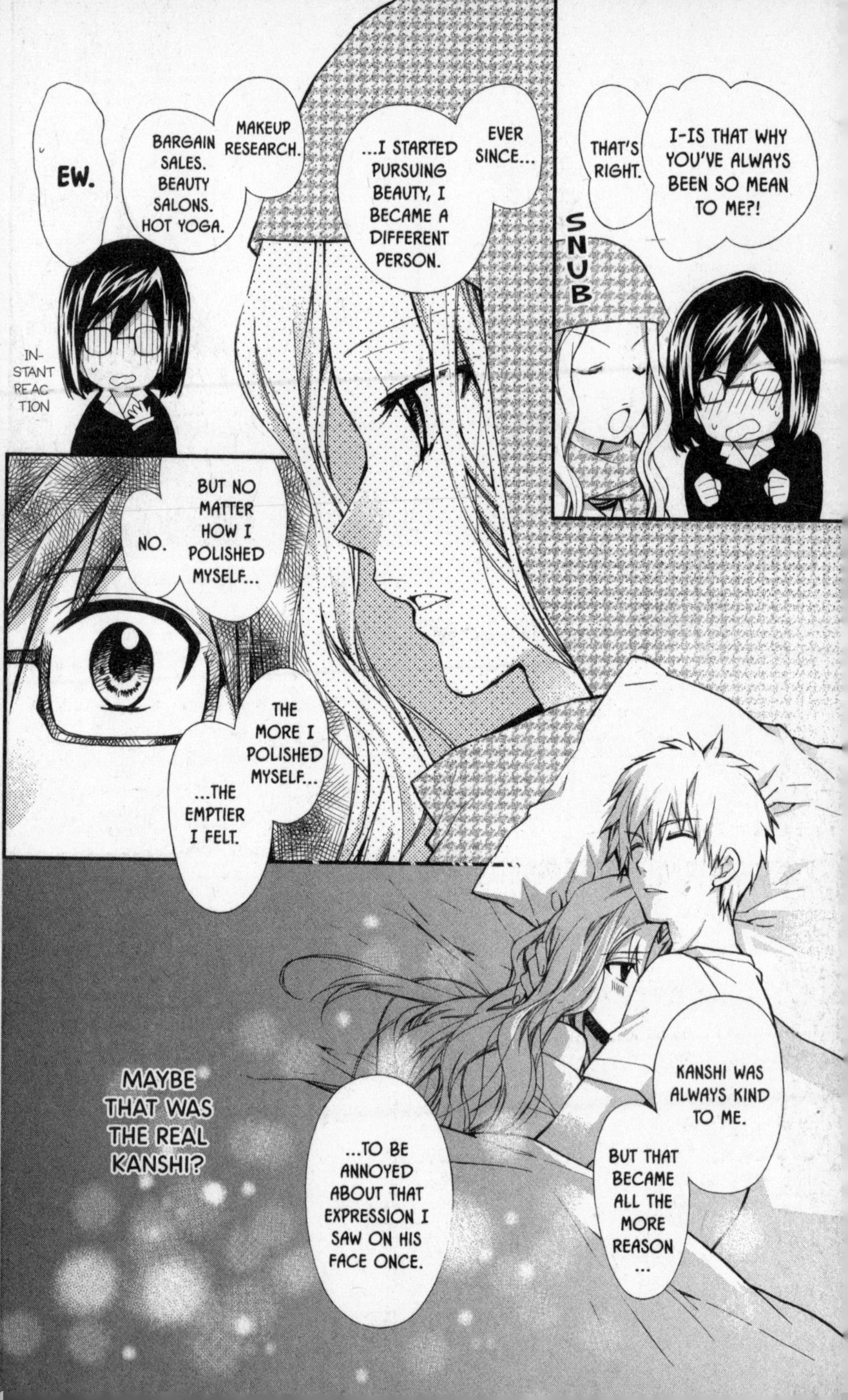
I-IS THAT WHY YOU'VE ALWAYS BEEN SO MEAN TO ME?!
THAT'S RIGHT.
SNUB
EVER SINCE...
...I STARTED PURSUING BEAUTY, I BECAME A DIFFERENT PERSON.
MAKEUP RESEARCH.
BARGAIN SALES. BEAUTY SALONS. HOT YOGA.
EW.
IN-STANT REAC-TION
NO.
BUT NO MATTER HOW I POLISHED MYSELF...
THE MORE I POLISHED MYSELF...
...THE EMPTIER I FELT.
KANSHI WAS ALWAYS KIND TO ME.
BUT THAT BECAME ALL THE MORE REASON ...
...TO BE ANNOYED ABOUT THAT EXPRESSION I SAW ON HIS FACE ONCE.
MAYBE THAT WAS THE REAL KANSHI?

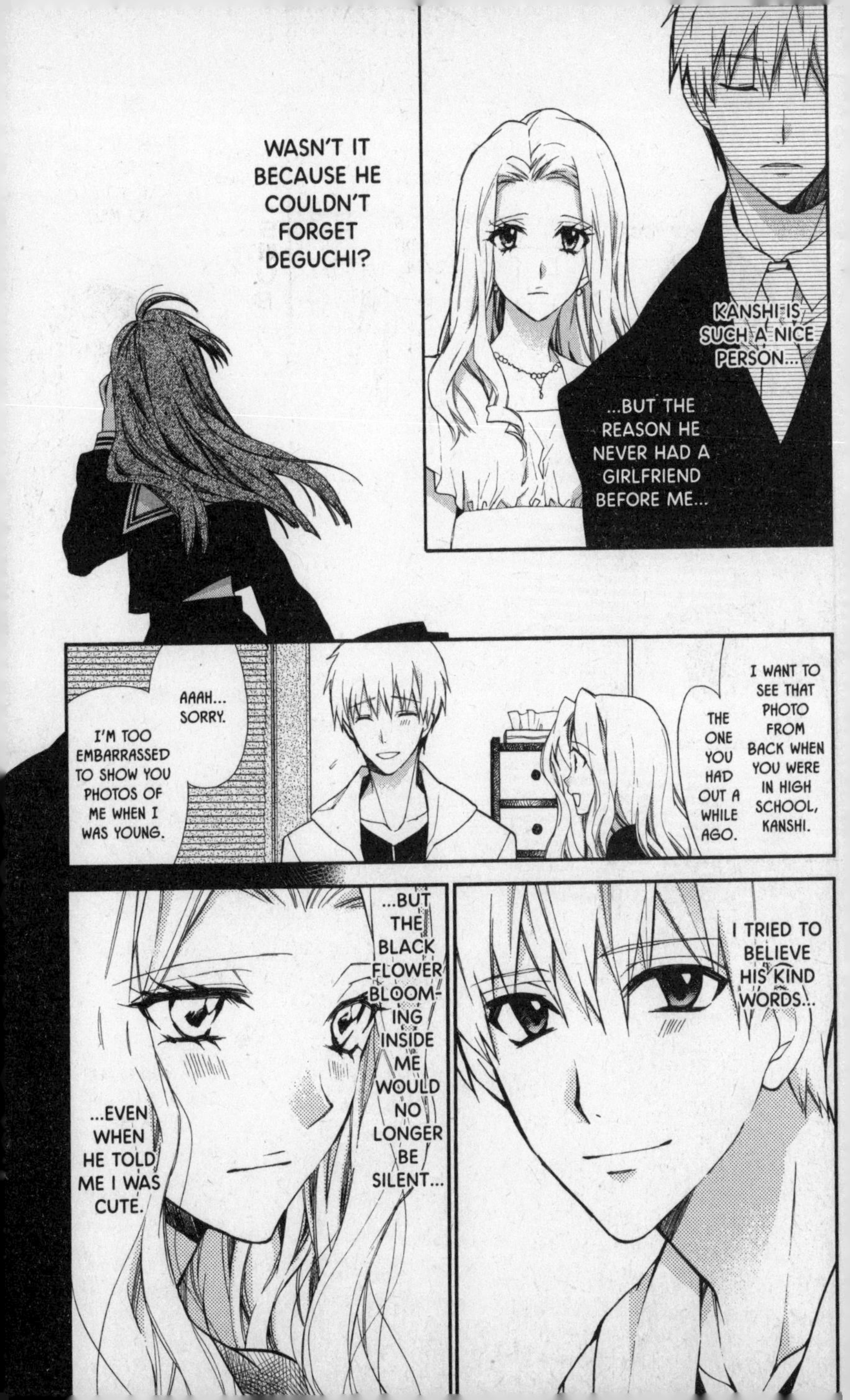
KANSHI IS SUCH A NICE PERSON...
...BUT THE REASON HE NEVER HAD A GIRLFRIEND BEFORE ME...
WASN'T IT BECAUSE HE COULDN'T FORGET DEGUCHI?
I WANT TO SEE THAT PHOTO FROM BACK WHEN YOU WERE IN HIGH SCHOOL, KANSHI.
THE ONE YOU HAD OUT A WHILE AGO.
AAAH... SORRY.
I'M TOO EMBARRASSED TO SHOW YOU PHOTOS OF ME WHEN I WAS YOUNG.
I TRIED TO BELIEVE HIS KIND WORDS...
...EVEN WHEN HE TOLD ME I WAS CUTE.
...BUT THE BLACK FLOWER BLOOMING INSIDE ME WOULD NO LONGER BE SILENT...

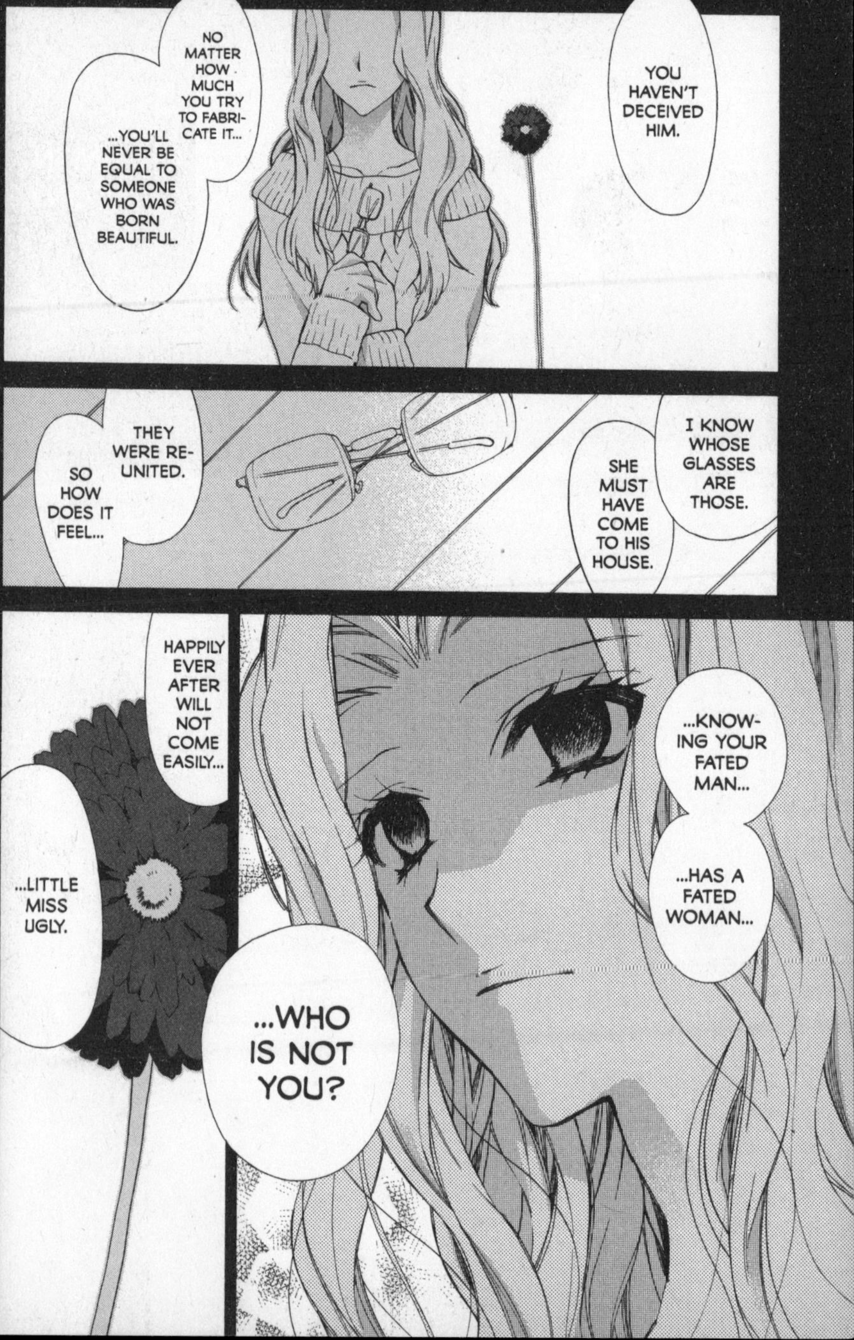
YOU HAVEN'T DECEIVED HIM.
NO MATTER HOW MUCH YOU TRY TO FABRI-CATE IT...
...YOU'LL NEVER BE EQUAL TO SOMEONE WHO WAS BORN BEAUTIFUL.
I KNOW WHOSE GLASSES ARE THOSE.
SHE MUST HAVE COME TO HIS HOUSE.
THEY WERE RE-UNITED.
SO HOW DOES IT FEEL...
...KNOW-ING YOUR FATED MAN...
...HAS A FATED WOMAN...
...WHO IS NOT YOU?
HAPPILY EVER AFTER WILL NOT COME EASILY...
...LITTLE MISS UGLY.

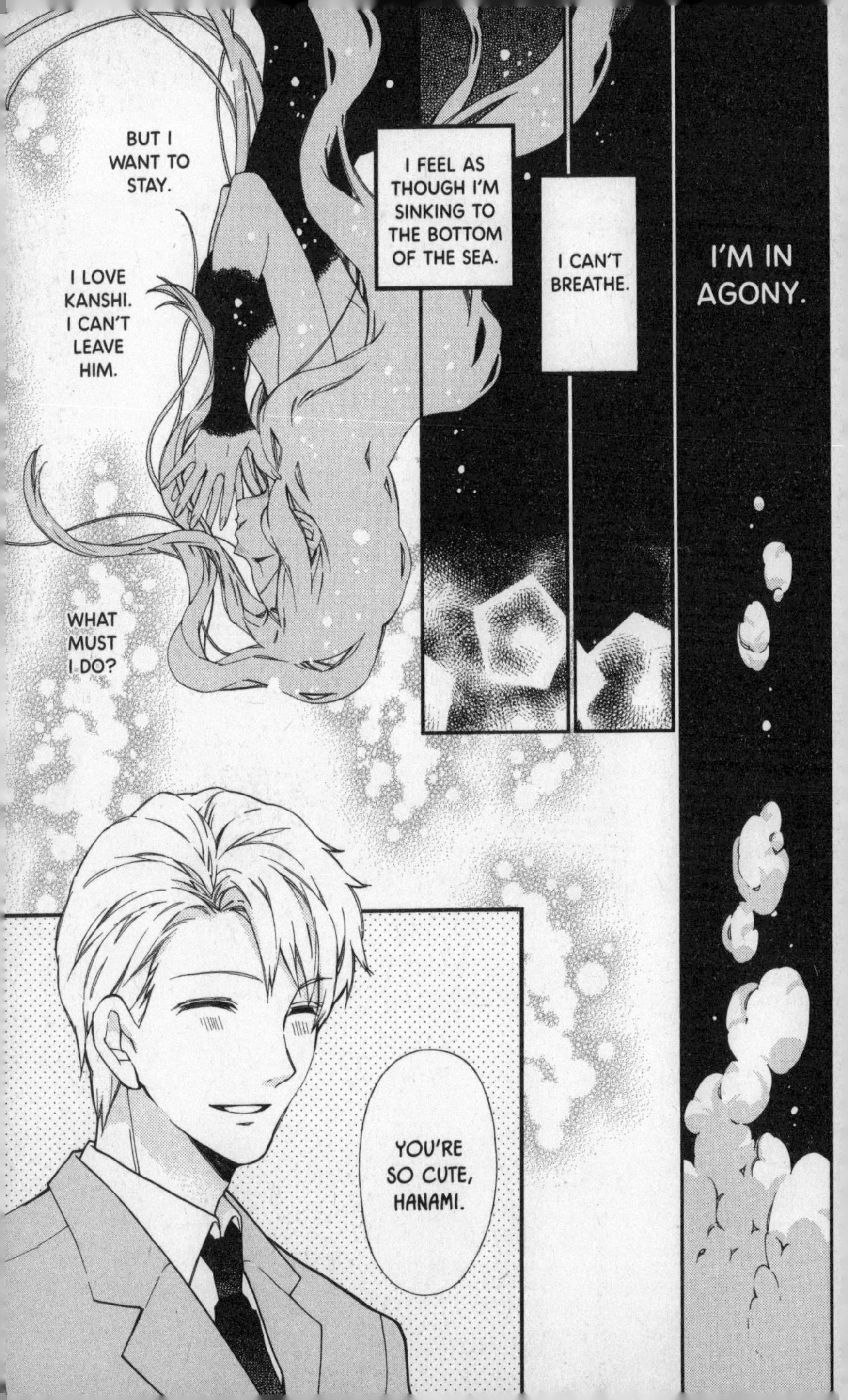
I'M IN AGONY.
I CAN'T BREATHE.
I FEEL AS THOUGH I'M SINKING TO THE BOTTOM OF THE SEA.
BUT I WANT TO STAY.
I LOVE KANSHI. I CAN'T LEAVE HIM.
WHAT MUST I DO?
YOU'RE SO CUTE, HANAMI.

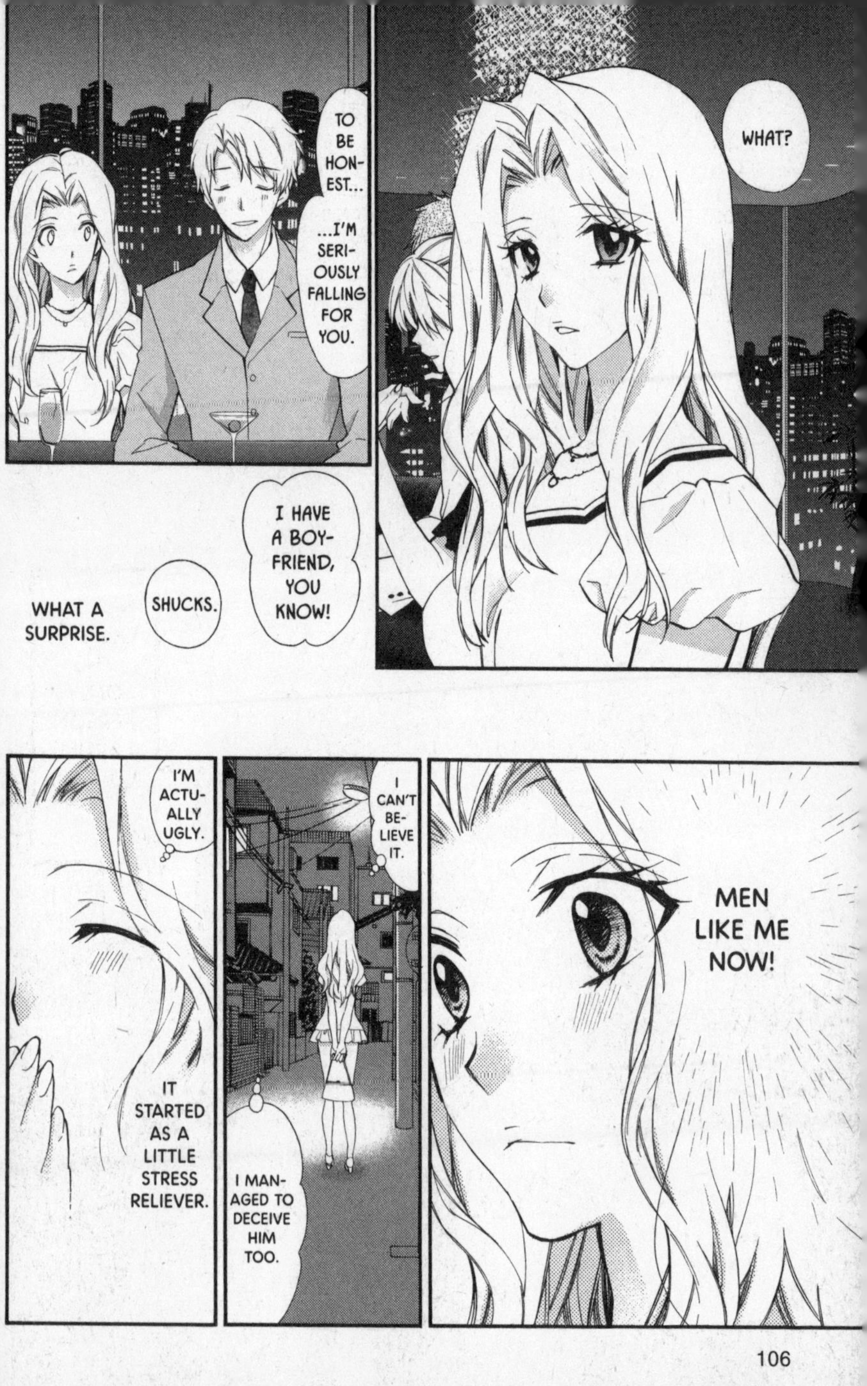
WHAT?
TO BE HONEST...
...I'M SERIOUSLY FALLING FOR YOU.
I HAVE A BOYFRIEND, YOU KNOW!
SHUCKS.
WHAT A SURPRISE.
MEN LIKE ME NOW!
I CAN'T BELIEVE IT.
I MANAGED TO DECEIVE HIM TOO.
I'M ACTUALLY UGLY.
IT STARTED AS A LITTLE STRESS RELIEVER.

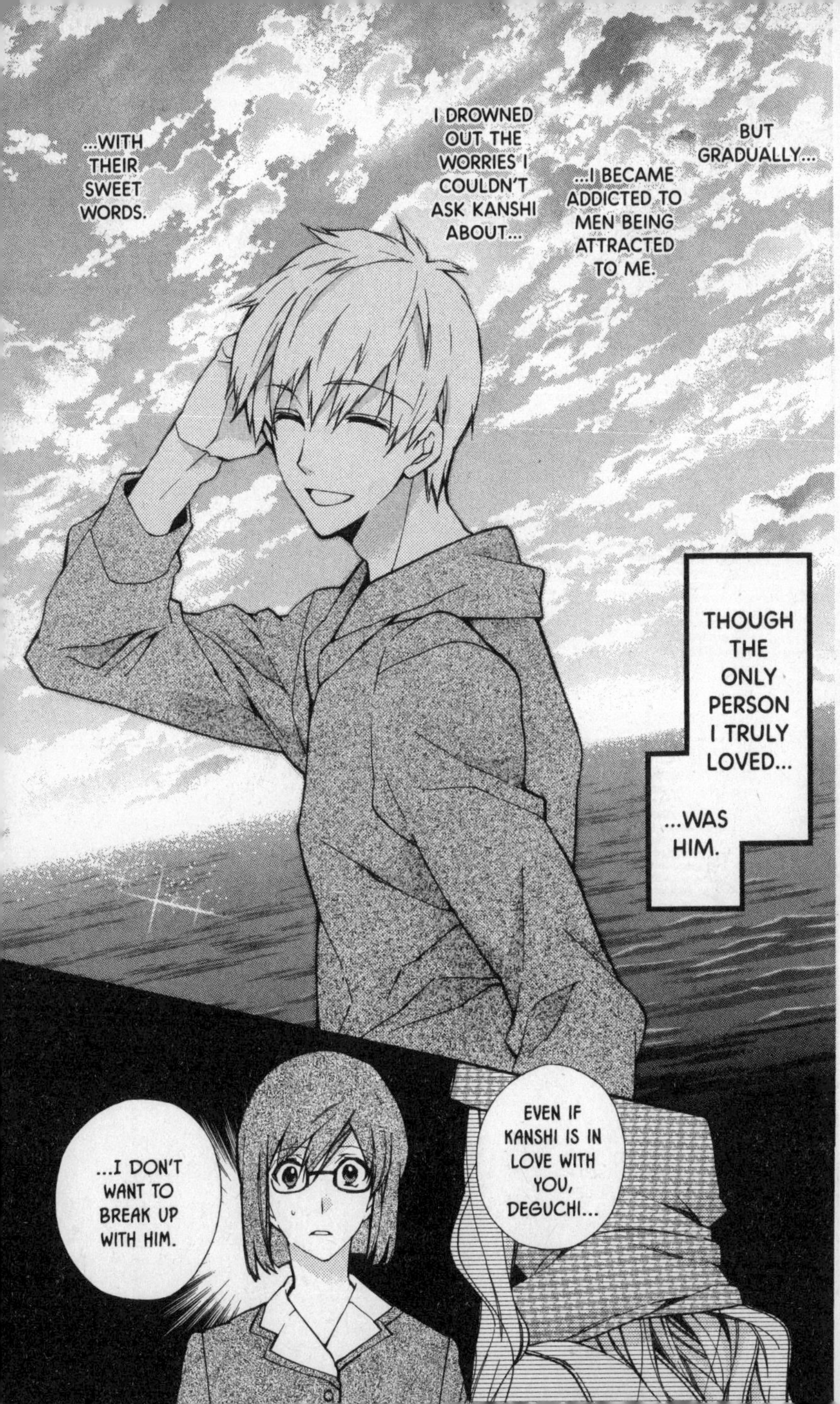
BUT GRADUALLY...
...I BECAME ADDICTED TO MEN BEING ATTRACTED TO ME.
I DROWNED OUT THE WORRIES I COULDN'T ASK KANSHI ABOUT...
...WITH THEIR SWEET WORDS.
THOUGH THE ONLY PERSON I TRULY LOVED...
...WAS HIM.
EVEN IF KANSHI IS IN LOVE WITH YOU, DEGUCHI...
...I DON'T WANT TO BREAK UP WITH HIM.

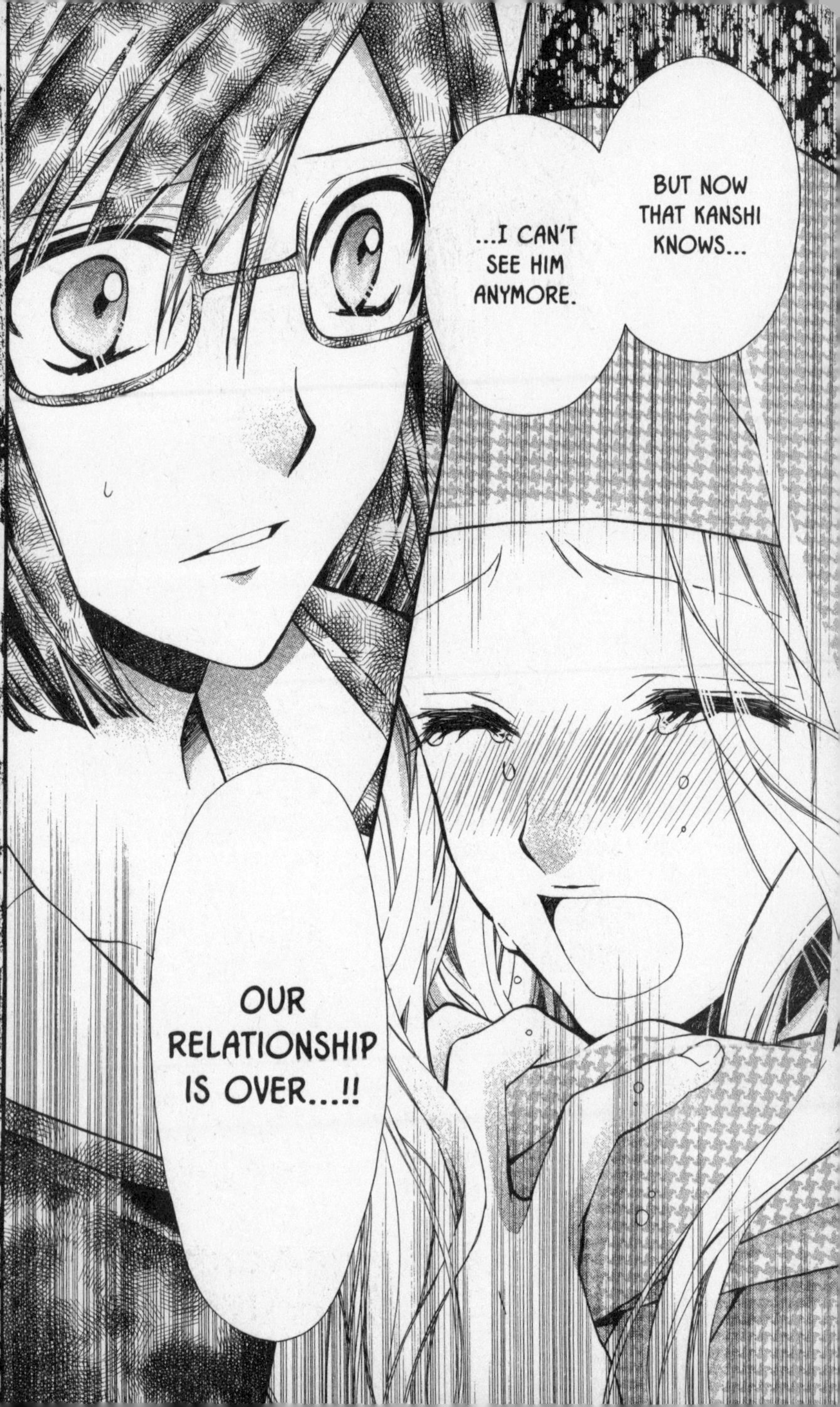
BUT NOW THAT KANSHI KNOWS...
...I CAN'T SEE HIM ANYMORE.
OUR RELATIONSHIP IS OVER...!!

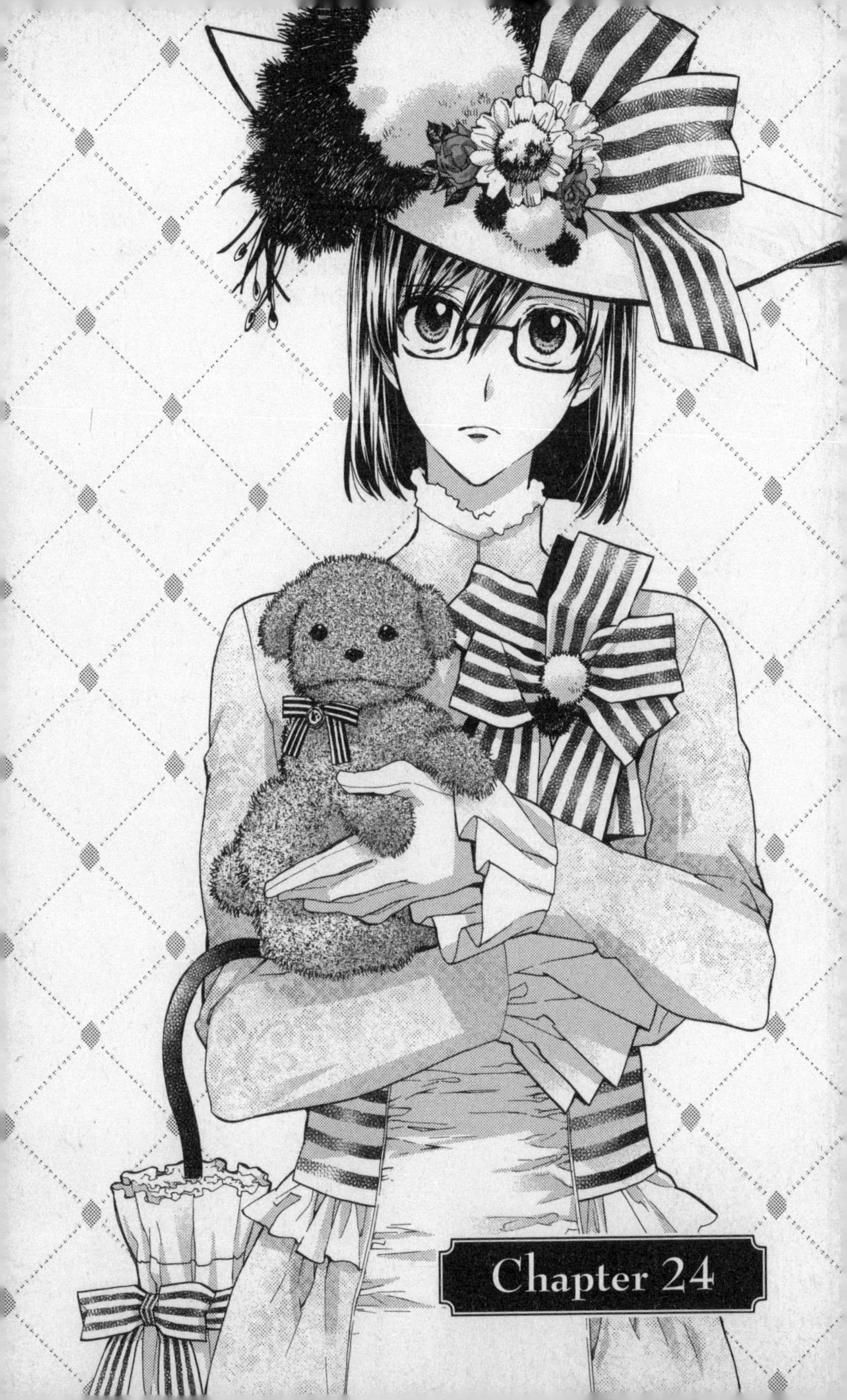
Chapter 24

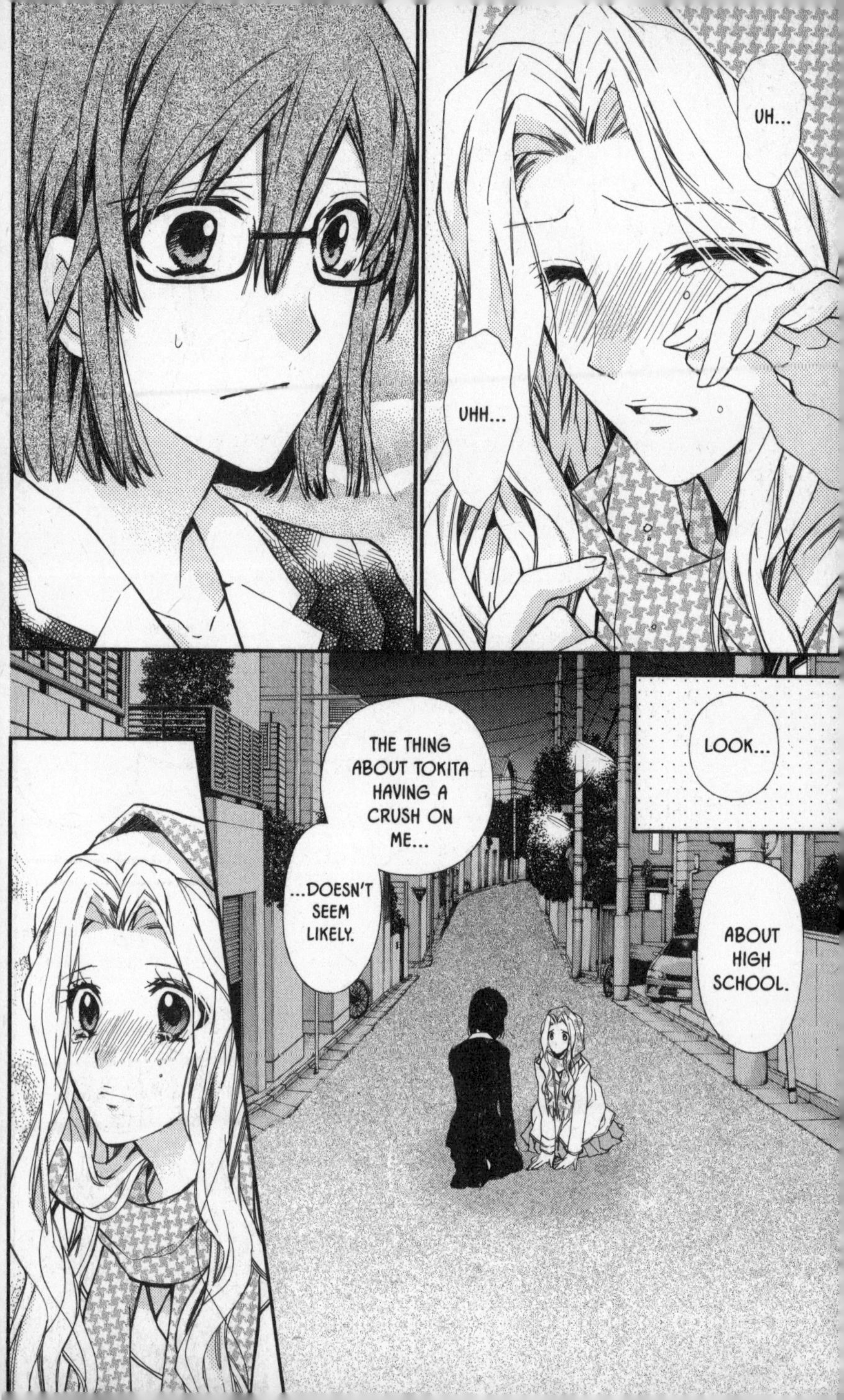
UH...
UHH...
LOOK...
ABOUT HIGH SCHOOL.
THE THING ABOUT TOKITA HAVING A CRUSH ON ME...
...DOESN'T SEEM LIKELY.

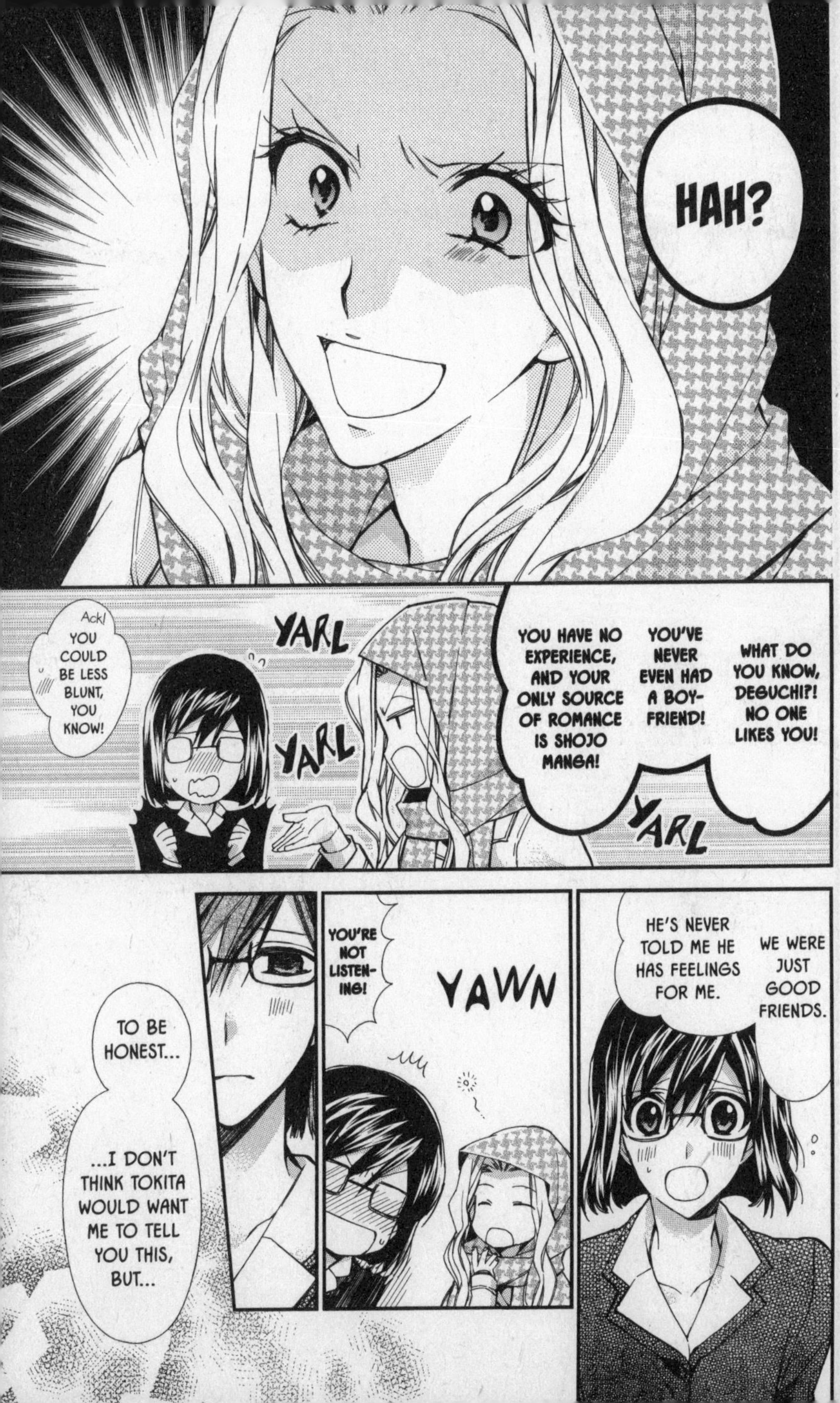
HAH?
WHAT DO YOU KNOW, DEGUCHI?! NO ONE LIKES YOU!
YOU'VE NEVER EVEN HAD A BOY-FRIEND!
YOU HAVE NO EXPERIENCE, AND YOUR ONLY SOURCE OF ROMANCE IS SHOJO MANGA!
YARL
YARL
YARL
Ack! YOU COULD BE LESS BLUNT, YOU KNOW!
WE WERE JUST GOOD FRIENDS.
HE'S NEVER TOLD ME HE HAS FEELINGS FOR ME.
YAWN
YOU'RE NOT LISTEN-ING!
TO BE HONEST...
...I DON'T THINK TOKITA WOULD WANT ME TO TELL YOU THIS, BUT...

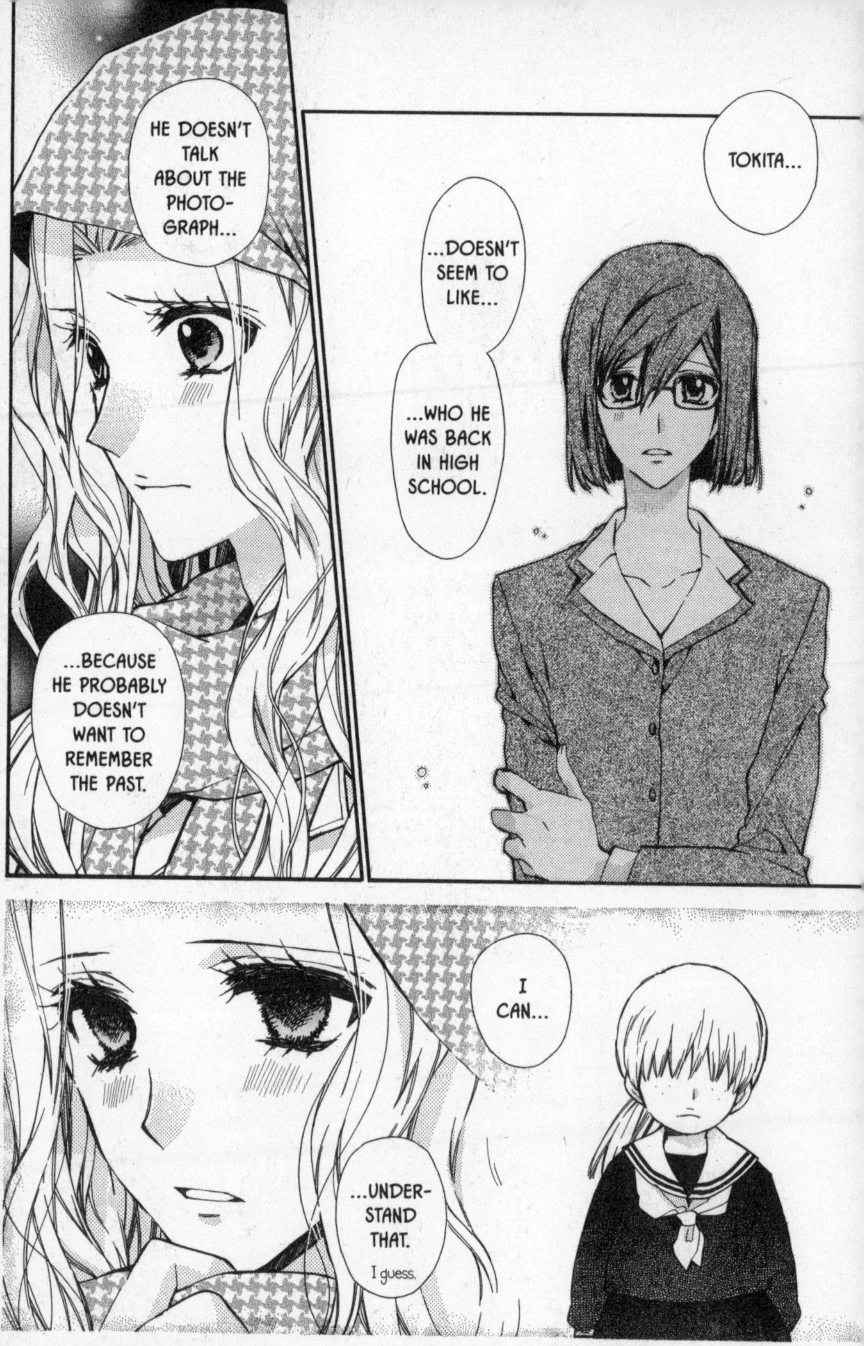
TOKITA...
...DOESN'T SEEM TO LIKE...
...WHO HE WAS BACK IN HIGH SCHOOL.
HE DOESN'T TALK ABOUT THE PHOTO-GRAPH...
...BECAUSE HE PROBABLY DOESN'T WANT TO REMEMBER THE PAST.
I CAN...
...UNDER-STAND THAT.
I guess.

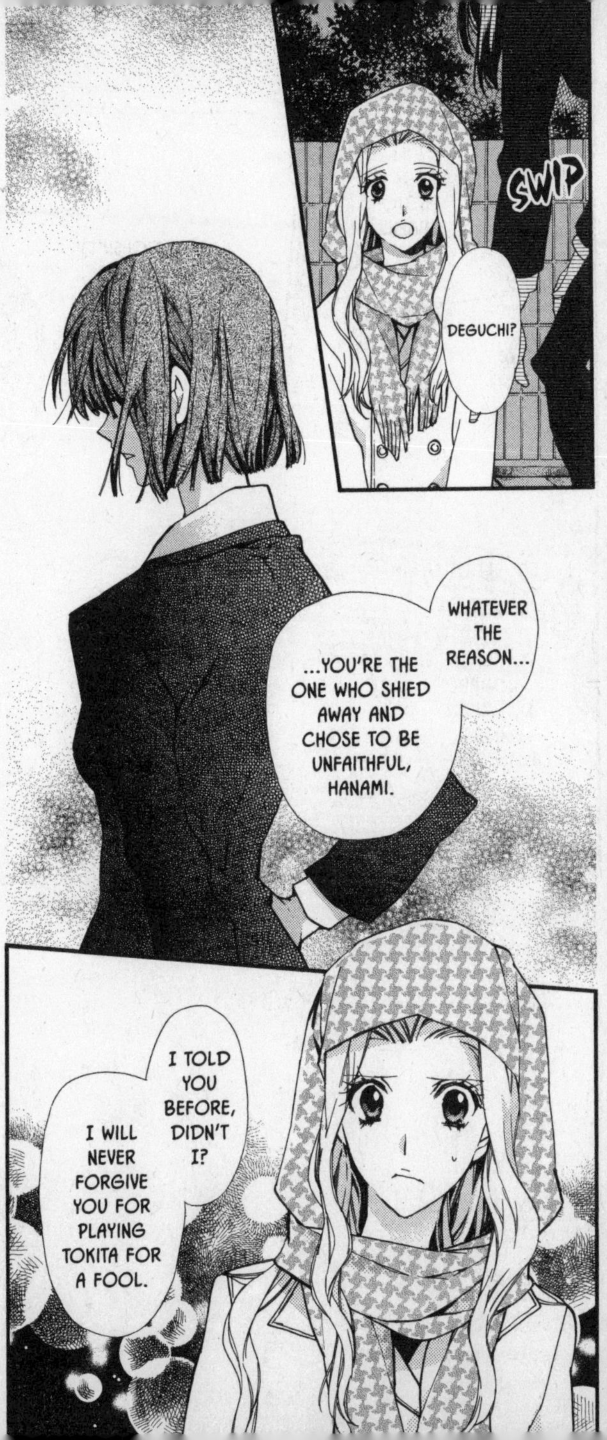
SWIP
DEGUCHI?
WHATEVER THE REASON...
...YOU'RE THE ONE WHO SHIED AWAY AND CHOSE TO BE UNFAITHFUL, HANAMI.
I TOLD YOU BEFORE, DIDN'T I?
I WILL NEVER FORGIVE YOU FOR PLAYING TOKITA FOR A FOOL.

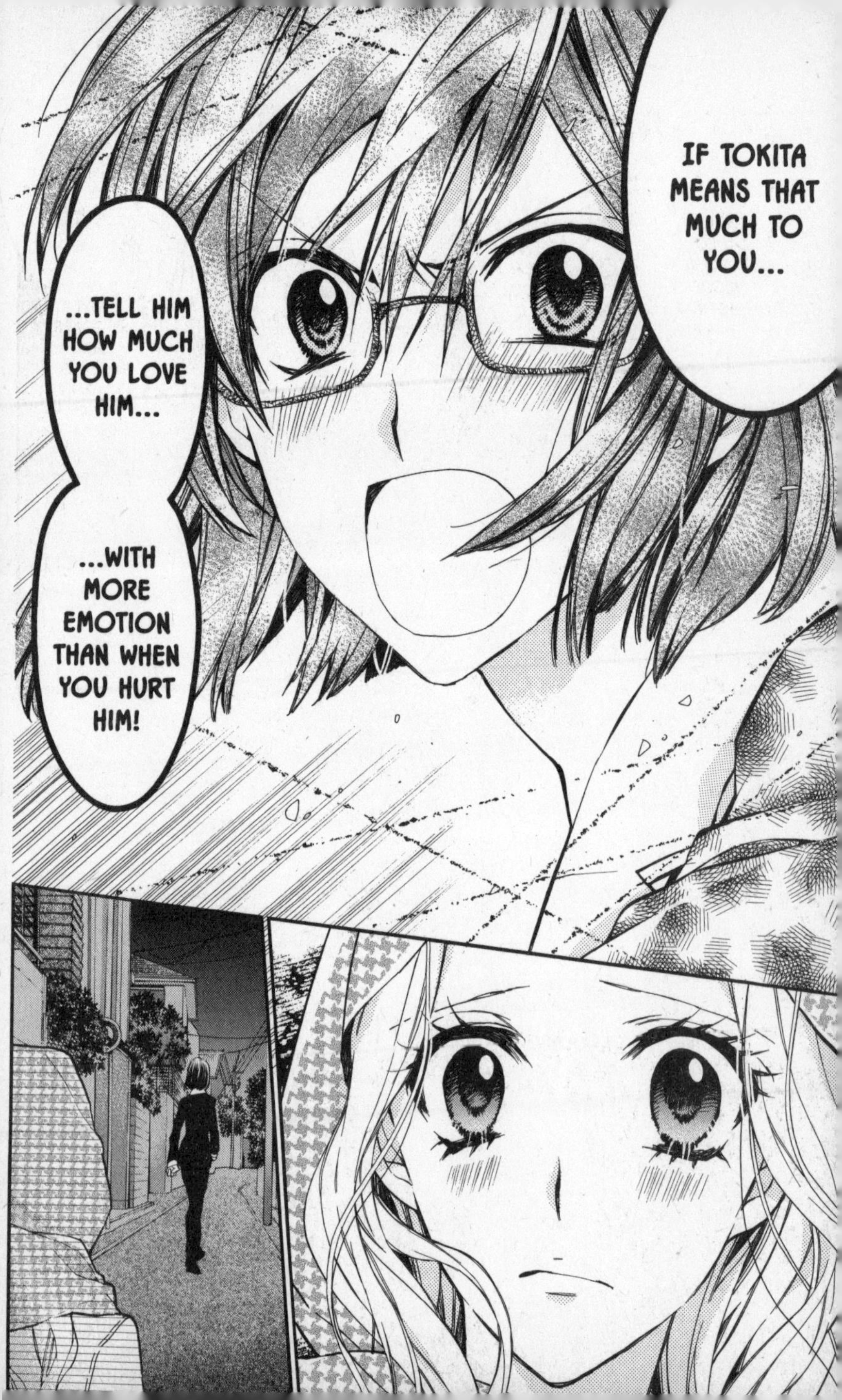
IF TOKITA MEANS THAT MUCH TO YOU...
...TELL HIM HOW MUCH YOU LOVE HIM...
...WITH MORE EMOTION THAN WHEN YOU HURT HIM!

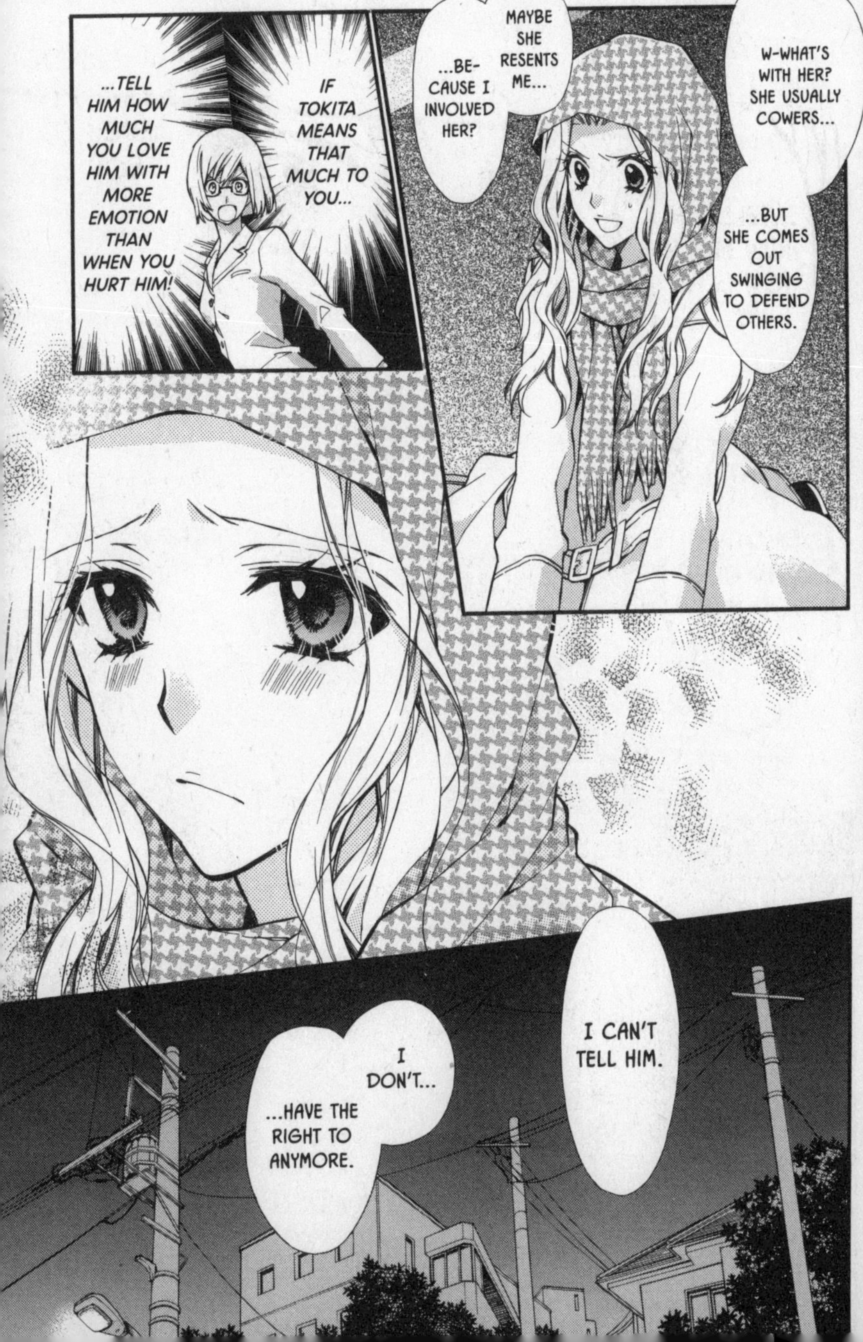
W-WHAT'S WITH HER? SHE USUALLY COWERS...
...BUT SHE COMES OUT SWINGING TO DEFEND OTHERS.
MAYBE SHE RESENTS ME...
...BE-CAUSE I INVOLVED HER?
IF TOKITA MEANS THAT MUCH TO YOU...
...TELL HIM HOW MUCH YOU LOVE HIM WITH MORE EMOTION THAN WHEN YOU HURT HIM!
I CAN'T TELL HIM.
I DON'T...
...HAVE THE RIGHT TO ANYMORE.

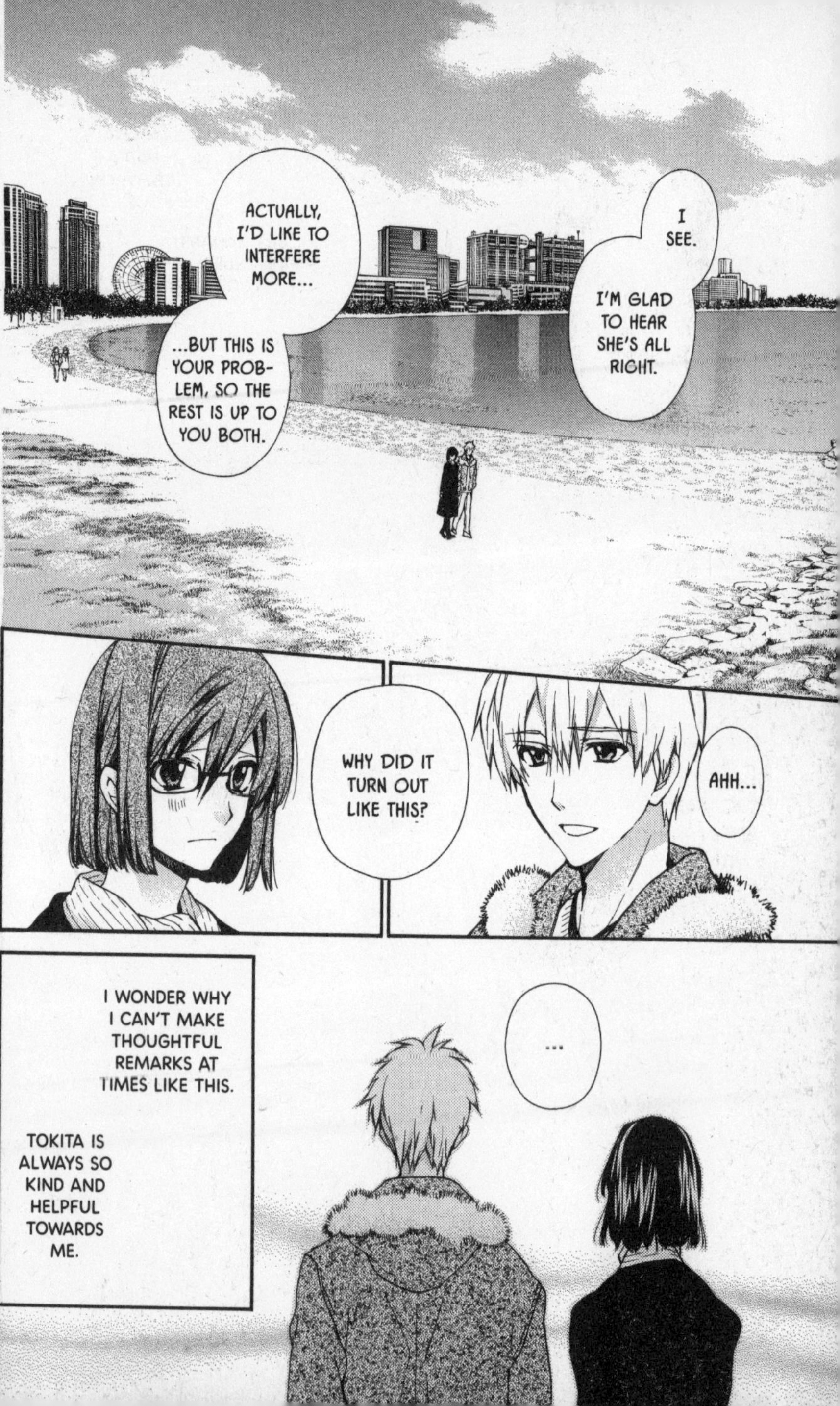
I SEE.
I'M GLAD TO HEAR SHE'S ALL RIGHT.
ACTUALLY, I'D LIKE TO INTERFERE MORE...
...BUT THIS IS YOUR PROBLEM, SO THE REST IS UP TO YOU BOTH.
AHH...
WHY DID IT TURN OUT LIKE THIS?
...
I WONDER WHY I CAN'T MAKE THOUGHTFUL REMARKS AT TIMES LIKE THIS.
TOKITA IS ALWAYS SO KIND AND HELPFUL TOWARDS ME.

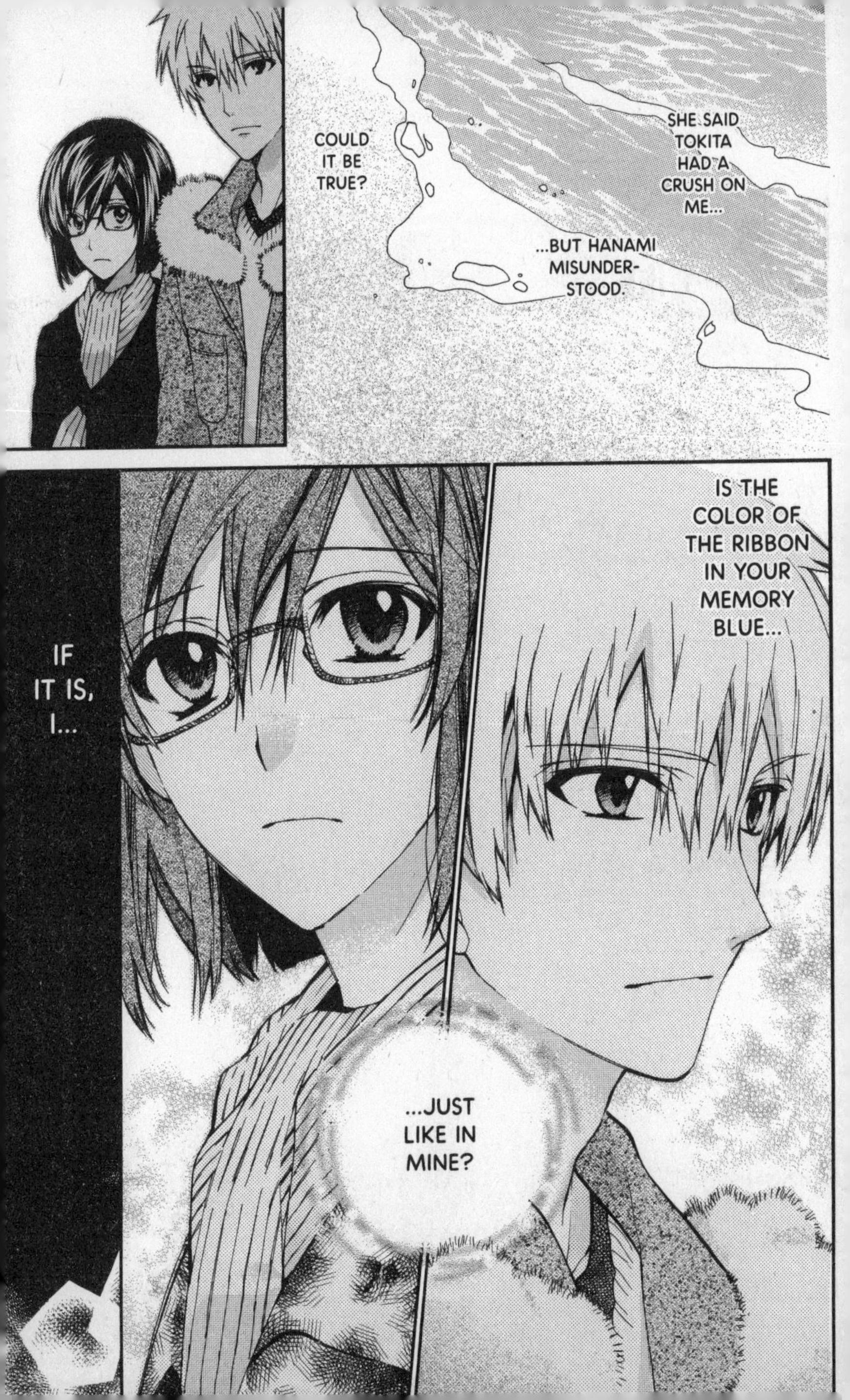
SHE SAID TOKITA HAD A CRUSH ON ME...
...BUT HANAMI MISUNDER-STOOD.
COULD IT BE TRUE?
IS THE COLOR OF THE RIBBON IN YOUR MEMORY BLUE...
...JUST LIKE IN MINE?
IF IT IS, I...

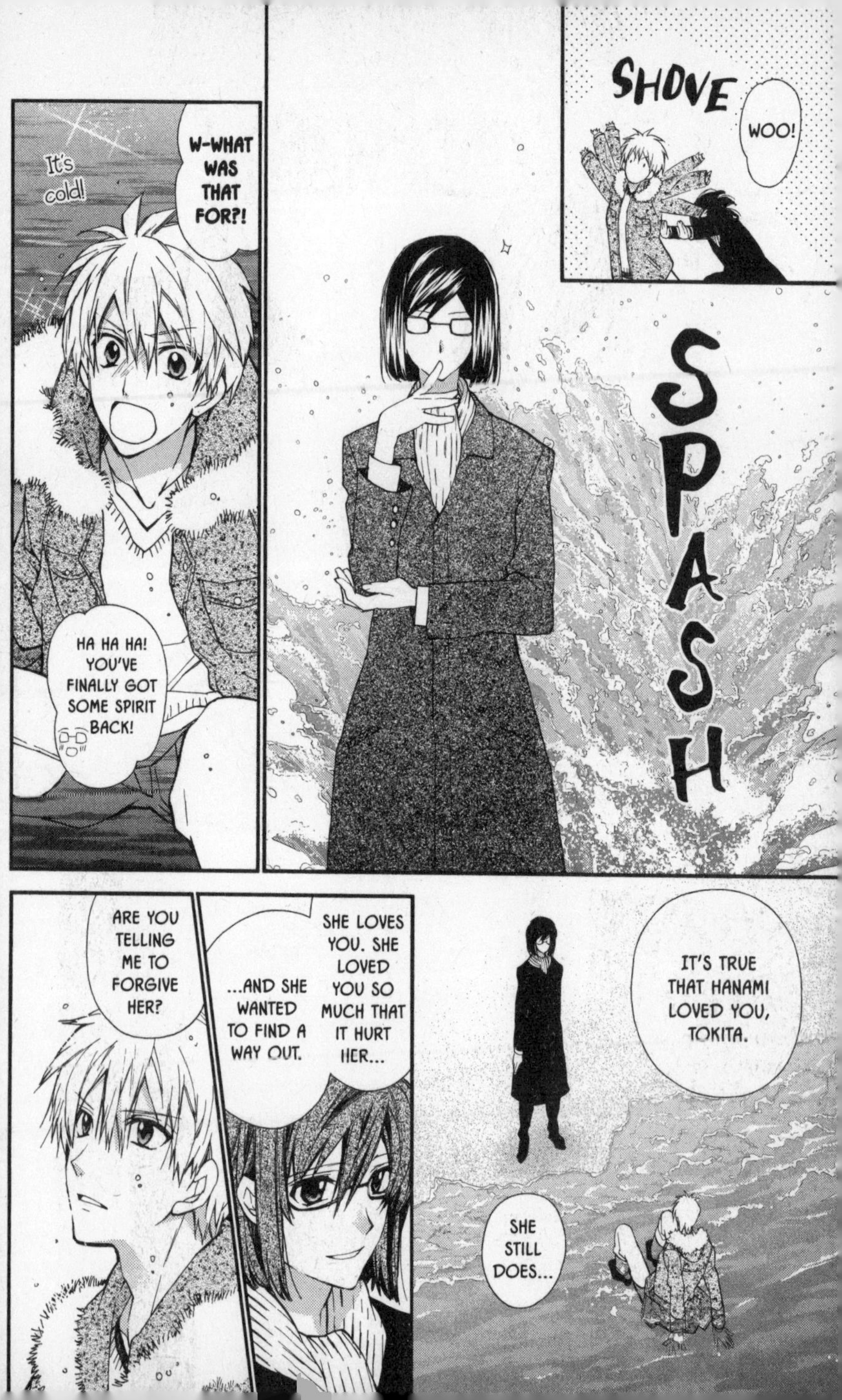
SHOVE
WOO!
SPASH
W-WHAT WAS THAT FOR?!
It's cold!
HA HA HA! YOU'VE FINALLY GOT SOME SPIRIT BACK!
IT'S TRUE THAT HANAMI LOVED YOU, TOKITA.
SHE STILL DOES...
SHE LOVES YOU. SHE LOVED YOU SO MUCH THAT IT HURT HER...
...AND SHE WANTED TO FIND A WAY OUT.
ARE YOU TELLING ME TO FORGIVE HER?

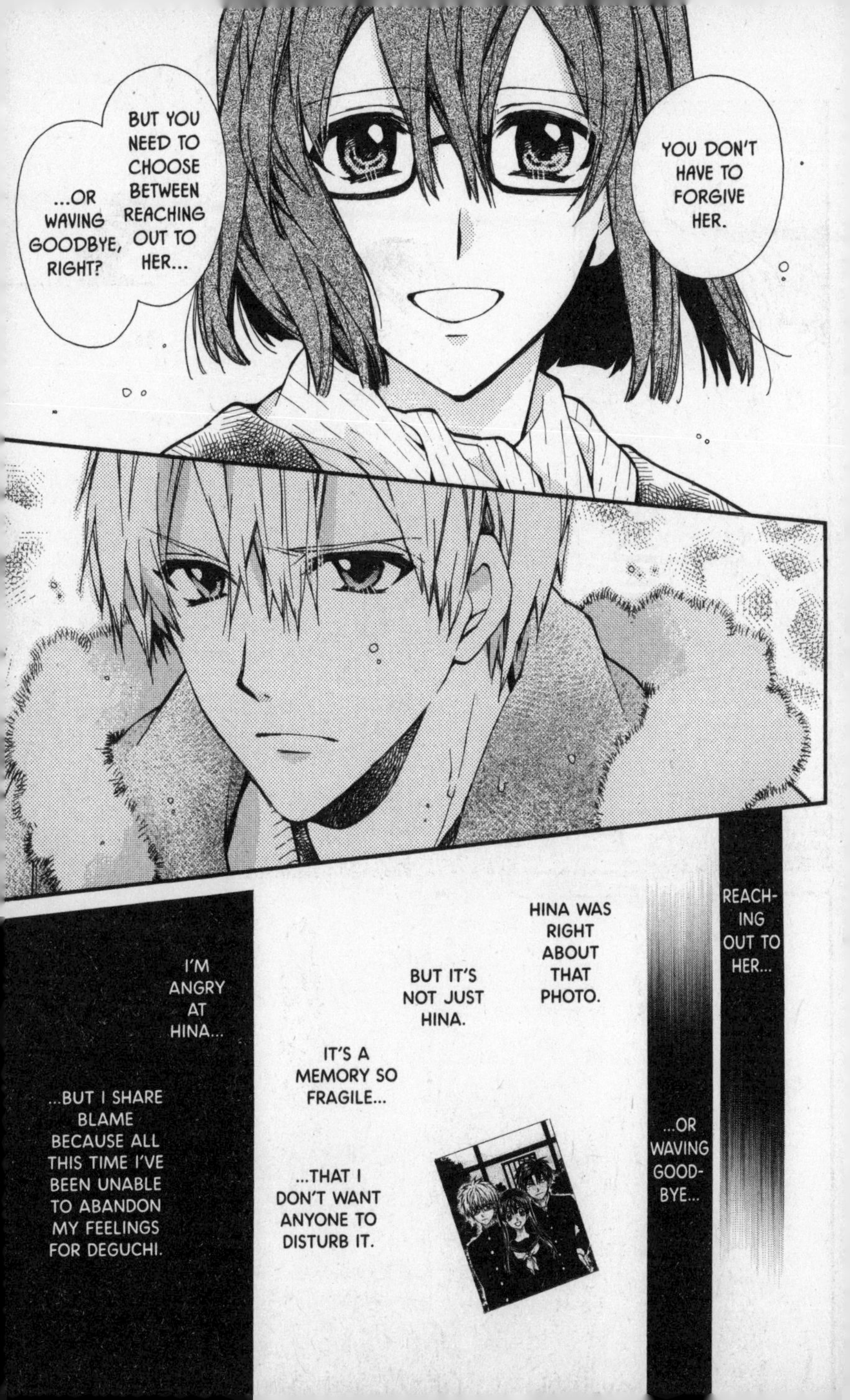
YOU DON'T HAVE TO FORGIVE HER.
BUT YOU NEED TO CHOOSE BETWEEN REACHING OUT TO HER...
...OR WAVING GOODBYE, RIGHT?
REACH-ING OUT TO HER...
...OR WAVING GOOD-BYE...
HINA WAS RIGHT ABOUT THAT PHOTO.
BUT IT'S NOT JUST HINA.
IT'S A MEMORY SO FRAGILE...
...THAT I DON'T WANT ANYONE TO DISTURB IT.
I'M ANGRY AT HINA...
...BUT I SHARE BLAME BECAUSE ALL THIS TIME I'VE BEEN UNABLE TO ABANDON MY FEELINGS FOR DEGUCHI.

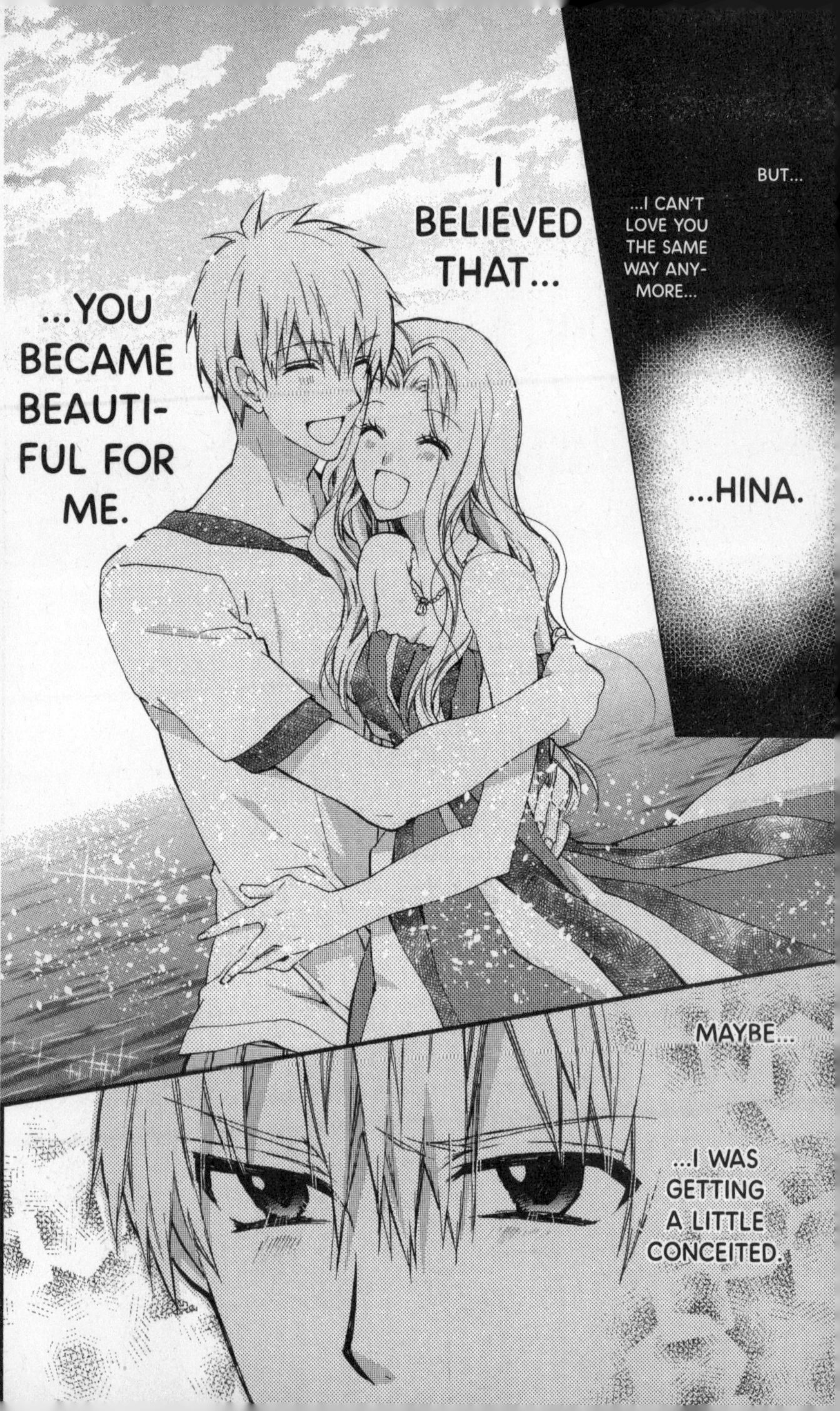
I BELIEVED THAT...
...YOU BECAME BEAUTIFUL FOR ME.
BUT...
...I CAN'T LOVE YOU THE SAME WAY ANY-MORE...
...HINA.
MAYBE...
...I WAS GETTING A LITTLE CONCEITED.

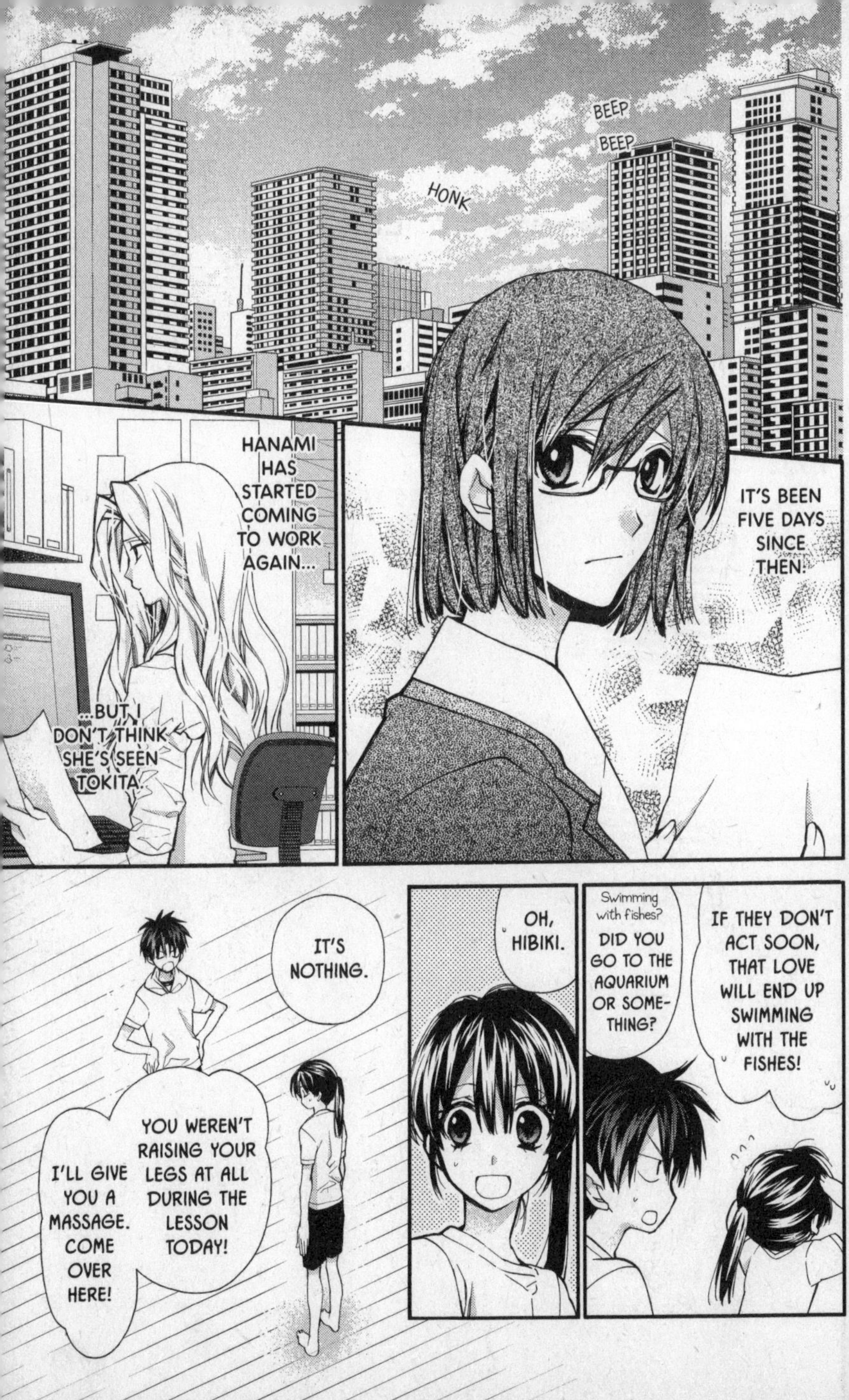
BEEP
BEEP
HONK
IT'S BEEN FIVE DAYS SINCE THEN.
HANAMI HAS STARTED COMING TO WORK AGAIN...
...BUT I DON'T THINK SHE'S SEEN TOKITA.
IF THEY DON'T ACT SOON, THAT LOVE WILL END UP SWIMMING WITH THE FISHES!
Swimming with fishes?
DID YOU GO TO THE AQUARIUM OR SOME-THING?
OH, HIBIKI.
IT'S NOTHING.
YOU WEREN'T RAISING YOUR LEGS AT ALL DURING THE LESSON TODAY!
I'LL GIVE YOU A MASSAGE. COME OVER HERE!

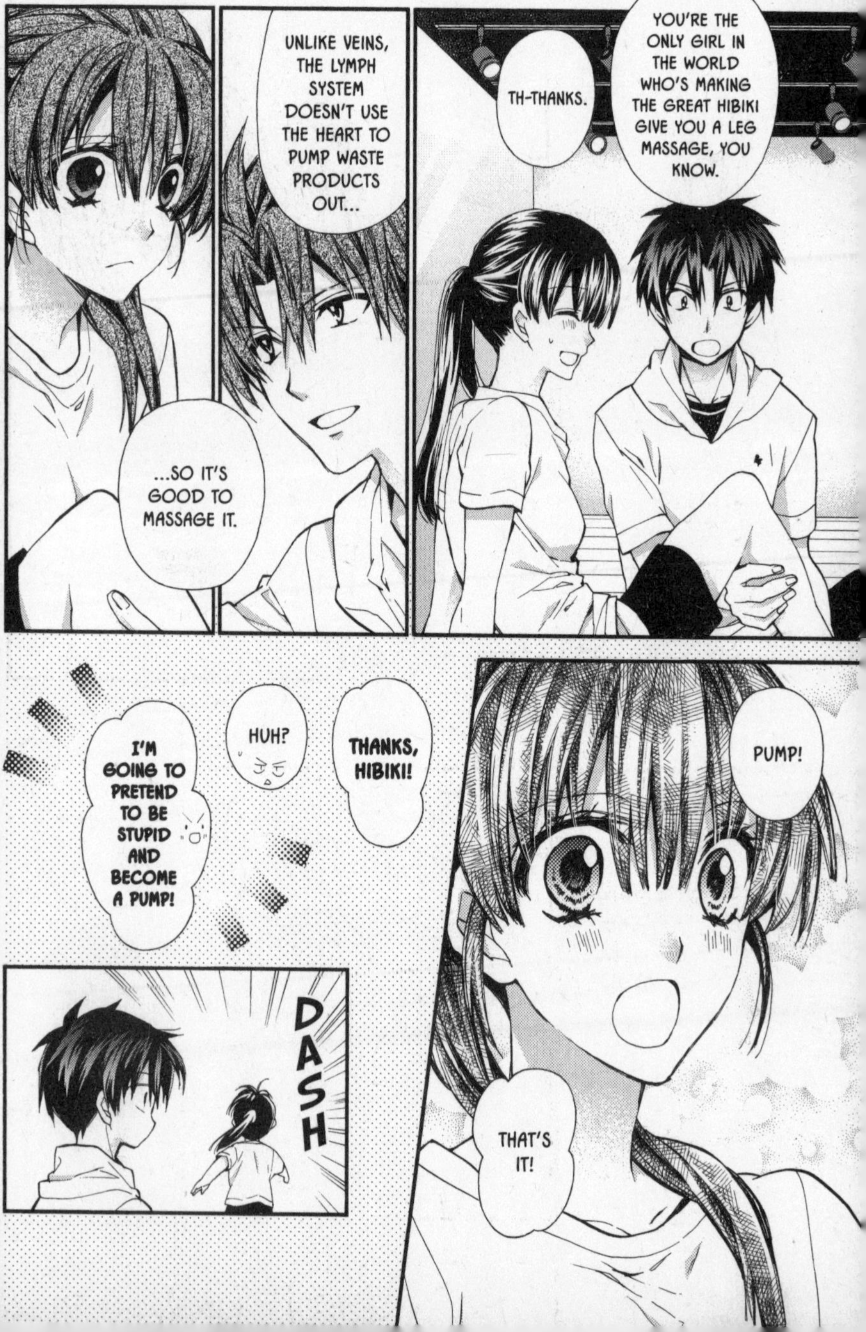
YOU'RE THE ONLY GIRL IN THE WORLD WHO'S MAKING THE GREAT HIBIKI GIVE YOU A LEG MASSAGE, YOU KNOW.
TH-THANKS.
UNLIKE VEINS, THE LYMPH SYSTEM DOESN'T USE THE HEART TO PUMP WASTE PRODUCTS OUT...
...SO IT'S GOOD TO MASSAGE IT.
PUMP!
THAT'S IT!
THANKS, HIBIKI!
HUH?
I'M GOING TO PRETEND TO BE STUPID AND BECOME A PUMP!
DASH

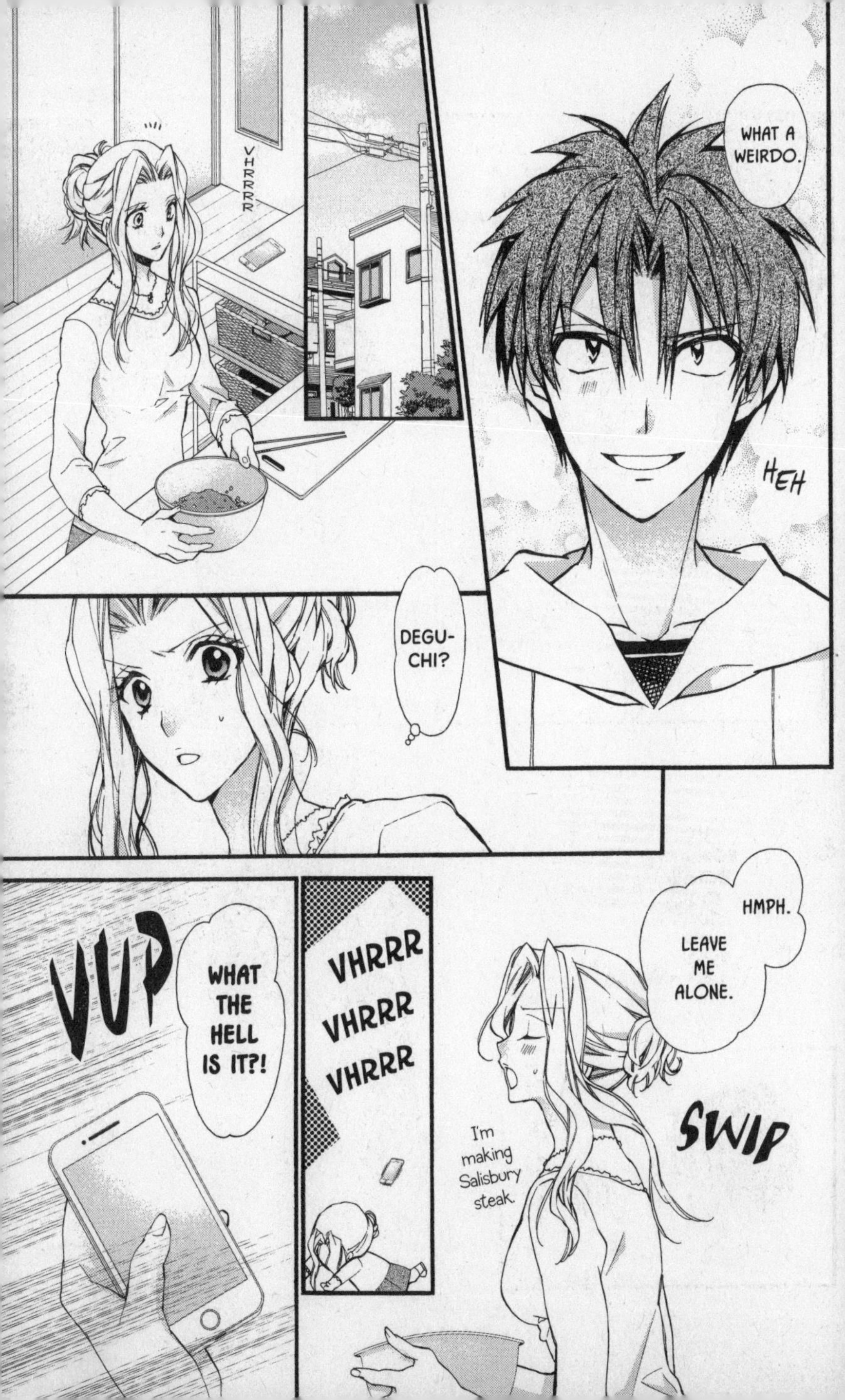
WHAT A WEIRDO.
HEH
VHRRR
DEGU-CHI?
HMPH.
LEAVE ME ALONE.
SWIP
I'm making Salisbury steak.
VHRRR VHRRR VHRRR
VUP
WHAT THE HELL IS IT?!

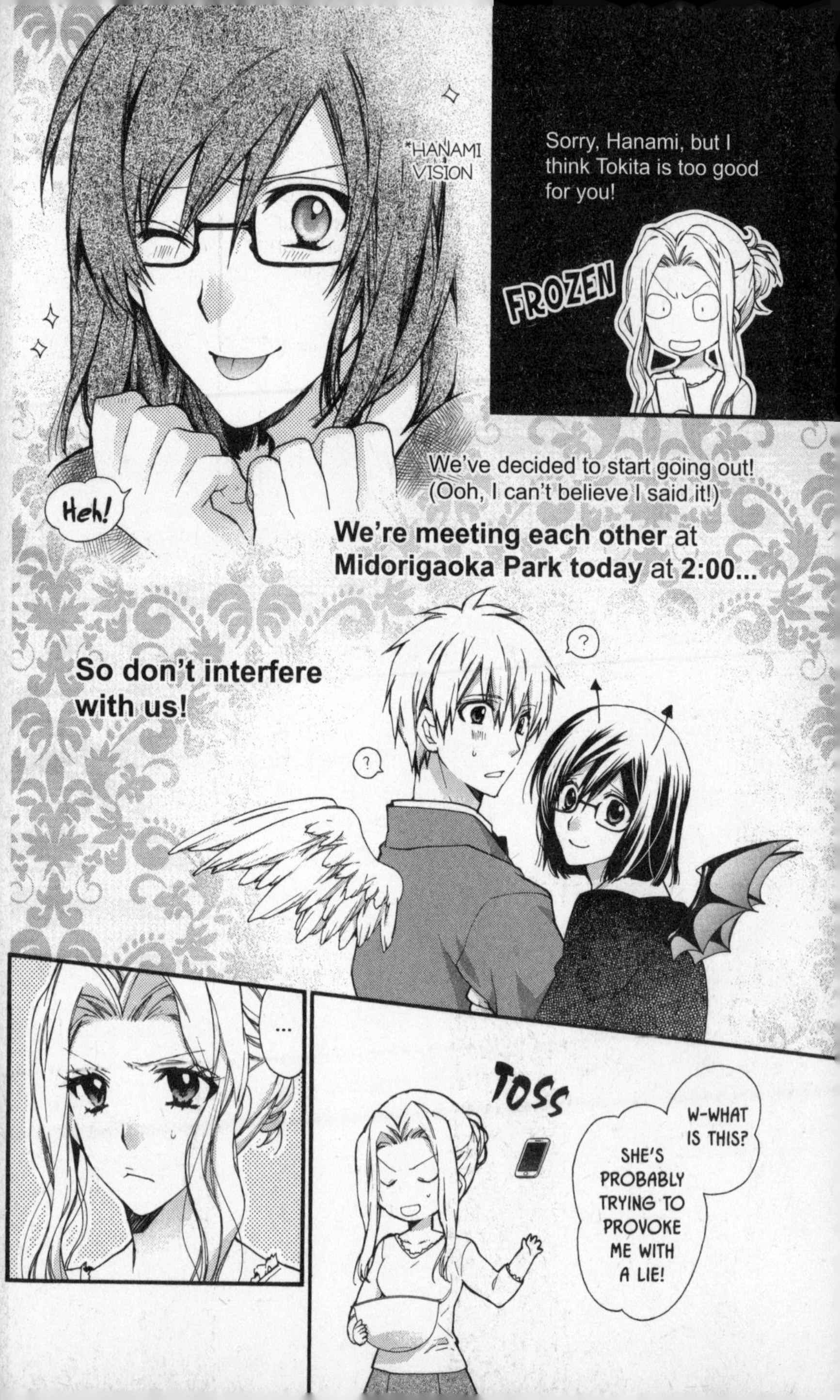
Sorry, Hanami, but I think Tokita is too good for you!
FROZEN
*HANAMI VISION
Heh!
We've decided to start going out! (Ooh, I can't believe I said it!)
We're meeting each other at Midorigaoka Park today at 2:00...
?
?
So don't interfere with us!
TOSS
W-WHAT IS THIS?
SHE'S PROBABLY TRYING TO PROVOKE ME WITH A LIE!
...

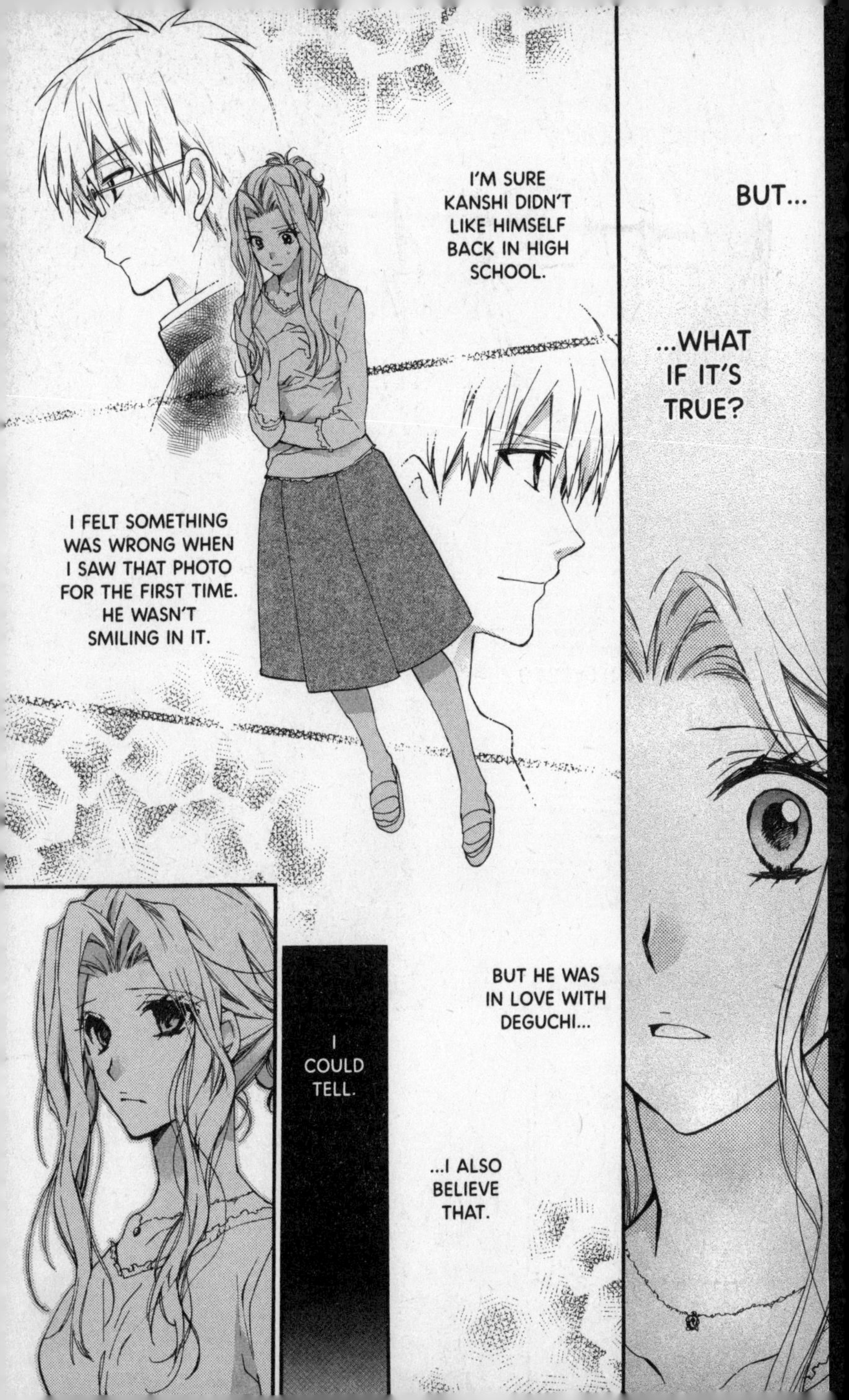
BUT...
...WHAT IF IT'S TRUE?
I'M SURE KANSHI DIDN'T LIKE HIMSELF BACK IN HIGH SCHOOL.
I FELT SOMETHING WAS WRONG WHEN I SAW THAT PHOTO FOR THE FIRST TIME. HE WASN'T SMILING IN IT.
BUT HE WAS IN LOVE WITH DEGUCHI...
I COULD TELL.
...I ALSO BELIEVE THAT.

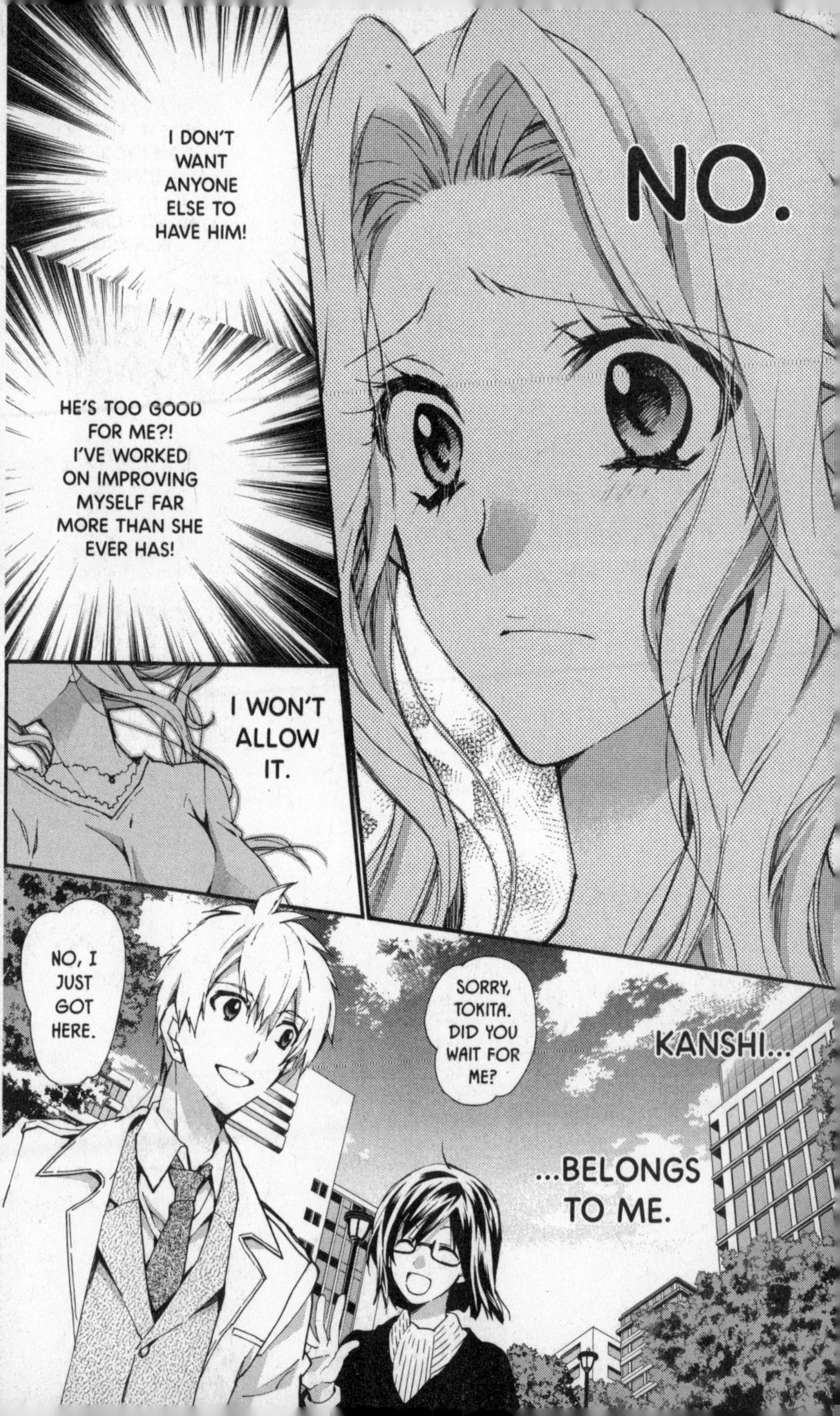
NO.
I DON'T WANT ANYONE ELSE TO HAVE HIM!
HE'S TOO GOOD FOR ME?! I'VE WORKED ON IMPROVING MYSELF FAR MORE THAN SHE EVER HAS!
I WON'T ALLOW IT.
SORRY, TOKITA. DID YOU WAIT FOR ME?
NO, I JUST GOT HERE.
KANSHI...
...BELONGS TO ME.

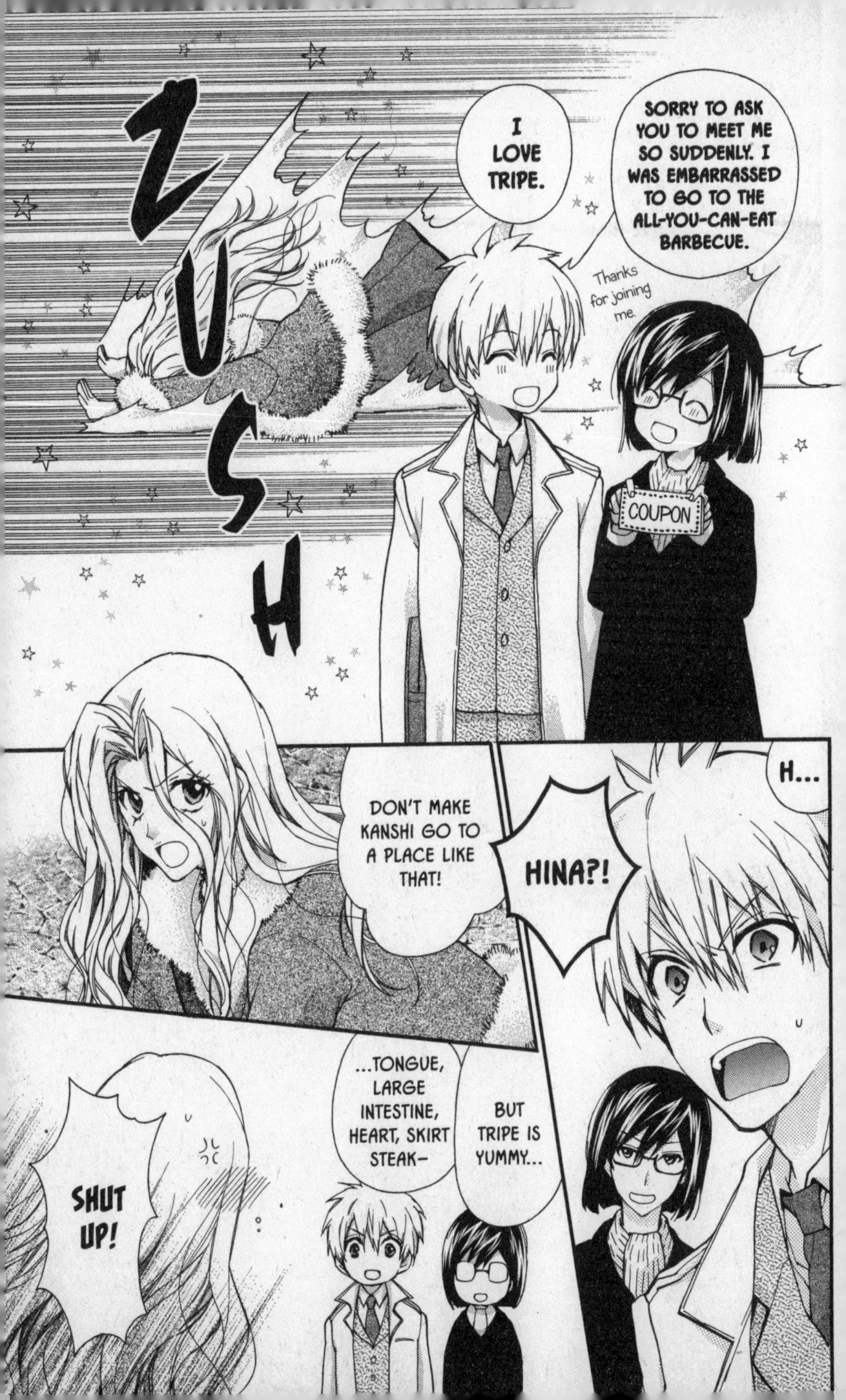
SORRY TO ASK YOU TO MEET ME SO SUDDENLY. I WAS EMBARRASSED TO GO TO THE ALL-YOU-CAN-EAT BARBECUE.
Thanks for joining me.
COUPON
I LOVE TRIPE.
ZUSH
H...
HINA?!
DON'T MAKE KANSHI GO TO A PLACE LIKE THAT!
BUT TRIPE IS YUMMY...
...TONGUE, LARGE INTESTINE, HEART, SKIRT STEAK–
SHUT UP!

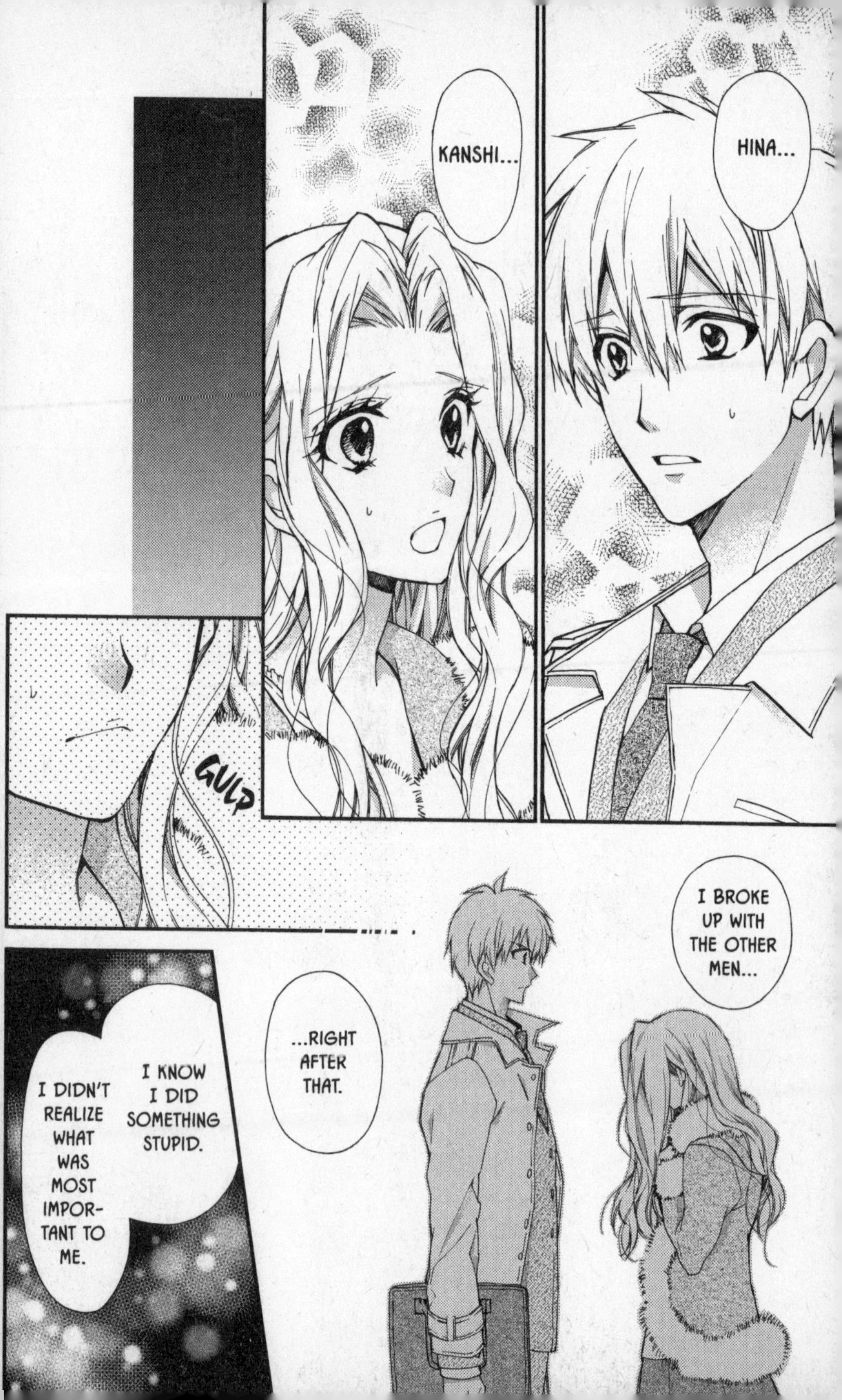
HINA...
KANSHI...
GULP
I BROKE UP WITH THE OTHER MEN...
...RIGHT AFTER THAT.
I KNOW I DID SOMETHING STUPID.
I DIDN'T REALIZE WHAT WAS MOST IMPORTANT TO ME.

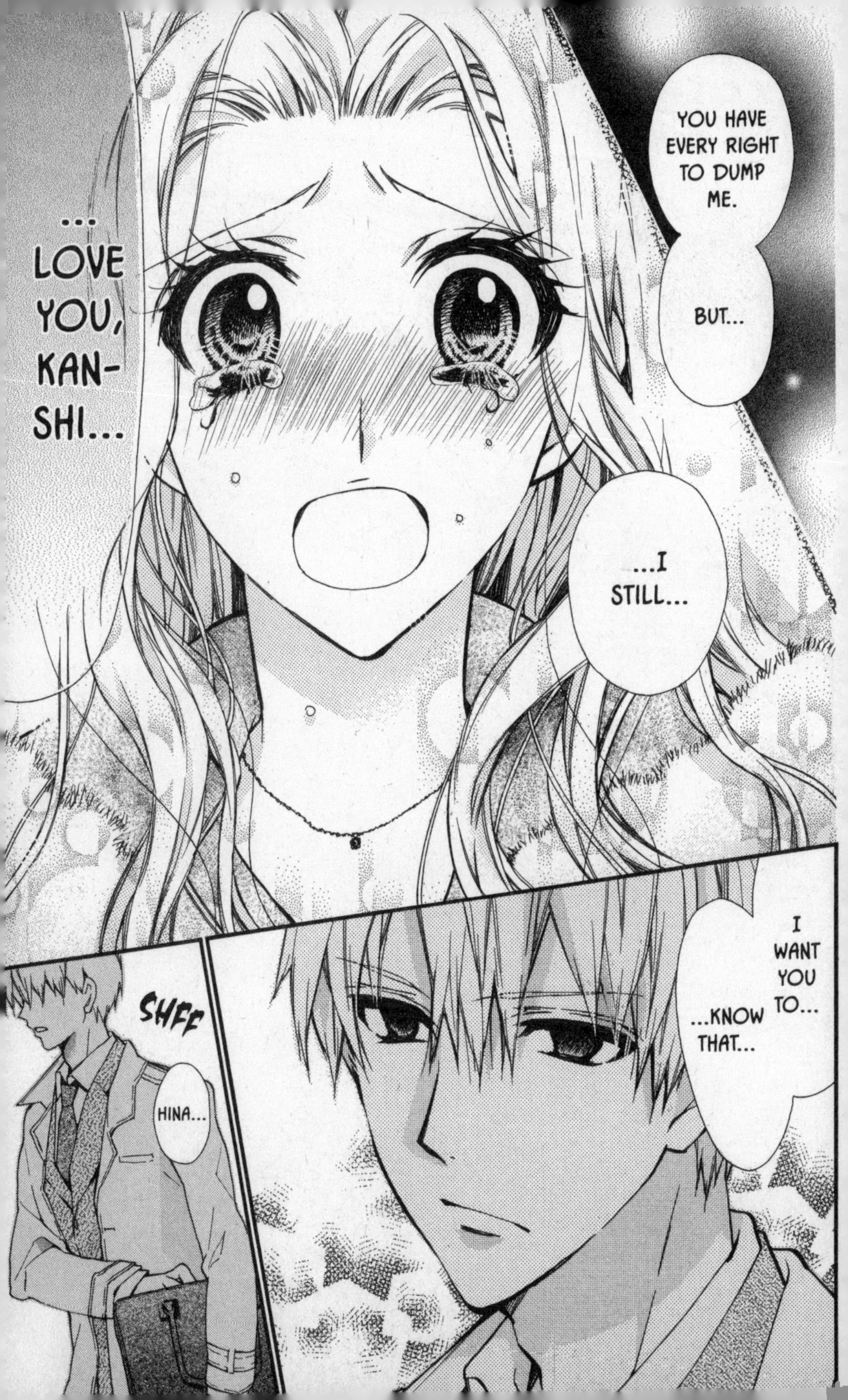
YOU HAVE EVERY RIGHT TO DUMP ME.
BUT...
...I STILL...
... LOVE YOU, KAN-SHI...
I WANT YOU TO...
...KNOW THAT...
SHFF
HINA...

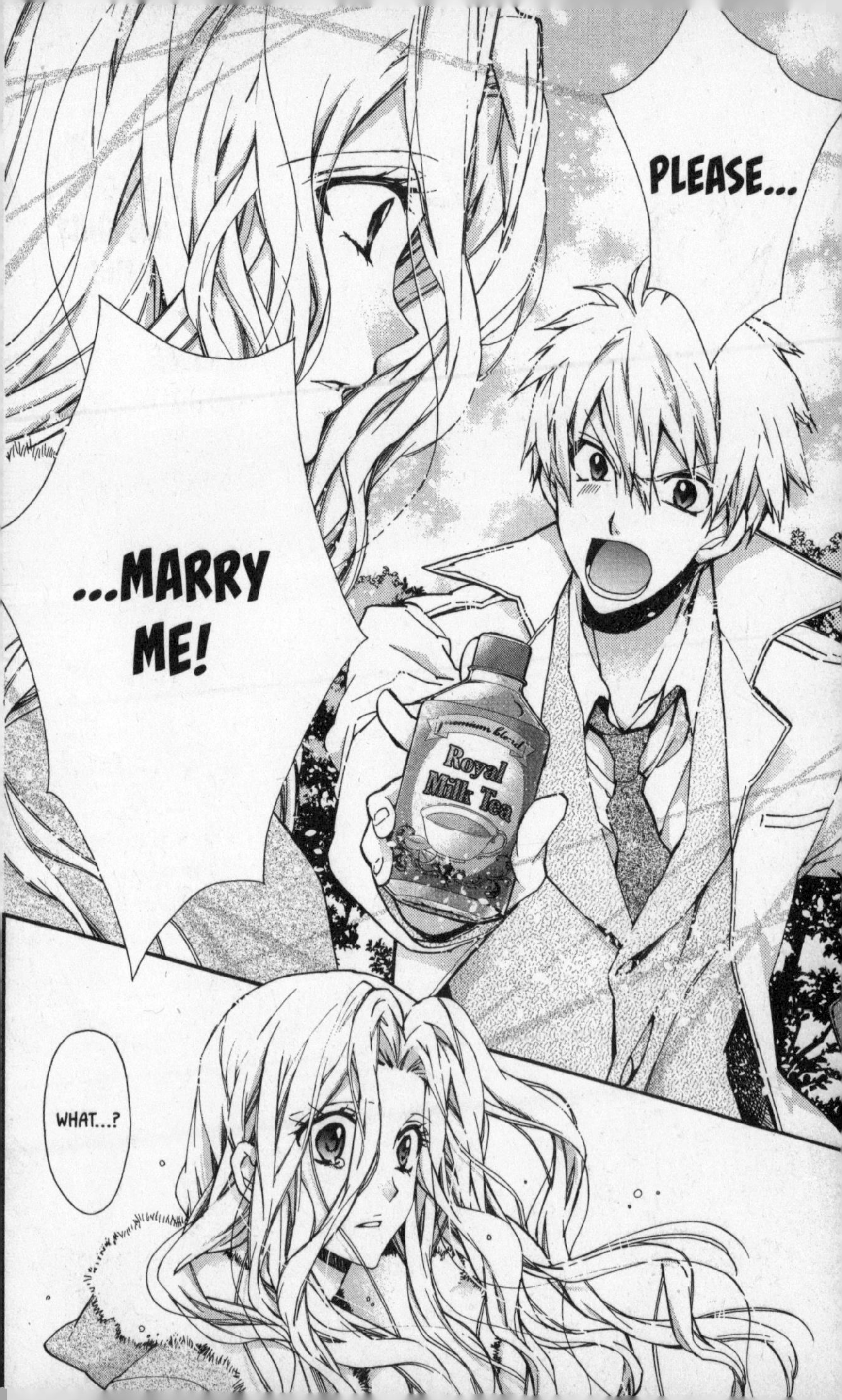
PLEASE...
...MARRY ME!
Royal Milk Tea
WHAT...?

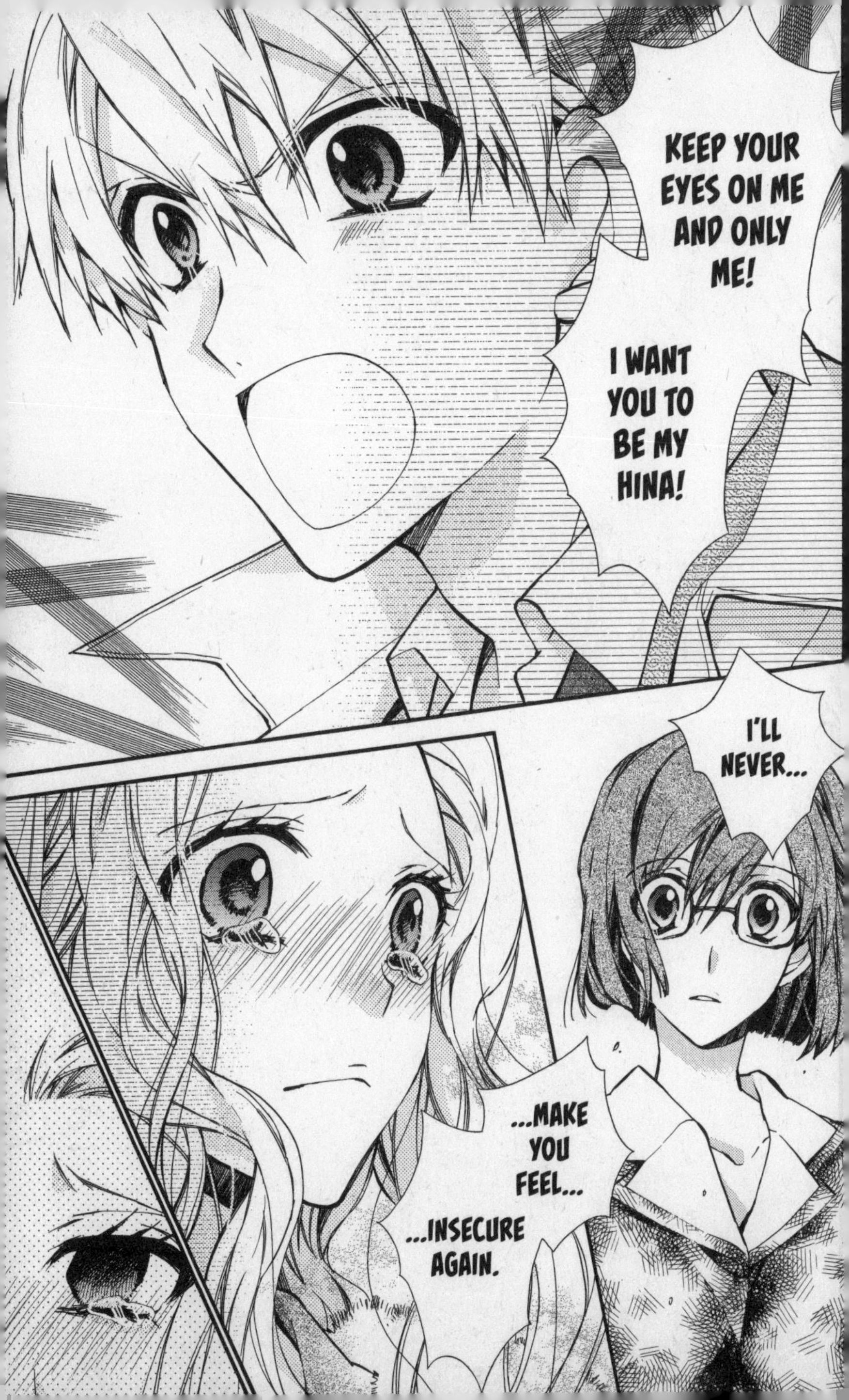
KEEP YOUR EYES ON ME AND ONLY ME!
I WANT YOU TO BE MY HINA!
I'LL NEVER...
...MAKE YOU FEEL...
...INSECURE AGAIN.

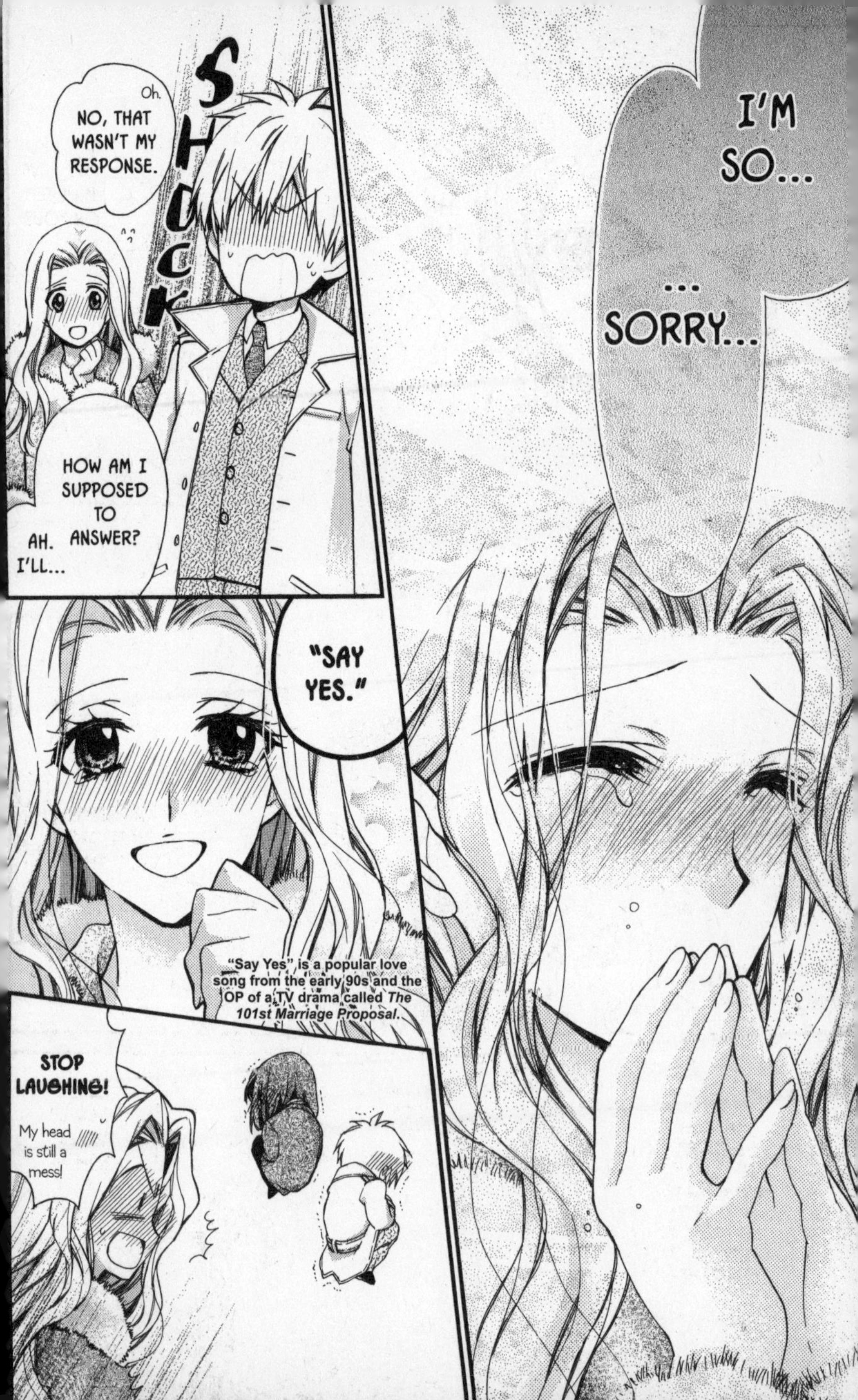
I'M SO...
... SORRY...
SHOCK
Oh. NO, THAT WASN'T MY RESPONSE.
HOW AM I SUPPOSED TO ANSWER?
AH. I'LL...
"SAY YES."
"Say Yes" is a popular love song from the early 90s and the OP of a TV drama called *The 101st Marriage Proposal*.
STOP LAUGHING!
My head is still a mess!

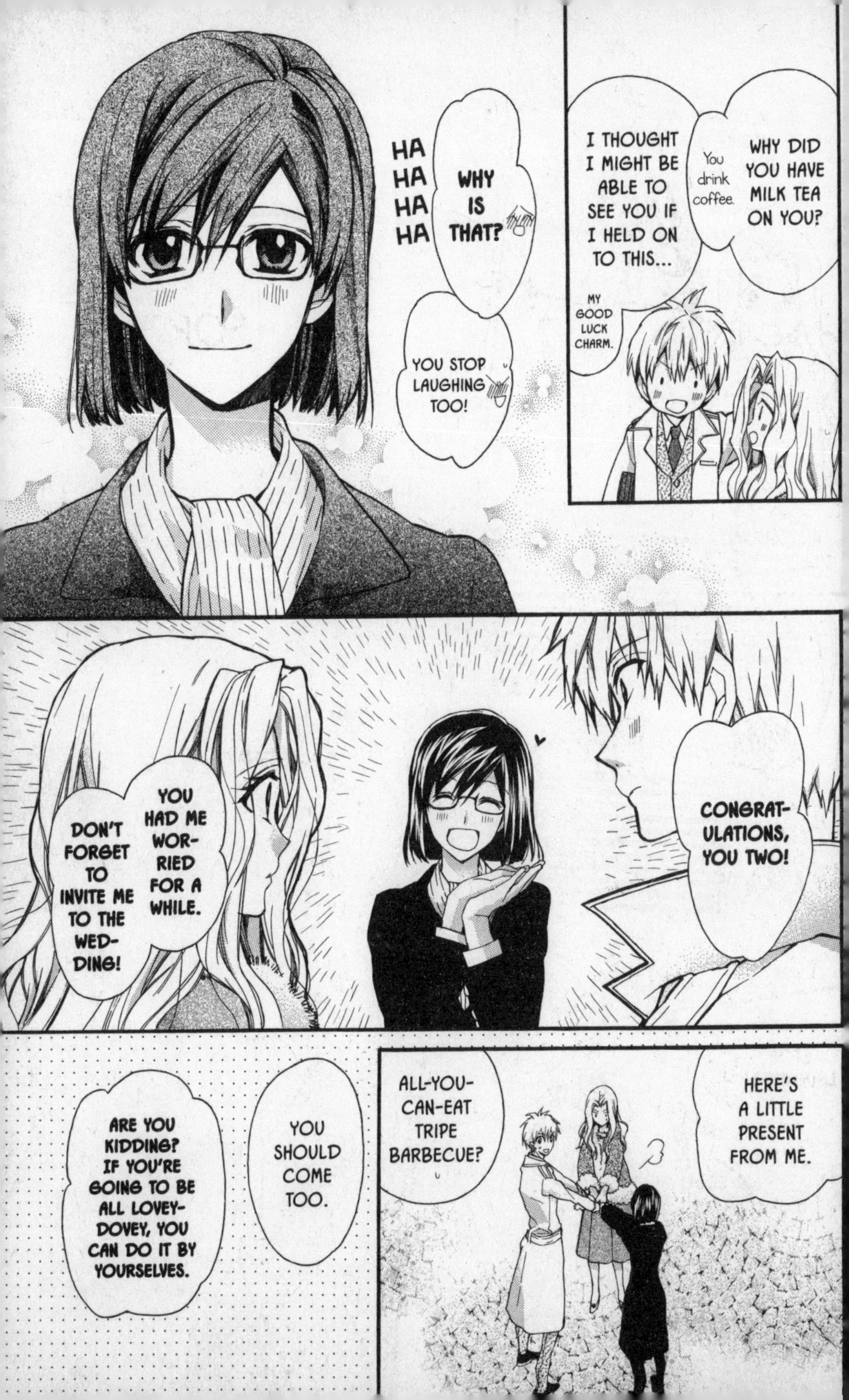
WHY DID YOU HAVE MILK TEA ON YOU?
You drink coffee.
I THOUGHT I MIGHT BE ABLE TO SEE YOU IF I HELD ON TO THIS...
MY GOOD LUCK CHARM.
WHY IS THAT?
HA HA HA HA
YOU STOP LAUGHING TOO!
CONGRAT-ULATIONS, YOU TWO!
YOU HAD ME WOR-RIED FOR A WHILE.
DON'T FORGET TO INVITE ME TO THE WED-DING!
HERE'S A LITTLE PRESENT FROM ME.
ALL-YOU-CAN-EAT TRIPE BARBECUE?
YOU SHOULD COME TOO.
ARE YOU KIDDING? IF YOU'RE GOING TO BE ALL LOVEY-DOVEY, YOU CAN DO IT BY YOURSELVES.

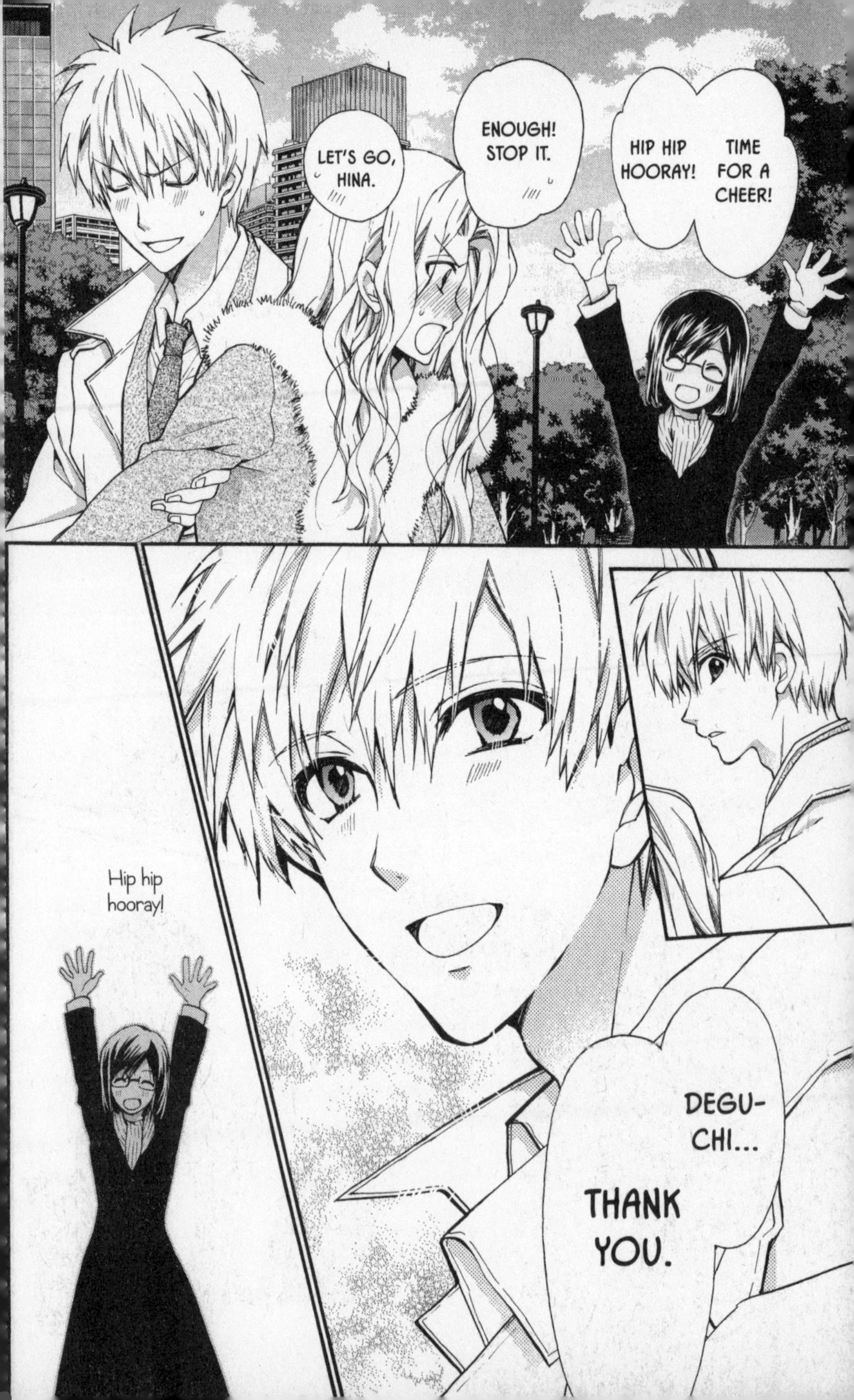
TIME FOR A CHEER!
HIP HIP HOORAY!
ENOUGH! STOP IT.
LET'S GO, HINA.
DEGU-CHI...
THANK YOU.
Hip hip hooray!

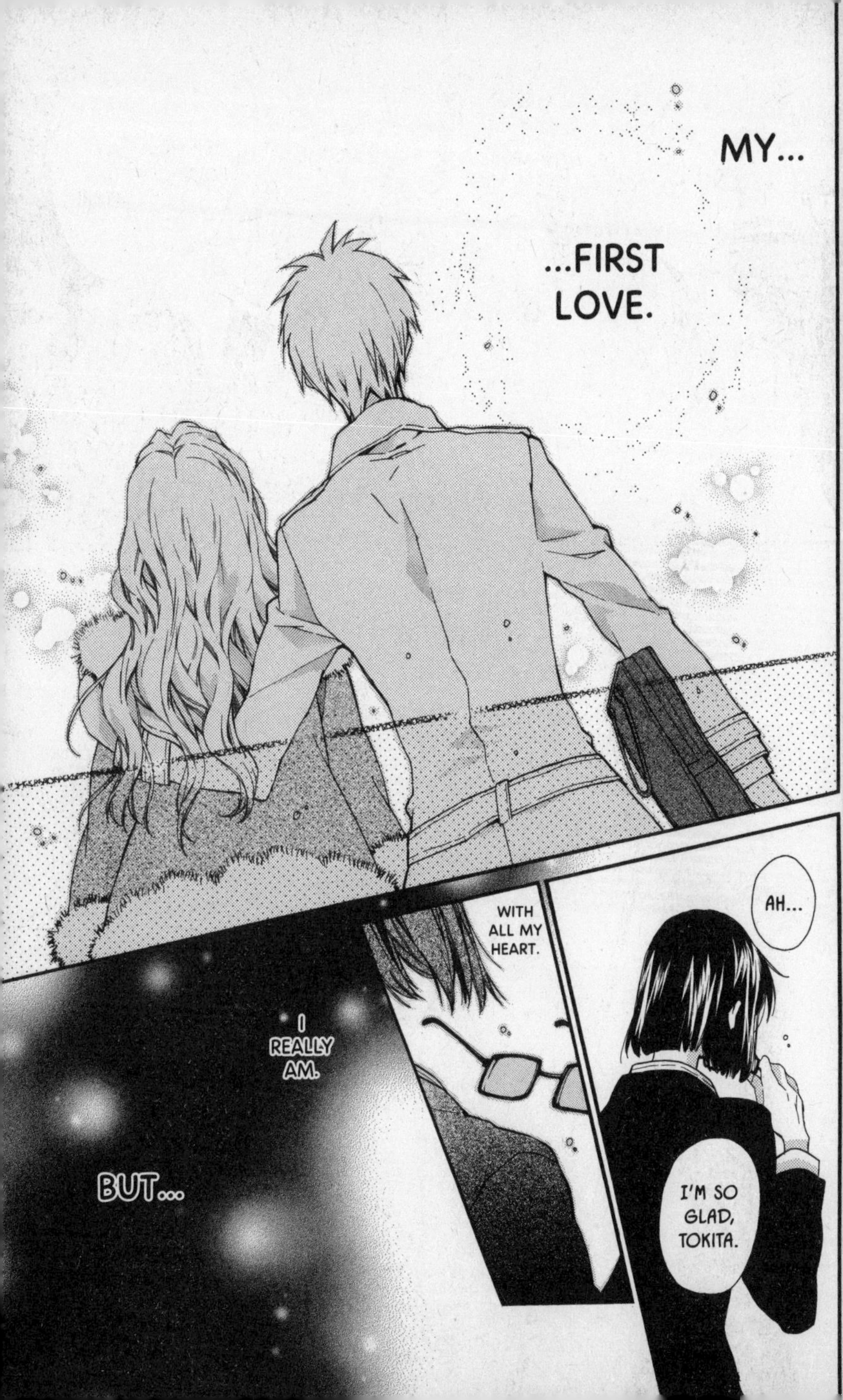
MY...
...FIRST LOVE.
AH...
I'M SO GLAD, TOKITA.
WITH ALL MY HEART.
I REALLY AM.
BUT...

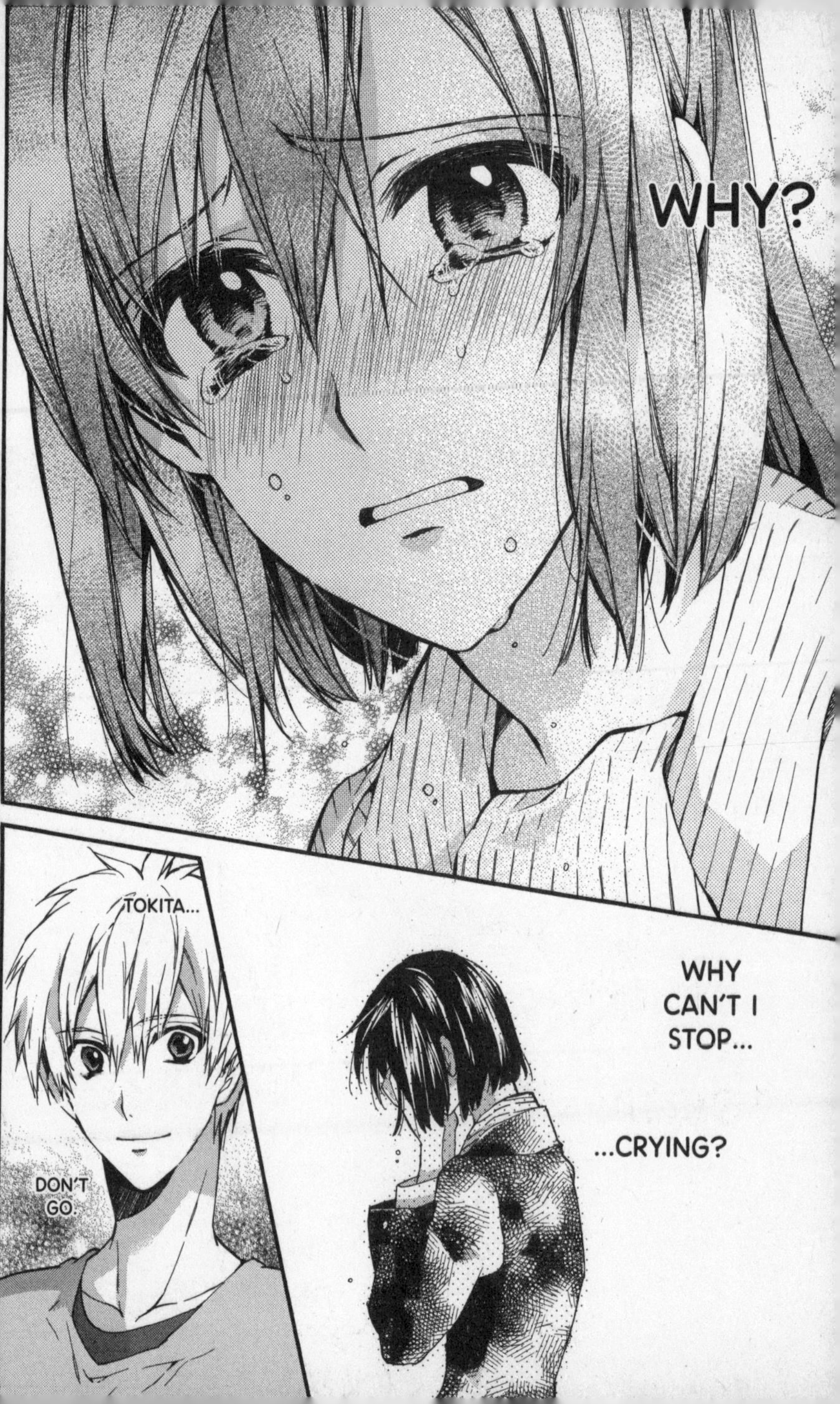
WHY?
WHY CAN'T I STOP...
...CRYING?
TOKITA...
DON'T GO.

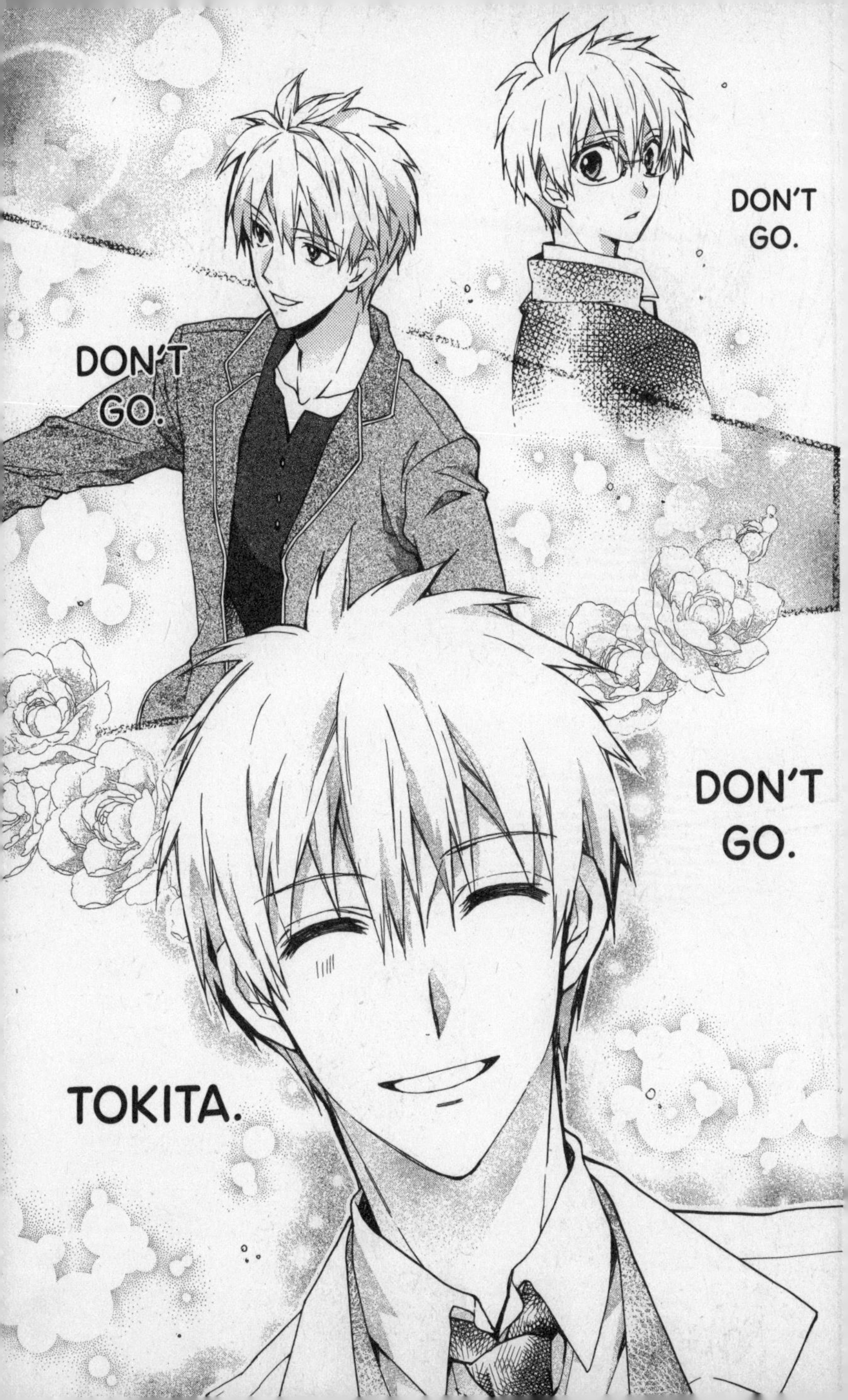
DON'T GO.
DON'T GO.
DON'T GO.
TOKITA.

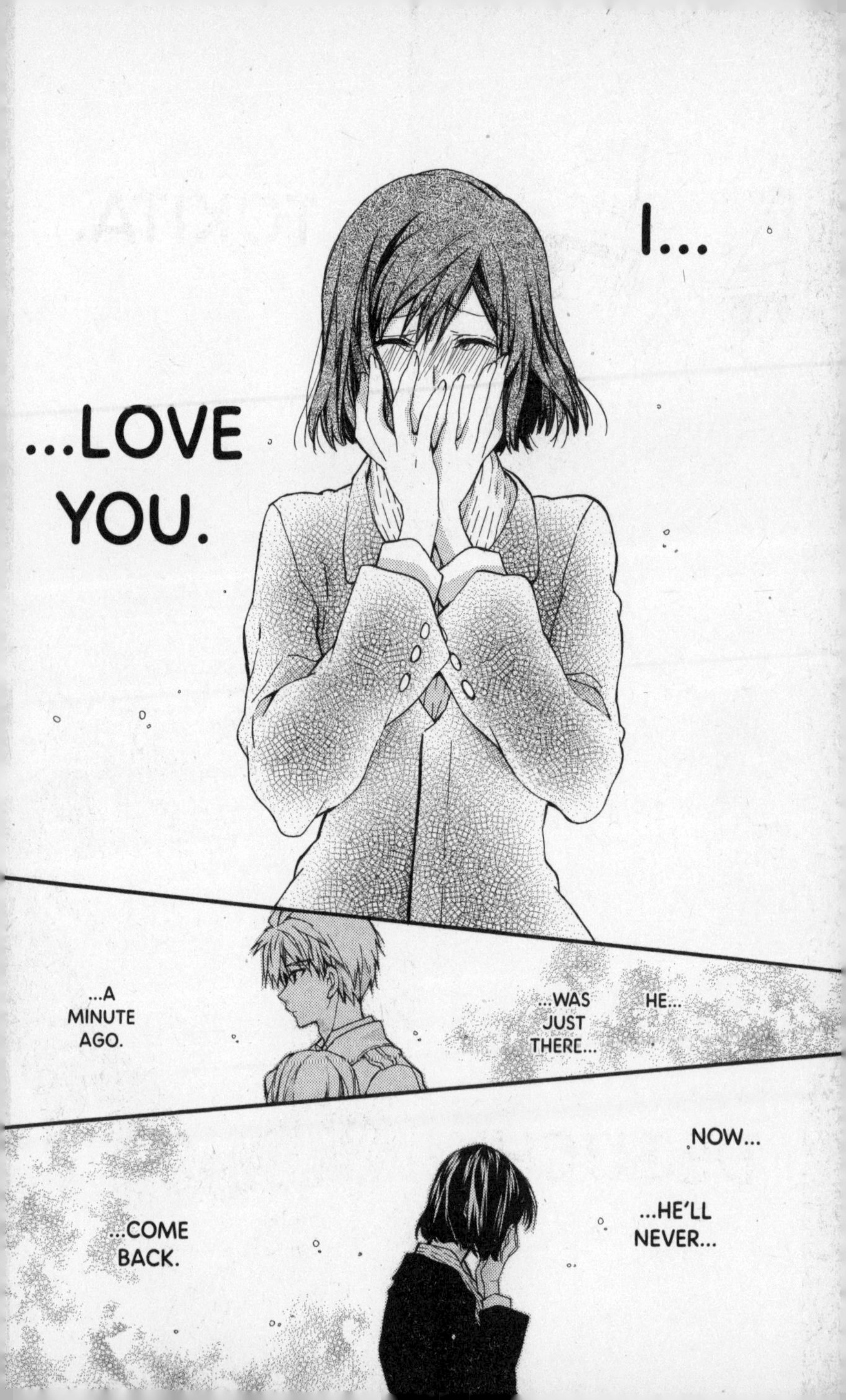
I...
...LOVE YOU.
HE...
...WAS JUST THERE...
...A MINUTE AGO.
NOW...
...HE'LL NEVER...
...COME BACK.

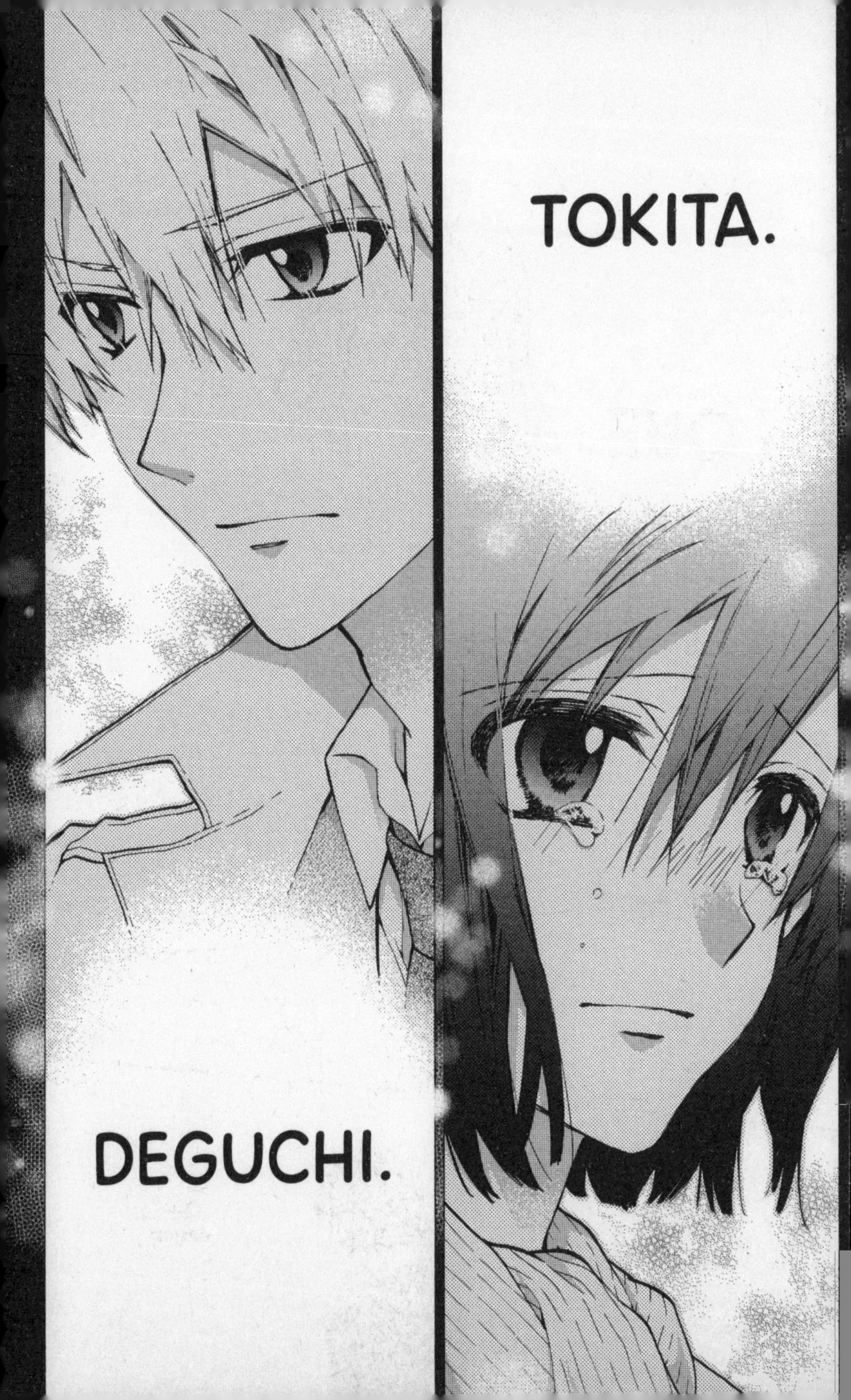
TOKITA.
DEGUCHI.

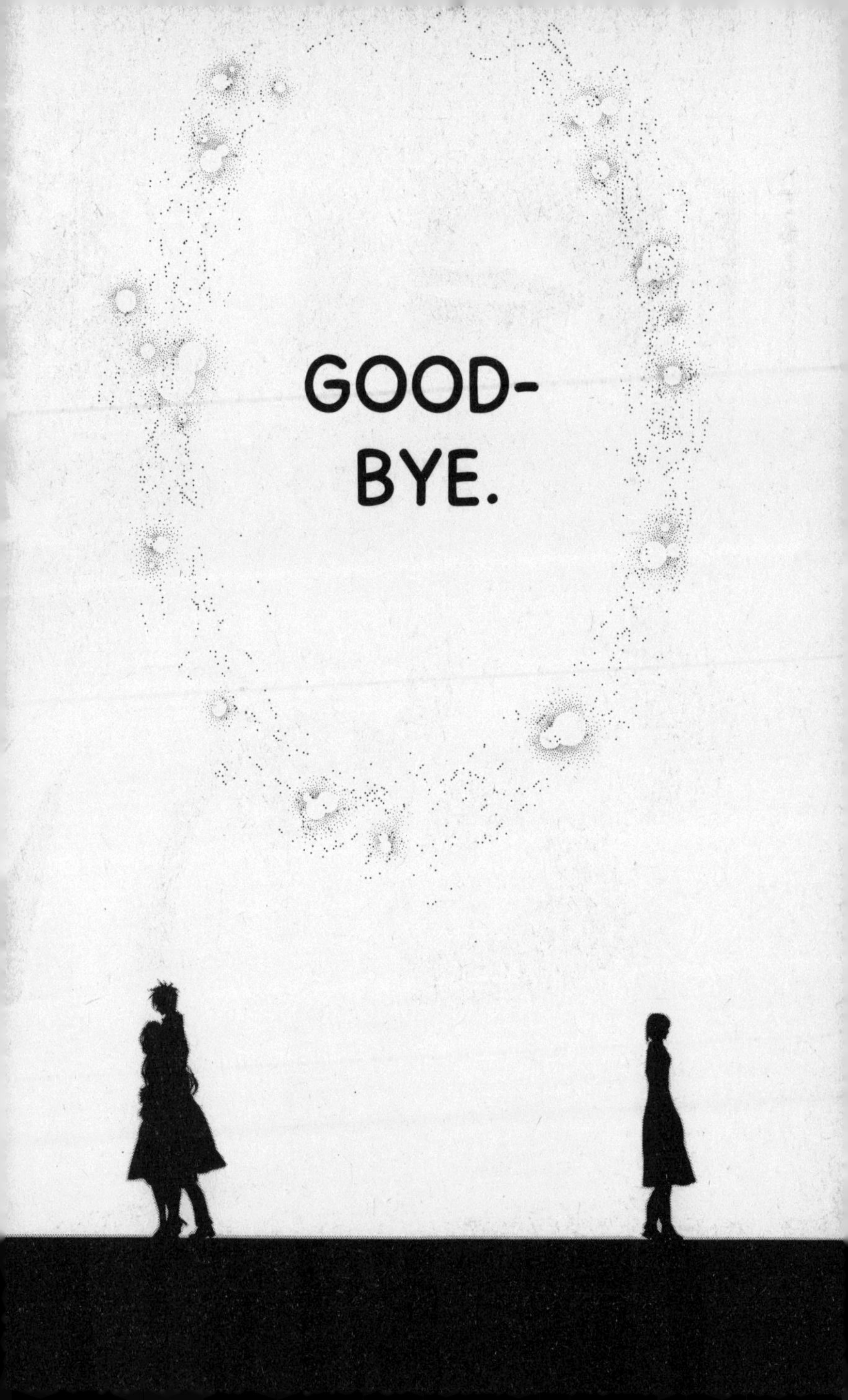
GOOD-BYE.

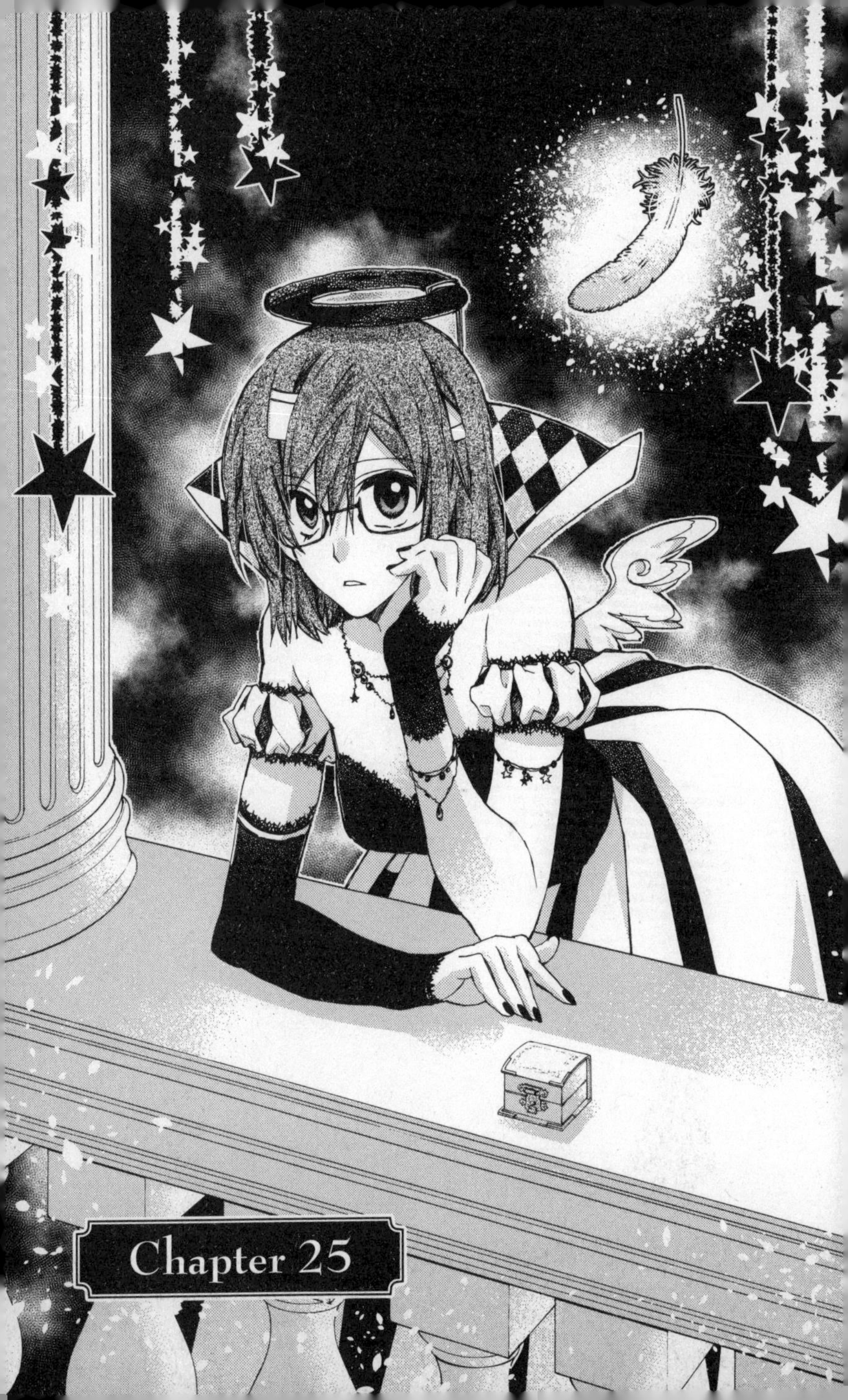
Chapter 25

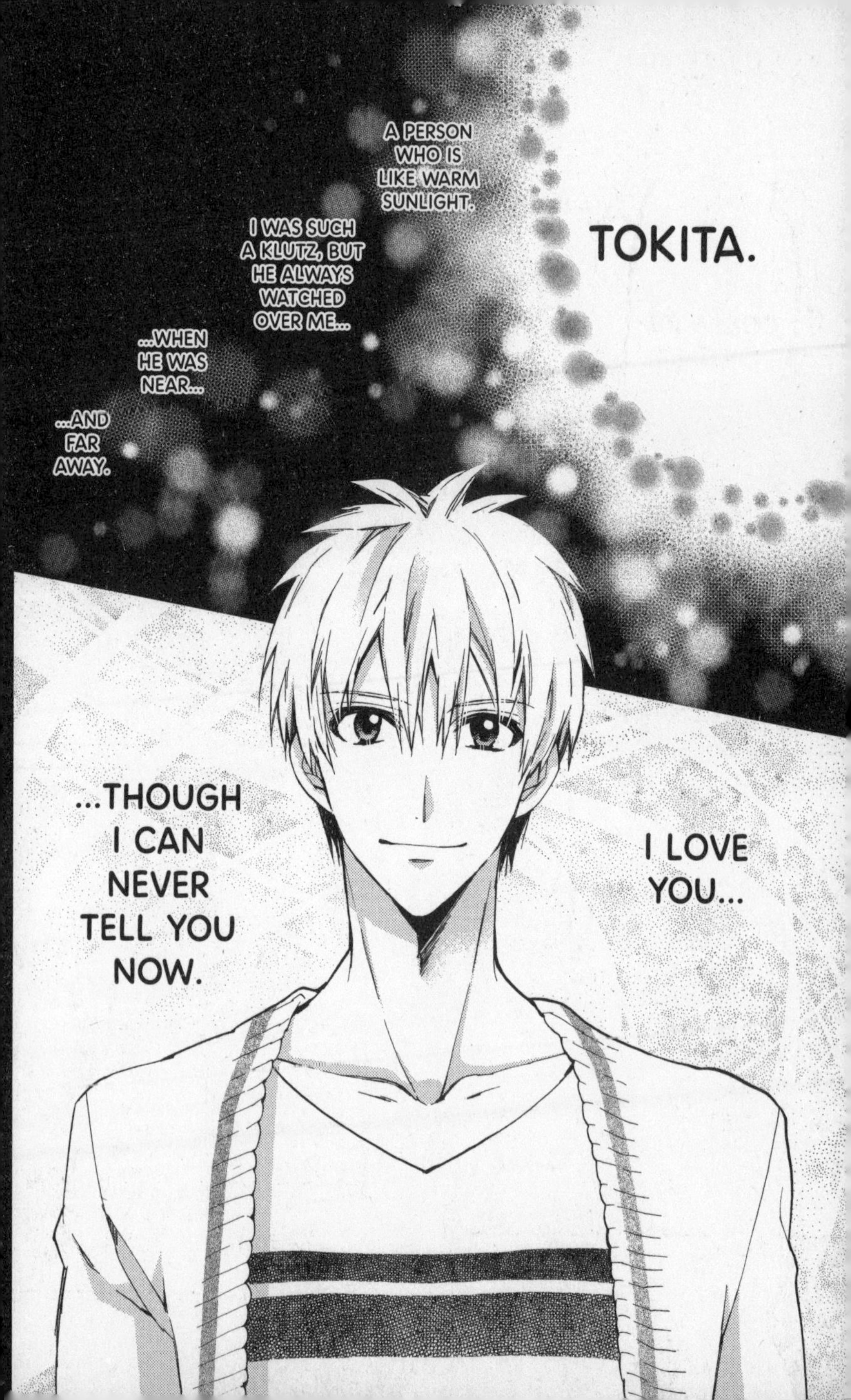
TOKITA.
A PERSON WHO IS LIKE WARM SUNLIGHT.
I WAS SUCH A KLUTZ, BUT HE ALWAYS WATCHED OVER ME...
...WHEN HE WAS NEAR...
...AND FAR AWAY.
I LOVE YOU...
...THOUGH I CAN NEVER TELL YOU NOW.

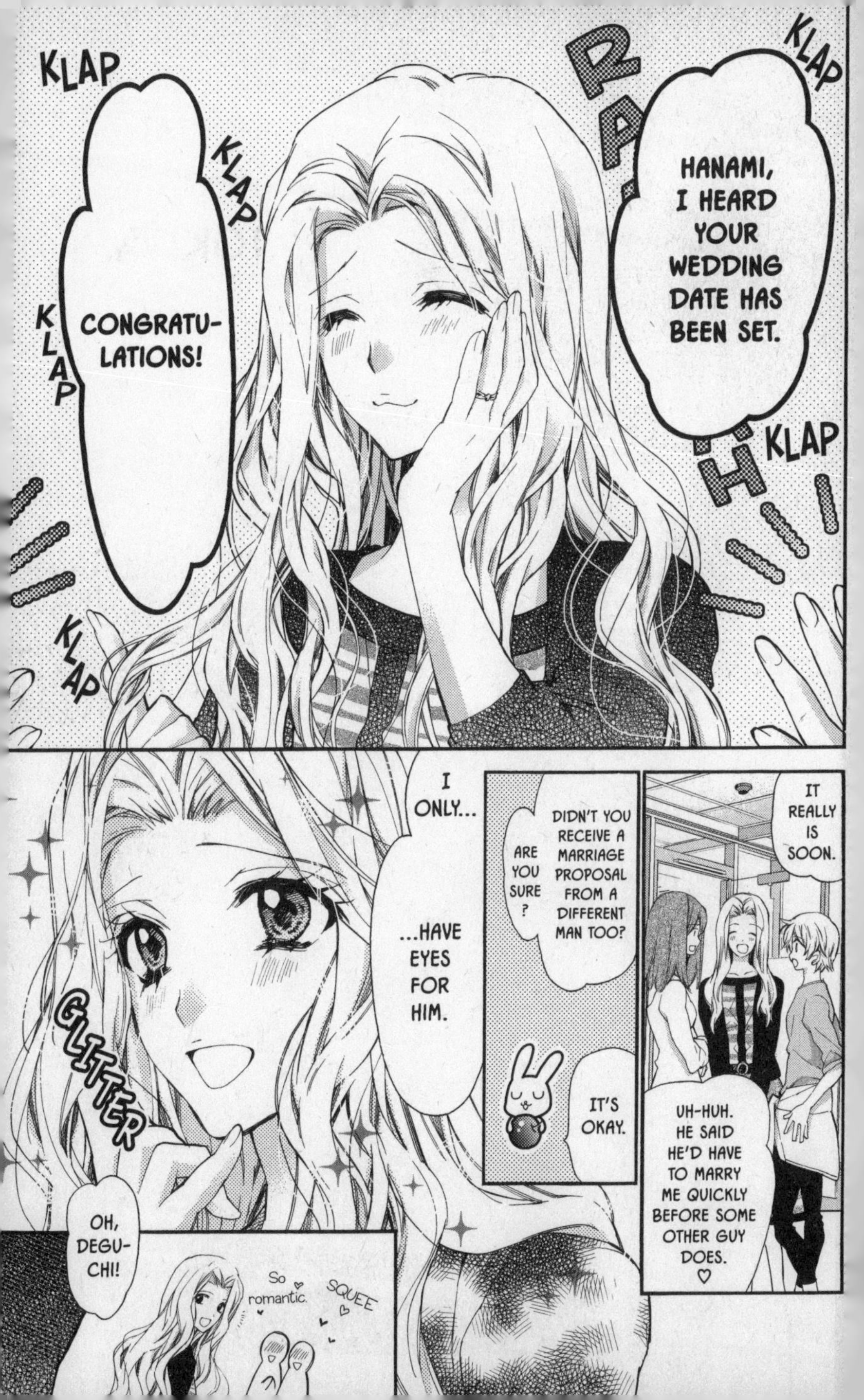
KLAP
HANAMI, I HEARD YOUR WEDDING DATE HAS BEEN SET.
KLAP
KLAP
CONGRATU-LATIONS!
KLAP
KLAP
KLAP
IT REALLY IS SOON.
UH-HUH. HE SAID HE'D HAVE TO MARRY ME QUICKLY BEFORE SOME OTHER GUY DOES. ♡
DIDN'T YOU RECEIVE A MARRIAGE PROPOSAL FROM A DIFFERENT MAN TOO?
ARE YOU SURE?
IT'S OKAY.
I ONLY...
...HAVE EYES FOR HIM.
GLITTER
OH, DEGU-CHI!
SQUEE
So romantic.

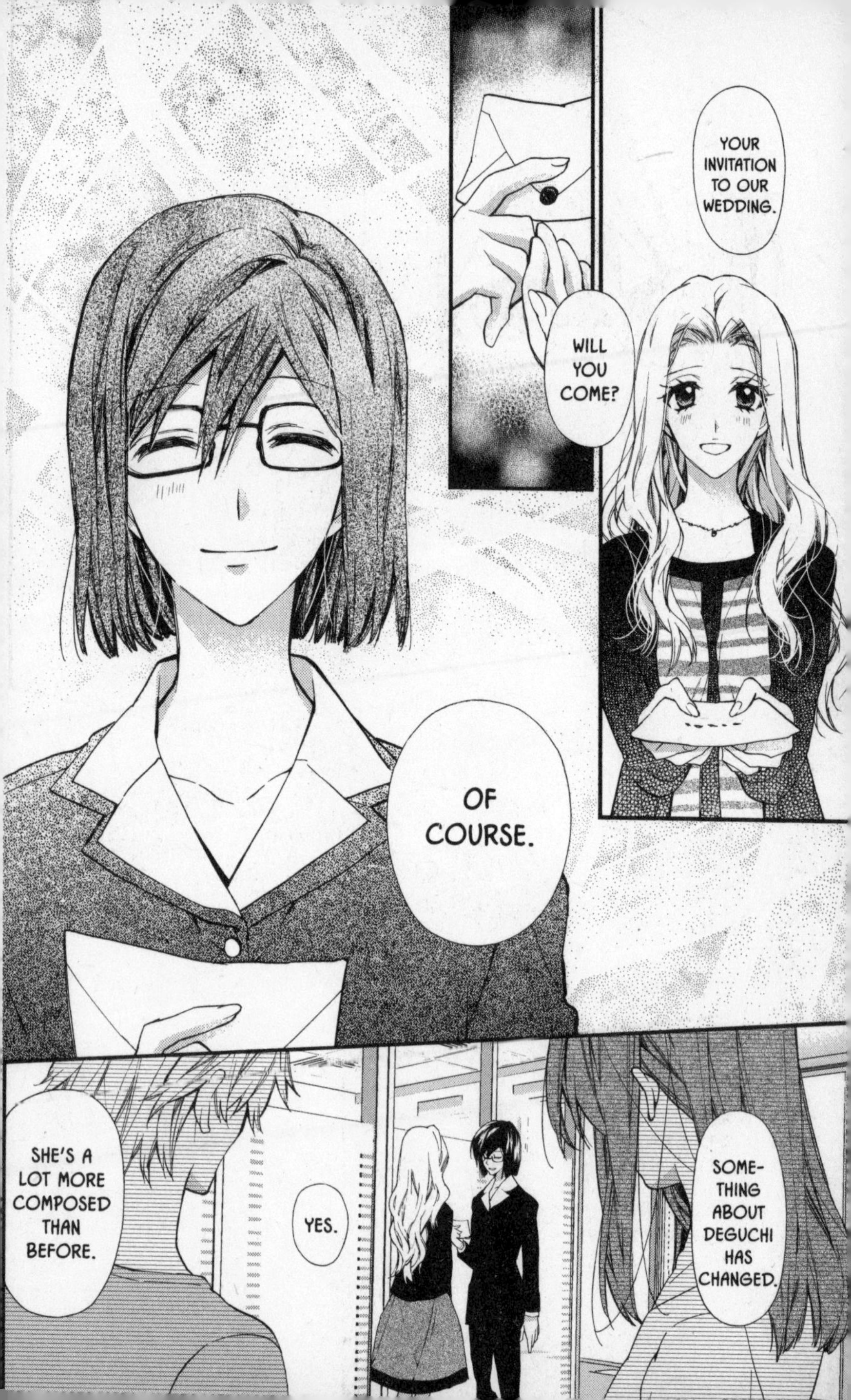
YOUR INVITATION TO OUR WEDDING.
WILL YOU COME?
OF COURSE.
SOME-THING ABOUT DEGUCHI HAS CHANGED.
YES.
SHE'S A LOT MORE COMPOSED THAN BEFORE.

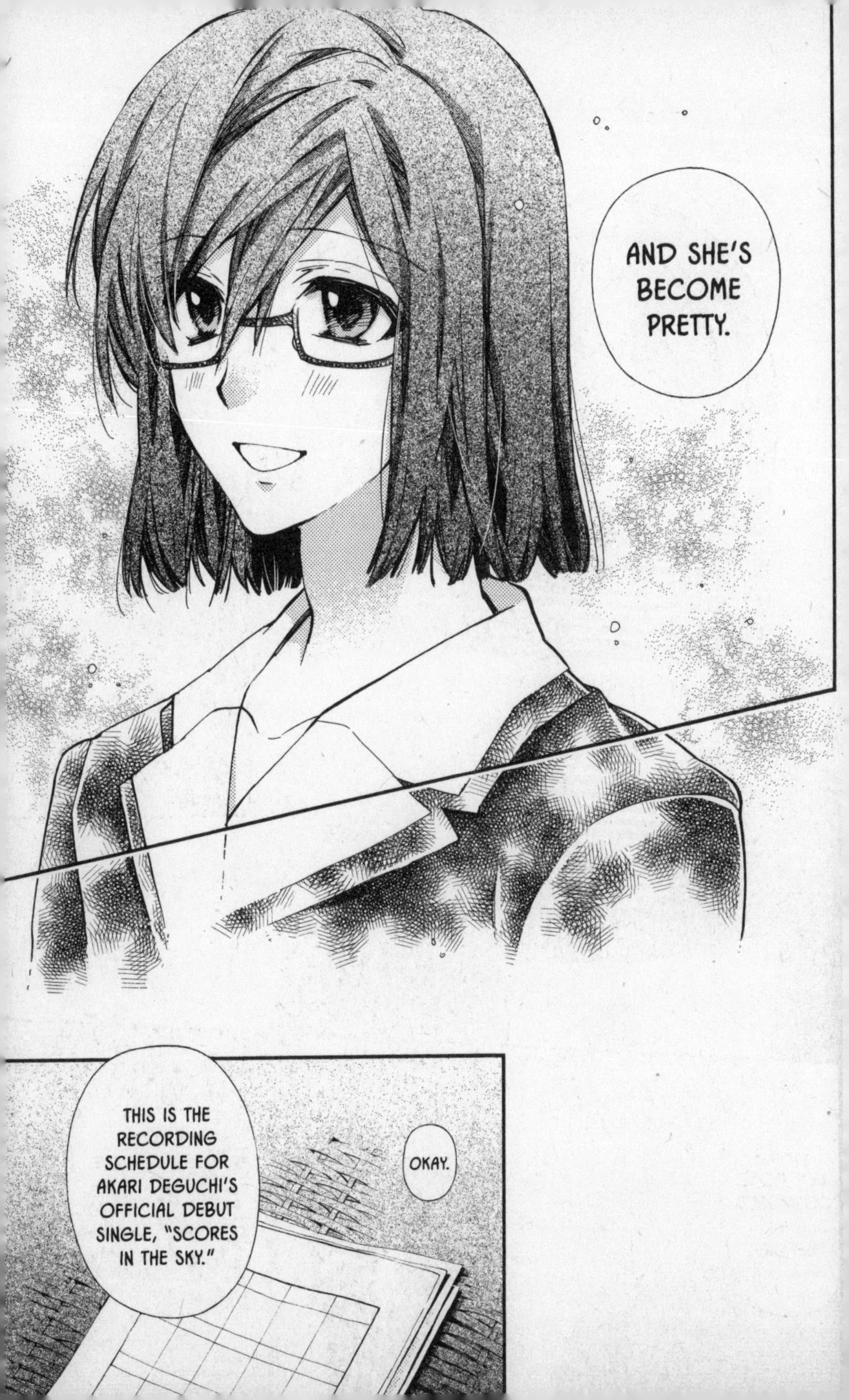
AND SHE'S BECOME PRETTY.
THIS IS THE RECORDING SCHEDULE FOR AKARI DEGUCHI'S OFFICIAL DEBUT SINGLE, "SCORES IN THE SKY."
OKAY.

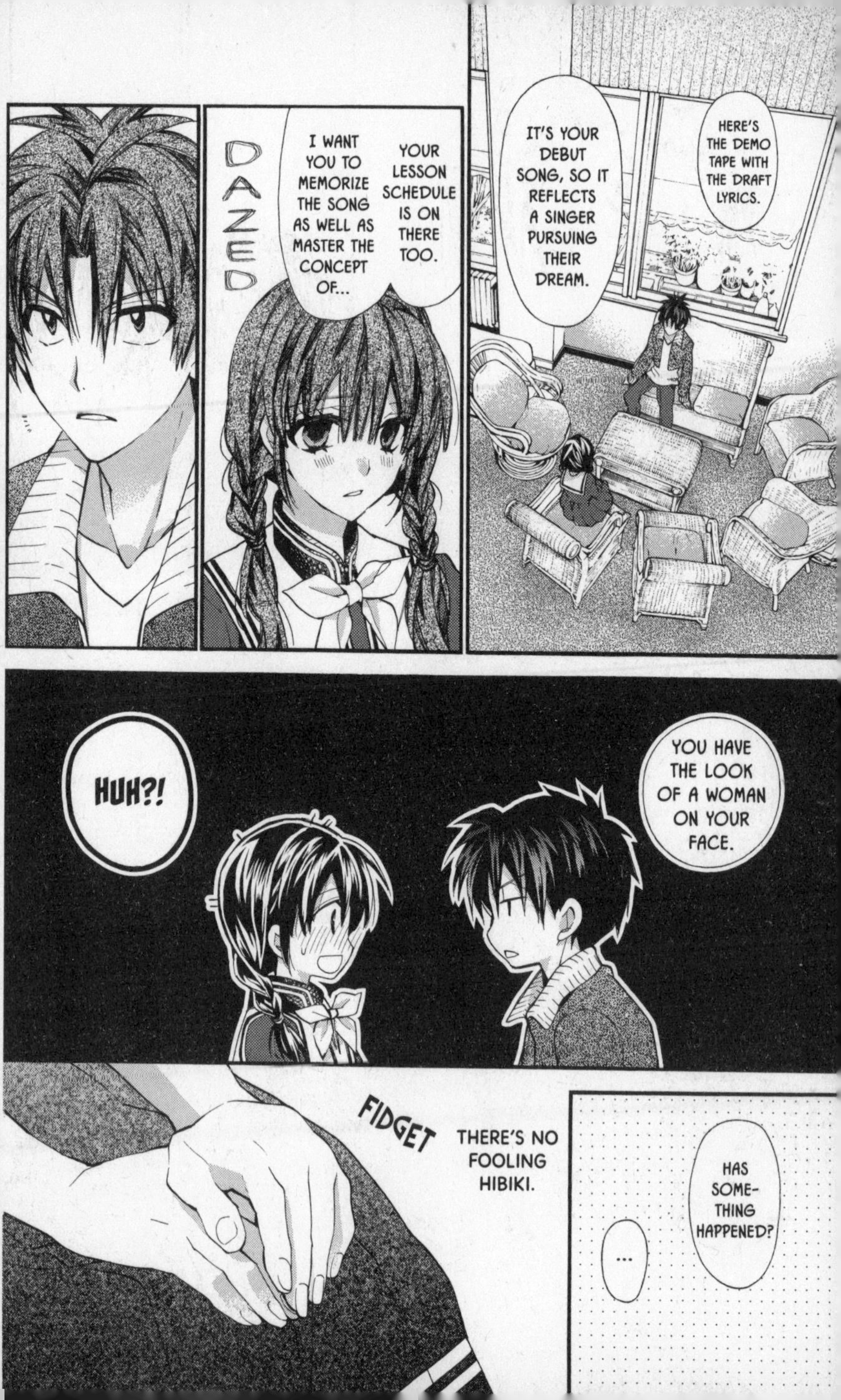
HERE'S THE DEMO TAPE WITH THE DRAFT LYRICS.
IT'S YOUR DEBUT SONG, SO IT REFLECTS A SINGER PURSUING THEIR DREAM.
YOUR LESSON SCHEDULE IS ON THERE TOO.
I WANT YOU TO MEMORIZE THE SONG AS WELL AS MASTER THE CONCEPT OF...
DAZED
YOU HAVE THE LOOK OF A WOMAN ON YOUR FACE.
HUH?!
HAS SOME-THING HAPPENED?
...
THERE'S NO FOOLING HIBIKI.
FIDGET

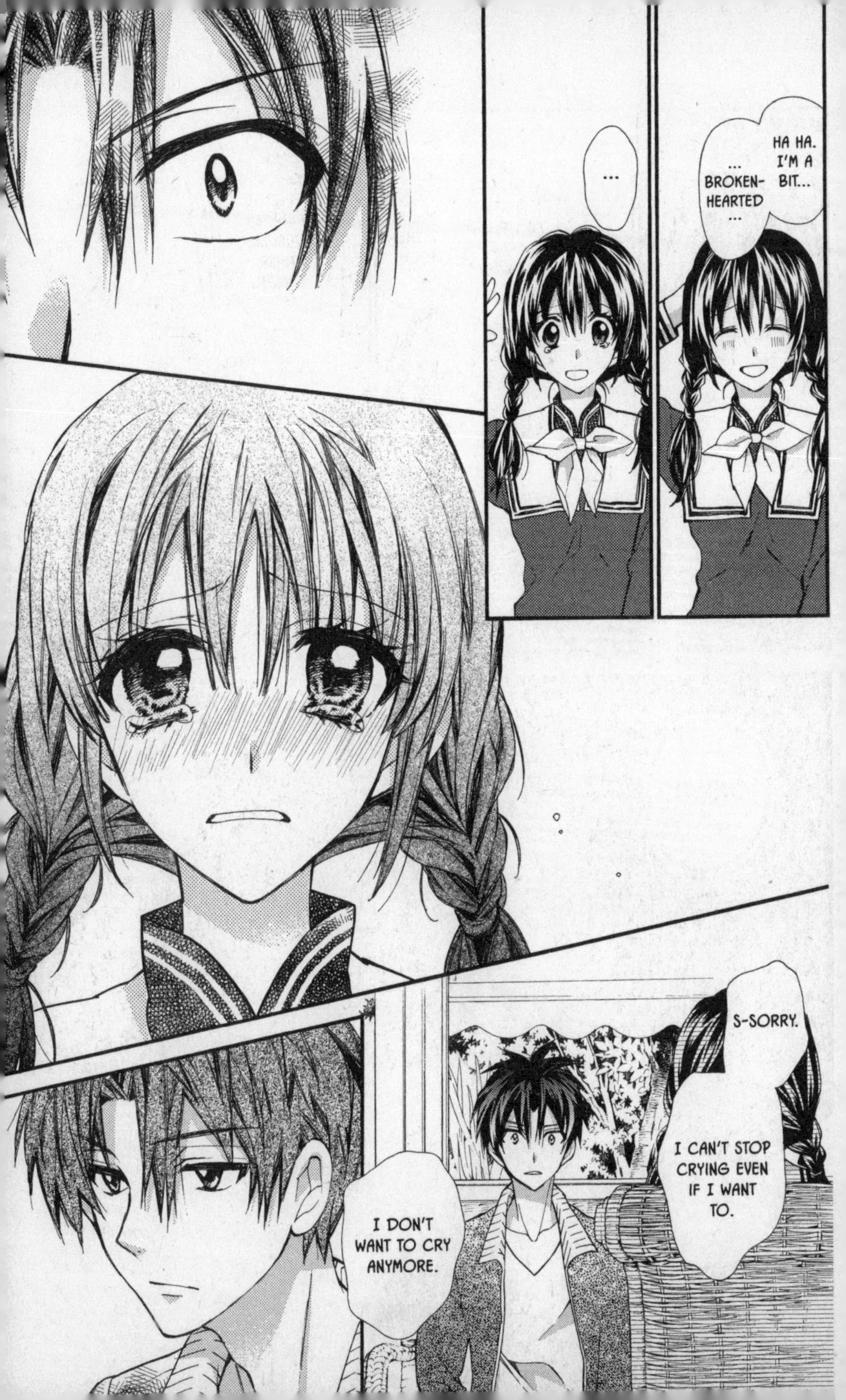
HA HA. I'M A BIT... ... BROKEN-HEARTED ...
...
S-SORRY.
I CAN'T STOP CRYING EVEN IF I WANT TO.
I DON'T WANT TO CRY ANYMORE.

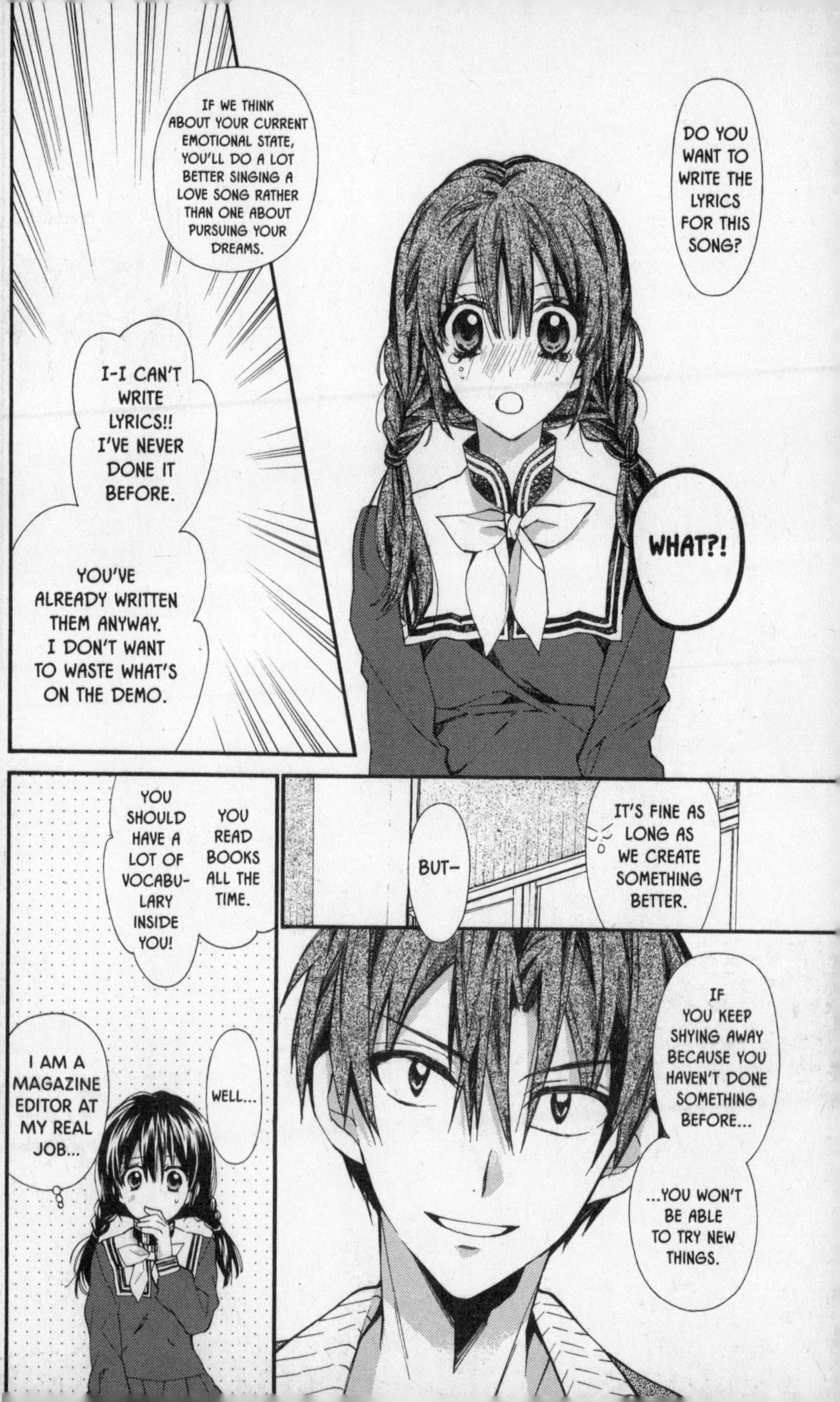

DO YOU WANT TO WRITE THE LYRICS FOR THIS SONG?
WHAT?!
IF WE THINK ABOUT YOUR CURRENT EMOTIONAL STATE, YOU'LL DO A LOT BETTER SINGING A LOVE SONG RATHER THAN ONE ABOUT PURSUING YOUR DREAMS.
I-I CAN'T WRITE LYRICS!! I'VE NEVER DONE IT BEFORE.
YOU'VE ALREADY WRITTEN THEM ANYWAY. I DON'T WANT TO WASTE WHAT'S ON THE DEMO.
IT'S FINE AS LONG AS WE CREATE SOMETHING BETTER.
BUT-
IF YOU KEEP SHYING AWAY BECAUSE YOU HAVEN'T DONE SOMETHING BEFORE...
...YOU WON'T BE ABLE TO TRY NEW THINGS.
YOU READ BOOKS ALL THE TIME.
YOU SHOULD HAVE A LOT OF VOCABU-LARY INSIDE YOU!
WELL...
I AM A MAGAZINE EDITOR AT MY REAL JOB...

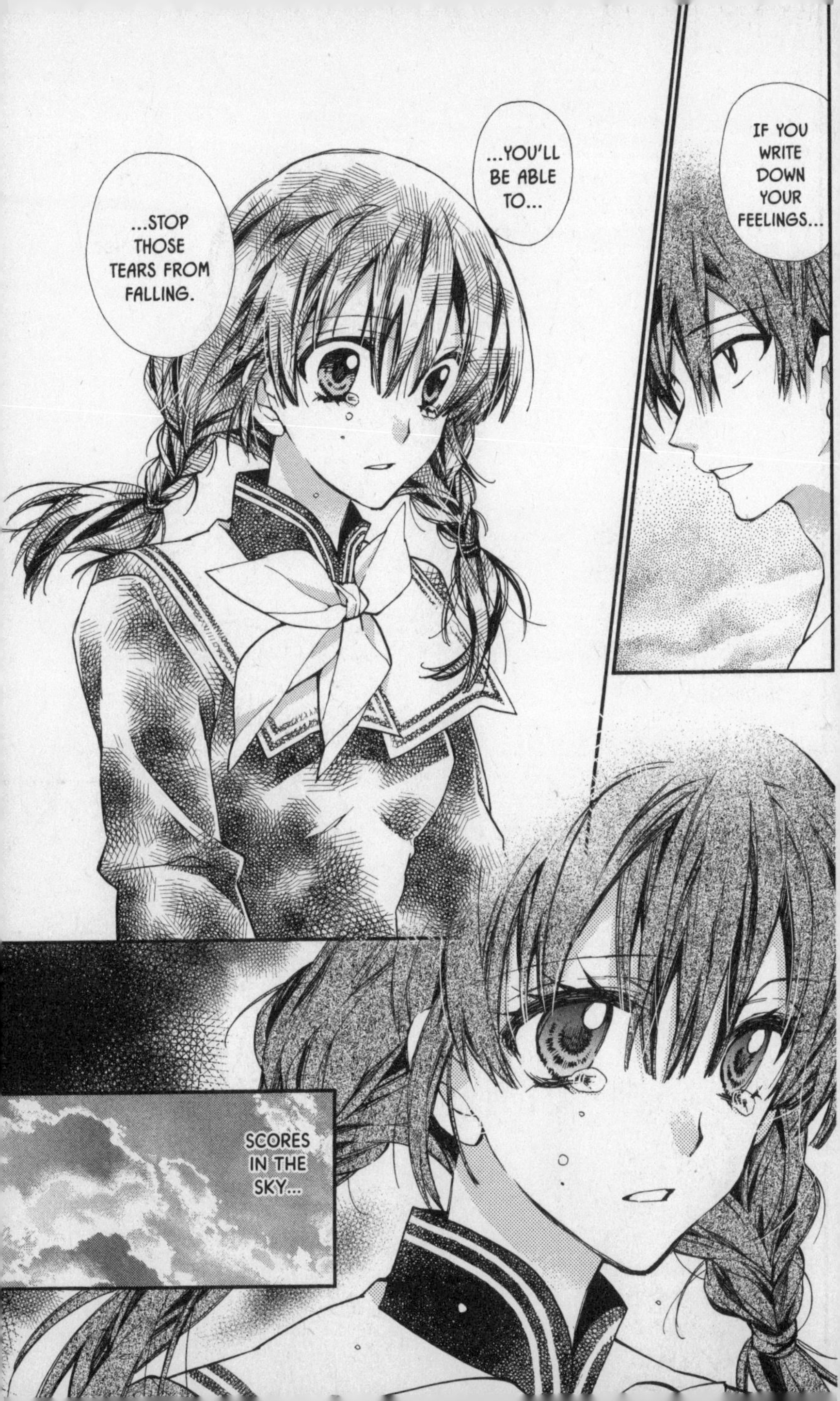
IF YOU WRITE DOWN YOUR FEELINGS...
...YOU'LL BE ABLE TO...
...STOP THOSE TEARS FROM FALLING.
SCORES IN THE SKY...

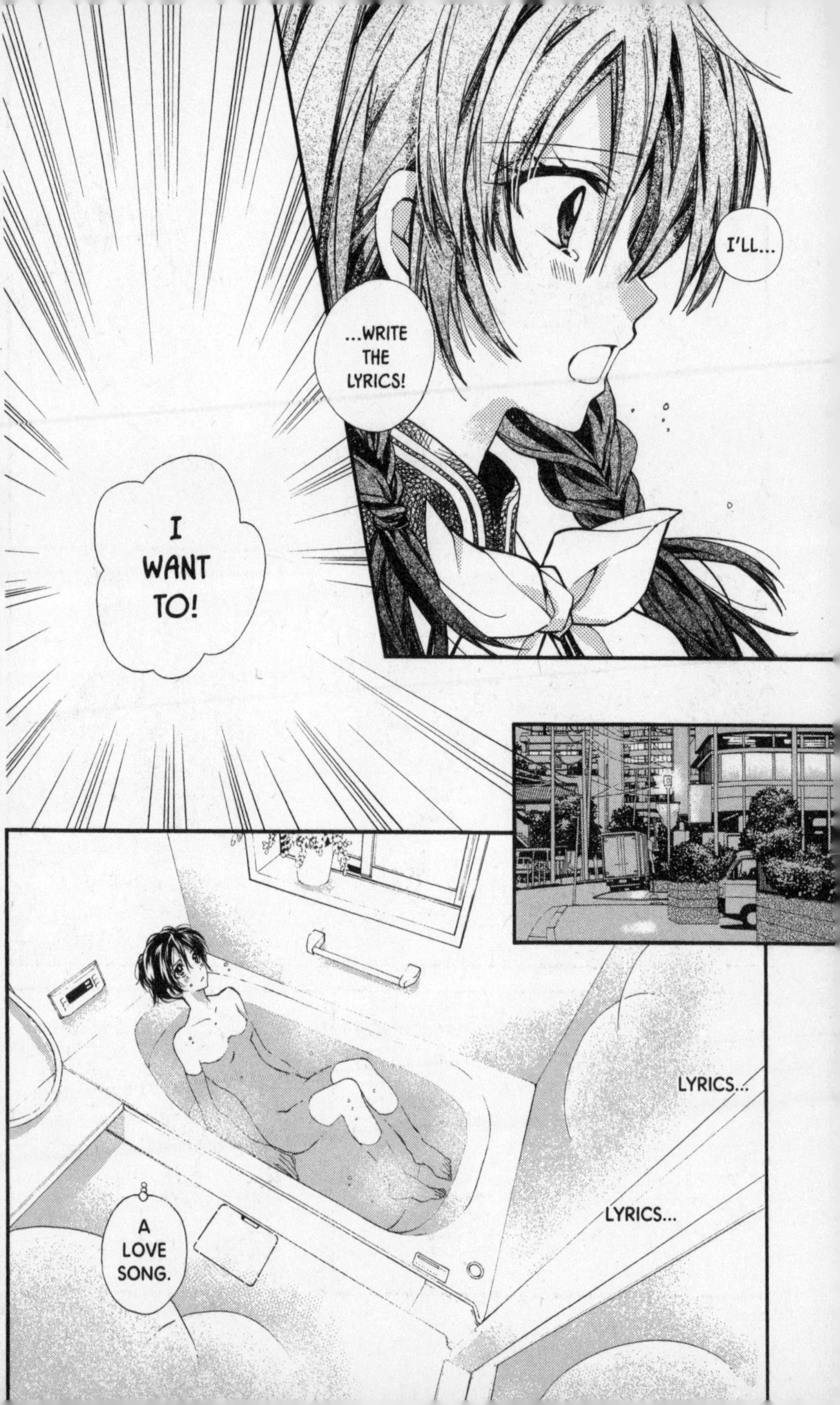
I'LL...
...WRITE THE LYRICS!
I WANT TO!
LYRICS...
LYRICS...
A LOVE SONG.

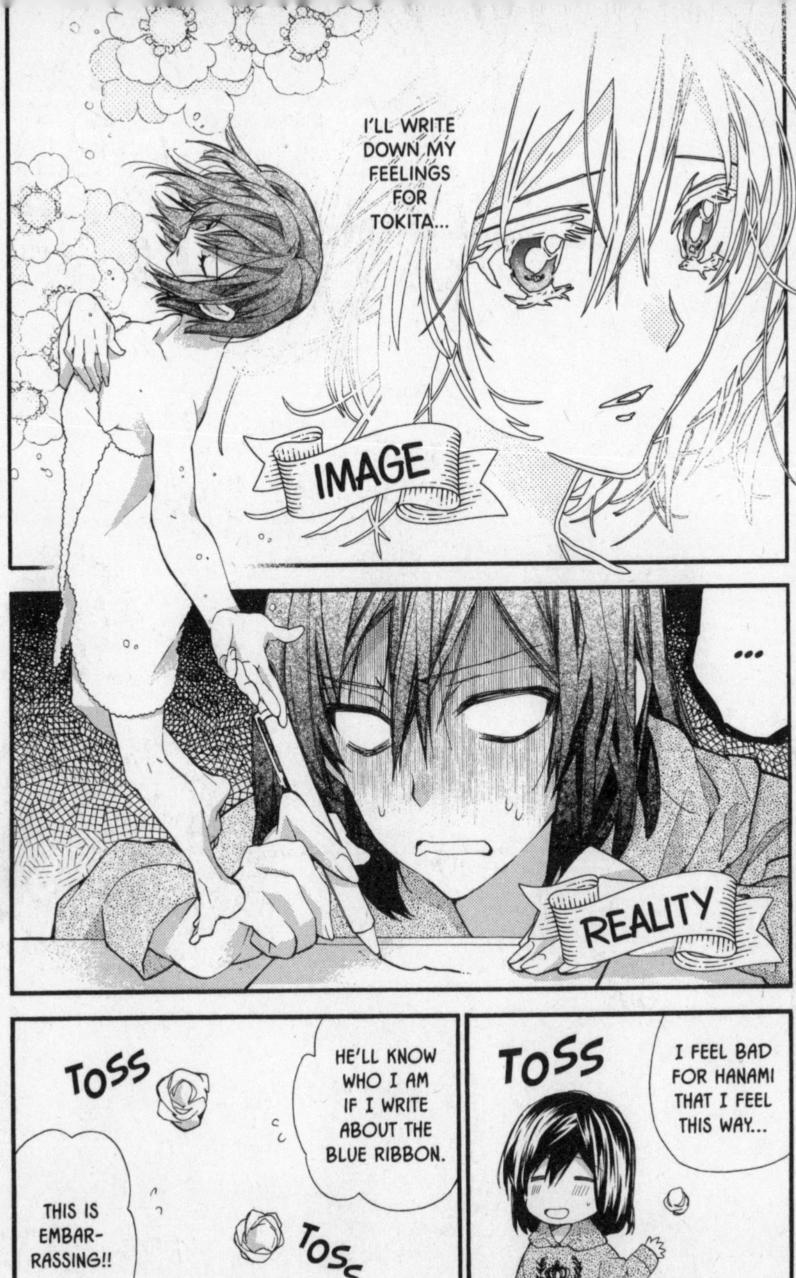
I'LL WRITE DOWN MY FEELINGS FOR TOKITA...
IMAGE
...
REALITY
I FEEL BAD FOR HANAMI THAT I FEEL THIS WAY...
TOSS
HE'LL KNOW WHO I AM IF I WRITE ABOUT THE BLUE RIBBON.
TOSS
TOSS
THIS IS EMBARRASSING!!

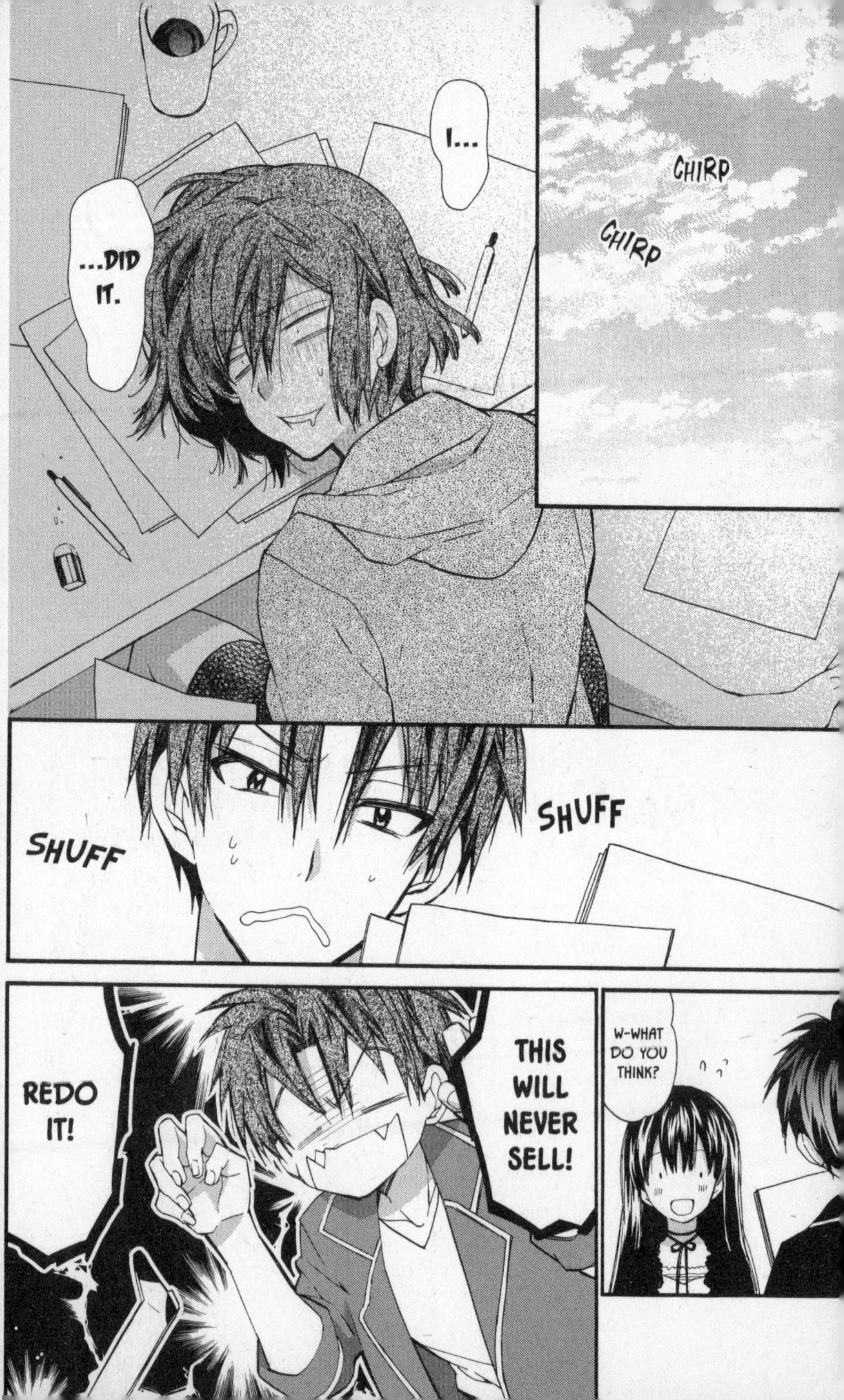
CHIRP
CHIRP
I...
...DID IT.
SHUFF
SHUFF
W-WHAT DO YOU THINK?
THIS WILL NEVER SELL!
REDO IT!

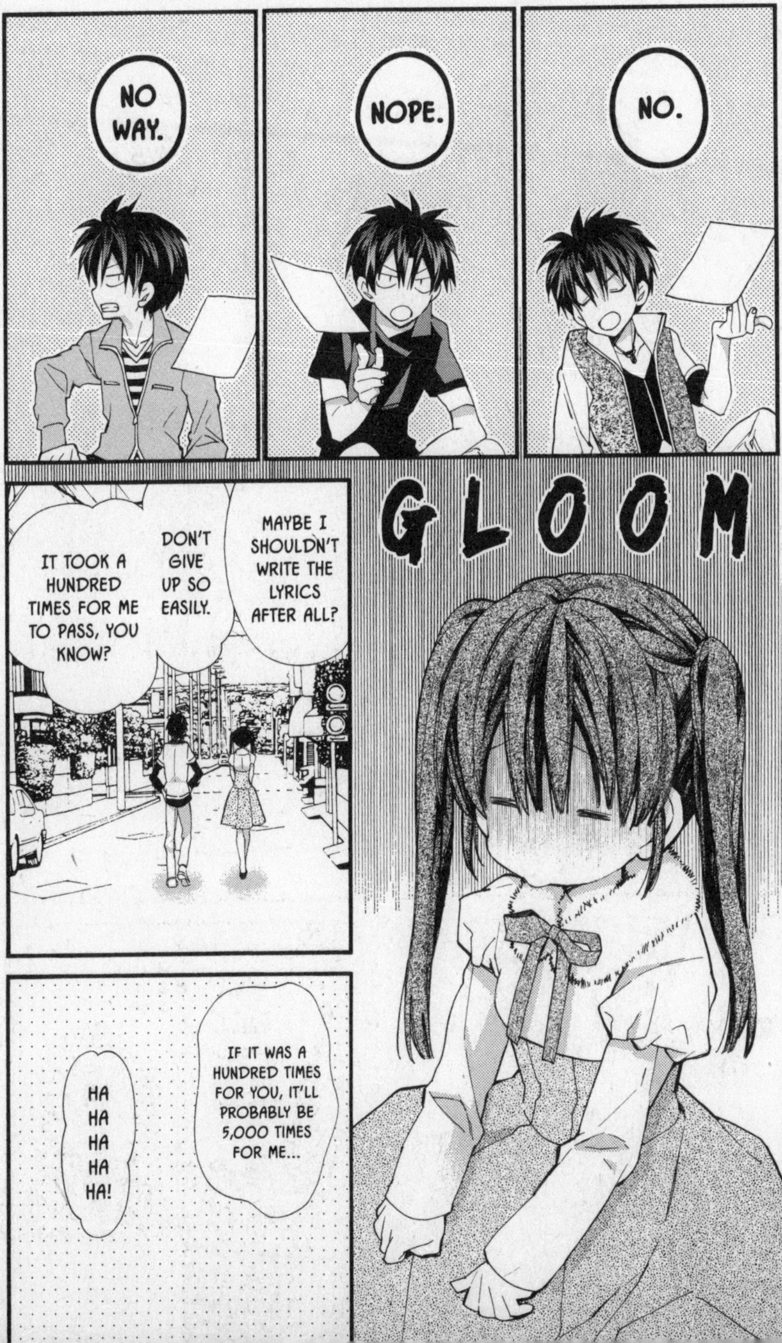
NO.
NOPE.
NO WAY.
GLOOM
MAYBE I SHOULDN'T WRITE THE LYRICS AFTER ALL?
DON'T GIVE UP SO EASILY.
IT TOOK A HUNDRED TIMES FOR ME TO PASS, YOU KNOW?
IF IT WAS A HUNDRED TIMES FOR YOU, IT'LL PROBABLY BE 5,000 TIMES FOR ME...
HA HA HA HA HA!

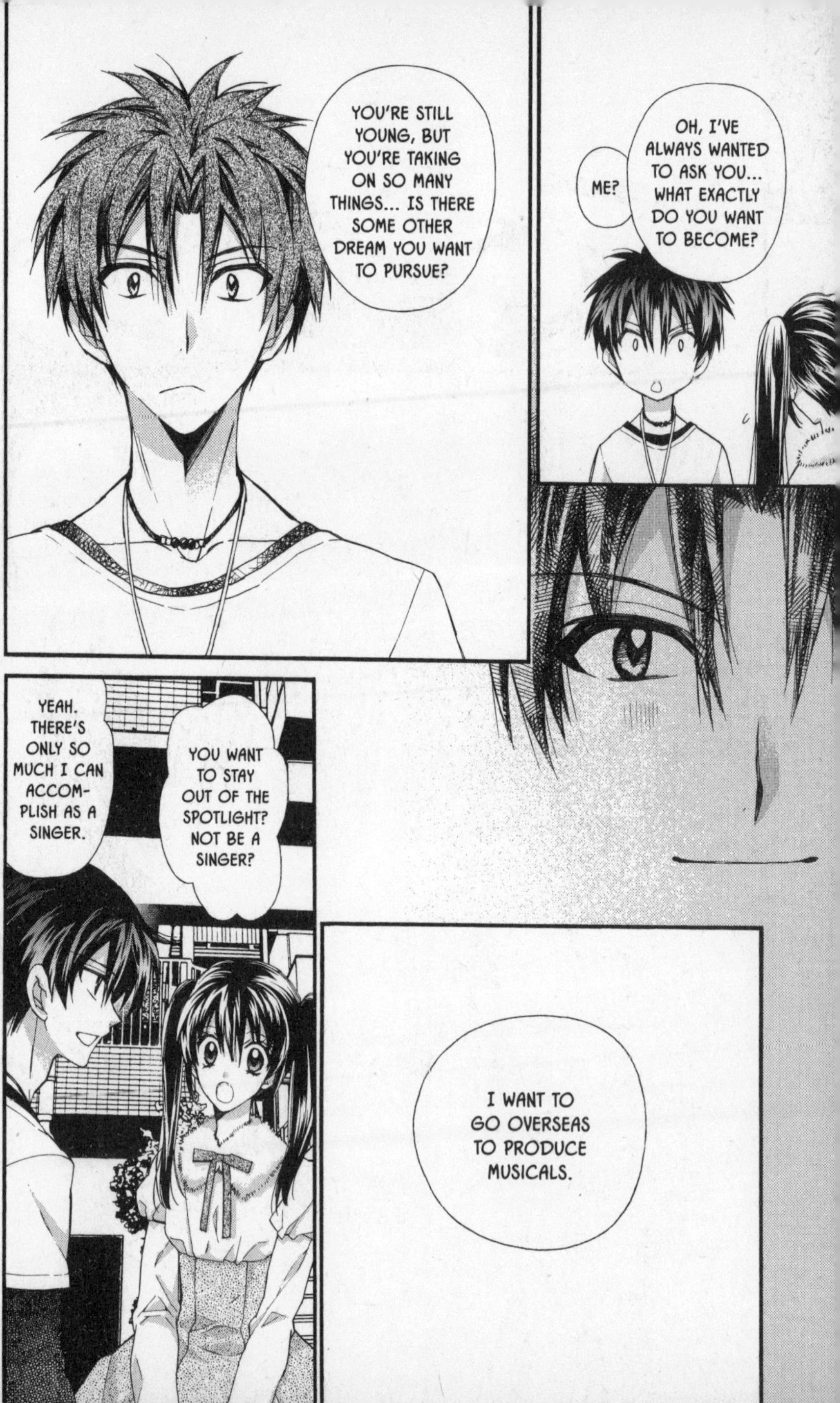
OH, I'VE ALWAYS WANTED TO ASK YOU... WHAT EXACTLY DO YOU WANT TO BECOME?
ME?
YOU'RE STILL YOUNG, BUT YOU'RE TAKING ON SO MANY THINGS... IS THERE SOME OTHER DREAM YOU WANT TO PURSUE?
I WANT TO GO OVERSEAS TO PRODUCE MUSICALS.
YOU WANT TO STAY OUT OF THE SPOTLIGHT? NOT BE A SINGER?
YEAH. THERE'S ONLY SO MUCH I CAN ACCOM-PLISH AS A SINGER.

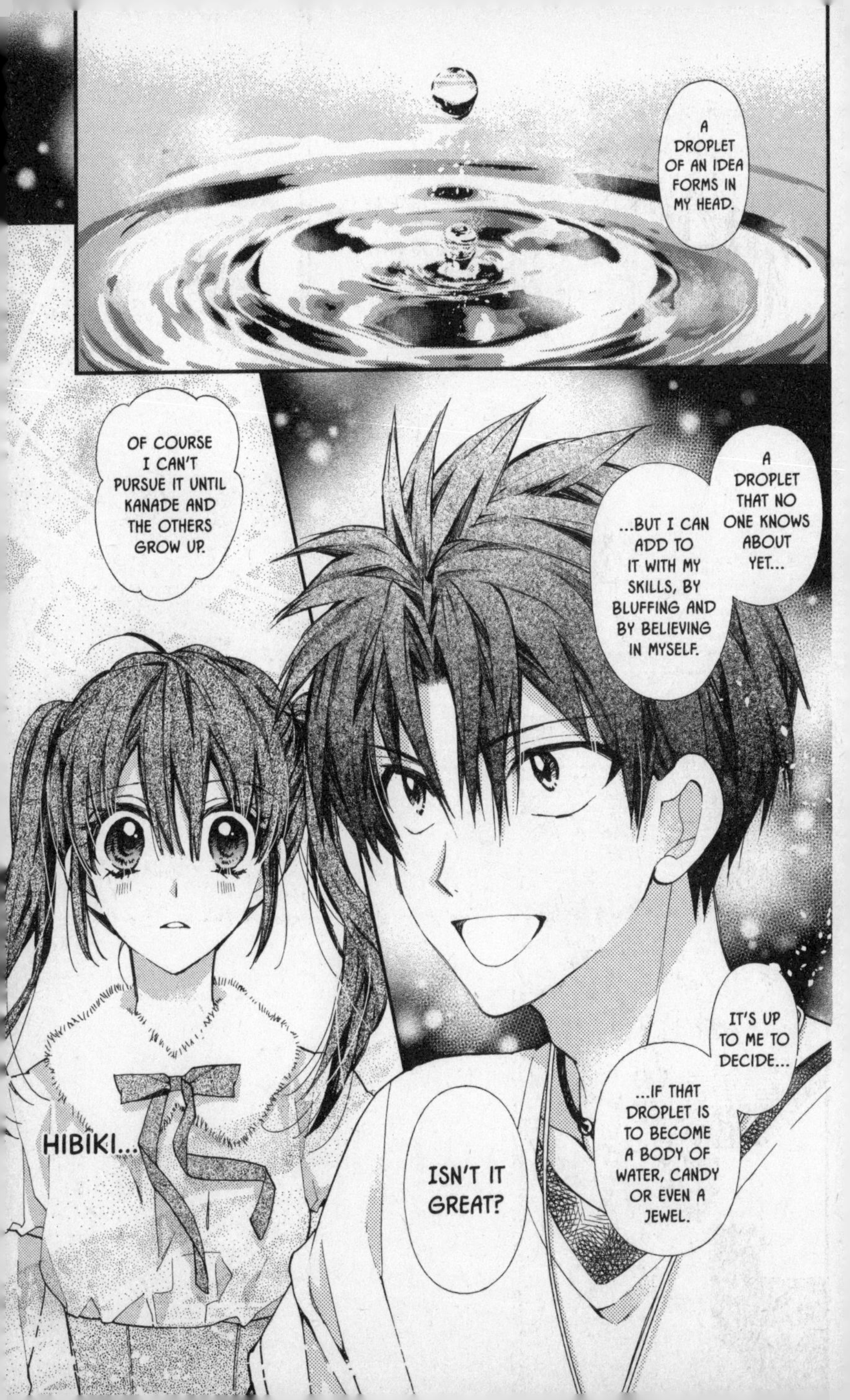
A DROPLET OF AN IDEA FORMS IN MY HEAD.
A DROPLET THAT NO ONE KNOWS ABOUT YET...
...BUT I CAN ADD TO IT WITH MY SKILLS, BY BLUFFING AND BY BELIEVING IN MYSELF.
OF COURSE I CAN'T PURSUE IT UNTIL KANADE AND THE OTHERS GROW UP.
IT'S UP TO ME TO DECIDE...
...IF THAT DROPLET IS TO BECOME A BODY OF WATER, CANDY OR EVEN A JEWEL.
ISN'T IT GREAT?
HIBIKI...

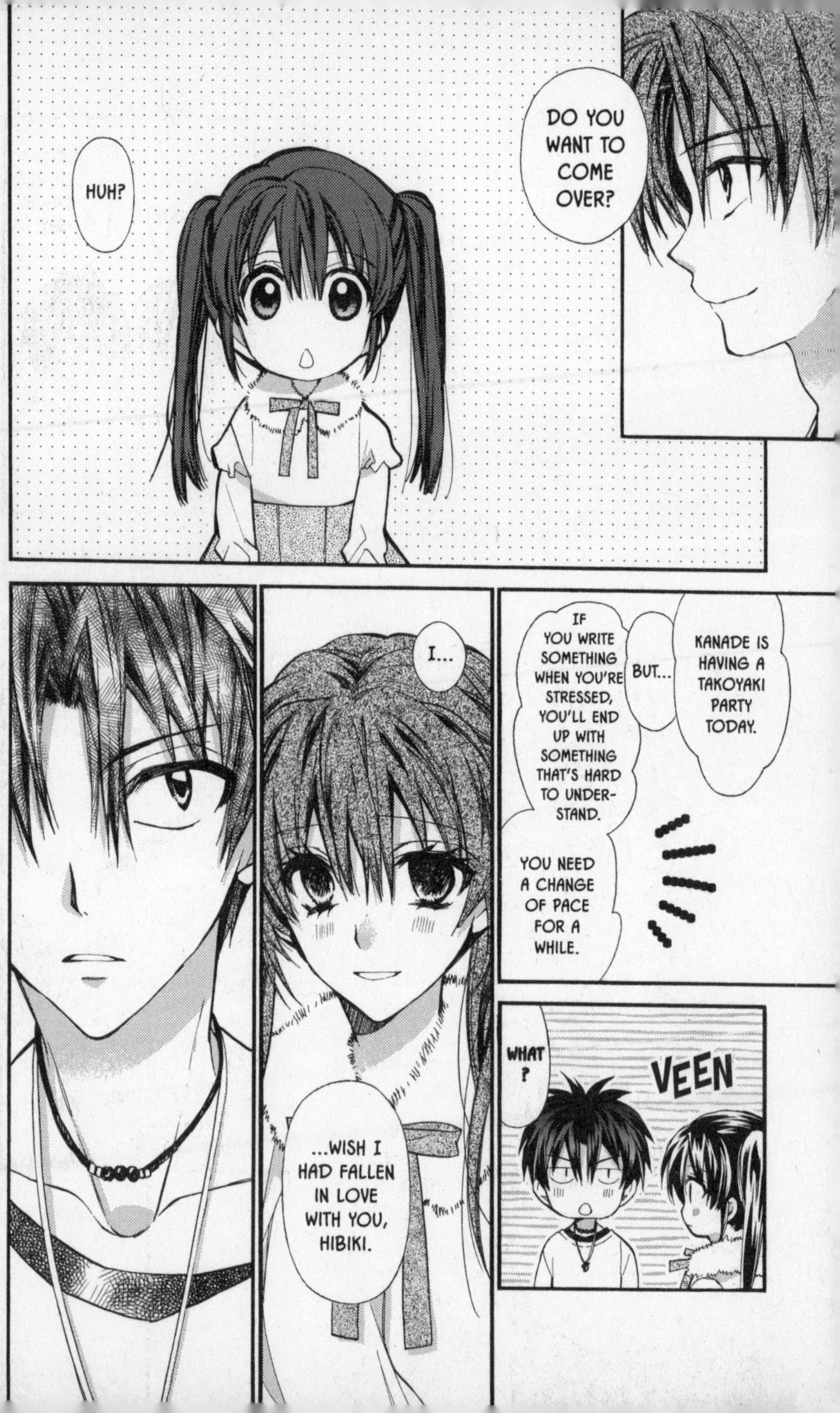
DO YOU WANT TO COME OVER?
HUH?
KANADE IS HAVING A TAKOYAKI PARTY TODAY.
BUT...
IF YOU WRITE SOMETHING WHEN YOU'RE STRESSED, YOU'LL END UP WITH SOMETHING THAT'S HARD TO UNDER-STAND.
YOU NEED A CHANGE OF PACE FOR A WHILE.
WHAT?
VEEN
I...
...WISH I HAD FALLEN IN LOVE WITH YOU, HIBIKI.

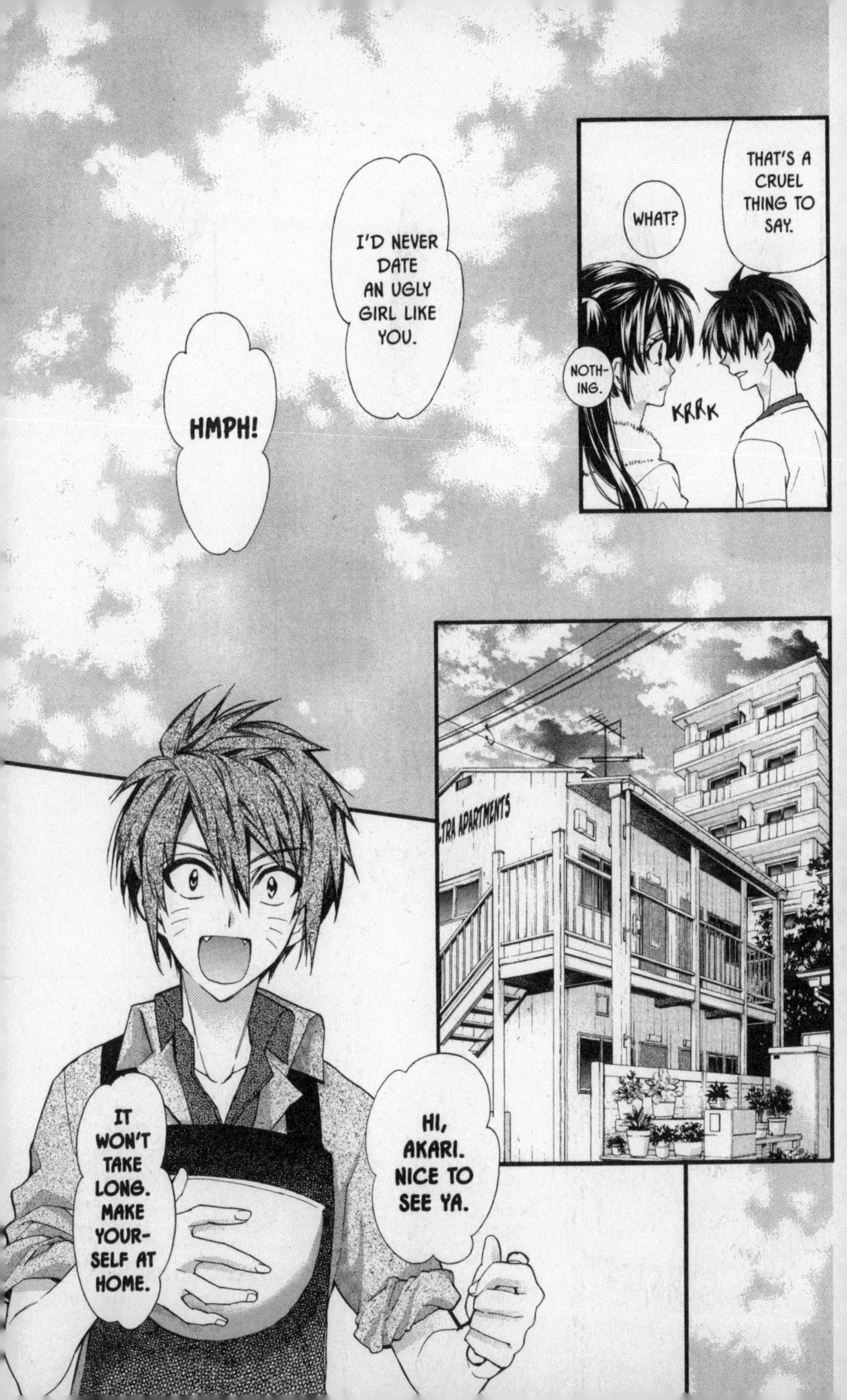
THAT'S A CRUEL THING TO SAY.
WHAT?
NOTH-ING.
KRRK
I'D NEVER DATE AN UGLY GIRL LIKE YOU.
HMPH!
LTRA APARTMENTS
HI, AKARI. NICE TO SEE YA.
IT WON'T TAKE LONG. MAKE YOUR-SELF AT HOME.

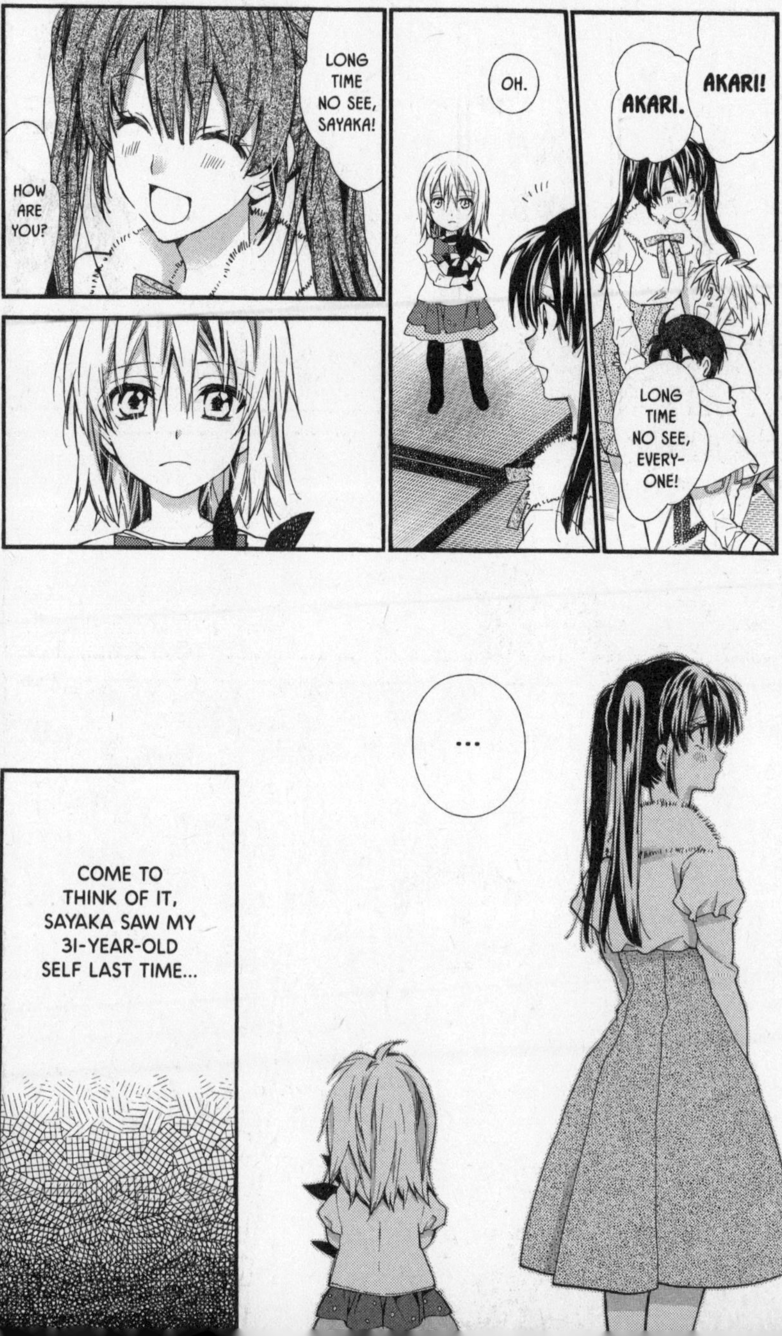
AKARI!
AKARI.
LONG TIME NO SEE, EVERYONE!
OH.
LONG TIME NO SEE, SAYAKA!
HOW ARE YOU?
...
COME TO THINK OF IT, SAYAKA SAW MY 31-YEAR-OLD SELF LAST TIME...

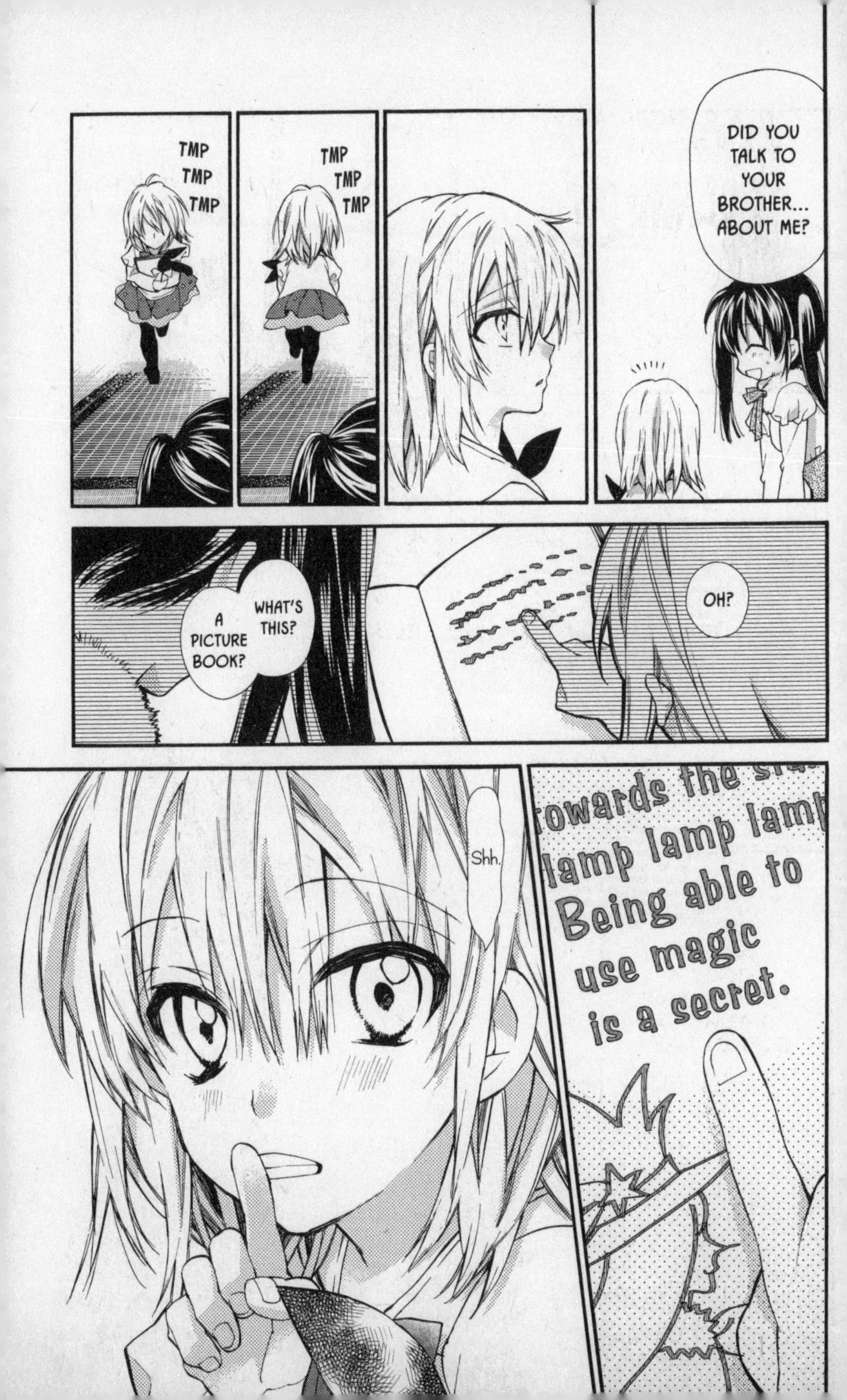
DID YOU TALK TO YOUR BROTHER... ABOUT ME?
TMP TMP TMP
TMP TMP TMP
OH?
WHAT'S THIS?
A PICTURE BOOK?
lamp lamp
Being able to use magic is a secret.
Shh.

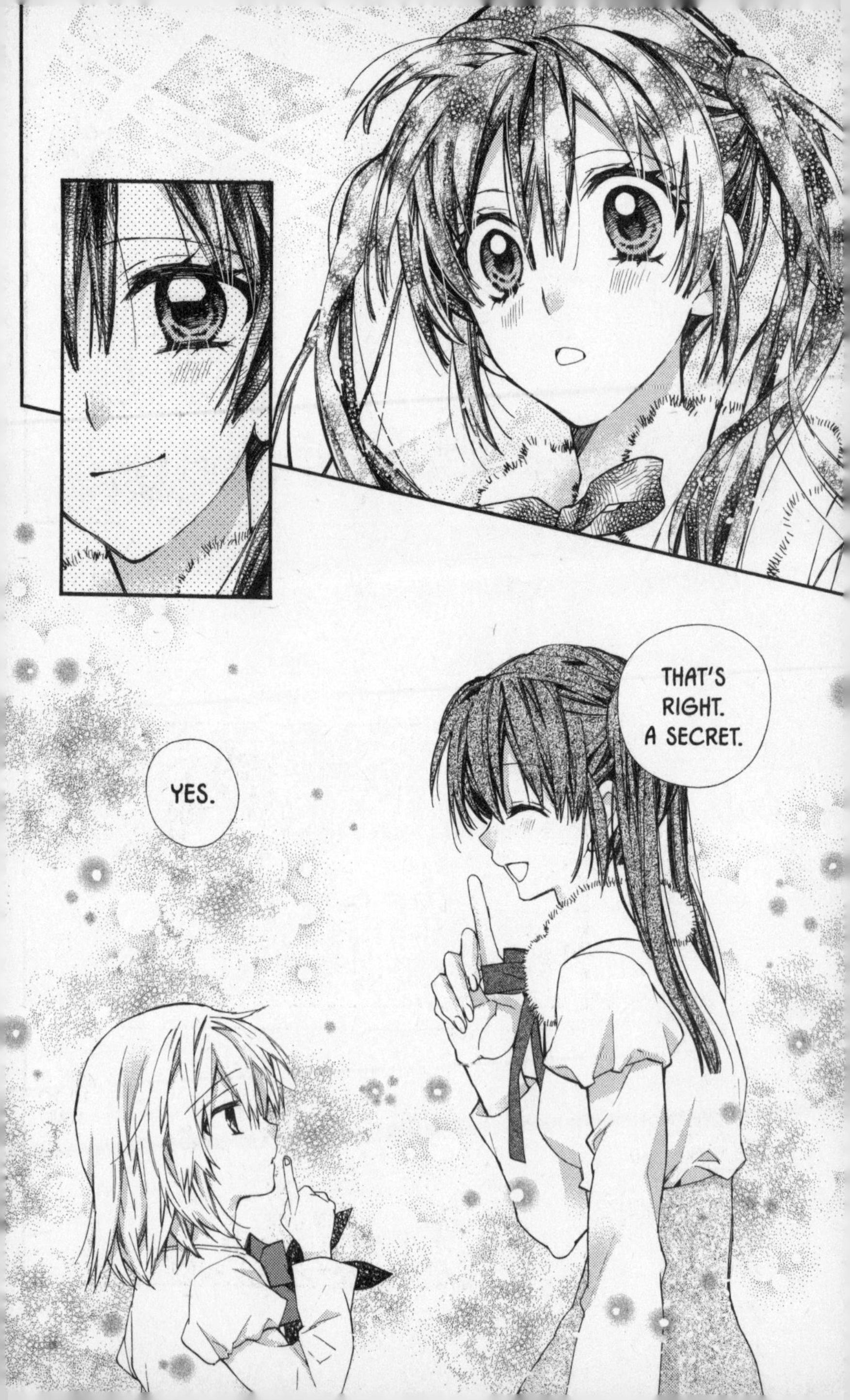
THAT'S RIGHT. A SECRET.
YES.

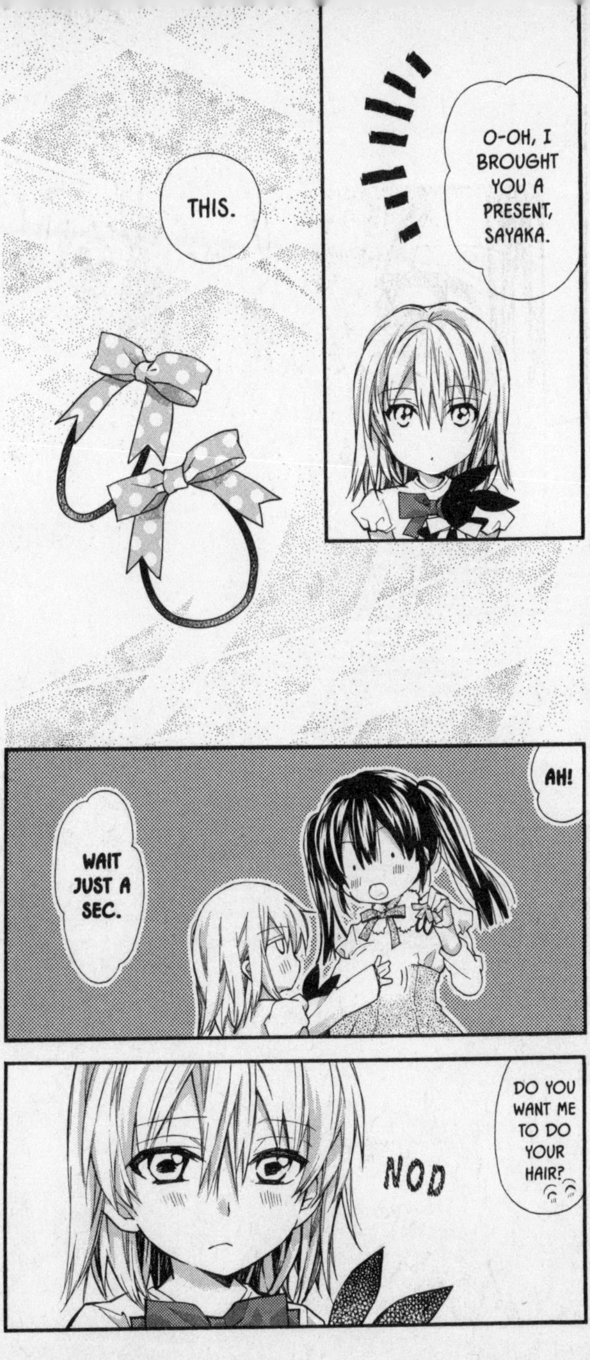
O-OH, I BROUGHT YOU A PRESENT, SAYAKA.
THIS.
AH!
WAIT JUST A SEC.
DO YOU WANT ME TO DO YOUR HAIR?
NOD

IDOL dreams

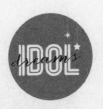

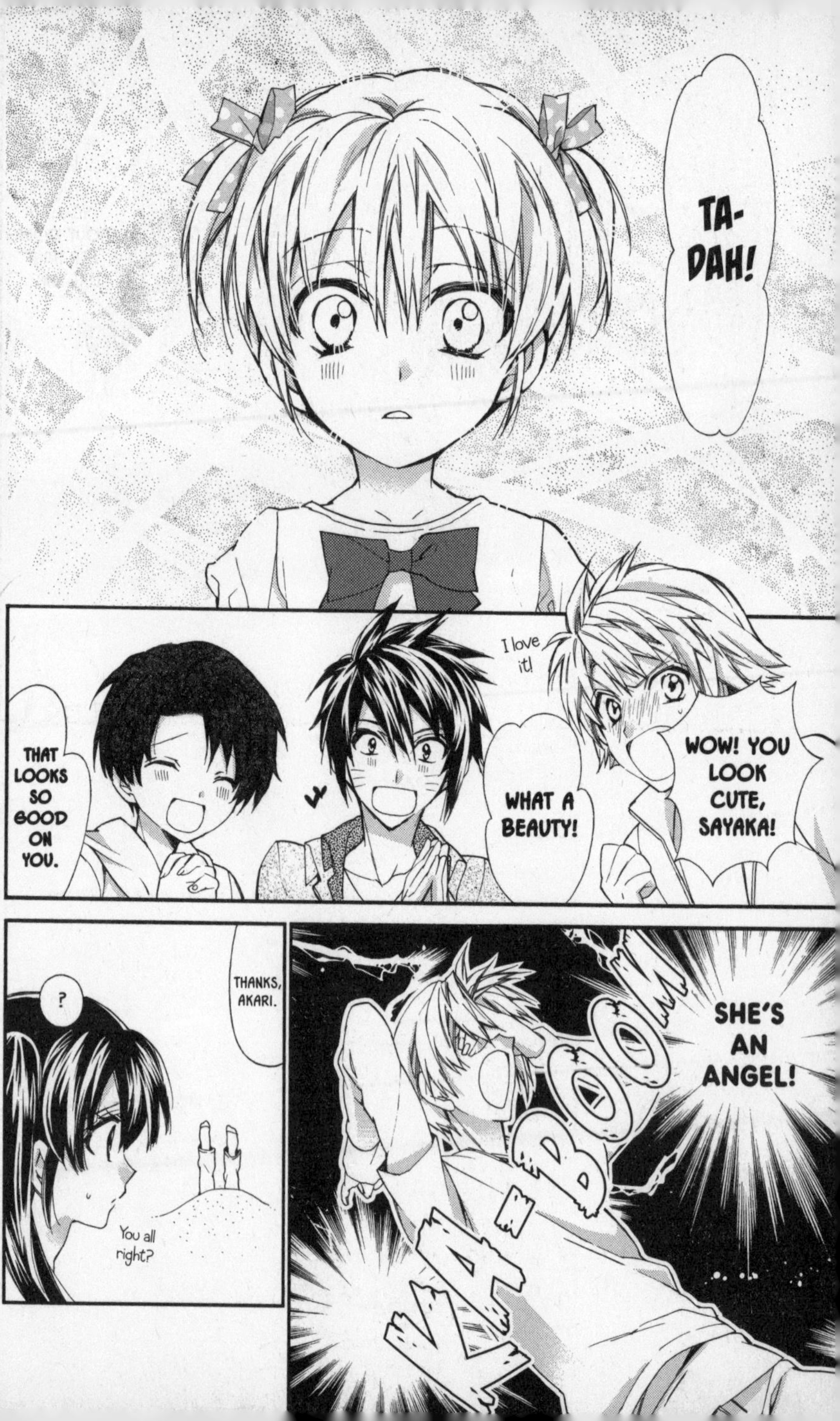
TA-DAH!
WOW! YOU LOOK CUTE, SAYAKA!
I love it!
WHAT A BEAUTY!
THAT LOOKS SO GOOD ON YOU.
SHE'S AN ANGEL!
KA-BOOM
THANKS, AKARI.
?
You all right?

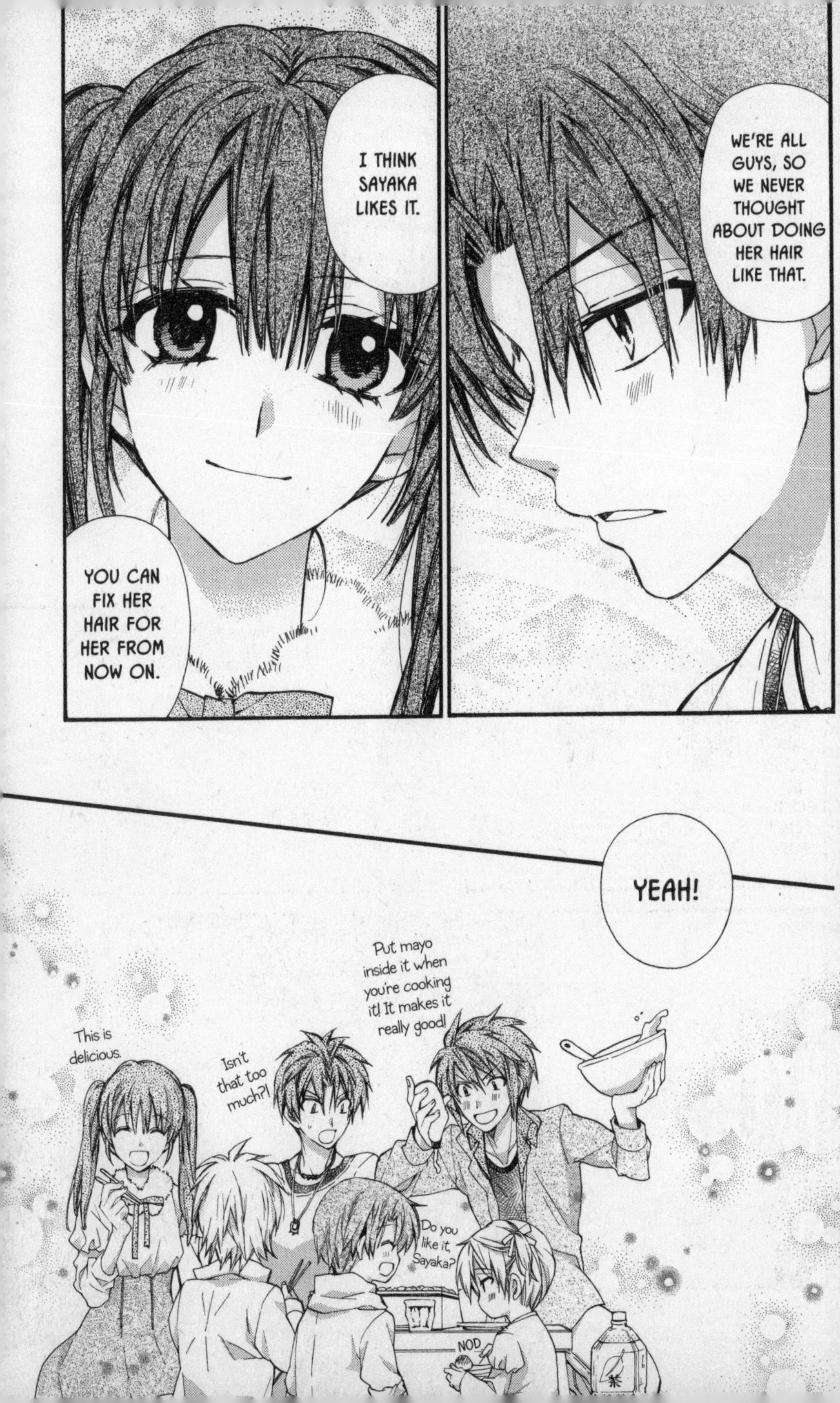
WE'RE ALL GUYS, SO WE NEVER THOUGHT ABOUT DOING HER HAIR LIKE THAT.
I THINK SAYAKA LIKES IT.
YOU CAN FIX HER HAIR FOR HER FROM NOW ON.
YEAH!
Put mayo inside it when you're cooking it! It makes it really good!
Isn't that too much?!
This is delicious.
Do you like it, Sayaka?
NOD

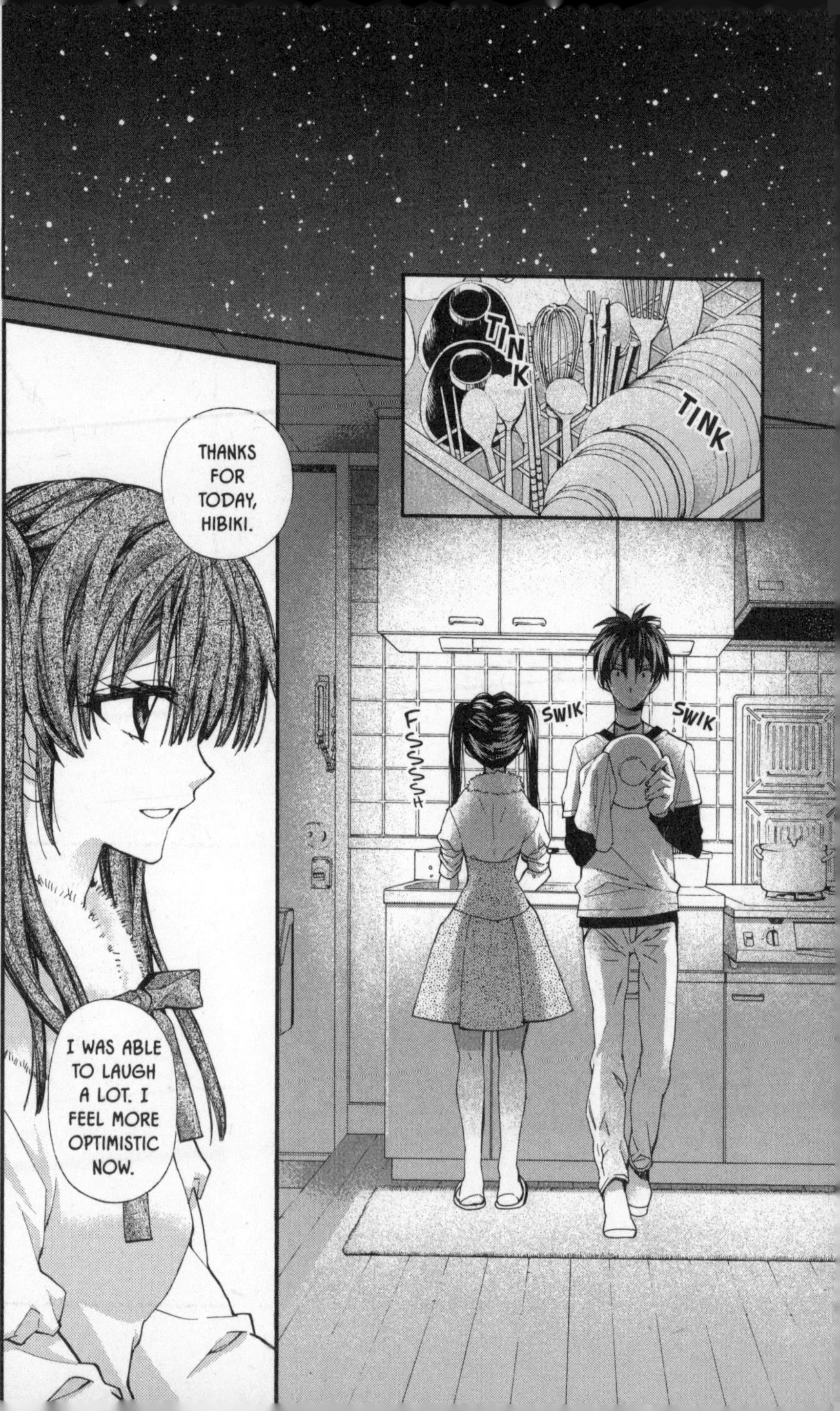
TINK
TINK
SWIK
SWIK
FSSSSSH
THANKS FOR TODAY, HIBIKI.
I WAS ABLE TO LAUGH A LOT. I FEEL MORE OPTIMISTIC NOW.

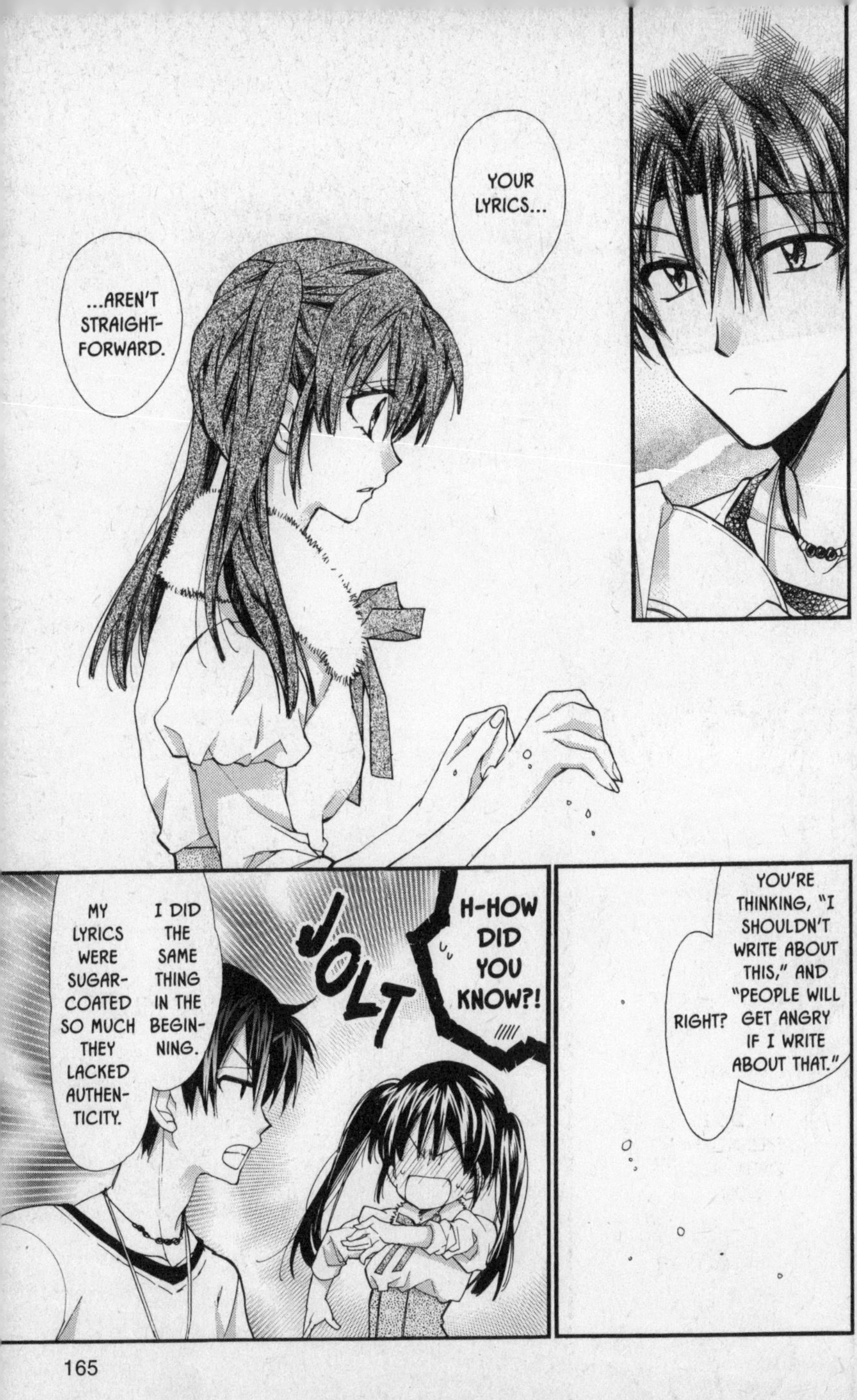
YOUR LYRICS...
...AREN'T STRAIGHT-FORWARD.
YOU'RE THINKING, "I SHOULDN'T WRITE ABOUT THIS," AND "PEOPLE WILL GET ANGRY IF I WRITE ABOUT THAT."
RIGHT?
H-HOW DID YOU KNOW?!
JOLT
I DID THE SAME THING IN THE BEGINNING.
MY LYRICS WERE SUGAR-COATED SO MUCH THEY LACKED AUTHENTICITY.

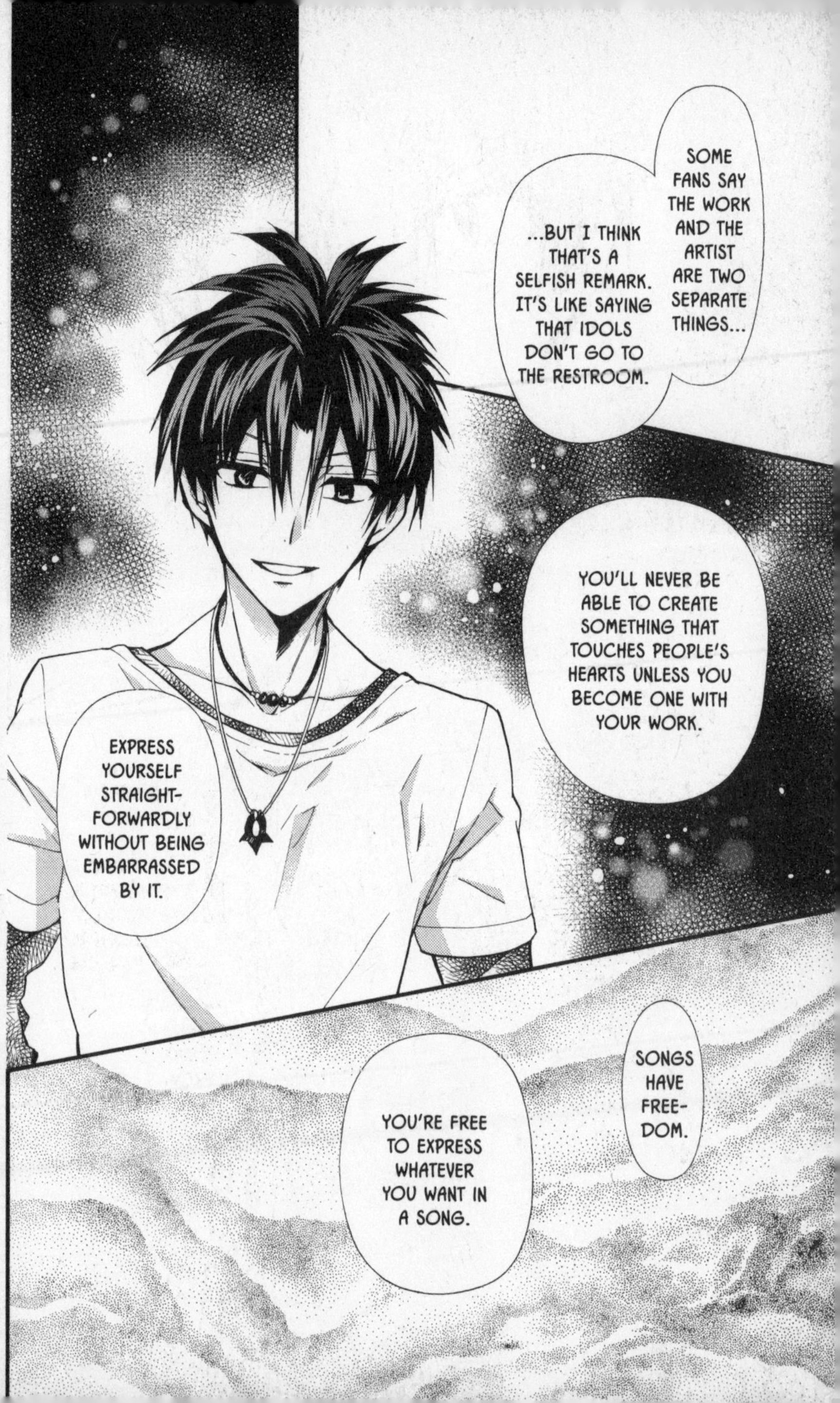
SOME FANS SAY THE WORK AND THE ARTIST ARE TWO SEPARATE THINGS...
...BUT I THINK THAT'S A SELFISH REMARK. IT'S LIKE SAYING THAT IDOLS DON'T GO TO THE RESTROOM.
YOU'LL NEVER BE ABLE TO CREATE SOMETHING THAT TOUCHES PEOPLE'S HEARTS UNLESS YOU BECOME ONE WITH YOUR WORK.
EXPRESS YOURSELF STRAIGHT-FORWARDLY WITHOUT BEING EMBARRASSED BY IT.
SONGS HAVE FREE-DOM.
YOU'RE FREE TO EXPRESS WHATEVER YOU WANT IN A SONG.

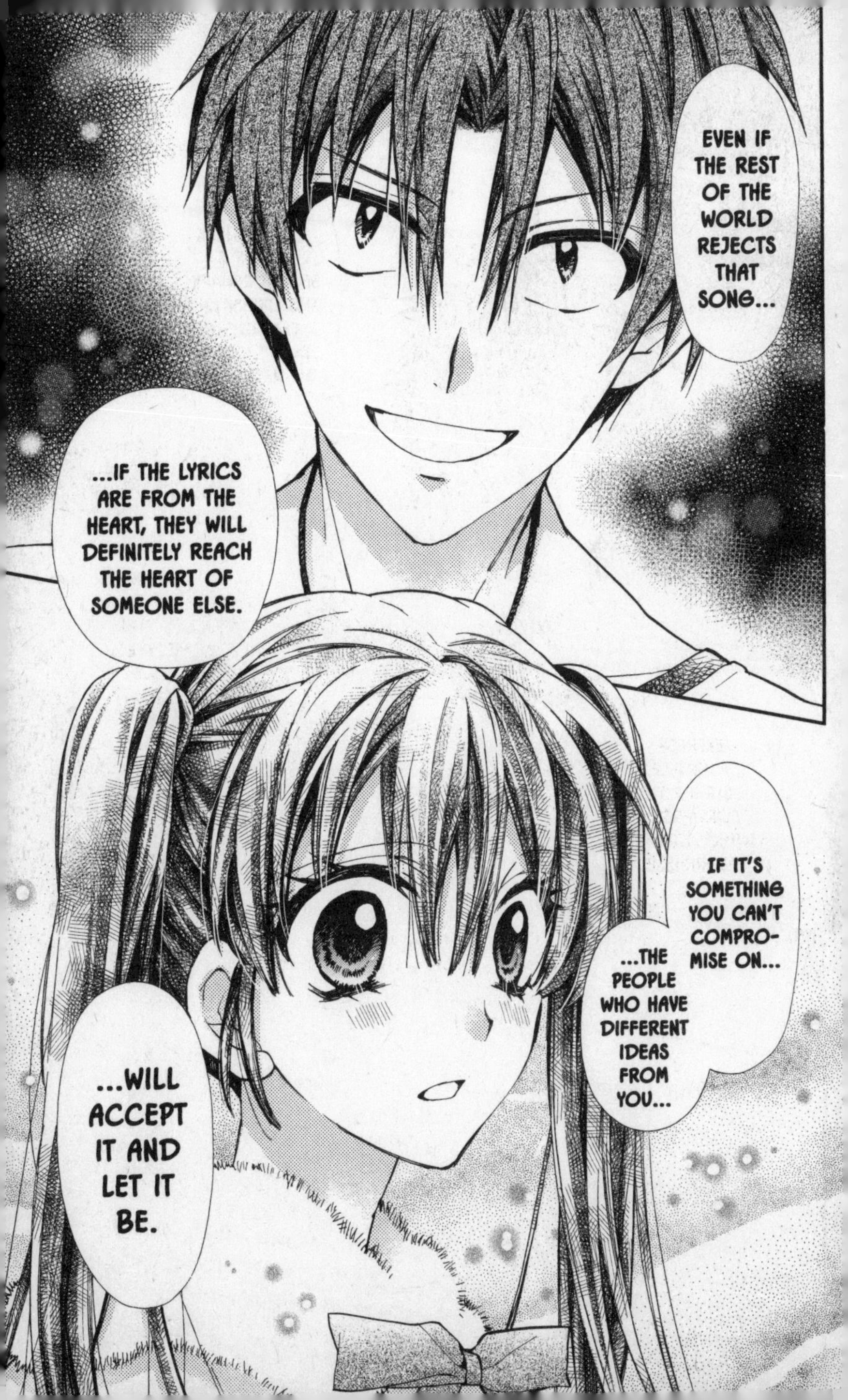
EVEN IF THE REST OF THE WORLD REJECTS THAT SONG...
...IF THE LYRICS ARE FROM THE HEART, THEY WILL DEFINITELY REACH THE HEART OF SOMEONE ELSE.
IF IT'S SOMETHING YOU CAN'T COMPRO-MISE ON...
...THE PEOPLE WHO HAVE DIFFERENT IDEAS FROM YOU...
...WILL ACCEPT IT AND LET IT BE.

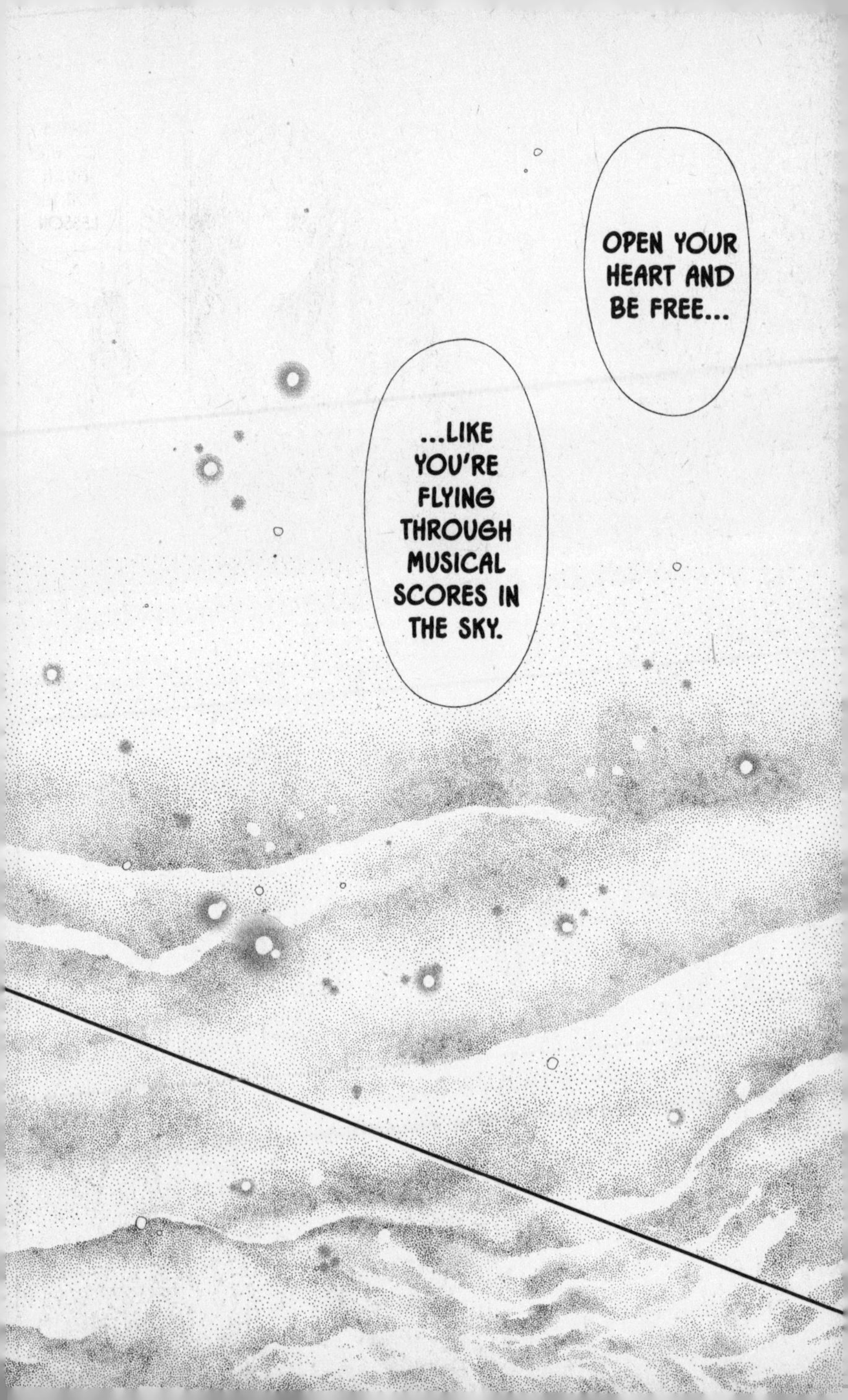
OPEN YOUR HEART AND BE FREE...
...LIKE YOU'RE FLYING THROUGH MUSICAL SCORES IN THE SKY.

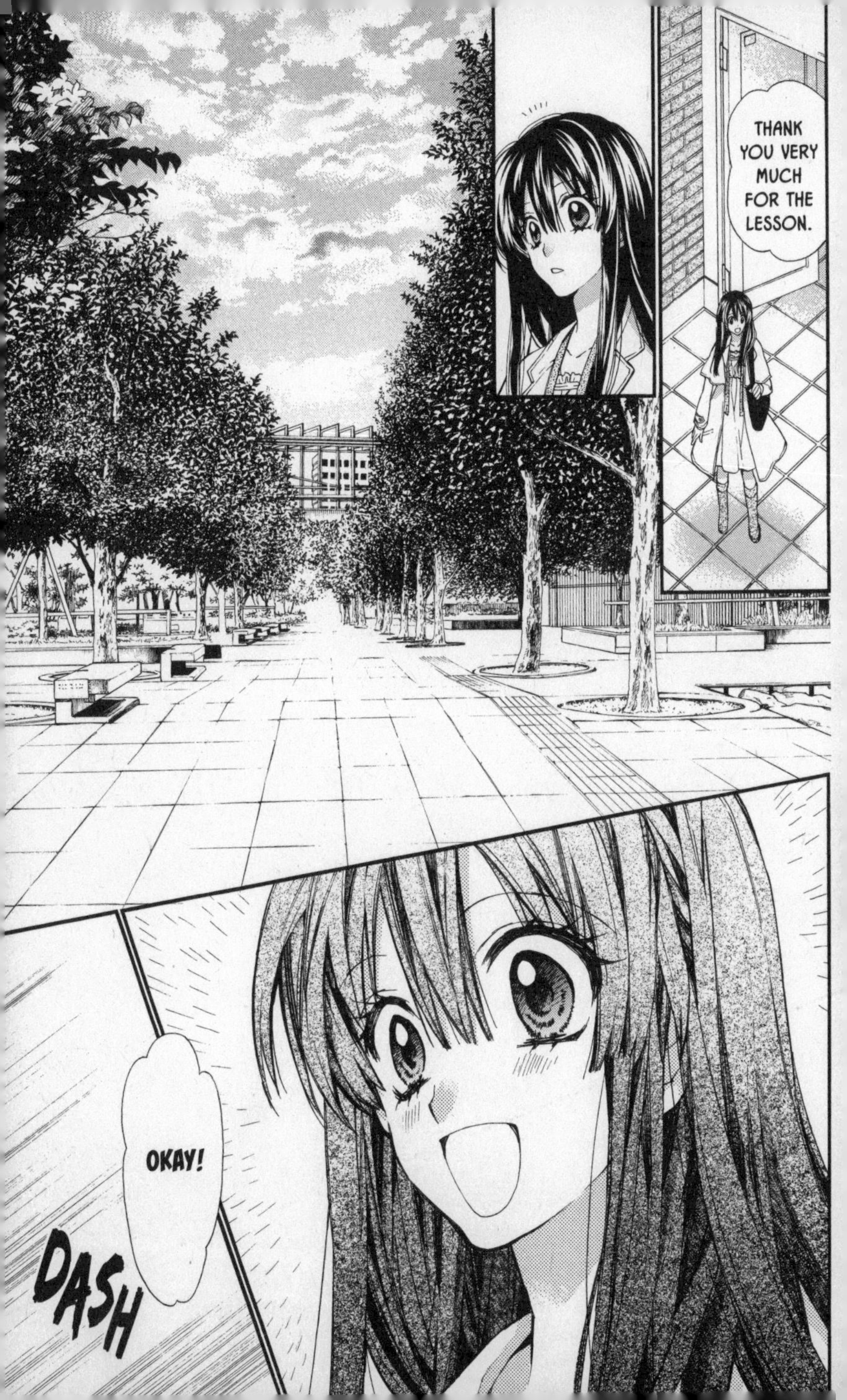
THANK YOU VERY MUCH FOR THE LESSON.
OKAY!
DASH

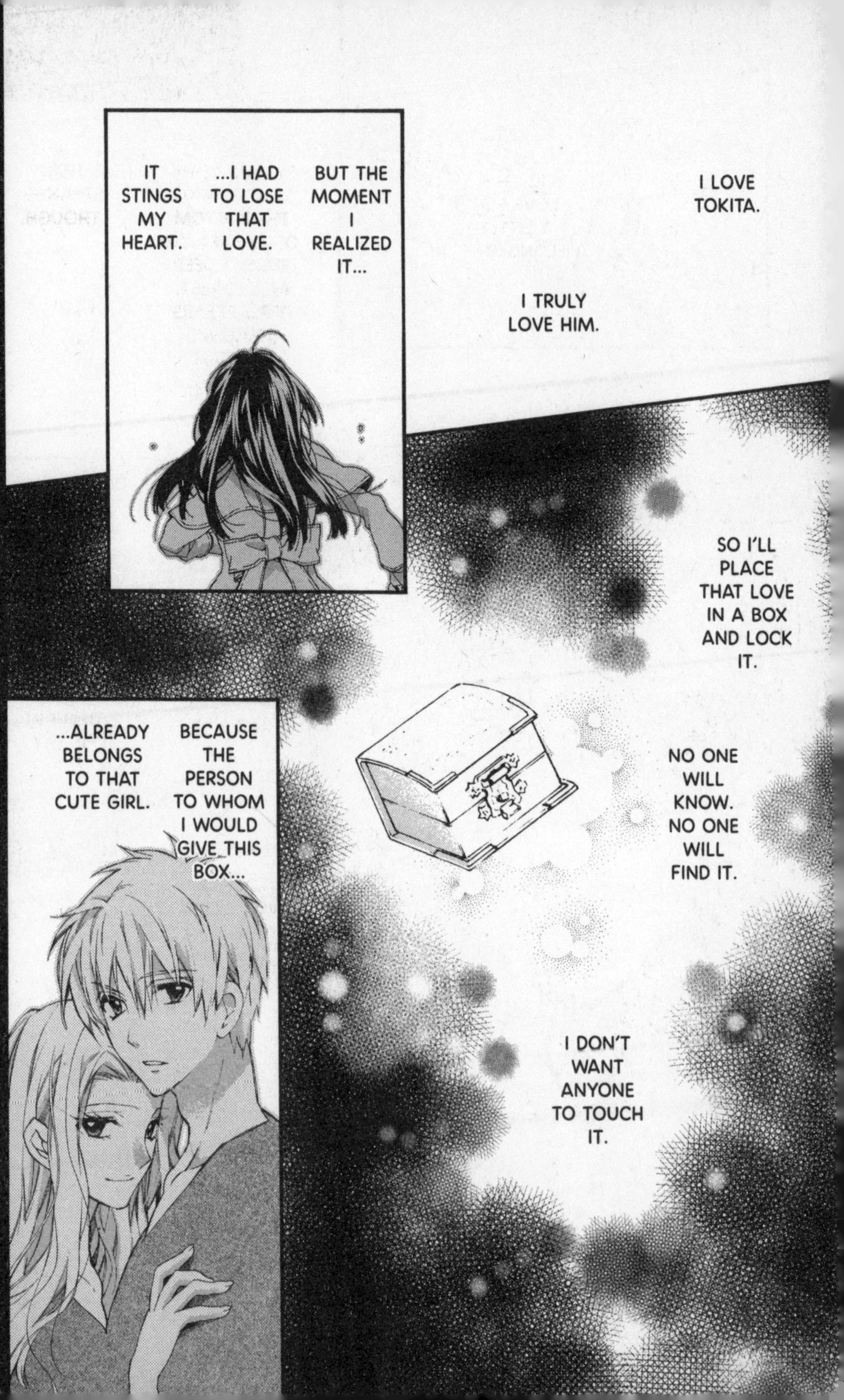
I LOVE TOKITA.
I TRULY LOVE HIM.
BUT THE MOMENT I REALIZED IT...
...I HAD TO LOSE THAT LOVE.
IT STINGS MY HEART.
SO I'LL PLACE THAT LOVE IN A BOX AND LOCK IT.
NO ONE WILL KNOW. NO ONE WILL FIND IT.
I DON'T WANT ANYONE TO TOUCH IT.
BECAUSE THE PERSON TO WHOM I WOULD GIVE THIS BOX...
...ALREADY BELONGS TO THAT CUTE GIRL.

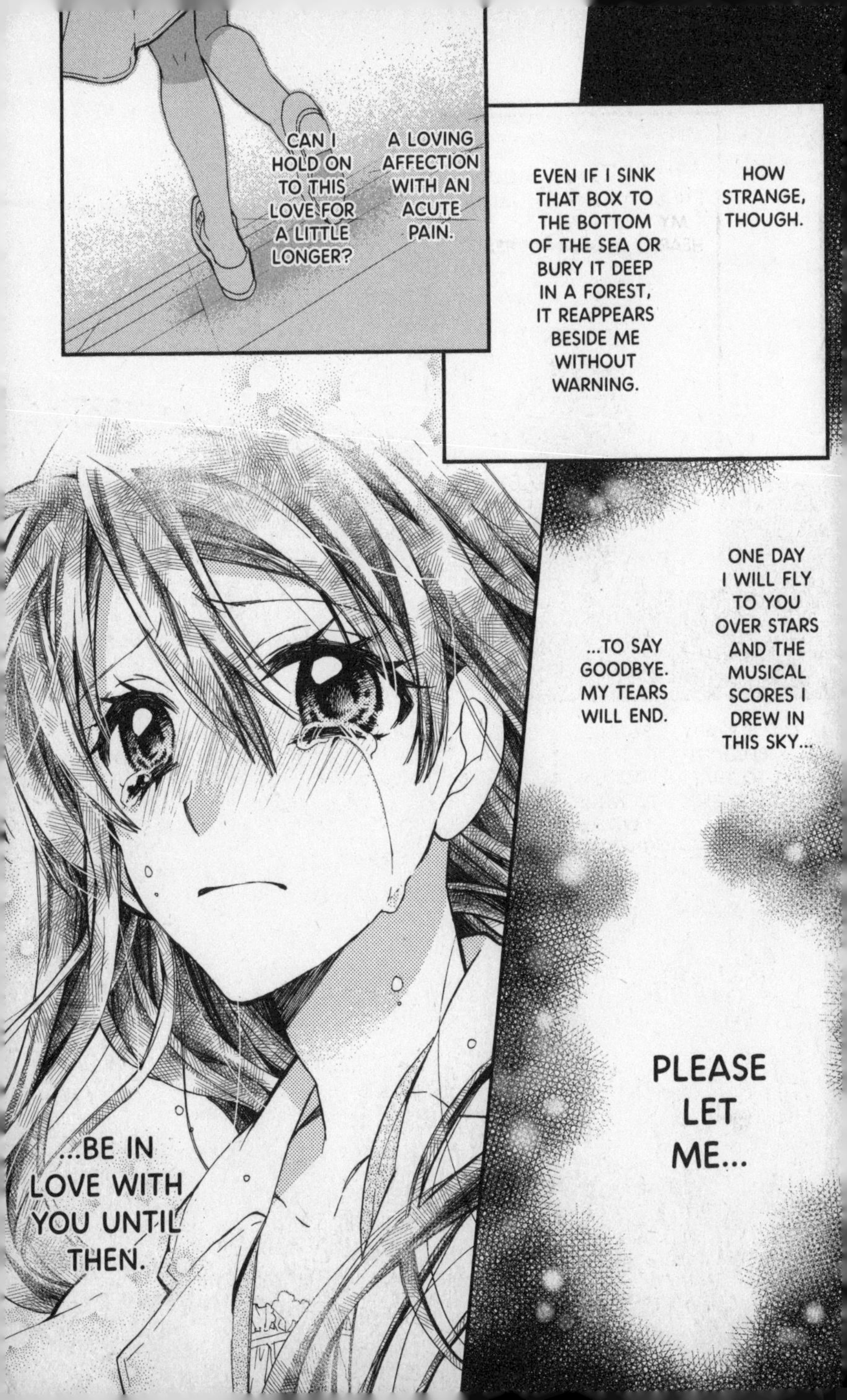
HOW STRANGE, THOUGH.
EVEN IF I SINK THAT BOX TO THE BOTTOM OF THE SEA OR BURY IT DEEP IN A FOREST, IT REAPPEARS BESIDE ME WITHOUT WARNING.
A LOVING AFFECTION WITH AN ACUTE PAIN.
CAN I HOLD ON TO THIS LOVE FOR A LITTLE LONGER?
ONE DAY I WILL FLY TO YOU OVER STARS AND THE MUSICAL SCORES I DREW IN THIS SKY...
...TO SAY GOODBYE. MY TEARS WILL END.
PLEASE LET ME...
...BE IN LOVE WITH YOU UNTIL THEN.

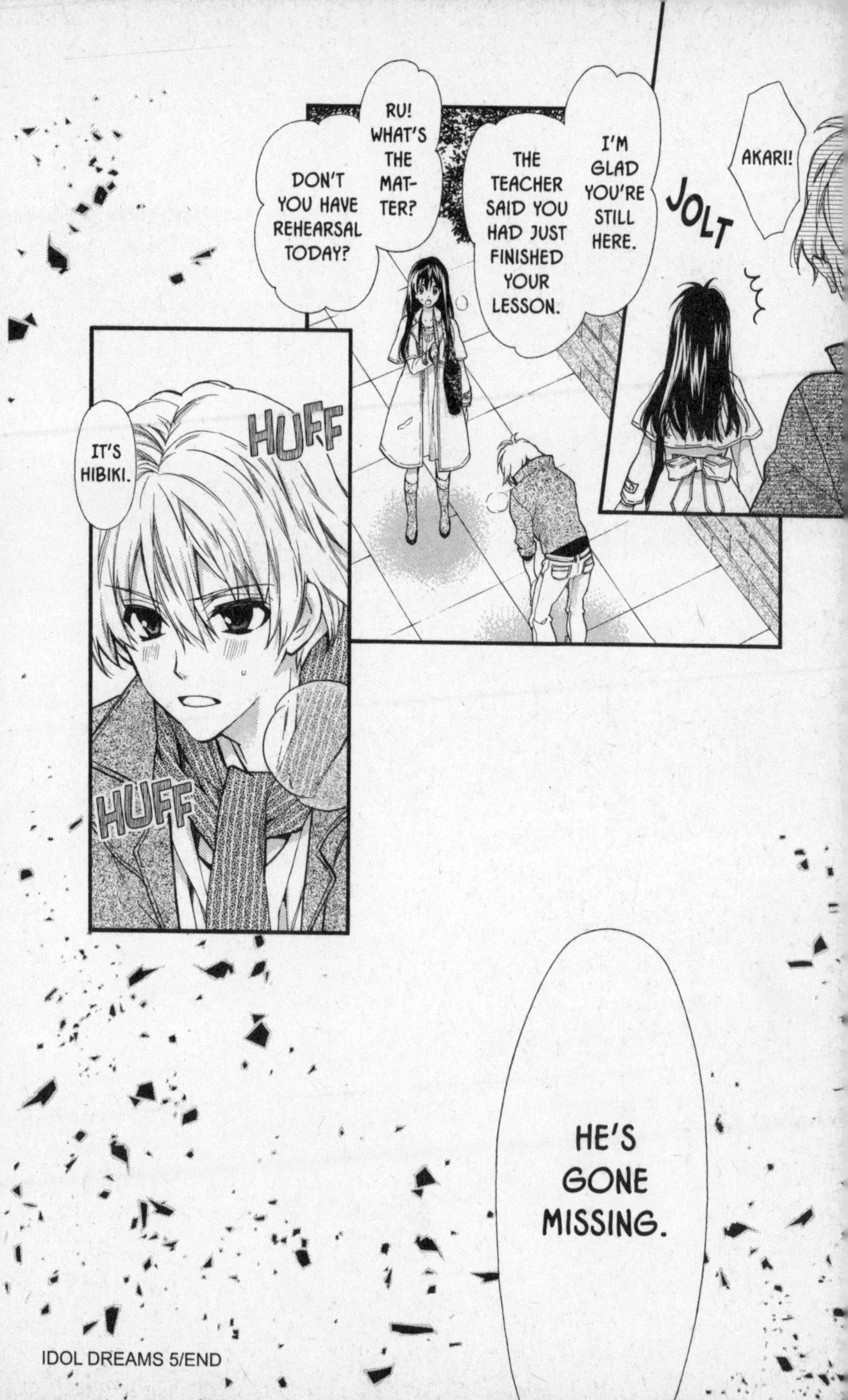
AKARI!
JOLT
I'M GLAD YOU'RE STILL HERE.
THE TEACHER SAID YOU HAD JUST FINISHED YOUR LESSON.
RU! WHAT'S THE MAT-TER?
DON'T YOU HAVE REHEARSAL TODAY?
HUFF
IT'S HIBIKI.
HUFF
HE'S GONE MISSING.

IDOL DREAMS 5/END

IDOL dreams

Tokita's girlfriend, who has been hiding in the dark since the beginning of the series, finally makes her appearance! Personally, I like them quite a lot as a couple, but what do you think? The scene at the convenience store was very tough to draw even when I was working on the rough draft, but thanks to my background artwork assistant, I managed to create something exactly as I had imagined in my head. Thank you so much!

ARINA TANEMURA

Arina Tanemura began her manga career in 1996 when her short stories debuted in *Ribon Original* magazine. She gained fame with the 1997 publication of *I•O•N*, and ever since her debut Tanemura has been a major force in shojo manga with popular series *Phantom Thief Jeanne*, *Time Stranger Kyoko*, *Full Moon*, *The Gentlemen's Alliance †* and *Sakura Hime: The Legend of Princess Sakura*. Both *Phantom Thief Jeanne* and *Full Moon* have been adapted into animated TV series.

IDOL dreams 5

SHOJO BEAT EDITION

STORY & ART BY ARINA TANEMURA

TRANSLATION **Tetsuichiro Miyaki**
TOUCH-UP ART & LETTERING **Inori Fukuda Trant**
DESIGN **Shawn Carrico**
EDITOR **Nancy Thistlethwaite**

Thirty One Idream by Arina Tanemura
© Arina Tanemura 2017
All rights reserved.
First published in Japan in 2017 by HAKUSENSHA, Inc., Tokyo.
English language translation rights arranged with HAKUSENSHA, Inc., Tokyo.

The stories, characters and incidents mentioned
in this publication are entirely fictional.

Printed in Canada

Published by VIZ Media, LLC
P.O. Box 77010
San Francisco, CA 94107

10 9 8 7 6 5 4 3 2 1
First printing, November 2018

STOP!
YOU MAY BE READING THE WRONG WAY!

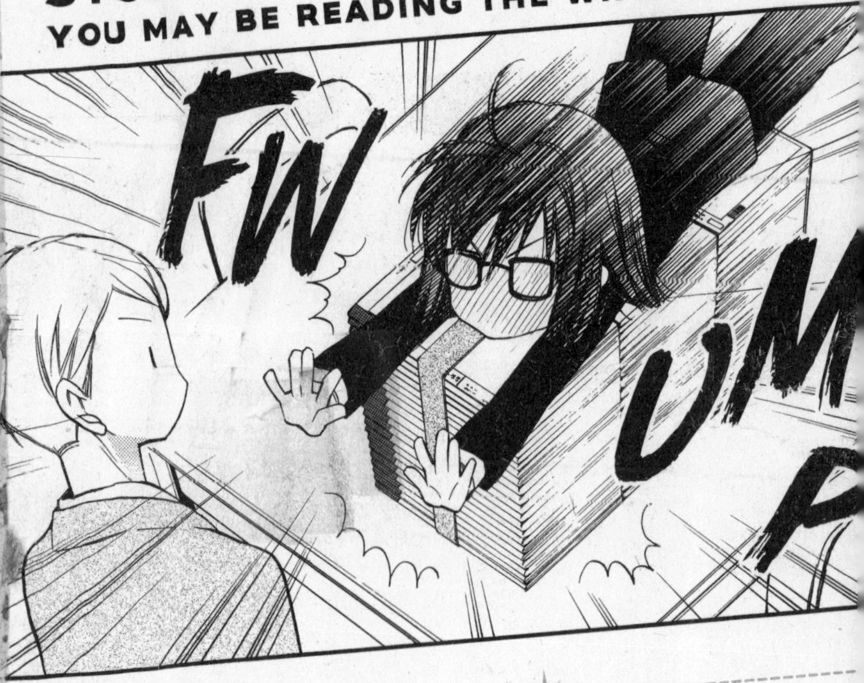
FWUMP

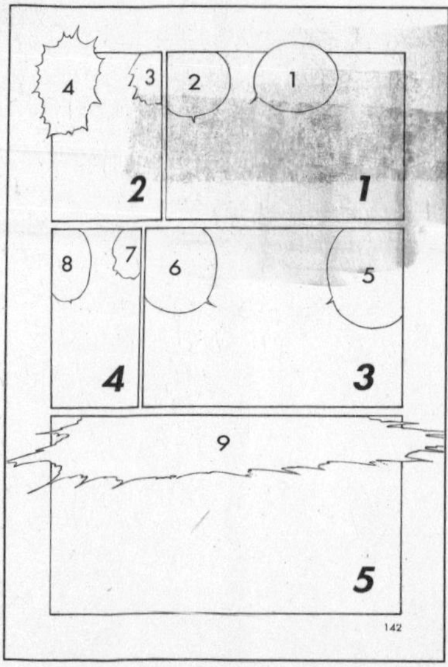
1
2
1
3
4
2
5
3
6
7
8
4
9
5
142

In keeping with the original Japanese comic format, this book reads from right to left—so action, sound effects and word balloons are completely reversed to preserve the orientation of the original artwork.

Check out the diagram shown here to get the hang of things, and then turn to the other side of the book to get started!